D1755633

# Representations of Political Resistance and Emancipation in Science Fiction

# Representations of Political Resistance and Emancipation in Science Fiction

Edited by Judith Grant and Sean Parson

LEXINGTON BOOKS
Lanham • Boulder • New York • London

Published by Lexington Books
An imprint of The Rowman & Littlefield Publishing Group, Inc.
4501 Forbes Boulevard, Suite 200, Lanham, Maryland 20706
www.rowman.com

6 Tinworth Street, London SE11 5AL, United Kingdom

Copyright © 2021 by The Rowman & Littlefield Publishing Group, Inc.

*All rights reserved.* No part of this book may be reproduced in any form or by any electronic or mechanical means, including information storage and retrieval systems, without written permission from the publisher, except by a reviewer who may quote passages in a review.

British Library Cataloguing in Publication Information Available

**Library of Congress Control Number: 2020943928**

ISBN: 978-1-7936-3063-6 (cloth : alk. paper)
ISBN: 978-1-7936-3064-3 (electronic)

∞™ The paper used in this publication meets the minimum requirements of American National Standard for Information Sciences Permanence of Paper for Printed Library Materials, ANSI/NISO Z39.48-1992.

The world is at a turning point where we face the choice first posed by Rosa Luxemburg, "Socialism or barbarism." With the realities of climate change, economic globalization, right-wing populism, entrenched white supremacy, technological displacement, social isolation, and growing alienation, the paths toward a more just, egalitarian, and socialist future seem harder to imagine than ever. This book is inspired by the writers, artists, musicians, dreamers, activists, and oppressed, who are both envisioning and building our collective paths forward. There are no road maps to lead us, but such visionaries are creating the star charts, imagining and forming new forms of community relationships, and reading against the dark scenarios of apocalypse to imagine new models of resistance that we need to write our unwritten future.

# Contents

Introduction: Capitalism, Modernity, and Science Fiction     1
   *Judith Grant and Sean Parson*

**Part I: Collapse and Rebuilding**     11

1. Dystopia, Apocalypse, and Other Things to Look Forward To: Reading for Radical Hope in the Fiction of Fear     13
   *Matthew Benjamin Cole*

2. Mirror, Mirror: The Tragic Vision of *Star Trek: Discovery*     33
   *Libby Barringer*

3. Beginning Again: *Jericho*, *Revolution*, and Catastrophic Originalism     53
   *Ira J. Allen*

**Part II: Resistance and Survival**     71

4. "We Survived You": Resisting Eugenicist Imaginaries through Feminist Science Fiction     73
   *Jess Whatcott*

5. Wakanda Forever: Black Panther in Black Political Thought     93
   *Debra Thompson*

6. Drowning Politics: Theorizing Resistance in the Anthropocene through JG Ballard's *The Drowned World*     113
   *Chase Hobbs-Morgan*

**Part III: Reconstructing Our World: Space and Place**  133

7  The Ambiguities of Critical Desire: Utopia and Heterotopia in Ursula K. Le Guin's *The Dispossessed* and Samuel R. Delany's *Trouble on Triton*  135
   *Michael Lipscomb*

8  Politicizing Cities in China Miéville's Speculative Fiction  153
   *Andrew Uzendoski and Caleb Gallemore*

9  Stranger than Fiction: Silicon Valley and the Politics of Space Colonization  175
   *Emily Ray*

**Part IV: Reconstructing Ourselves: Identity and Agency**  197

10  A Future Is Female: Loving Animals and Scientific Romance  199
    *Claire E. Rasmussen*

11  Finding Liberation and Futurity in the Sentient Spaceships of Leckie, Chambers, and Okorafor  219
    *Laurie Ringer*

12  What Do We Lose When We Become Posthuman?: "The People of Sand and Slag" and the Politics of Recognition  235
    *Michael Uhall*

Index  253

About the Contributors  257

# Introduction

*Capitalism, Modernity, and Science Fiction*

## Judith Grant and Sean Parson

The world today seems shrouded in dark clouds as large amounts of the world burn in forest fires, ethnonationalism grows and flourishes, and the stability of the post–cold war era seems to be resting on its deathbed. Not surprisingly, in a world in which political opportunity and liberation seem far away, the genre of science fiction grows in cultural importance and popularity. Few genres exceed science fiction's ability to evoke the expansive space of the imaginary. As Fredric Jameson has argued, the genre pushes hard against limits established in the context of modernity. In this, Jameson has argued, science fiction differs from the genre of fantasy, which deals with ahistorical, mythical concepts of good and evil, often offering magical resolutions. In contrast, science fiction novels, short stories, films provide venues for reflection and discussion about some of the most pressing issues raised by capitalist-modernity, science, technology while posing and exploring alternative futures.

Jameson writes in the tradition of German critical theory famously begun with the work of Adorno and Horkheimer in works such as *The Dialectic of Enlightenment* written in the first half of the twentieth century. Here the connection between modernity and capitalism is well-established. The Marxist critique of capitalism was mapped onto a critique of what first-generation critical theorists took to be the principles of modernity: Science, the individual, law, and reason. Capitalist productive practices, they argued, truncated, and mutilated the most progressive elements of modernity. Once one has this insight, as Horkheimer, Adorno, and others have argued, one can see that the regressive aspects of modernity were always-already latent in the modernist form. This argument moves the critique of capitalism beyond an analysis that centers the flow of capital or the exploitation of workers at the point of production and encourages us to also look to culture as a reflection of the core values and points of resistance in the imaginary.

Critical theory has linked the mutilation of the most progressive aspects of the high enlightenment (law, reason, science, etc.) to capitalism arguing that they have been brutally transformed both by capitalist economies, but also in political and cultural global events such as those that occurred in WWII and its aftermath. Rationality, once linked to ideas of justice, law, and science, is narrowed to become the positivist solving of particular problems absent any questioning of their normative status or connection to the structures of power linked to capitalism. Critical theory has also been central in developing claims about how the commodity form bleeds into every aspect of life, transforming subjectivity, consciousness, and ultimately flattening the imagination so that one can only conceive of the future as a repetition of the present, a point made forcefully by Herbert Marcuse in *One Dimensional Man*.

Similarly, Guy Debord in *The Society of the Spectacle* (1968) contended that the development of a society mediated by the image flattens time into what he calls, "semi-circular time." This shift alters the perception of humanity to one of a constantly repeating present, denying the role of agency and change. In effect, Debord argued, this turns all of us into spectators to a society and politics that is fed to us with a diminished possibility of democratic engagement. Taken all together, the commodity form transmutes progressive, modernist ideals with the entrenchment of its logic, thus deepening the levels of capitalist alienation that ultimately transform the human from subject to object and contribute to the origins and hegemonic status of technological rationality as a substitute for creative scientific inquiry.

All of this has only worsened with the rise of what David Harvey and others have termed "neoliberal" capitalism. David Harvey locates neoliberalism in the 1970s, where it became clear that the economic boom of the immediate postwar period was merely a blip as opposed to an ongoing trend toward increased prosperity. Harvey points specifically to globalization, a term that in neoliberalism becomes code for making the world hospitable to business. This coupled with the effective end of an oppositional labor movement (as achieved during this period by the "capitalist-labor accord" and the "European consensus") and the triumph of the logic of technological rationality that had been identified by earlier critical theorists. The hopeful utopic point of view of the Situationists, for example, who understood the problem of capitalist intransigence to be located in a blunted imaginary, was dashed with the crush of financial hardships that characterized the 70s and 80s. These include the rise of OPEC, the phenomenon of stagflation and the virtual end of the labor moment, all theorized by Harvey as neoliberalism that, he argues, builds on a capitalist /state partnership that had been firmly cemented in the nineteenth century.

In film, Jean-Luc Goddard's 1973, *Tout Va Bien* exemplifies the frustration of the May 1968 Left just before the moment of neoliberalism. His film critiques the communist party, trade unions, capitalism, and modernity in a plea for a return to the creative as an avenue for resistance. In the film, the character of the director explicitly references Bertolt Brecht in this regard, noting that the estrangement effects of avant-garde film date back to the German urge to revive the imagination and end the cycle of eternal reproduction and deepening of capitalist logics. Importantly, the film notes the expansion of capitalist and modernist partnership into the white-collar work in the deepening penetration of neoliberal expansionist ideals into every aspect of life. As with the discussion of capitalism and modernity above, there are a vast number of illustrations of this link between capitalism, modernity, and neoliberalism. To give just one more example, one might turn to cultural theorist Stuart Hall. Hall explicitly points to the economic factors which we now call neoliberalism in returning to culture as a site of contestation in his extraordinary and prescient essay, "The Great Moving Right Show," published in the late 1970s.

All of these thinkers arrived at a similar conclusion with regard to the imagination and the political. That is, moments of political transformation require critical, creative, and visionary thinking. As the logics that structure outcomes from capitalist-modernist systems crack, crumble, and potentially unravel old theories and even our physical environment, the need for visionary imagination becomes more powerful. The rise of right-wing nationalism, left-wing opposition, absurdism and nihilism, and the collapse of mainstream/center parties certainly appears to repeat familiar patterns from the first half of the twentieth century.

## SCIENCE FICTION AS RESISTANT IMAGINATION: RETHINKING THE HUMAN, THE MACHINE, AND THE NATURAL WORLD

As the quip goes, "it is easier to imagine the end of the world than to imagine the end of capitalism." Furthermore, while few examples of science fiction directly attack capitalism, a discussion of modernity that is very consistent with critical theory is evident in a myriad of science fiction works. The political imaginary presented in science fiction is often a bleak vision full of destruction, pain, imprisonment, fear, death, or even annihilation to the point that one is hard-pressed to think of many compelling works of utopian science fiction. Dystopian visions far outweigh the utopian in science fiction, probably because the genre in its most political manifestation is mostly a reflection of cultural anxieties about modernity, capitalist social relations, politics, and power. A truly great science fiction novel like *1984*, for instance, paints a harrowing picture of totalitarianism. By the novel's end, not only is Winston Smith betrayed and broken, but the truth itself is destroyed. It is a novel detailing the destruction of both the individual and of reason; a destruction that can become genuinely horrific only in the context of a modernist dream that situates those two ideas as foundational pillars. Dystopian novels such as *1984, Brave New World, Oryx and Crake, Fahrenheit 451, Neuromancer, Parable of the Sower, Snow Crash*, and countless others have fruitfully illustrated the evils of political power, the possibilities of the ends of freedom, truth, and justice. Such works highlight the parameters of modernity as well as possibilities that hint at ways to reach beyond its limits to read moments of resistance into dystopian narratives.

While the majority of political theory focuses on the philosophic work of writers and activists largely from certain historical defined philosophic traditions, this work treats fictive sources as forms of philosophic inquiry. Octavia Butler, for example, evokes ideas from feminist, black liberation, and environmentalist thinkers which she synthesizes in compelling and powerful stories that are also theoretical positions. The authors in this work, in applying these principles, treat the works of speculative fiction they engage with, as philosophically valid and powerful theories. In so doing, they imagine political futures.

This collection's narrative structure is mindful of the usefulness of science fiction to such discussions and coalesces around two themes. First, authors have been asked to read texts for messages of political resistance even as they may appear in stories of crisis and collapse, thus reading to reimagine the possibility of hope amidst despair. This theme has become especially relevant given the recent rise of the global ultra-right. Second, the chapters will highlight science fiction's propensity for questioning the centrality of a fixed concept of the human, as well as Anthropocentric definitions of political agency, a theme clearly made relevant both by climate emergency and by scientists' continuing revelations about the softening boundary between human and animal intelligences. Various chapters in this collection illustrate one or more moments evident in the ongoing critique of humanism as it appears in science fiction. For example, twentieth-century critiques of humanism centered around its essentialism and sought to create discourses of inclusion featuring points of view that acknowledged gender, race, disability, and so on. Later developments more properly thought of as "posthumanism" sought to include nonhuman animals and machines in discussions of political agency and ethics. Finally, the relatively new idea of the "Anthropocene" contends that human domination has transformed the entire planet, from ecosystems to natural cycles, in unalterable and alarming ways.

Both Marx and Engels were both enamored of the possibilities of the machine, industrialization, and technology because they thought technology moved the world forward by creating the more leisure, increased production, and ultimately, the end of work. They recognized too, of course, that, in the short term, it deepened the immiseration of workers and contributed to the transformed consciousness of the creative human species into a passive arm of the productive apparatus. This point about the mechanization of human labor is made beautifully in the scene in Fritz Lang's film *Metropolis* where the movements of workers during a shift change is choreographed to depict the worn bodies of increasingly homogenized workers moving with metronomic precision in time with their machine masters. Like Marx, second-wave feminist Shulamith Firestone famously embraced technological changes to the body and human reproduction as a possible solution for sex/gender discrimination that she believed was rooted in the women's physical connection to maternity. These examples of left valorization and critique of technology rest alongside contemporary news stories about Silicon Valley capitalists like Elon Musk who have fixated on technological innovation as a means to overcome the limits of the human body. In addition, the modern moment is one in which human life is constantly embedded with the machine world. We are all Donna Haraway's cyborgs. From cell phones and WIFI enabled cardiac implants to facial recognition software and "deep fakes" our lives are shaped, regulated, managed, and extended through our intimate connection with technology. These new technological innovations have empowered what, McKenzie Wark (2019) calls the "Vectoralist" class; the new economic super elite who use consumer data driven analytics as their form of "surplus value." While many mourn the death of privacy and fear the Authoritarian application of these technologies, other embrace it. Biohackers use CRISP technology to alter their bodies, gun rights libertarians use 3D printing to circumvent gun regulations, and media pirates torrent and stream endless contact off the Internet. From this new class antagonism might be developing as activists, theorists, and novelists confront the rise of this new Technosphere. As Mao said, "Everything under heaven is in utter chaos; the situation is excellent." That said, liberation is far from certain as the new technological systems have created an excellent situation for liberation, oppression, and everything in-between.

These are provocative juxtapositions. They explain why this collection takes a dialectical approach to technology in understanding that it contains both liberatory and repressive possibilities. We, with Marx, understand the Janus face of technology. Contemporary critiques of technology do not merely come from Greta Thunberg, but also from activists like Edward Snowden, formerly of the security state and himself a lover of technology who is nonetheless cognizant of its dangers. Multitudes of recent news stories illustrate Foucault's point about biopower and the uses it makes of technology (e.g., modern prisons, China's treatment of the Uyghurs largely via technology, Facebook, etc.).

The problem of technology must be reimagined. It is not quite beside the point to speculate about whether one is for or against technology. We are already saturated with it. There is no point in resisting it as a concept, and it is also not a new problem. Technological innovation calls for us to conceptualize it as no longer its own sphere, but insofar as it is integral to the human. Luddite attempts to dispense with it are bound to fail as are naïve calls to ignore the necropolitics that it often yields. The key is to understand it dialectically, to embrace the cyborg while resisting the turn to technology's dominance over human agency.

We must be mindful too of the fact that many progressive moments of capitalism have been rooted in a specific version of humanism, a version that this book heavily criticizes. The kind of humanism embraced by us in this book is a Marxian or radical humanism, which argues, in short, that humans are self-creative on the level of species. The decentering of human that intrigues us includes work such as that done in animal liberation studies or in Donna Haraway's recent work on the "Capitalocene." It foregrounds the need for a raised consciousness about how the centering of humans as world subject, without regard to class, gender or other differences, allows capitalist ideas of progress to drive the very construction and the very future of the human and the planet itself. The examples of climate change and the current mass extinction event wherein humans have killed an estimated 83 percent of all mammals and half of all plants make it imperative to dislodge the version of human that is linked to capitalism and modernism. We must reimagine the human in relation to this and other yet to be created worlds. We must understand that technology in its full ramifications is not a dismissal of the human, but rather an understanding of the Marxian, dialectical meaning of nature as man's inorganic body.

As with the concepts of technology and the human, the origin of the term "the Anthropocene" is heavily debated within the literature. The Anthropocene, a concept promoted by Nobel winner Paul Crutzen, contends that the planet has entered a new geologic era; the era of the human altered world. At the core of the Anthropocene is a claim that humans have so drastically impacted the world that we are, collectively changing basic ecological feedback loops and impacting all corners of the planet, from the bottom of the Mariana Trench to the exosphere at the limits of our atmosphere. Some scholars locate it in 1950 with the development of nuclear power, plastic, concrete, and bioengineering. Others have argued that the period started with the development of industrialism in the late eighteenth century and others the colonization of the Americas by Europe and the development of the trans-Atlantic slave trade. No matter when the Anthropocene began, the concept requires us to rethink the relationship that humans have with the world around us, and the way that complex webs of responsibility restructure politics, ethics, and science. By focusing on the themes above, the authors in this book, read science fiction through unique lenses that provide timely and powerful perspectives to the political problems facing the planet.

The authors in this book deal with stories in which radical transformations have occurred. These transformations are not always the ones that have historically been envisioned by progressives, but rather ones created by the ravages of capitalism, the military and prison industrial complexes, state violence, or environmental degradation. Nonetheless, these are changes that force a confrontation with what it means to be human and how one might resist and maintain hope in the face of catastrophe. The volume's unique contribution comes from the discussion of the themes of resistance and the invitation to decenter various notions of the human. While methodologically framed as a work of political theory, the proposed book includes authors with degrees and teaching positions in rhetoric, communication studies, disability studies, environmental studies, women's studies, queer studies, and African American studies. Though the majority of the writers hold positions in departments of political science, a diverse selection of subfields is represented herein, including offerings from political theory, international relations, comparative politics, law, and public administration while we have resisted using race, class, and gender as organizational categories, but have made sure to include the full complement of gendered, racial, international and other related normative categories within this volume.

## MAPPING THE STARS

We have divided the book into four sections. Part one, "Collapse and Rebuild," begins with Matthew Cole's chapter that explores the ways that fear is deployed in science fiction scenarios. He asks us to consider how that anxiety then challenges us to preserve the idea of human relationships in the event of "pervasive instrumentalism." Radical hope, he argues, transcends our current framework for understanding human interactions and depicts a resilient world that is at once human and posthuman. In this same section, author Libby Barringer uses *Star Trek Discovery* to counter the recent turn to realist theories in international relations theory that point to the limits of human political action. Combining early IR realist thinkers with a reading of Nietzsche, Barringer argues that the series "Discovery may be 'read' in a way that offers an alternative political vision useful for contemporary politics; one where humanist, rational optimism does not ever escape the paradoxical conflicts which tragedy invites us to attend." Finally, Ira Allen looks at alternate discourses of foundings as they are portrayed post-catastrophe in science fiction, asking us to consider how science fiction has imagined social renewal amid collapse. Looking to the TV series *Jericho* and *Revolution*,

Allen "examine[s] the grimly proleptic, and yet not wholly dark, future-thinking available today."

In part two, "Resistance and Survival," Jess Whatcott uses feminist, queer, and disability theories to good effect in her discussion of the bioethics of eugenics as displayed in the television show, *Orphan Black*. Through its device of an ethic of responsibility and a reconceptualized understanding of the family, its discussion of clones moves us to consider new norms of obligation. Next, Debra Thompson reads the film *Black Panther* as an example of Afrofuturism and relates to the theoretical work on black nationalism, both in the United States and globally. The section concludes with Chase Hobbs-Morgan, who offers a chapter that sets the tone for the book's narrative by provocatively linking the idea of the anthropocene to politics. He considers environmental catastrophe as a metaphor for the demise of the anthropocene, the loss of political agency, and what he calls the "slow degradation of politics" in his analysis of the work of JG Ballard. He argues that the anthropocene and ideas about a drowned world can be read as metaphors for a "drowned politics," and a loss of political agency.

Revolutions, destruction, and rebirth all take place in a particular space, though this aspect of revolution is often given short shrift. In part three, "Space and Place," spaces of resistance, both literal and metaphorical, are considered. The chapter by Andrew Uzendoski and Caleb Gallemore centers on urban politics and the future of the city. In this chapter, the city becomes a situation in which differences are brought together, producing new agencies. Likewise, Damian White uses works by Kim Stanley Robinson and Cory Doctorow to ask how they might offer us materials for thinking about "an emancipatory politics of radical ongoingness in a warming world." The chapter uses critical design theory to explore this point. Emily Ray's chapter concentrates on the literature of interdisciplinary space studies, specifically looking to the planet Mars. Novels about Mars allow us to consider ideology in the context of new world-building, as well as providing scenarios about how humans could live through climate change. Finally, Michael Lipscomb's chapter reads Leguin and Delaney to explore what he terms "ambiguous utopia and an ambiguous heterotopia." The very idea of utopia is, after all, a desire for the construction of a new space that, Lipscomb writes, might "provide a materialist anchor" to help "us better figure the necessary and proper utopian elements of any critical-liberatory political project," of resistance.

In part four, the crucial roles of "Identity and Agency" in political resistance are considered with particular attention to posthuman iterations of agency. The first two chapters consider two categories that bound the human, animal, and machine. Claire Rasmussen reads against the use of animals as metaphors to consider them as subjects in their own right. This way of considering the nonhuman animal shows how their existence exposes the central human problem; namely, defining the boundaries of human nature.

On the other side, Laurie Ringer explores how machines bound the human. Her chapter explores the idea of sentience in machines that we do not normally associate with AI; in this case, spaceships. She writes, "their diverse, cyborg materialities also empower forms of resistance and politics that offer hope at the edge of survival." The section concludes with Michael Uhall's chapter about the extraordinary and brutal, Nebula-nominated 2004 novelette, *People of Sand and Slag* by Paolo Bacigalupi. The story is a stark meditation on the unusual potential realities of a posthumanist world that pits the biological against the technological in ways that are stunning and surprising. The story, he argues, creates a site in which we can question just how far we are willing to go in the destruction of nature and the maintenance of some version of the anthropocene.

Why science fiction? Because it is one of the few genres that takes the modernist problematics of science, rationalism, and technology and through imagination, projects them forward as imaginaries in which humans defy domination. Much of this genre involves dystopias. Moreover, one might read these as unproductive art forms in the sense that they reproduce despair, hopelessness, fear, and power. In contrast, the goal of this book is to read these works against the grain to find moments of radical alterity and imagination inside despair. We have already explained why we believe culture to be central to the project of a reawakened radical imaginary. The current global political situation warrants art that provides paths to resistance and creative, transformative engagement in the face of crushing power and looming disasters that include big data collection and surveillance, climate change, AI, deepening state/capital partnerships, truncated notions of rationality, and the rise of conspiratorial and magical thinking. They also demand ways for us to think about technology in positive and useful ways that underscore its potential for human emancipation.

*Part I*

# Collapse and Rebuilding

*Chapter One*

# Dystopia, Apocalypse, and Other Things to Look Forward To

*Reading for Radical Hope in the Fiction of Fear*

Matthew Benjamin Cole

In the first two decades of the twenty-first century, there has been a major revival of dystopian and apocalyptic fiction drawing on a panoply of technological, political, and ecological doomsday scenarios. Among them are works like Margaret Atwood's *Oryx and Crake* (2003), Kazuo Ishiguro's *Never Let Me Go* (2005), and Cormac McCarthy's *The Road* (2006), which established the trend of "serious" literary novelists, whose preceding works had been largely realist, now populating their novels with bioengineered chimeras, sentient clones, and marauding cannibal hordes. At the same time, classic works of speculative fiction—from perennials like *Brave New World* (1932), *1984* (1949), and *The Handmaid's Tale* (1985) to cult favorites by the likes of J.G. Ballard, Phillip K. Dick, and Octavia Butler—have benefited from popular rediscovery and critical reevaluation. And this is to speak only of the relatively high-brow examples. In comic books, video games, and young adult novels, dystopian or post-apocalyptic worlds are practically a default setting. *The Walking Dead* (2010), by some measures the most popular television series of the last decade, is a bleak saga of survival in a world overrun by bloodthirsty zombies and often bloodthirstier humans, while acclaimed streaming series like *Black Mirror* (2011) and the adapted *Handmaid's Tale* (2017) deliver dystopian drama in bingeable portions.

Despite their apparent pessimism, I argue that these prophecies of doom can play a constructive role in orienting our ethical imagination toward the future. The fiction of fear is not a fiction of despair; at its best, it extends its own radical and desperate hope that even amidst inhuman conditions, humanity may not only survive, but flourish. To make this case, I consider several recent examples of literary fiction that deploy apocalyptic and dystopian scenarios in terms of how they contribute, both negatively and positively, to our ethical understanding of the human. In the first part of the chapter, I consider some exemplary works in the dystopian and apocalyptic modes as instances of what the philosopher Hans Jonas has called the "heuristics of fear": ethical inquiries which seek to refine our normative conception of the human by imagining its destruction or distortion. I aim to show in the second part of the chapter that the value of such works is not only in what they warn against. In examining McCarthy's *The Road* and Atwood's *MaddAddam* (2003–2013) trilogy, I argue that we can uncover an ethos of "radical hope" uniquely suited to those who aspire to survive the end of their world. Radical hope orients not toward concrete plans or probabilities, but instead toward future possibilities which transcend current frameworks of understanding. The protagonists of *The Road* and *MaddAddam* exhibit radical hope insofar as they anticipate and enable the renewal of human life even as the ethical criteria by which they define it are thrown into doubt. These works also demonstrate that storytelling itself is a critical method for sustaining hope, as narrative provides a means for projecting cherished values and practices into an uncertain future. Read in this way, we will find that the fiction of fear, though it does not promise salvation or disclose alternatives, may nonetheless extend the enduring mission of the utopian social imagination: "to map, to warn," and even "to hope."[1]

## "TO MAP": THE TWENTY-FIRST-CENTURY FICTION OF FEAR

If the boundaries between science fiction and realistic fiction have grown more difficult to discern over the last few decades, perhaps it is because our hallucinatory new reality seems to have come straight from the pages of science fiction. Ursula K. Le Guin, whose work has done more than anyone's to legitimize science fiction in literary circles, insists that science fiction is "less a mythological genre than a realistic one . . . a way of trying to describe what in fact is going on, what people actually do and feel, how people relate to everything else."[2] "It is a strange realism," she concedes, "but it is a strange reality." Likewise for Bruce Sterling, who in 1989 coined the term "slipstream" to refer to a nebulous family of fictions "which simply makes you feel very strange, the way that living in the twentieth century makes you feel strange, if you are a person of a certain sensibility."[3] Sterling's eclectic canon of slipstream fictions includes some major dystopian fictions—*The Handmaid's Tale*, Marge Piercy's *Woman on the Edge of Time* (1976)—alongside literature with explicit science-fiction elements (such as the Kurt Vonnegut of *Slaughter-house Five* (1969)), literature that is typically classified as magical realism (Gabriel Garcia Marquez, Salman Rushdie), fantasy horror (Anne Rice), as well as other kinds of mind-bending experimental fiction (William Burroughs, Thomas Pynchon). Nonetheless, a trend emerges beginning in the middle of the twentieth century. Writers working within a variety of cultural and genre traditions rebelled against realism, straining instead for new images and metaphors that could do justice to the character of contemporary life.

Of course, one could appropriate the symbolic elements of science fiction to tell an optimistic story about the future. H.G. Wells wrote of utopian futures as well as dystopian ones. Kim Stanley Robinson's minutely rendered and mind-expanding stories of the future have tended to foreground wonder, ingenuity, and resilience. Still, visions of peace and plenty are a hard sell in the current intellectual climate. Instead, apocalypse and dystopia are the dominant forms of future fiction. The distinction between these modes is worth drawing out. While both dystopia and apocalypse imagine a world changed for the worse, they diverge in how they depict the nature of the change and the consequences thereof: "In the most basic political terms, dystopia is a nightmare of authoritarian or totalitarian rule, while the end of the world is a nightmare of anarchy."[4] In apocalyptic fictions, the world as we have known it comes to an end. The whole edifice of civilization is stripped away and society crumbles, leaving the survivors in a Hobbesian state. In dystopian fiction, society persists, forever entrenched and unshakeable, with the population either bullied into submission, pace Orwell, or pacified and indifferent, pace Huxley, or some of each.

Apocalypses, stories of the end times, have been part of the mythical and religious traditions of most cultures going back to antiquity: Ragnaroks, Last Judgments, Second Comings. Though the works to be discussed in this piece tend not to be interested in eschatology, they are more accurately characterized as post-apocalyptic than apocalyptic, as their principle focus is not on the reckoning but on those who survive it. In *The Road*, for example, we never learn what caused the world to collapse, just that it did so quickly and violently and that few survived. Humanity does not always directly cause the apocalypse—the collapse could be caused by plague, as in Mary Shelley's *The Last Man* (1826)—but the retribution doled out in these stories tends to be mundane rather than divine. During the Cold War, the apocalyptic imaginary was vexed by nuclear annihilation, as in Vonnegut's *Cat's Cradle* (1963) or Stanley Kubrick's *Dr. Strangelove* (1964). Today, the cause of collapse is more likely to be ecological. But in either case, the fault lies deep in modern civilization, whose startling technological potency seems only to amplify, rather than to contain or transform, the impulses toward conflict and consumption. As Heather Hicks explains, "with the emergence of modernity in the eighteenth century, apocalypse shifted from its origins as the story of the annihilation of the sinful human world to become, in novel form, the story of the collapse of modernity itself."[5] Aside from *The Road*, this terrain has recently been explored in Atwood's *MaddAddam* novels, in Emily St. John Mandel's *Station Eleven* (2014), Sophie Mackintosh's *The Water Cure* (2018), and in other popular media such as *Mad Max: Fury Road* (2015), *The Walking Dead*, and the *Fallout* video game franchise.

Dystopias, on the other hand, are exclusively modern, a dubious token of the twentieth century's darkened horizon of expectations. Utopias have thrived in the cultural imagination and occasionally even in real social life for centuries, but up until the tail end of the nineteenth century, no one had bothered to write a dystopia. The reasons why the turn of the century necessitated such a form of writing are complex and difficult to summarize.[6] It is easier to say, at first, why no dystopias were written prior to modernity. This was because, up until the time of the Enlightenment, expectations about the possibility of enduring, human-driven change were narrowly bounded.[7] First, the idea of progress had to overtake the static and fatalist visions of history which had predominated in the Ancient and Medieval worlds. At that point, utopia could transform from a heuristic to a blueprint. Plato, for example, had located his ideal republic in speech, while More's *Utopia* was displaced spatially, on a remote island. The first utopia to be located in *the future*, to make utopia into "euchronia" was Mercier's *L'ann 2440* (1771).[8] Once it is conceivable that the society of the future could be radically better than that of the present, it doesn't take long to get to the idea that it could also be radically worse. By now, we all know the story of how the traumas of the early twentieth century irreparably damaged the confidence in progress that had united the Enlighteners with their socialist successors, how the century of Saint-Simon, Comte, Fourier, Marx, and Bellamy gave way to the century of Zamyatin, Huxley, and Orwell. Decades of total war and totalitarian domination drove home the salience of the latter works, with dystopias quickly eclipsing utopias in significance. Landmark utopias of the twenty-first century, such as Le Guin's *The Dispossessed* (1974) are more likely to interrogate the whole concept than to make earnest proposals for the future. Only a few brave or foolish souls would now aver that utopia lies ahead or that progress is inevitably leading to such an outcome.

By contrast, dystopian novels have never lost their power to shock, nor they have ever been in short supply. Ayn Rand and Kurt Vonnegut each wrote their own political dystopias, dealing, respectively, with the evils of collectivism and technocracy. Science fiction writers such as Dick, Ballard, and Butler wrote vivid and unsettling accounts of modernity gone awry, and today's dystopias, which find new ways of triangulating corporate power, technological hubris, and political subjugation, follow more directly in that lineage. A partial roll call of twenty-first-century dystopias would have to include Atwood's *Oryx and Crake*, Ishiguro's *Never Let Me Go*, Dave Egger's *The Circle* (2013), Chang-rae Lee's *On Such a Full Sea* (2014), Naomi

Alderman's *The Power* (2016), Omar El Akkad's *American War* (2017), and countless others besides. There is also at least a separate chapter's worth of young adult dystopias, some of which, such as *The Hunger Games* (2012) trilogy, have become influential well beyond their target demographic.

At their core, apocalyptic and dystopian fiction speaks to a characteristically modern concern with the future of humanity, "how fundamental features of the human condition may change or remain constant in the long run."[9] The resurgence of these forms in the twenty-first century, the attraction they exert on some of the most original and penetrating literary voices of our era, and the popularity and prestige they have found in culture at large, all indicate that this concern is one which remains critical to our sense of where we are headed and who we are becoming. Some commentators worry that the fiction of fear has become yet another commodified arm of the entertainment industry, where grim futuristic settings and aesthetics are as likely to advance slick nihilism as any kind of coherent social protest.[10] And yet there is no shortage of examples where dystopian fiction has succeeded at motivating precisely the stance of resistance which critics suggests it will quash. From Washington, DC, to Belfast to Beunos Aires, demonstrators have donned the crimson robes and white bonnets of Atwood's handmaid*'s* as they protest in defense of reproductive rights.[11] For these demonstrators, the final meaning of the novel lies in its slogan of defiance—*"don't let the bastards grind you down"*—not in its lurid scenes of violation and subjugation. Likewise, some of the readers who responded to Trump's inauguration by stockpiling their own dystopian libraries—*1984* and *Brave New World* shot to the top of the bestseller lists, Sinclair Lewis' *It Can't Happen Here* (1935) went out of stock—may well have intended to curl up, helpless and hopeless, but it seems just as likely they sought to be forewarned and forearmed by those who, give or take a few details, seemed to have seen it coming. These books are not for readers who have given up on their future, they are for those who intend to fight for it.

## "TO WARN": HUMANISM AT THE BRINK

It may seem apparent the primary function of much of what I am calling the fiction of fear is to warn. But even in their capacity as warnings, such works do more than alert humanity to the moral hazard of the day, be it cloning, surveillance, or climate change. By making us aware of the vulnerabilities in our ethical conceptions of the human, the fiction of fear underscores the importance of asserting just such a conception, and even provides insight into what such a conception must consist of. This is no small feat, given that the cogency of "the human" as a category and, relatedly, the possibility or desirability of defending any normative conception of the human, has been challenged from a variety of anti-essentialist, anti-humanist, and post-humanist positions.[12] This is fraught territory, and the arguments raised are not easy to counter. They range from prudent insights about the difficulties and occasional dangers of articulating the human as an array of substantive value positions, to more rhetorically and theoretically flamboyant arguments for the deconstruction, displacement, or transcendence of the human. Into this fray, where theoretical arguments typically lead to aporia or impasse, the fiction of fear enters a distinctive appeal to the imagination.

The ethical claims raised by the fiction of fear can be clarified with reference to what Hans Jonas has called the "imaginative-anticipatory *heuristics of fear*."[13] Jonas developed this concept as part of his own ethics of responsibility, which he intended to respond to the unique ethical stakes of modernity, what he termed the problem of an endangered future. His inquiry is fundamentally concerned with how to make responsible use of our power to reshape the natural and human world through technology, and Jonas himself notes that science fiction is an exemplary source of "well-informed thought experiments, whose vivid imaginary results may assume the heuristic functions here proposed."[14] The fundamental question, then, is how are we to guide our actions responsibly given the long-term, cumulative character of the changes that we are now introducing into the world? Which principles should bound, direct, and constrain this power?

Jonas contends that our reflection ought to begin with the heuristics of fear:

> [I]n our search after an ethics of responsibility for distant contingencies, it is an anticipated *distortion* of man that helps us to detect that in the normative conception of man which is to be preserved from it. . . . As long as the danger is unknown, we do not know what to preserve and why. Knowledge of this comes, against all logic and method, from the perception of what to *avoid*.[15]

The most apparent threat to humanity would be a literal doomsday scenario: a nuclear war, ecological catastrophe, plague, or some other event which raised the possibility of human extinction. These are the types of scenarios which pervade the apocalyptic imagination, but as we have seen, the contemporary post-apocalyptic genre is defined by near-extinction experiences rather than the genuine article—for there must be someone left to write about. More to the point, such literature contends with the survivors' struggle to maintain their humanity in a collapsing world. Survival is a necessary condition for any ethical conception of the human, and therefore must come first among the preconditions which Jonas calls on us to preserve. However, even this premise is not absolute: "the policy of survival must beware lest the existence finally saved will have ceased to be human."[16]

Extinction and a dehumanized existence, apocalypse and dystopia, are the Scylla and the Charybdis that humanity must navigate, the ethics of survival "a ridge between two abysses, where means can destroy the end." Post-apocalyptic fiction is often rich in its commentary on these dilemmas, where the victory of survival is hollowed out by the brutality of a survivalist ethos. Indeed, it calls into question what it even means for humanity to survive *as humans*. In *The Road*, the protagonist's wife commits suicide for fear of a life worse than death. "We're not survivors," she declares, "We're the walking dead in a horror film."[17] As I will discuss further, much of the novel's moral potency comes from its characters' struggle to survive while adhering to a code of ethics: aspiring in some legible way to be "good guys" in a world where goodness is a weakness. Similarly, the defining mantra of *Station Eleven* (following an episode of *Star Trek: Voyager*), is that "survival is insufficient." The novel concerns the odyssey of a Shakespearean troupe who persists in traveling and performing amidst a plague-stricken world. The ethical conception of the human they defend therefore extends beyond the minimal ethics of *The Road* (though the situation is correspondingly less dire). In this novel to persist as human in the ethical sense, as opposed to surviving as a species in the biological sense, means to carry forward the art, values, and culture of the human world, and to preserve a link with the past so that the dead are not forgotten. "We want to be remembered," says the narrator, but this is only a possibility if remembrance is taken up as an ethical task by the survivors.[18]

Perhaps the most persistent dangers raised in contemporary dystopian novels are those pertaining to the instrumentalization of human beings. This danger may issue from new forms of hierarchy, such as the exploitation of cloned human beings in *Never Let Me Go*, or the reemergence of familiar ones, such as the patriarchal theocracy of *The Handmaid's Tale* or the twenty-first-century slave economy in Ben Winter's *Underground Airlines* (2016). In *Never Let Me Go*, the cloned humans are "donors," their purpose in life to provide organs to the humans from whom their DNA was copied. In *The Handmaid's Tale*, women selected for their fertility following a population crisis are raped and forcibly impregnated by male Governors. And in *Underground Airlines*, slavery persists as a cornerstone of the American economy. Compared with the post-apocalyptic novels, the violence of dystopia is systematic and cruelly predictable. To the extent that the personhood of the exploited is recognized, it establishes no limit to the pain and degradation that can be inflicted in the name of creating a secure and comfortable existence for others. In Ishiguro's novel, the donors' claim to moral personhood is dismissed not because it is metaphysically or ontologically specious, but because the benefits of their exploitation became too appealing to give up. The idea that the donors are less than human is not the *reason* for their exploitation, it is an excuse given after the fact. This is explained to the protagonists near the end of the novel:

> However uncomfortable people were about your existence, their overwhelming concern was that their own children, their spouses, their parents, their friends, did not die from cancer, motor neurone disease, heart disease. So for a long time you were kept in the shadows, and people did their best not to think about you. And if they did, they tried to convince themselves you weren't really like us. That you were less than human, so it didn't matter.[19]

The donor's ultimate end, to be harvested then switched off and discarded, is an open secret and a banal evil: "It's horror movie stuff, and most of the time people don't want to think about it."[20] The outrage is not only that such atrocities occur, but that the society which benefits from them refuses to acknowledge or accept responsibility for the cruelties administered in its name.

Dystopian writers also imagine societies where individuals become complicit in their own instrumentalization and the price of participation in the modern world is one's willingness to make oneself a resource: Big Brother meets Big Data. In *The Circle*, Eggers satirizes Silicon Valley's cheery totalitarian drive to optimize through social media and surveillance. The titular company, an amalgam of Facebook and Google, seeks to "close the circle" by constructing a minutely detailed profile of every voting-age citizen of the United States. Users are further incentivized, on pains of ostracization, to surveil themselves with the Circle's proprietary fiber-optic cameras, ensuring a constant flow of information to their digital audience—and of course, to the Circle itself. Eggers presents a plausible future in which individuals facilitate their own exploitation and all is justified by a passive-aggressive ideology of mandatory interconnectedness: "Sharing is caring. Privacy is theft. Secrets are lies."[21] Eggers' concerns resonate with other critics of social media. Zadie Smith argues that platforms like Facebook reduce our interior life down to their parameters, such that we come to resemble the flattened digital personae we share online. What is lost, Smith fears, is the notion of the "private person, a person who is a mystery to the world and—which is more important—to herself."[22] If the person of the new media age is the sum total of their likes, views, shares and mention, perhaps in the future a person will be little more than a number reflecting their aggregate social utility. This outcome was forecasted in "Nosedive" (2016), *Black Mirror*'s pastel nightmare of digital status anxiety, and has more recently surfaced in discussions of China's Social Credit System. At stake is a future where intrusive technology and hyper-socialization reduce a person's worth to their instrumental value, now objectively quantifiable and updated in real-time. Rather than being coerced, we learn to surveil and censor ourselves, and we face an array of social and technological "pushes" to participate in our own commodification.

This instrumentalization of human life keeps pace with, and may be seen as an outgrowth of, the instrumentalization of external nature. Atwood explores this terrain in her *MaddAddam* novels, each of which presents a nesting doll of calamities: a character's journey in a post-apocalyptic world, interspersed with flashbacks to the dystopian society which precipitated the near-extinction event. Atwood has described the dystopia as "a technocracy and an anarchy," referring to the distinction between the Compounds, which house the privileged employees of powerful corporations—mainly bioengineering firms—and the Plebelands, where the rest of humanity is walled off.[23] In the Plebelands, "things were unpredictable," while the Compounds curate normalcy and stability.[24] In the first novel, *Oryx and Crake*, we learn about this two-tiered society from the viewpoint of Jimmy, the son of a highly sought after "genographer." For Jimmy's father, life in the Compounds is "the way it used to be . . . before things got so serious," but for his mother, who experiences intensifying doubts about the cost of her family's comfort, it is "artificial," "a theme park." The Compounds are protected by private security firms which, we learn in the second novel, *The Year of the Flood*, have mostly replaced the police and military forces whose resources proved inadequate to the increasingly unstable world of the Plebelands.

The "kings and dukes" of this neo-feudal arrangement, the residents of the Compounds also benefit from genetic advances to prevent disease and aging, courtesy of firms like NooSkins, HelthWyzer, and OrganInc Farms which extend bioengineering into every area of human and nonhuman life. Jimmy's father works on OrganInc Farms' most controversial and lucrative project: the design of the "ss multiorganifier," otherwise known as the "pigoon." These animals, which end up playing a significant role in the third novel, are pigs which have been genetically modified to grow human organ tissue for transplant purposes. A brief but horrifying aside indicates that the type of wholesale exploitation of human beings depicted in *Never Let Me Go* is on the near horizon, blocked not so much for ethical reasons as by a (temporarily) prohibitive price tag: "It was much cheaper than getting yourself cloned for spare parts—a few wrinkles to be ironed out there, as Jimmy's Dad used to say—or keeping a for-harvest child or two stashed away in some illegal baby-orchard."[25] Eventually, the pigoon project extends to the cultivation of "genuine human neo-cortex tissue," an experiment which will ultimately allow the animals to attain sentience.[26] In a society that has already accepted that nonhuman life exists only to be exploited, the line being crossed here is impossible to articulate. While Jimmy's mother calls it "immoral" and "sacrilegious," his father can't believe an "educated person" could make such an objection.[27] Jimmy finds himself in the same position as he begins to object to Crake's experiments, feeling that "some line has been crossed, some boundary transgressed" but unable to explain why.[28] In any event, Crake is unmoved by Jimmy's concerns, asserting that he doesn't believe in nature—"Or not with a capital N." The instrumentalization of all life, up to and including human life, unites Crake's Frankenstein-like hubris with the broader patterns of consumption and exploitation that characterize their culture. Looking back on this ruinous trajectory from the post-apocalyptic future, the surviving humans can only explain it as the consequence of an unconscionable blindness: a disregard for nonhuman life that ends with humanity itself being fed into the vast destructive machinery they have built.

Atwood indicates that an ethical conception of the human may have more vulnerabilities than we might initially imagine if we consider only what it means for humans themselves to be treated with dignity. An ethical conception of the human must also fill out the way we relate to nature with orienting principles as well as boundaries and limitations. This warning also complicates the task of a humanist ethics, as the very humanisms which assert the sanctity of the human species have frequently entailed the elevation of the human as master and possessor of nature. According to Heidegger, humanity exalts itself to the "posture of lord of the earth" in an anthropo-solipsism that collapses into nihilism and brings humanity "to the brink of a precipitous fall."[29] As contemporary critics of anthropocentrism point out, many influential ethical conceptions of the human have, in their turn, contributed to humanity's total domination of nature, and in that way contribute to our precarious predicament today.[30] This means that in order for humanity to persist, our ethical conception of the human must not only be articulated and preserved, but also reimagined in new terms, if it is to continue on any terms.

## "TO HOPE": PERIL AND POSSIBILITY IN ATWOOD'S *MADDADDAM* AND MCCARTHY'S *THE ROAD*

What then, can the fiction of fear teach us about the struggle to preserve, or even imagine, a human future? With this question in mind, let us return to Atwood's *MaddAddam* novels and McCarthy's *The Road*, each of which dramatizes their protagonist's struggle against despair. For prior to even to their physical struggle to survive, the remnants of humanity must avoid falling into hopelessness. They have to believe that there is some reason to keep surviving and that giving up would foreclose meaningful possibilities which they may yet persist to actualize. If we are attentive to this thin filament of possibility, then each novel sustains an inquiry into hope in dark times.

By reading Atwood's and McCarthy's novels as confrontations between hope and despair, I argue that we can uncover an ethos of what Jonathan Lear has called "radical hope," a desperate hope necessitated by dire circumstances. Lear develops his account of radical hope by reflecting on the experiences of the Crow people of North America. He is haunted by the words of their last great chief, Plenty Coup, who witnessed as the Crow's traditional way of life became an impossibility in the course of the nineteenth century. What Plenty Coup describes is a kind of apocalypse: the end of *a* world, if not *the* world, what Lear refers to as the collapse of a way of life. Lear is particularly interested in the practice of "counting coups," a ritual by which Crow warriors celebrated feats of courage in battle. Crow warriors typically fought with members of other tribes over hunting grounds as they pursued a nomadic existence in the present-day American West. But once the buffalo are eliminated, there is no hunt; once nations are confined to reservations, there is no cause for territorial dispute; and once there is no war between tribes there are no coups to count. Lear emphasizes that the practice of counting coups did not just become impossible, it became *unintelligible:* "Counting coups makes sense only in the context of a world of intertribal warfare; and once that world breaks down, *nothing* counts as counting coups."[31] Tellingly, Plenty Coup himself derives his name from this practice, such that his very identity and place of honor among his people is tied to it. This illustrates the dilemma of cultural devastation as, per Lear, one in which the impossibility of a way of life evacuates the concepts once used to make sense of one's self and one's world. The Crow seem to suffer a similar fate as a collective subject capable of relating their history from their own point of view. "The issue is that the Crow have lost the concepts with which they would construct a narrative" and the result is a "breakdown in what might count as happening."[32] This gives meaning to Plenty Coup's pronouncement that "nothing happened" to the Crow once they were confined to the reservations—their story had come to an end.

Much in Lear's account of cultural devastation resonates with the fiction of fear, particularly the post-apocalyptic strand. The survivors whose stories are told in these works have likewise experienced the shattering dislocation of their worlds and their identities. What they confront is not just the loss of their identity as members of a tribe, nation, or faith, but as human beings of any kind. We can observe this breakdown in both *MaddAddam* and *The Road*, where the protagonists' understanding of what it means to be human is thrown into crisis. It is unclear whether there is any future for humanity, whether extinction can be avoided, and if so, whether the remnants of humanity have any prospects beyond the daily struggle for survival against inhospitable conditions. This struggle has both physical and psychological dimensions, but the aspect of the struggle which most interests me, and which I find Lear's work most helpful for distilling, is its existential dimension: whether an ethical understanding of humanity can be extended into the future, whether a human world is still possible, in short whether there is any purpose to be found in survival besides the postponement of the final extinction event.

The precarity of the human is emphasized from the opening pages of *The Road*. We find the novel's protagonists, referred to only as the man and the boy, on a night pitch dark and cold. The man has just awakened from a dream in which he stands across a black lake from a "creature . . . with eyes dead white and sightless as the eggs of spiders . . . pale and naked and translucent."[33] What is this creature? McCarthy describes it in terms that sound humanoid, though not quite human: "Its bowels, its beating heart. The brain that pulsed in a dull glass bell." It is an evolutionary nightmare, a creature well-adapted to its lightless, heatless environment. If we take the man's dream as an augury of what humanity may yet become, then the opening of the novel is a stake-setting piece: will *homo sapiens*, like the creature, disappear "soundlessly into the dark?"[34] The Darwinian predicament is underscored throughout the novel. Humanity, McCarthy asserts, is "a creation perfectly evolved to meet its own end," and the novel gives ample reason to believe the end has come.[35] For in the "scablands" wandered by the man and the boy it is no good fortune to meet with human company. The first time the novel alludes to the possibility of other human survivors they are "blood-cults" and "marauders," "men who would eat your children in front of your eyes."[36]

When McCarthy gestures toward the civilizational markers by which time and space are rendered comprehensible on a human scale, they occur as relics of a half-forgotten epoch. The man cannot explain the "state roads" on the map because the boy has no memory of the world where "what used to be called states" were meaningful entities.[37] Watching his son run his fingers idly along a map, the man reflects on the simple reassurance of finding one's city on a map or one's name in the phonebook. The old world had been organized into a cohesive ensemble of things and persons, "[t]hemselves among others, everything in its place."[38] *The Road*'s language is not so much spare as starved, capturing the phenomenological decay of a world "shrinking down about a raw core of parsible entities."[39] Appropriately, McCarthy's stylistic plunge into the void underscores this essential fragility of world, enacting the collapse of meaning in sentences that register subjectivity as a flickering in a dead circuit.

Atwood's *Oryx and Crake* likewise posits its extinction event as a linguistic extirpation. Jimmy, like McCarthy's man, is stranded amidst the "absence of official time," and the unworlding in which he is caught up indexes to the growing number of "blank spaces in his stub of a brain, where memory used to be."[40] One of Atwood's signature devices is to have Jimmy recall a word, usually a proper noun, that remains lodged in his mind even though he no longer has any context in which to use it. "This is happening too much lately, this dissolution, of meaning, the entries on his cherished wordlists drifting off into space."[41] Since he once considered himself a writer, Jimmy is particularly attuned to this bleeding out of meaning. The sudden futility of language is not simply a personal loss, however, it reflects the deterioration of the human species, "once so ingenious with language."[42] Unlike the countless species which have already gone extinct, once humanity meets its end there will be no one to add it to the list, and in this sense the oblivion faced by humanity is total.

As Atwood and McCarthy conceptualize the apocalypse, the decimation of the human population is most significant for how it severs the continuity of the human world, revealing the tenuousness of its concepts and constructs. For this reason, one reading for hope in these works might begin by considering Lear's prescriptions for avoiding despair amid cultural devastation. In Lear's estimation, Plenty Coup is not only a witness to the collapse, but an exemplar of radical hope. Surviving the end of his world, he becomes the protagonist of his own post-apocalyptic story. His dilemma, as Lear explains, is that his way of life cannot be projected into the future, at least not as he had previously known or defined it. The alternative to despair therefore cannot be any concrete possibility: "The commitment is only to the bare possibility that, from this disaster, something good will emerge: the Crow shall somehow survive. Why that will be or how that will be is left open. The hope is held in the face of the recognition that, given the abyss, one cannot really know what survival means."[43] This uncertainty, however terrible to live within, also turns out to be a bulwark against premature fatalism. "What makes this hope *radical*," Lear argues, "is that it is directed toward a future goodness that transcends the current ability to understand what it is. Radical hope anticipates a good for which those who have the hope as yet lack the appropriate concepts with which to understand it."[44]

In *The Road,* the man and the boy are sustained by their hope that some semblance of a human world can be reestablished. This hope is almost always embodied by the boy, with his curiosity about "the world that for him was not even a memory" and his expectation that they will encounter other companions on the road—other children, or a dog, or other "good guys."[45] The man's own struggle to hope is bound up in his effort to live by a moral code, "to seek out the upright," even as the decay of civilization prompts him to wonder, "Upright to what?"[46] The man persists because he still believes that his actions are of consequence, and though he struggles to articulate this belief, his hope is efficacious in that it provides an orientation toward the future in which the man and the boy can discern better or worse possibilities for action. One point which Lear does not emphasize enough is that hope must be able to sustain action and inform practice if it is to be anything more than a compensatory fiction. "When your dreams are of some world that never was or of some world that will never be," the man tells the boy, "then you will have given up."[47] Here, McCarthy is instructive, as the hope which the man and boy cling to becomes a guide for their actions in the post-apocalyptic world, allowing them to "keep trying" and to consider, albeit with some irony, their "long-term goals."[48] The preservation of hope for a human world even takes precedence over survival. By establishing limits on what they will do to survive, McCarthy's protagonists safeguard the possibility of ethical life and manifest their hope for a renewal of the human world. Such decisions are critical to their sense that they are the "good guys," the ones "carrying the fire," with the implication being that the fire would go out, perhaps once and for all, were they to descend to the level of inhumanity that their circumstances seemingly demand.[49] These mantras are repeated whenever the man and the boy face a decision between their chances of survival and their hope for a better future: in the first instance to refrain from killing and eating a dog, or later when the man promises the boy that they would starve before engaging in cannibalism.[50] To partake of such brutality would be a fate worse than death: letting the fire go out.

At the novel's end, this hope is rewarded. The man dies, but not before he can entrust the boy with the first family they have encountered, a man and woman with children and a dog, who assure the boy that they do not eat people, and, though initially "weirded out" by his question, that they too are carrying the fire.[51] The novel's closing lines invoke once more the paradox of radical hope. On the one hand, McCarthy speaks of "a thing which could not be put back. Not be made right again," but also of "the world in its becoming," of places where "all things were older than man and they hummed of mystery."[52] Though the world that once was can never be "made right again," there are still possibilities, however impervious to human comprehension, which have yet to be realized.

If McCarthy's novel reads as a paean to hope, Atwood offers a more intensive interrogation. Particularly in *Oryx and Crake*, the story most rooted in the dystopian world of the Compounds, hope is an ambiguous good, and it is not always clear if the boldness it inspires is a virtue. To Crake, hope is yet another illusion that leads humanity to ruin. At one point he muses that "human beings hope they can stick their souls into someone else, some new version of themselves, and live on forever."[53] This, too, is hope borne of desperation, from the recognition of our morality and the imagination of our own deaths. The outcome, as far as Crake can tell, is overpopulation amidst dwindling resources. It seems to him that humanity would be better off with no sense of the future at all. When Jimmy tells Crake that "[w]e are doomed without hope," Crake replies that this is true "[o]nly as individuals." Nonetheless, Jimmy persists on hope, even if it is the bare hope that he is not the last of his kind.

Hope takes on a different character in *The Year of the Flood* and *MaddAddam*, whose perspective departs from the brooding, masculine pessimism of the first novel. As Le Guin observes their events are seen "largely through the eyes of women, powerless women" in contrast with *Oryx and Crake*, where women are a fugitive presence.[54] In that novel, Jimmy's mother abandons the meaningless life of the Compounds much as the mother in *The Road*, while the titular Oryx remains unknowable. This makes it all the more intriguing that the following novels are principally concerned with a woman's hopes. Toby, their primary protagonist, is an archetypal Atwood woman: a resourceful realist who responds to danger with cunning and grit. Her misadventures in the Plebelands lead her to the movement known as God's Gardeners, and while she joins out of desperation, she comes to find real meaning in their practices. *Oryx and Crake* introduces this group in passing as "a bunch of wackos" whose demonstrations against the biotech firms are outlawed and violently suppressed (it is also speculated that Jimmy's mother may have joined them when she fled the Compounds).[55] God's Gardeners reject the crass materialism of the Compounds and try to preserve what is left of humanity's connection to nature: growing their gardens on rooftops amid the Plebelands, they act as stewards of an ecological consciousness which most seem as eccentric at best. Toby herself initially considers them "fugitives from reality."[56] Unlikely as it seems, it is these fugitives who are key to what Le Guin calls the "hidden heart of the novel": its "irrational affirmation" of hope.[57] The Gardeners' gospel of restoration emphasizes possibilities of hope and renewal even as they reject much of civilization as monstrous. Their leaders preach a Jeremiad in which humanity will be laid low by a "Waterless Flood," "a massive die-off of the human race . . . due to overpopulation and wickedness."[58] As they see it, humanity has failed its "sacred task of Stewardship" by contributing to the extinction of the Earth's species.[59] Following the flood, the Gardeners believe they will replenish the Earth and begin anew. Though few Gardeners, in fact, survive the flood, it is because she has been initiated in their ways that Toby is able to weather the despair and guilt she feels as a survivor. "She ought to trust that she's here for a reason," she reminds herself, "to bear witness, to transmit a message, to salvage at least something from the general wreck."[60] In moments of crisis, she remembers what she learned from her mentors: "When the Flood rages, you must count the days . . . do not descend to a level that is too deep for any resurgence, or the Night will come in which all hours are the same to you, and then there will be no Hope."[61] What the Gardeners teach Toby is not really how to grow mushrooms or make potions (though these skills eventually prove useful), but how to preserve a way of life.

In a commentary on *Radical Hope,* Hubert Dreyfus draws on Heidegger to develop the idea of being a steward of a way of life.[62] He argues, with Heidegger, that this will entail sensitivity to marginal practices. For when a culture collapses, its central practices are no longer intelligible. With her Gardeners, Atwood demonstrates how a new culture can be built from the margins. Their practices are comical, corny and New Agey in all the wrong ways. But the virtues they instill nonetheless turn out to be essential for rebuilding the human world. Many of them are virtues like those that sustain the hopes of the man and boy in *The Road*: solidarity with human and nonhuman life, gratitude for what is given by nature or left behind by humanity, contrition for the harm one must sometimes do in the name of survival. They are habits, though not the only ones, by which we can exist in a cruel world without becoming cruel people. And in the context of a dystopian modernity, they are habits that should bound and direct our relentless instrumentalization of other, self, and world. Such virtues may in some sense preserve or retrieve humanity amid inhuman conditions, but from another vantage point they require a reimagining of the human—a retelling of the human story.

## CONCLUSION: SURVIVORS' STORIES

How do we carry on when worlds collapse and hope is all but lost? According to Lear, the Crow had to look for new ways of being Crow since the old ways had become impossible. This would require "a new Crow poet: one who could take up the Crow past and—rather than use it for nostalgia or ersatz mimesis—project it into vibrant new ways for the Crow to live and to be."[63] Similarly, Atwood and McCarthy illuminate how humanity can hold out hope for a human existence where flourishing once again becomes a possibility. For this to happen, death must be avoided, but so must despair. There must be some possibility of drawing creatively on the meanings, practices, and traditions that constitute a human life, out of which a new understanding of how to live may emerge even in the face of novel challenges. Lear, Atwood, and McCarthy all suggest that the tether across the abyss may at times be nothing more than a story.

For in each of these works, storytelling is one of the ways in which the survivors connect their struggles to the unfolding of the human narrative, even as they inaugurate a new chapter. Together, they suggest that to be human is not to share in an essence but to belong to a story. Atwood tells us that "even a castaway assumes a future reader, someone who'll come along later and find his bones and his ledger, and learn his fate."[64] Stories rescue the past from oblivion and overlay the present with meanings and continuities. Early in *The Road*, the boy asks to be read a story, and likewise the man understands their struggle "an old chronicle."[65] In Atwood's saga, Jimmy knits Crake's posthuman progeny into the human community by telling them, in mythicized form, the events of the first novel. By the end of *MaddAddam*, the Crakers will hand down the myth as well—the third novel is framed as a public reading of the Story of Toby. This telling is significant and dangerous because Crake had not wanted the Crakers to read. Crake believed, rather like Rousseau, that language and symbol lead inevitably to the dead-end of civilization. And so to initiate the Crakers into the world of stories is to wager that Crake was wrong and that humanity can find futures other than dystopia.

To do so, it will have to tell a different story. As its title slyly suggests, *MaddAddam* is nothing less than a creation myth for a community that is, on the one hand, post-human and, on the other, more human than the humanity they have replaced. Bizarre and visionary, the books could be read as a retelling of *Frankenstein*, itself a retelling of Prometheus, on a civilizational scale, or a sci-fi reimagining of the Book of Genesis. Humanity survives in the novel on the condition that its position be radically decentered. Humankind no longer dominates the natural world, instead it once again struggles to survive. And it gathers with it the products of its bioengineering, entities which blur the lines between human and animal, born and made, natural and unnatural. To the extent that *MaddAddam* connects the renewal of civilization with a return to nature, it is an impure nature, irrevocably altered by science and technology. In Shelley's *Frankenstein*, Victor disowns his Adam, but in Atwood's story humankind must embrace its monstrous fabrications, at least those which can exist without endangering humanity or the planet.

Atwood's narrative speaks to us from within this tangle of mythologies, and indeed her book seems to affirm that to be human is to be caught up in the telling and hearing of stories. At one point in *Oryx and Crake*, Jimmy tries to convince Crake of this point: "When any civilization is dust and ashes . . . art is all that's left over. Images, words, music. Imaginative structures. Meaning—human meaning, that is—defined by them. You have to admit that."[66] Crake does not admit that. But Atwood's novels vindicate Jimmy. He and Toby preserve humanity by telling its story in a new way. Their hope is that their story will be told as well. "People need such stories," Toby reflects, "because however dark, a darkness with voices in it is better than a silent void."[67]

## NOTES

1. Junot Diaz, "Editor's Note," in *Boston Review: Global Dystopias*, ed. Junot Diaz (Cambridge: MIT Press, 2017), 6. See also Tom Moylan, *Scraps of the Untainted Sky: Science Fiction, Utopia, and Dystopia* (Boulder: Westview, 2000) and Lyman Towers Sargent, "The Three Faces of Utopianism Revisited," *Utopian Studies* 5, no. 1 (1994).

2. Ursula K Le Guin, *Dancing at the Edge of the World: Thoughts on Words, Women, Places* (New York: Grove Press, 1989), 170.

3. Quoted in James Patrick Kelly and Kohn Kessel, *Feeling Very Strange: The Slipstream Anthology* (San Francisco: Tachyon, 2006), viii.

4. Benjamin Kunkel, "Dystopia and the End of Politics," *Dissent* 55, no. 4 (2008): 90.

5. Heather Hicks, *The Post-Apocalyptic Novel in the Twenty-First Century: Modernity Beyond Salvage* (London: Palgrave Macmillan, 2016), 2.

6. But one could begin with Gregory Claeys, *Dystopia: A Natural History* (Oxford: Oxford University Press, 2017); and Krishan Kumar, *Utopia and Anti-Utopia in Modern Times* (London: Blackwell, 1987).

7. See Robert Heilbroner, *Vision of the Future: The Distant Past, Yesterday, Today, and Tomorrow* (Oxford: Oxford University Press, 1995).

8. See Kumar, *Utopia and Anti-Utopia in Modern Times*, 38.

9. Nick Bostrom, "The Future of Humanity" in *New Waves in Philosophy of Technology*, eds. Jan Kyrre Berg Olsen, Evan Selinger, and Soren Riis (London: Palgrave Macmillan, 2009), 186.

10. For example, Kunkel, "Dystopia and the End of Politics," and Jill Lepore, "A Golden Age for Dystopian Fiction," *New Yorker*, June 5, 2017.

11. Peter Beaumont and Amanda Holpuch, "How The Handmaid's Tale Dressed Protests across the World," *Guardian*, August 3, 2018. https://www.theguardian.com/world/2018/aug/03/how-the-handmaids-tale-dressed-protests-across-the-world

12. For a lucid overview, see Anne Phillips, *The Politics of the Human* (Cambridge: Cambridge University Press, 2015).

13. Hans Jonas, *The Imperative of Responsibility* (Chicago: University of Chicago Press, 1984), 26.

14. Jonas, *Imperative of Responsibility*, 30.

15. Jonas, *Imperative of Responsibility*, 26–27.

16. Jonas, *Imperative of Responsibility*, 81.

17. Cormac McCarthy, *The Road* (New York: Knopf, 2006), 45.

18. Emily St.-John Mandel, *Station Eleven* (New York: Knopf, 2014), 33.

19. Kazuo Ishiguro, *Never Let Me Go* (New York: Vintage International, 2005), 263.

20. Ishiguro, *Never Let Me Go*, 279.

21. Dave Eggers, *The Circle* (New York: Knopf, 2014), 303.

22. Zadie Smith, "Generation Why?" in *Feel Free: Essays* (New York: Penguin, 2018), 60–61.

23. Margaret Atwood, *In Other Worlds: SF and Human Imagination* (New York: Doubleday, 2011), 91.

24. Margaret Atwood, *Oryx and Crake* (New York: Doubleday, 2003), 27.

25. Atwood, *Oryx and Crake*, 23.

26. Atwood, *Oryx and Crake*, 56.

27. Atwood, *Oryx and Crake*, 57.

28. Atwood, *Oryx and Crake*, 206.

29. Martin Heidegger, "The Question Concerning Technology," in *The Question Concerning Technology and Other Essays* (London: HarperCollins, 1977), 27.

30. For example, see Bill McKibben, *The End of Nature* (New York: Random House, 1989); and *Enough: Staying Human in an Engineered Age* (New York: Henry Holt, 2003); or Yuval Noah Harari, *Homo Deus: A Brief History of Tomorrow* (New York: HarperCollins, 2016).

31. Jonathan Lear, *Radical Hope: Ethics in the Face of Cultural Devastation* (Cambridge: Harvard University Press, 2006), 31–32.

32. Lear, *Radical Hope*, 32, 35.

33. McCarthy, *Road*, 1.

34. McCarthy, *Road*, 2.

35. McCarthy, *Road*, 50.

36. McCarthy, *Road*, 14, 152.

37. McCarthy, *Road*, 36.

38. McCarthy, *Road*, 153–54.

39. McCarthy, *Road*, 75.

40. Atwood, *Oryx and Crake*, 3–5.

41. Atwood, *Oryx and Crake*, 39.

42. Atwood, *Oryx and Crake*, 99.

43. Lear, *Radical Hope*, 97.

44. Lear, *Radical Hope*, 103.

45. McCarthy, *Road*, 46.

46. McCarthy, *Road*, 13.

47. McCarthy, *Road*, 160.

48. McCarthy, *Road*, 116, 135.

49. McCarthy, *Road*, 70.

50. McCarthy, *Road*, 108–9.

51. McCarthy, *Road*, 238–39.
52. McCarthy, *Road*, 249.
53. McCarthy, *Road*, 120.
54. Ursula K. Le Guin, "Margaret Atwood: *The Year of the Flood*," in *Words Are My Matter: Writings on Life and Books, 2000–2016* (Boston: Mariner Books, 2019), 197.
55. Atwood, *Oryx and Crake*, 213.
56. Margaret Atwood, *The Year of the Flood* (New York: Doubleday, 2009), 47.
57. Le Guin, "Margaret Atwood," 197.
58. Atwood, *Year of the* Flood, 47.
59. Atwood, *Year of the* Flood, 53.
60. Atwood, *Year of the* Flood, 95.
61. Atwood, *Year of the* Flood, 163.
62. Hubert Dreyfus, "Comments on Jonathan Lear's *Radical Hope*," *Philosophical Studies* 144, no.1 (2009).
63. Lear, *Radical Hope*, 51.
64. Atwood, *Oryx and Crake*, 41.
65. McCarthy, *Road*, 13.
66. Atwood, *Oryx and Crake*, 167.
67. Margaret Atwood, *MaddAddam* (New York: Doubleday, 2013), 154.

## BIBLIOGRAPHY

Atwood, Margaret. *Oryx and Crake*. New York: Doubleday, 2003.
———. *The Year of the Flood*. New York: Doubleday, 2009.
———. *In Other Worlds: SF and the Human Imagination*. New York: Doubleday, 2011.
———. *MaddAddam*. New York: Doubleday, 2013.
Bostrom, Nick. (2009) "The Future of Humanity." In *New Waves in Philosophy of Technology*, edited by Jan Kyrre Berg Olsen, Evan Selinger, and Soren Riis. London: Palgrave Macmillan, 2009.
Claeys, Gregory. *Dystopia: A Natural History*. Oxford: Oxford University Press, 2017.
Beaumont, Peter and Amanda Holpuch. "How The Handmaid's Tale Dressed Protests across the World." *Guardian*, August 3, 2018. https://www.theguardian.com/world/2018/aug/03/how-the-handmaids-tale-dressed-protests-across-the-world
Diaz, Junot, "Editor's Note." In *Boston Review: Global Dystopias*, edited by Junot Diaz. Cambridge: MIT Press, 2017.
Dreyfus, Hubert. "Comments on Jonathan Lear's *Radical Hope*." *Philosophical Studies*, 144, no. 1 (2009): 63–70.
Eggers, Dave. *The Circle*. New York: Knopf, 2013.
Harari, Yuval Noah. *Homo Deus: A Brief History of Tomorrow*. New York: HarperCollins, 2017.
Heidegger, Martin. "The Question Concerning Technology." In *The Question Concerning Technology and Other Essays*. London: HarperCollins, 1977.
Heilbroner, Robert. *Visions of the Future: The Distant Past, Yesterday, Today, and Tomorrow*. Oxford: Oxford University Press, 1995.
Hicks, Heather. *The Post-Apocalyptic Novel in the Twenty-First Century: Modernity beyond Salvage*. London: Palgrave Macmillan, 2016.
Ishiguro, Kazuo. *Never Let Me Go*. New York: Vintage International, 2005.
Jonas, Hans. *The Imperative of Responsibility*. Chicago: University of Chicago Press, 1984.
Kelly, James Patrick and John Kessel. *Feeling Very Strange: The Slipstream Anthology*. San Francisco: Tachyon, 2006.
Kumar, Krishan. *Utopia and Anti-Utopia in Modern Times*. London: Blackwell, 1987.
Kunkel, Benjamin. "Dystopia and the End of Politics." *Dissent* 55, no. 4 (2008): 89–98.
Le Guin, Ursula K. *Dancing at the Edge of the World: Thoughts on Words, Women, Places*. New York: Grove Press, 1989.

———. "Margaret Atwood: *The Year of the Flood*." In *Words Are My Matter: Writings About Life and Books, 2000–2016*. Boston: Mariner Books, 2019.
Lear, Jonathan. *Radical Hope: Ethics in the Face of Cultural Devastation*. Cambridge: Harvard University Press, 2006.
Lepore, Jill. "A Golden Age for Dystopian Fiction." *New Yorker*, June 5, 2017.
Mandel, Emily St. John. *Station Eleven*. New York: Knopf, 2014.
McCarthy, Cormac. *The Road*. New York: Knopf, 2006.
McKibben, Bill. *The End of Nature*. New York: Random House. 1989.
McKibben, Bill. *Enough: Staying Human in an Engineered Age*. New York: Henry Holt, 2003.
Moylan, Tom. *Scraps of the Untainted Sky: Science Fiction, Utopia, Dystopia*. Boulder: Westview Press, 2000.
Phillips, Anne. *The Politics of the Human*. Cambridge: Cambridge University Press, 2015.
Sargent, Lyman Towers. "The Three Faces of Utopianism Revisited." *Utopian Studies* 5, no.1 (1994): 1–37.
Smith, Zadie. "Generation Why?" In *Feel Free: Essays*. New York: Penguin, 2018.

*Chapter Two*

# Mirror, Mirror

*The Tragic Vision of* Star Trek: Discovery

## Libby Barringer

*Star Trek* stands out among science fiction offerings for its optimistic celebration of diplomacy, scientific achievement, and human intrepidness. Yet the first season of its most recent iteration—*Star Trek: Discovery* (2017)—provides a darker, more self-consciously "tragic" treatment of these themes. In this respect, the show reflects a recent turn in International Relations (IR) theory toward classical tragedy and the vision of politics it provides. Often referencing IR theorists such as Reinhold Neibuhr and Hans Morgenthau, tragedy is presented in this turn as the proper framework for a "classical realist" understanding of human relations; a corrective for excessive liberal optimism and for neo-realist theories which champion the rationalist pursuit of power at the expense of moral principle.[1] *Discovery*'s first season dramatizes these concerns, illustrating the value of ethical commitments for political survival—also the costs these exact—through the tragic suffering of its protagonists.

Yet as I argue here, *Discovery* also illustrates how a too-rigid understanding of tragedy can lead agents to fall prey to their own vision of political reality, one ruled by incommensurable, zero-sum conflicts between identities and values; a perspective which, itself, drives many tragic plots. Read alongside Friedrich Nietzsche's depiction of the transfiguring Dionysian "mirror" of the tragic stage in the *Birth of Tragedy,* I suggest that *Discovery* provides a useful diagnosis of this danger, also resources for a productive response. As we will see, the political and personal *failures* of different characters throughout *Discovery*'s first season challenge, rather than support, the stability of identities and their conflicts, exposing the dangers of overly rigid optimistic, or realist, worldviews. These themes are particularly present in

*Discovery*'s "Mirror Universe" plotline, where characters confront dystopian versions of themselves to Nietzschean effect.

*Discovery* thus shows how tragedy is perhaps too easily coopted in ways that "mirror" the hubristic excess of optimistic, rationalist faith it claims to combat. Tragedy's tendency to undermine clean binaries of political and ethical opposition allows us to find on *Discovery* an alternative political vision useful for contemporary politics; one where humanist, rational optimism never escapes the paradoxical conflicts and transformative potentials which tragedy invites us to attend. Rather than leading to a politics of despair, this Nietzschean reading reminds viewers they are active creators of their worldviews. They are therefore capable political agents, responsible for the outcomes their political visions create.

## TRAGIC REALISM

When *Star Trek* debuted in 1966, creator Gene Rodenberry imagined a United Federation of Planets bound by utopian, humanist principles. The series celebrates racial diversity, rational secularism, and Rodenberry's progressive ideals: "If man is to survive, he will have learned to take delight in the essential differences between men and between cultures. He will learn that differences in ideas [. . .  are] part of life's exciting variety, not something to fear."[2] Roddenberry's vision threads through the many permutations of *Star Trek*, with spinoffs such as *Star Trek: The Next Generation* and *Star Trek: Voyager* following a similar formula: with economic scarcity and war a relic of Earth's past, a principled Starfleet captain leads a diverse crew across the moral and political frontiers of the galaxy, seeking out new life and new civilizations; boldly going where no one has gone before.

Set several years before Rodenberry's original *Star Trek*, *Discovery* departs from its predecessors in a few ways. Formally, the series shifts from an episodic to a serialized plot. The season follows the titular USS Discovery through a disastrous war with the Klingons (an isolationist, aggressive alien race) and an excursion into the Terran Empire (a fascist regime from the "Mirror Universe"). Where earlier *Treks*' ensemble plots shift between lead characters every week, *Discovery* focuses on a single hero, Michael Burnham (Sonequa Martin-Green). These changes allow *Discovery* to wade into deeper narrative waters. While *Star Trek* has always engaged philosophically demanding subject matter—including the ethics of war, racism, torture, and sexual violence—these plots are typically contained to one or two episodes. *Discovery*, in contrast, lingers on the painful consequences of high-stakes decision making.

Indeed, the largest difference between *Discovery* and its predecessors is tone. *Discovery* is literally darker, with moody, stylish lighting, costume, and set designs that depart from the primary tones of other *Trek* series. *Discovery*'s costume designer Gersha Phillips comments that "Our mandate was to do something that felt real."[3] *Discovery*'s narrative content is also "realist." *Discovery*'s producers abandoned a long-standing rule of Roddenberry's to avoid personal conflicts between Starfleet officers, and violence on *Discovery* is more viscerally brutal, psychologically intimate, and posed in edgier, more visually explicit ways. "It's about how you portray war" executive producer Akiva Goldsman comments. "And war has real losses. If you're going to start with the proposition that the Federation is going to be exposed to the pressures of war, it should be real."[4]

"Realism" is a contested term. As Duncan Bell puts it, in casual speech realism "implies the will, and perhaps even the ability, to grasp that 'reality'—however it might be understood—and not to be misled by ephemera. It also suggests wariness of easy answers, and of unreflective optimism."[5] *Political* realism reflects this ethos and has been a dominant (if controversial) paradigm in IR for over seventy years. Derived from midcentury authors such as E. H. Carr, Reinhold Neibuhr, and Hans J. Morgenthau, realists typically agree on several fundamental premises.[6] First, that the international arena is structurally anarchic, unbound by higher authority. Second, that the survival of states depends on their material capabilities and alliances. Finally, and following these premises, realists hold that states must be fundamentally concerned with power—its forms, sources, and material effects—and that the demands of maintaining power in the international arena can conflict with the moral and legal limits which define domestic politics.

To varying degrees realists are therefore skeptical of the progressive view that secular liberal institutions, scientific advancement, and humanitarian legalism can yield a peaceful international order.[7] Some "neo-realists" reject normative questions from the calculus of state security entirely, or narrowly bind such concerns to state interest.[8] The pervasiveness of these beliefs has real world implications. As Richard Ned Lebow comments, speaking of the ubiquitous use of realist justifications in foreign policy briefs, "Realism is not another arcane academic doctrine. As currently formulated, it offers an intellectual justification for a range of policies at odds with core democratic and humanitarian values."[9]

Realism and *Star Trek* thus might seem strange bedfellows. Nonetheless, *Discovery*'s first season depicts a realist clash of civilizations between Klingon, Federation, and Terran "states"; an existentially fraught venture where Federation idealism is continually thrown against the demands of war. In this way *Discovery* engages what has been termed the "tragedy" of IR. Nicholas Rengger comments,

> It is a common place, after all, that realist accounts of politics depict the political realm of 'recurrence and repetition' where the dichotomy between

human moral self-understanding and the necessities of successful political action is unavoidably confronted to the detriment of the former of the collapse of the latter. The recognition of this permanent tension in human experience is one of the aspects of realist thinking that gives it its real intellectual, also moral, power; and without denying that there is considerable variety within the realist tradition of political thought, the word that is often used to refer to this condition, by many realists, in many different contexts, is tragedy.[10]

The use of classical tragedy as realism's privileged metaphor has been well documented.[11] In the tragic heroes of fifth-century Athens realists find "magnificent but flawed actors [who] are forced to confront the limits of their power" making "critical but unavoidable errors in their relations with other states and thereby producing violence, great pain, suffering, and sometimes their own demise."[12] Tragedy provides a fictive construct that exposes basic truths about the political reality states must navigate, and sometimes suffer.

IR theorists have lately returned to tragedy as critics and reformers of realist thought. These authors argue that classical tragedy could supply an important corrective for realist and neo-realist accounts which focus too narrowly on the pursuit of material power. For Lebow, and others such as Mervyn Frost and Toni Erskine, classical tragedy illustrates why ethical considerations must be reclaimed for realist thinking. Responding critically to neo-realists such as Kenneth Waltz, Lebow suggests tragedy "provides the basis for an ethical and intellectual framework with which to confront life" one which shows "no amount of knowledge or power can protect against the kinds of reversals tragic heroes encounter or the suffering they bring on." In fact, a narrow reliance on power to the exclusion of all else makes "reversals more likely by encouraging hubris."[13]

For many, tragedy's value rests in the political condition it depicts: "the tragic," a reality of conflicting, incommensurable identities and practices.[14] By this view tragedies like Aeschylus' *Oresteia,* and especially Sophocles' *Antigone*, illustrate how equally valid norms may sit in direct opposition, necessitating agonizing choices for political actors between right and might—or right and *right*. Tragedy, therefore, also addresses liberal optimism, offering what James Mayall calls "a necessary antidote to the hubris of progressive thought and the constant liberal temptation to avoid accepting responsibility for well-intentioned actions that go wrong."[15] These authors suggest adopting a tragic outlook could mitigate morally disastrous outcomes between states—an optimistic end made possible by tragic education.[16]

Yet many hesitate over this turn. A central worry is that tragedy's political vision is enervating and fatalist, undermining the grounds of ethical agency. Rengger thus warns that replacing utopian visions of liberal progress with tragedy's unrelenting pessimism commits the same error in reverse, "throwing the reasonable baby out with the rationalist bathwater."[17] Others, such as J. Peter Euben and Tracy Strong note these objections concern the way tragedy—or "the tragic"—is read, often simplified to a kind of existentially loaded value pluralism.[18] Viewing tragedy as structural conflict where a hero—or a state—stands doggedly "for" one set of values, colliding against others to disastrous effect, yields a political vision both overly tidy and overly determined.[19] As Paige duBois notes, such readings ignore the relational, polyphonous qualities of tragedy; its tendency to undermine, rather than affirm, the "intractable character, the hero, the subject."[20] Or, as Euben succinctly argued: "For tragedy to work, it must master you before you master it."[21]

As I will argue, *Discovery* dramatizes central themes from this turn, using Burnham's tragic fall to illustrate the necessity of ethical practices for a secure, sustainable politics. The conflict between the isolationist, aggressive Klingons; the fascist, imperialist Terrans; and the progressive, humanist Federation is presented as a tragedy that might be avoided by future others educated by the hard-earned wisdom of Discovery's crew. *Discovery*'s optimistic ending thus endorses a humbled "tragic realism" in terms similar to Lebow, Erskine, and Frost. Yet in keeping with critiques by duBois, Euben, and Strong, I argue this way of reading tragedy—and this way of reading *Discovery*—overlooks tragedy's critical potential to unsettle and dissolve rigid oppositions. And, with reference to Friedrich Nietzsche, we will see it does so in a particularly tragic way.

## "CONTEXT IS FOR KINGS"

Episode one of *Discovery* begins in the desert. Captain Phillipa Georgiou (Michelle Yeoh) and Burnham become stranded on an alien planet, unable to contact their ship. Georgiou cheerfully suggests they take a walk: "follow in my footsteps, even lines." As they walk Georgiou optimistically looks to the future. Burnham, meanwhile, worries about surviving an approaching sand storm. She expresses frustration when they arrive back where they started. "You've walked us in a circle!" "Not *exactly* a circle" Georgiou responds. The camera pans back to reveal Georgiou's ship, the USS Shenzhou, appearing to beam them safely away. As the ship speeds off we see Georgiou's path has traced the Starfleet insignia in the sand—a sigil locating them in the wasteland [1:1].

This opening sequence anticipates the themes of *Discovery*'s first season, which push a Federation crew into the moral wastelands of war. To tell this story, *Discovery* borrows formal conventions from tragic emplotment: an admirable hero struggles with a dramatic reversal of fortune (*peripeteia*), resulting from a violation of sacred boundaries due to mistaken judgment (*hubris*, *hamartia*); the consequences unravel the fortunes of the play's characters (*lysis*) yielding suffering (*pathos*) and tragic understanding (*anagnori-*

sis).[22] A human raised by Vulcans, Burnham is an exemplary Starfleet officer. Yet early in the season she mutinously orders a preemptive attack against the Klingons in violation of Starfleet principles. Fallout leads to Georgiou's death, the destruction of the Shenzhou, and a devastating war with the Klingons. Stripped of her rank and conscripted as a wartime asset, *Discovery*'s first season follows Burnham as she comes to recognize the saving power of the principles she has violated.[23]

*Discovery* uses these tragic conventions to dramatize the dangers of a narrowly power-centric politics. But *Discovery* also explores the difficulty of staying true to one's values when confronted by other principled actors—a double-bind often emphasized by IR scholars. As Mervyn Frost puts it, "At the heart of the tragic sequence—from ethical struggle, to act, to negative consequences—is an *agon* which is a conflict between the ethical values embedded in rival practices, both of which are fundamentally constitutive of the protagonist as he or she values him or herself to be."[24] These concerns form the moral stakes of *Discovery*'s first season, and are explored through Discovery's interactions with Klingon and Terran cultures, alongside Burnham's personal attempts to rebuild her life.

Particularly important is Burnham's relationship with Captain Gabriel Lorca (Jason Isaacs), under whom she is stationed aboard Discovery with her former Shenzhou crewmates. In contrast to the humanitarian Georgiou, Lorca is laser focused on his war mission and prone to bending rules. He provides a foil for Burnham—having already violated Federation principles in the name of survival once, will she continue down that path? Lorca presents these stakes when he recruits Burnham:

> I did choose you, but not for the reasons you think. Your assumption that the Klingons were waiting in ambush at the Binary Stars was predictive. You chose to do the right thing over and above what was sanctioned even at great cost to yourself. And that is the kind of thinking that wins wars [1:3].

Here Lorca echoes neo-realist logic, erecting "a firewall between foreign affairs and domestic politics."[25] Lorca's argument that correctly predicting violence *justifies* illegal acts neatly exempts intergalactic action from the legal boundaries governing Federation politics. Second, Lorca explicitly redefines Burnham's mutiny as "the right thing." For Lorca, the demands of war determine the rightness of an act: moral principles are not independently or universally valid. He drives this point home with a realist credo. "Universal law is for lackeys. Context is for kings."

Burnham accepts Lorca with reservations: "Before I was a mutineer I was a first officer in Star Fleet [. . .] it is who I am and who I will always be" [*ibid*]. This response articulates a recurring tension on Discovery between identity and survival, seen particularly in the presentation of Klingon and

Terran cultures. The Klingon T'Kuvma, for instance—a religious leader who seeks Klingon unification—presents the Federation threat in structural, existential terms: "Remain Klingon or die!" It is not hostility which makes the Federation an enemy, but the *fact* of their existence as a rival community. Indeed, T'Kuvma's disciples repeatedly warn of the "assimilation" that coexistence with the Federation will bring.[26] "Here is the great lie!" T'Kuvma says to gathered Klingons as a hologram of Georgiou proclaims, "We come in peace" [1:1,2]![27] For the Klingons, intergalactic politics are defined by existential oppositions which are, at heart, zero-sum.[28]

The second half of the season extends these themes by revealing Lorca is not actually Starfleet, but Terran. We learn early in the show that Discovery is equipped with an experimental "spore" drive that uses inter-dimensional fungal networks to move laterally through space. Lorca manipulates Discovery's crew into jumping to his home dimension, the Mirror Universe, where he promptly attempts to overthrow the Terran Emperor—the "mirror" Georgiou [1:10]. The Terran Empire is a brutal, supremacist regime maintained through fascist displays of dominance; a reflection of the Federation stripped of its principles. Like the Klingons, the Terrans enact a politics of existentially defined sovereignty and zero-sum conflict, but they discard all pretense of moral justification. Theirs is a world of unrepentant *machtpolitik*, friends and enemies. "Are you with me," the Empress demands, "or are you against me" [1:15]?

*Discovery* treats both Klingon and Terran worldviews as politically insufficient and morally dangerous, exposing tragically how, for each, "the search for security can lead to insecurity."[29] Throughout the course of the season viewers watch as violence initiated for the reasonable end of protecting existence comes to define it. Values like honor, cooperation, and trust are sacrificed in the name of securing power—cynically, for the Terrans; inadvertently for the Klingons. Crucially, however, as the season progresses Starfleet *also* begins to adopt survivalist rationality, denying their ethical agency through reference to the structural, existential threats of the international arena.

This tendency is critiqued in the season's climax. Facing the immanent destruction of Earth, Starfleet leadership turns to deposed Emperor Georgiou (who Burnham has impulsively rescued). Georgiou explains the Terrans defeated the Klingons through genocide, detonating a bomb in their home planet's core. Starfleet leadership desperately adopts her strategy. When the plan is revealed Burnham confronts Starfleet Admiral Katrina Cornwall (Jayne Brook).

> Burnham: "Is this how Starfleet wins the war? Genocide?"

Cornwall: "[. . .] Terms of "atrocity" are convenient, after the fact. The Klingons are on the verge of wiping out the federation. [. . .] We do not have the luxury of principles."
Burnham: "That *is all we have*, admiral. A year ago, I stood alone, and I believed our survival was more important than our principles. I was wrong. Do we need a mutiny today, to prove who we are?" [1:15]

Preparing to commit mutiny for the second time—this time in *support* of Starfleet principles—the Discovery crew stands with Burnham. "We are Starfleet!" each of them announces as they rise, refusing Cornwall's plan [*ibid*].

*Discovery* thus dramatizes how moral disasters are often seductive because they are rational. Because the Klingon Empire is seen as existentially opposed to the Federation, the question of genocide is not one of moral limits but logical necessity. "All are agreed that we have no choice but to proceed." The Vulcan Ambassador Sarek (James Frain) reports to Cornwall. "Our very existence hangs in the balance" [1:14]. Indeed, nearly every major violation of Federation principles on Discovery involves Vulcan influence—a race known for their advanced rationalism. It is Sarek who tells Burnham (he is also her adoptive father) that the Vulcans preemptively shot any Klingon cruisers they encountered to establish peace. This "Vulcan Hello" provides the template for Burnham's mutiny. "The Klingon threat is always immanent, and inevitable" Burnham tells Georgiou [1:1]. It is similarly Sarek who is persuaded by the Terran Empress's genocidal reasoning. "You face annihilation." She argues. "Is it not logical to do anything you can to ensure the survival of your people?" [1:14]

Viewed through the lens of tragic realism, *Discovery* shows how rationalization proceeds from whichever premises it starts from, and continues without regard for moral or political boundaries. Constraining reason's excesses requires strong ethical practices capable of interrupting its processes. The trap into which Sarek and Cornwall fall (and which the Terrans embrace) is to mistakenly ignore that acting according to the logic of violent power confines one, politically, to power's limited resources. *Discovery* thus offers its audiences a lesson similar to what Lebow draws from tragedy: "interests and justice are inextricably connected and mutually constitutive. On the surface they appear to be in conflict [but . . .] interests cannot be intelligently considered, formulated, or pursued outside a community and the identities it constructs and sustains."[30]

*Discovery*'s closing episode articulates this conclusion explicitly. Having narrowly avoided moral disaster, Burnham and Cornwall hand over their explosive device to L'Rell (Mary Chieffo), a former spymaster of T'Kuvma turned reluctant ally. L'Rell uses this power to unify the Klingons, who ally with the Federation. The war is thus ended, and for her heroic efforts Burnham's rank is restored. In the finale, Burnham reaffirms Federation values before Starfleet command:

> No, we will not take shortcuts on the path to righteousness. No, we will not break the rules that protect us from our basest instincts. No, we will not allow desperation to destroy moral authority. I am guilty of all these things. Some say that in life there are no second chances. Experience tells me that this is true, but we can only look forward. We have to be torchbearers, so we can see the path to lasting peace. We will continue to explore, discovering new worlds, new civilizations. Yes, that is the United Federation of Planets. *Yes.* That is Starfleet! [1:15]

Here military power is rhetorically linked to the enlightened self-interest of a commitment to Starfleet's moral code. These values make the Federation an ally capable of honoring Klingon integrity and resisting Terran shortcuts—the only true "path to lasting peace."

This conclusion is given a tragic frame. Rather than excusing her former actions or the losses of the war, Burnham pointedly acknowledges her guilt. Yet the staging of the final award ceremony conveys a "cautious [hope] for progress, tempered by awareness of forgetting the inherent limitations of human beings."[31] The implications of the scene—a bright set with soaring music, staged as a lecture hall with Burnham "teaching" Starfleet Command—is that tragic suffering has granted Discovery's crew the moral authority to guide Starfleet to a better future. The season thus resolves by folding its realist, tragic commitments *into* Rodenberry's progressive vision: optimism enabled by tragic education. "Yes," Burnham concludes, smiling, "that is who *we are . . . and who we will always be*" [1:15].

While appealing, we might hesitate over the ease with which this conclusion restores Starfleet's moral identity and settles *Discovery*'s tragic events as steps along a progressive path. "Every planet of the Federation has made the odyssey out of darkness into light. So too have the Klingons" Burnham says. "[. . .] But make no mistake: these were bleak times, times we cannot repeat, times we cannot forget" [1:15]. There is a troubling disjuncture here between this optimistic conclusion and the "bleak times" which the viewing audience has just born witness. Most disturbing is that L'Rell enforces the Klingon-Federation alliance with the same genocidal technology the Federation refuses on moral grounds. Burnham's speech brackets this fact, glossing L'Rell's coup as progress. Both Federation and Klingon identities are reasserted here, but not in comfortable ways.

As I will argue, the disjuncture between *Discovery*'s optimistic conclusion and the troubling moral and political failures chronicled in its first season provides a tragic insight of its own. By focusing on the very real dangers of abandoning ethical identity for expediency, it is easy to miss that a too-rigid commitment to one's values is also a tragic error. It is one of the most potent forms of *hamartia*, the devastating mistake resulting from a failure to acknowledge other perspectives. As Tracy Strong comments, "In tragedy, that which is tragic is not the *confrontation* of two non-commensurable values [. . .but] rather that which is *consequent* to the insistence that one's own stance and point of view is the only admissible one."[32] To see what we might gain by rereading *Discovery* along these lines, let us turn to Friedrich Nietzsche.

## DIONYSIAN MIRRORS

Nietzsche's early book *The Birth of Tragedy* traces the origins and "death" of tragedy in ancient Greece, ending with a meditation on the political significance of tragic culture, and the possibility for a similar achievement in his own time.[33] For Nietzsche, tragedy acts as a "transfiguring mirror," enabling a uniquely active, healthy political culture by providing a distinctive critical orientation toward the fixedness of cultural identity while simultaneously honoring its importance; an orientation I argue we can productively seek on Discovery. This perspective unsettles the assumption that conflict *must* result between distinct identities—and is thereby natural or inherently justified. Nietzsche famously explains this perspective as the synthesis of two countervailing worldviews: the Dionysian and the Apollonian.

The Apollonian, taken from Nietzsche's (idiosyncratic) view of the god Apollo, places self-knowledge at its heart, affirming those social and political boundaries that shape the identities of individuals or whole peoples. Drawing on phrases adorning Apollo's temple at Delphi, "know thyself" and "nothing in excess," Nietzsche associates the Apollonian above all with the *principum individuationes,* the individuating principle [BT:2]. Dionysus, in contrast, was the god of drunkenness, sex, madness, excess, and paradox. The Dionysian orientation views life as part of the continuous, chaotic flux of natural existence writ large, the "fundamental knowledge of the oneness of everything existent, the conception of individuation as the primal cause of evil" [BT:10; WP:585; TI:110].[34] Dionysian awareness is ecstatic: it takes persons out of themselves, collapsing Apollonian, individuating distinctions in favor of continuity with the joyful, frightening, and unstable whole.

The achievement of tragedy—quickly overcome by the rise of Socratic rationalism—was to productively synthesize these countervailing orientations. To understand the stakes here, first consider a pre-tragic version of their dynamic. For Nietzsche tragedy supplants the world of Homeric myth, itself an Apollonian response to Dionysian reality: "The same impulse which calls art into being," he comments "[. . .] was also the cause of the Olympian world which the Hellenic 'will' made use of as a transfiguring mirror"

[BT:3]. Why describe myth as a 'transfiguring mirror'? Earlier in this passage Nietzsche comments,

> The Greeks knew and felt the horror of existence. That he could endure this terror at all he had to interpose between himself and life the radiant birth dream of the Olympians [. . . this terror] was again and again overcome by the Greeks with the Olympian *middle world* of art. [BT:3]

As a "mirror," Homeric myth reflects reality back to its adherents in altered form: poetic art overcomes the "horror of existence" by organizing one's experience of reality in a meaningful way [BT:7; WP:585]. Myths depict, create, and legitimate distinctions—god/human/animal, citizen/foreigner, glorious/shameful, just/unjust—providing stable sources of meaning that differentiate an individual's existence from the continuous natural cycles of creation and destruction Dionysian awareness reveals. As "mirror images" of human life, Olympian myths thereby make mortal existence meaningful. "Thus the gods justify life: they themselves live it—the only satisfactory theodicy" [BT:3]!

For Nietzsche the tragic stage was also a transfiguring mirror. Yet where Olympian myth *veils*, tragedy *exposes* Dionysian reality by "repeating in miniature, as it were, the tendency of the whole" [WP:617]. Nietzsche especially identifies this function of tragedy with the tragic chorus, a mass of dancers he describes dressed as satyrs who stood between the Athenian spectators and the action of the stage:

> The Greek man of culture felt himself nullified in the presence of the satiric chorus; and this is the most immediate effect of Dionysian tragedy, that the state and society and, quite generally, the gulfs between man and man give way to an overwhelming feeling of unity leading back to the very heart of nature. [BT:7]

What does it mean to say the man of culture is "nullified"? For Nietzsche tragedy assaults the naturalness, or necessity, of one's identity. The entire design of the ancient theater provoked this nullification [BT:7]. The choral mass of half-human, half-man creatures blends into the crowd of spectators, blurring the distinctions between natural animal life and "cultured" existence, simultaneously connecting and separating viewers and the choral figures on stage.[35] These blurred distinctions provoke an ecstatic response: by identifying with the chorus, persons are thrown out of their ordinary perspectives which take their value commitments and worldviews as given. These are thus revealed as the products of cultural "dreaming"—which is to say, they are exposed as *art*.

When Nietzsche writes of "art as the joyous hope that the spell of individuation may be broken" [BT:3], he references how tragedy reveals identity as human creation. Cultural values give meaning to mortal life, but they also impose logical, stable orders on a reality, and beings, which are fundamentally characterized by change. No single theoretical framework or cultural order can universally accommodate Dionysian reality. Losing sight of this insufficiency invites disaster: "[. . .] the high tide of the Dionysian destroyed from time to time all those little circles in which the one-sidedly Apollonian "will" had sought to confine the Hellenic spirit" [BT:9]. The tragic chorus provides the "mirror image in which the Dionysian man contemplates himself" because it "represents existence more truthfully, really, and completely than the man of culture does *who ordinarily considers himself as the only reality*" [BT:8 my emphasis].

This last point indicates the critical perspective which the "mirror" of tragedy provides. For Nietzsche, tragedy reminds audiences that one's cultural framing of the world is distinct from Dionysian *reality as such*. Tragedy shows the struggles of Apollonian individuals, each "with right on his side" who suffer because they treat as natural—as the only, complete reality—what is merely one possible organization of it [BT:9]. As Tracy Strong notes, Nietzsche defines this error as a kind of "tyranny." Imposing one's worldview on reality as universal truth arises "from *the failure to remember* that we live in worlds that we have made: tyranny is thus a forgetting of human agency."[36]

Nietzsche is not suggesting here that we can simply do away with cultural norms, or that our identities are "fake." On the contrary, these make our experience of reality meaningful and intelligible: we cannot do without them. Nietzsche makes this point by comparing the Dionysian man to Hamlet, paralyzed by his existential awareness. We require art to transform "these nauseous thoughts about the horror or absurdity of existence into notions with which one can live" [BT:7]; but this yields a double bind. On the one hand, no stable cultural framework can encapsulate Dionysian becoming; clinging to these too rigidly invites disaster. On the other, culture cannot be changed without "sacrilege"—that is, without assaulting the sources of meaning for our own lives and, crucially, what is meaningful for others [BT:9]. What tragedy captures for Nietzsche is thus "an existential social condition" generated by "the self-constitutive processes through which social agents create meaningful interpretations of the world."[37]

This double bind gives tragedy its political power as an emancipating, frightening institution. Tragedy is emancipating because it suggests we can be other than what we are. Nietzsche thus points to Prometheus alongside Dionysus as the original tragic hero, a titan who steals fire and liberates mankind from Olympian control. But Prometheus, and humanity, suffer terribly for this violation [BT:9,10]. Tragedy is thus also frightening. As creatures of becoming we alone are responsible for what we engender; but what we can become encompasses the full spectrum of human-animal capacities, gracious and horrific. Tragedy teaches that "all that exists is just and unjust and equally justified in both" [BT:9]. The Dionysian mirror of tragedy exposes the mutability of our sacred commitments *and* the costs of their violation. It enables audiences to recognize themselves as creatures of becoming, with all the destabilizing, frightening, and liberating potential that implies.

I argue below that *Discovery* stages tragic, Dionysian "nullifications" through a similarly Nietzschean device: the transfiguring mirror. Through its Mirror Universe plotline, *Discovery* exposes how identity-constituting worldviews are constructed and obliterated in ways which complicate an overly rigid reading of *Discovery*'s central conflicts—and of tragedy itself. From this Nietzschean perspective, *Discovery* continually explores how rigid identities fail to accommodate the complex world of becoming. These failures transform the celebratory ending of *Discovery* into a moment of tragic uncertainty which exposes the power of community and identity, also the frightening, liberating potential for each to be remade.

## "THE WAR WITHOUT, THE WAR WITHIN"

To survive the Mirror Universe, Discovery's crew must act like Terrans. Through a series of impersonations and confrontations with Mirror colleagues (and Mirror versions of themselves) *Discovery* shows how identities are both powerful and limited; a Nietzschean perspective which destabilizes perceived structural conflicts between cultures—and the realist politics they justify—on Discovery as a whole. These confrontations are explicitly set against a Dionysian background: the inter-dimensional fungal network which connects all realities and all iterations of individuals to each other, living and dead [1:12]. Against this Dionysian framing the interactions between Federation, Terran, and Klingon transform from tidy structural oppositions into unstable continuums.

Cadet Tilly (Mary Wiseman), for instance, a kind and principled science officer, transforms into her Terran counterpart "Captain Killy." *Discovery* introduces this change by showing Tilly facing a hyper-realistic mirror of herself dressed as a Terran. "You are a captain now." Burnham says, comforting. "No, *I'm* not." Tilly responds. "*She* is [. . .] I'm going to have nightmares about myself now." The effect here is nullifying. Tilly's sense of herself as "the only reality" is undone by her Mirror self, who exposes a frightening capacity to be other while remaining inescapably her reflection. "You achieved your rank by stabbing your rival in bed." Burnham says, briefing Tilly. "That's not possible!" Tilly objects [1:10]. Indeed, the longer Discovery's crew remains in the Mirror Universe, the more unstable the distinctions between Starfleet and Terran become. This discomforting slide is summed up by Burnham, impersonating Empress Georgiou's adopted daughter. While playing this role, she *actually* commits several morally dubious deeds: killing a crewmate (in self-defense), overseeing executions, even feasting on a sentient species. "Every moment is a test." She narrates. "[. . .] Can you continue to pretend to be one of them, even as little by little it kills the person you really are?" [1:11]

These Dionysian nullifications illustrate that staying true to oneself is not a simple matter. How do you stay true—for or against—an identity which cannot be taken for granted as knowable, or fixed? Here it is helpful to consider *Discovery*'s central romance between Burnham and Ash Tyler (Shazad Latif), Discovery's security officer. Both Tyler and Burnham undergo transformations on Discovery. Through flashbacks we see Burnham as a child on Vulcan, purging her human traits; later she arrives on the Shenzhou speaking dismissively of human emotion [1:2]. While this Vulcan persona softens under Georgiou's humane (and human) mentorship, the process is painful. "All my life the conflict has been between logic and emotion." Burnham tells Tyler, "and now it's my emotions that I'm fighting [. . .] I want to cry, but I have to smile; I'm angry, but I want to love; and I'm hurt, but there's hope. What is this?" Tyler laughs. "It's just being human" [1:6]. Burnham echoes this confusion in the Mirror Universe. Now lovers, Burnham makes the Dionysian observation to Tyler that she does not truly know herself. "We all start out with the same drives, the same needs," she says. "Maybe all of us, no matter where we are from, we never really know what darkness is waiting inside" [1:11].

The irony of these moments is quickly revealed: Tyler is a Klingon sleeper agent and quite literally *not* human inside. He is T'Kuvma's disciple Voq, who has had his psyche and skeleton grafted into a human body. As Burnham struggles to reconcile herself to "being human," we watch as Tyler is psychologically torn between "being human," a victim of Klingon torture and Burnham's lover, and (re)becoming Voq, who despises Starfleet and loves L'Rell. This process comes to a head when Tyler literally confronts himself in the Mirror Universe. Listening to his Mirror self argue for Federation-like values provokes a mental crisis Tyler-Voq resolves by trying to kill his opposite, then Burnham [1:10,11]. Once stabilized, he encompasses both human and Klingon identities. Tyler's story concentrates *Discovery's* Nietzschean questions: what does it mean to *always be* Starfleet, or to *remain Klingon*? Put more generally, what does it mean to belong to a community, or to define oneself against others, when as creatures of becoming such identities face infinite transgressions from without and within?

The Nietzschean "agonies of individuation [BT:10]" which *Discovery* chronicles suggest a tragic response to these questions. Commenting on the "necessity of sacrilege" Nietzsche notes, how un-Apollonian this pessimistic notion [of tragic suffering] is. For Apollo wants to grant repose to individual beings precisely by drawing boundaries between them and by again and again calling these to mind as the most sacred laws of the world, with his demands for self-knowledge and measure. [BT:9]

Here Nietzsche describes the comfort of viewing our identities as fixed. These grant us "repose" when viewed as naturally immutable because they stabilize the world in ways we need not, ultimately, bear responsibility for. Yet the tragic suffering of agents like Burnham and Tyler—also Tilly, Cornwall, and Georgiou—is not due to a fated clash of opposed values. It emerges through commitments to, and transgressions of, identities which are contingent, prone to failure, and the products of human, all too human art.

It is important, then, that *Discovery* presents these psychological struggles alongside the realist dynamics analyzed above where structural, existential conflict *defines* the relations between Federation, Klingon, and Terran states. The effect is tragic in a Nietzschean sense. On the one hand, the interpersonal struggles of Discovery's crew undermine the naturalness of these identities— and their conflicts—by showing how they fall short of the complex, changing persons they claim. Indeed, *Discovery* is full of characters who inhabit multiple identities: Voq becomes Tyler; Burnham becomes Vulcan, then Terran; and Empress Georgiou and Lorca become Starfleet captains. On the other hand, the differences between Federation, Klingon and Terran are not "fake." Characters like Georgiou, Voq, and Burnham show repeatedly they are willing to stake their lives, and the lives of others, on their commitments. The result is to expose how "sacred" identities generate political consequences that spill over each other in painful, liberating, and unexpected ways.

A Nietzschean reading of *Discovery* thus points beyond the danger, exposed by tragic realism, of jettisoning moral principle for survival. It suggests that while persons cannot meaningfully "survive" without formative, moral identities, it is equally disastrous to forget these are creations of mutual projects one participates in, and which one remains responsible for. Returning to Burnham's second, climactic mutiny, Cornwall's insistence that "terms of moral atrocity are convenient after the fact" thus mistakenly mirrors the Terran rejection of Federation values as "childish delusions." Both confuse their realist *visions* of political reality, with its existential, structural conflicts between identities, for *political reality as such*. There is no room to question whether political decisions involving these "others"—Burnham's initial mutiny, Cornwall's genocidal plan, or more subtly, the enabling of L'Rell's coercive regime—might be made differently. Defining political reality as *necessitating* morally costly conflict is itself a tragic error; the sort a Nietzschean reading of *Discovery* exposes to sight.

*Discovery* also suggests an alternative perspective. In the final episode before parting ways, Burnham reveals to Tyler that Klingon raiders killed her parents. Tyler asks "How can you not hate them? And me, for what I've become?" Burnham shrugs. "[. . .] I look around [. . .] I see people living their lives. Maybe it's not normal to us, but in their own way, ordinary." He responds, "I can see both sides *literally*. The side I've chosen is where you stand, where it's possible to feel compassion and sympathy for your enemy. But I can guarantee no Klingon ever felt that way toward you." Burnham corrects him: "*You did*" [1:15]. Where Tyler praises tragic empathy, he also reasserts Klingon and Human opposition. Burnham insists on agency. Her perspective is thus closer to the "middle path" Nietzsche identifies with tragedy. Poised between paralyzing Dionysian capaciousness and tyrannizing Apollonian individuation, this perspective recognizes the power of the identities given to us, shaping our sense of "ordinary." But it also insists these identities are not determined; nor do they determine us.

## CONCLUSION: "WHAT'S PAST IS PROLOGUE"

I have argued that *Discovery* presents a meditation on realist politics. Through the tragic conflicts between Federation, Terran, and Klingon worldviews, *Discovery* demonstrates the importance of ethical identity for political survival, reflecting a recent turn toward tragedy in IR theory. Yet *Discovery* also reveals how an overly narrow appropriation of tragedy can yield a tragic error. For Nietzsche, tragedy exposes the dangers of forgetting our roles as creators of the worldviews we inhabit. Read in a Nietzschean way, I argue *Discovery* provides a similar exposure, and a productive response. Against the fatalist dangers of moral enervation which critics of tragedy in IR theory warn, Nietzschean tragedy reminds us of our agency.

This reading also transforms *Discovery*'s ending, casting its optimistic resolution in a more uncertain light. Indeed, each commitment Burnham reaffirms—to uphold Federation law, to refuse to let fear "destroy moral authority"—has been dramatically violated over the season by the very individuals she addresses. Even the peace she celebrates is morally tenuous, guaranteed by the threat of genocidal destruction. When listening to Burnham reassert Starfleet identity—"this is who we are, and *who we will always be*"—after a season's worth of failures, we may seem to have walked in a circle; clinging to optimism in the wasteland. But, importantly, the individuals who *affirm* Starfleet identity have changed. The Klingon L'Rell, the hybrid Tyler-Voq, and the deposed Empress Georgiou are not exiled at the end of *Discovery*'s first season, but incorporated into a new Federation reality. Likewise, Burnham's final speech incorporates Klingon identifiers: "we must be torchbearers" she states, using Voq's former title, "so we can see the path to lasting peace" [1:15].

Here the Federation is reaffirmed in keeping with a Nietzschean middle way: a community bound by principles that never transcend the creatures of becoming who enact them, defined but not determined. By the same token, the moral failures of *Discovery*'s first season do not repudiate its hopeful vision. Burnham's chronicling of Starfleet principles is a reminder of failure *and* potential. For Nietzsche, tragedy exposes the ways our lives are shaped by uncontrollable, sometimes unredeemable, commitments and events; but we are also reminded of our agency and responsibility within these contexts. Rather than tragic fatalism, a Nietzschean read of *Discovery* offers a reminder that the world we encounter is meaningfully of our making.

## NOTES

1. Richard Ned Lebow, *The Tragic Vision of Politics* (Cambridge: Cambridge University Press, 2003); Richard Ned Lebow and Toni Erskine (eds), *Tragedy and International Relations* (New York: Palgrave 2012); and John J. Mearsheimer, *The Tragedy of Great Power Politics* (New York: Norton 2001). On tragedy's recent uses (and abuses) in political theorizing, see Rita Felski (ed), *Rethinking Tragedy* (Baltimore: Johns Hopkins University Press, 2008).

2. Lance Arkin, *The Impossible Has Happened: The Life and Work of Gene Rodenberry* (London: Aurum Press 2016), 206.

3. Gavia Baker-Whitelaw, "How Lululemon and Balgencia Influenced the Look of Star Trek: Discovery," *Daily Dot* (February 11, 2018), accessed January 15, 2019. https://www.dailydot.com/.

4. Daniel Holloway, "Star Trek: Discovery: Akiva Goldsman on Spock, What's in Store for Season 1," *Variety* (Septemper 25, 2017), accessed January 15, 2019. https//variety.com/.

5. Duncan Bell, "Under an Empty Sky," in *Political Thought and International Relations* (Oxford, 2009), 1.

6. E. H. Carr, *The Twenty Year Crisis, 1919–1939: An Introduction to the Study of International Relations* (New York: St. Martin's Press, 1952); Han J. Morgenthau, *Politics among Nations: The Struggle for Power and* Peace (New York: Alfred A. Knopf, 1948). For a survey of contemporary realists "types," Colin Elman, *Recovering Realism* (London: Routledge 2011).

7. James Mayall, "Tragedy, Progress, and the International Order," in ed. Erskine and Lebow, *Tragedy and International Relations* (New York: Palgrave 2012), 48–49.

8. Kenneth Walz, "Realist Thought and Neorealist Theory," *Journal of International Affairs*, 44 (1990) 21–38; Robert D. Kaplan, *Warrior Politics: Why Leadership Demands a Pagan Ethos* (New York: Random House 2001).

9. Lebow, *The Tragic Vision of Politics*, 16.

10. Rengger, "Tragedy or Skepticism? Defending the Anti-Pelagian Mind in World Politics," in *Tragedy and International Relations*, 53–54.

11. Vassilios Paipais, "Necessary Fictions: Realism's Tragic Theology" *International Politics,* 50:6 (2013) 848–50; Michael Spirtas, "A House Divided: Tragedy and Evil in Realist Theory," in Benjamin Frankel (ed) *Realism: Restatements and Renewal* (London: Frank Cass, 2006), 385–424.

12. Paipais, "Necessary Fictions," 849

13. Lebow, *The Tragic Vision of Politics*, 364–65.

14. Duncan Bell, "Under an Empty Sky," 7–9.

15. Mayall, "Tragedy, Progress and the International Order," 45.

16. Mervyn Frost, "Tragedy, Ethics, International Relations," in *Tragedy and International Relations,* 42.

17. Rengger, "Tragedy or Skepticism?" 60.

18. Strong notes a "pluralism" approach to "the tragic" reflects Judeo-Christian notions of sin more than tragedy's *agon*. "Nietzsche and Questions of Tragedy, Tyranny, and International

Relations," 145–46 in *Tragedy and International Relations*. Also, J. Peter Euben, "The Tragedy of Tragedy," in *ibid.*, 86–87. Simon Goldhill, "Generalizing about Tragedy," in *Rethinking Tragedy*, 45–65.

19. Tragedy is often read in IR in traditionally schematic "Aristotelian" ways. As duBois comments, however, this tradition forces "upon [Aristotle and . . .] tragedy, the 'tragic hero' and his 'fatal flaw'" a tendency redoubled by Hegel's dialectical conflict *between* heroes. "Toppling the Hero: Polyphony in the Tragic City," in *Rethinking Tragedy*, 132–34.

20. *Ibid*, 136.

21. Euben, "The Tragedy of Tragedy," 86.

22. *Discovery* is also heavily defined by the conventions of genre action and melodrama. In this sense, *Discovery*'s "tragedy" is formally limited. My concern here is less with proper tragic form than whether *Discovery* might have a tragic effect on its viewers of the sort Nietzsche outlines.

23. Kurtzman notes, "The whole season was reverse engineered from the ending. [. . .] Really the big driver there was [Burnham's] arc and [. . . her realization] that it's much more important to protect [Federation] ideals than to protect herself." in Joe Otterson, "*Star Trek: Discovery*: Alex Kurtzman Breaks Down Major Finale Reveal," in *Variety* (2018), accessed 1/15/2019 https://variety.com/

24. Frost, "Tragedy, Ethics, International Relations," 27–28.

25. Lebow, *The Tragic Vision of Politics*, 15.

26. On *Star Trek* the language of "assimilation" is typically reserved for the Borg; a species that absorbs—and thereby destroys—all they encounter. Its transference to the Federation indicates a startling reversal. I owe this observation to Melvin Rogers.

27. *Discovery* cold opens with T'Kuvma railing against Starfleet whose "fatal greeting is *we come in peace.*" This line is emphasized by T'Kuvma breaking the fourth wall, speaking in English. The next shot cuts to Burnham: "We come in peace! We're the Federation. That's why we're here. Isn't that the whole idea of Starfleet?"

28. These themes are reinforced visually. The set and costume redesign of the Klingons evoke Tudor and Conquistador silhouettes, whose valor and religion-based sovereigntist principles the Klingons reenact. The fascist Terran aesthetic was inspired by the brutalist and art-deco movements of the 1930s and 1950s. See Baker-Whitelaw, ". . . the Look of Star Trek: Discovery."

29. Chris Brown, "Tragedy, Tragic Choices, and Contemporary Political Theory," in *Tragedy and International Relations*, 76.

30. Lebow, "The Tragic Vision of Politics," 166.

31. Lebow, "Tragedy, Politics, and Political Science," in *Tragedy and International Relations*, 70.

32. Strong, "Tragedy, Tyranny, and International Relations," 145.

33. Friedrich Nietzsche, *The Birth of Tragedy and the Case of Wagner*, (trans.) Walter Kaufman (New York: Vintage Books 1967) Hereafter BT, cited by section number. Other Nietzsche works cited include *The Will to Power*, Ed., Walter Kaufman (Vintage Books, New York) [WP]; and *Twilight of the Idols and the Anti-Christ,* trans. J. Hollingdale (New York: Penguin Classics 1990) [TI]. Nietzsche is often cited by realists [especially TI: ". . . Ancients" 2] but his 'realism' is deeply idiosyncratic. See Jean-Francois Drolet, "Ennobling Humanity: Nietzsche and the Politics of Tragedy" *The Journal of International Political Theory,* 10:3 (2014) 233; Daniel Conway "The Birth of the State" in H. W. Seimens and V. Roodt *Nietzsche, Power, and Politics: Rethinking Nietzsche's Legacy for Political Thought* (De Gruyter 2009) 37.

34. Joshua F. Dienstag, "Tragedy, Pessimism, Nietzsche," in *Rethinking Tragedy*, 108–11.

35. Here Nietzsche engages contemporary debates about the ancient chorus. David B. Allison, *Reading the New Nietzsche* (New York: Rowan & Littlefield 2001), Ch. 1.

36. Strong, "Tragedy, Tyranny, and International Relations," 147.

37. Drolet, "Ennobling Humanity," 252.

# BIBLIOGRAPHY

Allison, David B. *Reading the New Nietzsche*. New York: Rowan & Littlefield, 2001.
Arkin, Lance. *The Impossible Has Happened: The Life and Work of Gene Rodenberry*. London: Aurum Press, 2016.
Baker-Whitelaw, Gavia. "How Lululemon and Balgencia Influenced the Look of Star Trek: Discovery." *Daily Dot*, February 11, 2018. https://www.dailydot.com/parsec/star-trek-discovery-costume-designer-interview/.
Bell, Duncan. "Under an Empty Sky," In *Political Thought and International Relations*, edited by Duncan Bell, 1–25. Oxford: Oxford University Press, 2009.
Brown, Chris. "Tragedy, Tragic Choices, and Contemporary Political Theory," in *Tragedy and International Relations*, edited by Richard Ned Lebow and Toni Erskine, 75–85. New York: Palgrave, 2012.
Carr, E. H. *The Twenty Year Crisis, 1919–1939*: *An Introduction to the Study of International Relations*. New York: St. Martin's Press, 1952.
Conway, Daniel. "The Birth of the State." In *Nietzsche, Power, and Politics: Rethinking Nietzsche's Legacy for Political Thought*, edited by H. W. Siemens and V. Roodt, 37–68. Berlin: De Gruyter, 2009.
Dienstag, Joshua F. "Tragedy, Pessimism, Nietzsche." In *Rethinking Tragedy*, edited by Rita Felski, 104–23. Baltimore: Johns Hopkins University Press, 2008.
Drolet, Jean-Francois. "Ennobling Humanity: Nietzsche and the Politics of Tragedy." *The Journal of International Political Theory*, 10:3 (2014): 231–60.
duBois, Paige. "Toppling the Hero: Polyphony in the Tragic City." In *Rethinking Tragedy*, edited by Rita Felski, 127–47. Baltimore: Johns Hopkins University Press, 2008.
Elman, Colin. *Recovering Realism*. London: Routledge, 2011.
Euben, J. Peter. "The Tragedy of Tragedy." In *Tragedy and International Relations*, edited by Richard Ned Lebow and Toni Erskine, 86–96. New York: Palgrave, 2012.
Felski, Rita (ed). *Rethinking Tragedy*. Baltimore: Johns Hopkins University Press, 2008.
Frost, Mervyn. "Tragedy, Ethics, International Relations." In *Tragedy and International Relations*, edited by Richard Ned Lebow and Toni Erskine, 21–43. New York: Palgrave, 2012.
Goldhill, Simon. "Generalizing about Tragedy." In *Rethinking Tragedy*, edited by Rita Felski, 45–65. Baltimore: Johns Hopkins University Press, 2008.
Holloway, Daniel. "Star Trek: Discovery: Akiva Goldsman on Spock, What's in Store for Season 1." *Variety*, September 25, 2017. https://www.yahoo.com/entertainment/star-trek-discovery-akiva-goldsman-spock-store-season-175835359.html.
Kaplan, Robert D. *Warrior Politics: Why Leadership Demands a Pagan Ethos*. New York: Random House 2001.
Lebow, Richard Ned and Erskine, Toni (eds.) *Tragedy and International Relations*. New York: Palgrave, 2012.
Lebow, Richard Ned. "Tragedy, Politics, and Political Science." In *Tragedy and International Relations*, edited by Richard Ned Lebow and Toni Erskine, 63–71. New York: Palgrave, 2012.
———. *The Tragic Vision of Politics*. Cambridge: Cambridge University Press 2003.
Mayall, James "Tragedy, Progress, and the International Order." In *Tragedy and International Relations*, edited by Richard Ned Lebow and Toni Erskine, 43–52. New York: Palgrave, 2012.
Mearsheimer, John J. *The Tragedy of Great Power Politics*. New York: Norton, 2001.
Morgenthau, Hans J. *Politics among Nations: The Struggle for Power and* Peace. New York: Alfred A. Knopf, 1948.
Nietzsche, Friedrich. *The Will to Power*, edited by Walter Kaufman. New York: Vintage Books, 2011.
———. *Twilight of the Idols and the Anti-Christ.* Translated by J. Hollingdale. New York: Penguin Classics, 1990.
———. *The Birth of Tragedy and the Case of Wagner*. Translated by Walter Kaufman. New York: Vintage Books, 1967.

Otterson, Joe. "*Star Trek: Discovery*: Alex Kurtzman Breaks Down Major Finale Reveal." *Variety*, February 2, 2018. https://variety.com/2018/tv/news/star-trek-discovery-finale-cbs-all-access-1202694405/.

Paipias, Vassilios. "Necessary Fictions: Realism's Tragic Theology." *International Politics*, 50:6 (2013): 846–62.

Rengger, Nicholas. "Tragedy or Skepticism? Defending the Anti-Pelagian Mind in World Politics." In *Tragedy and International Relations*, edited by Richard Ned Lebow and Toni Erskine, 53–62. New York: Palgrave, 2012.

Spirtas, Michael. "A House Divided: Tragedy and Evil in Realist Theory." In *Realism: Restatements and Renewal*, edited by Benjamin Frankel, 385–424. London: Frank Cass, 2006.

Strong, Tracy. "Nietzsche and Questions of Tragedy, Tyranny, and International Relations." In *Tragedy and International Relations*, edited by Richard Ned Lebow and Toni Erskine, 144–57. New York: Palgrave, 2012.

Walz, Kenneth. "Realist Thought and Neorealist Theory." *Journal of International Affairs*, 44 (1990): 21–38.

*Chapter Three*

# Beginning Again

Jericho, Revolution, *and Catastrophic Originalism*

Ira J. Allen

Whether nasty, brutish, and short or nostalgically communal, human prehistory was of great interest to Enlightenment future-thinkers. In their different ways, Hobbes, Locke, Herder, and Rousseau all looked to a time-before-stories for *conditions that must have prevailed* in order for political associations to have emerged—each in search of future-resources for his own philosophy. Their speculative prehistories served as bases for the construction of politics. Historical origins prefigured each thinker's vision of the possibilities of collective decision making and life-in-common, of *politeia* or constitution in the Attic Greek sense—at once both a system for living together and the materialized actuality of collective being-together.[1] In more recent times, Rawls' original situation, especially as rejuvenated by Nussbaum, has presented one of the strongest expressions of the urge to found new origins upon some speculative variant of the old. For Rawls and other idealistic originalists, more just futures were to be grounded in *ideal founding situations*, not history as such. With this move, nostalgia for a prelapsarian world and disgust for irredeemable "human nature" alike disappear into a speculatively ahistorical void.[2] The liberal future-thinking that formed an important horizon for late-twentieth-century visions of politics depended on stipulation of an ideally empty past that has become increasingly unpersuasive.

For liberals up to the present moment as for the *philosophes* of various iterations of Enlightenment, the aim of thinking origins was to articulate the conjoint spaces of possibility and impossibility that constitute the political from behind, so to speak. This aim of finding bases for political futures in origins real or ideal is perhaps central to political theory, as Anne Norton notes in *95 Theses on Politics, Culture, and Method* (Yale University Press,

2004). Making meaning of the past, whether imagined or unearthed or abstracted, is crucial to determining how the political present and future may each be constituted. Norton observes in this vein that "The past constitutes the present but the present also constitutes the past" (92). The past, that is, serves as a well-worn tool that is itself continually in the process of being reworked. We invent the pasts, real and ideal (and to come) that make our present and future seem habitable, projecting those invented pasts forward. Norton thus notes, "The work of politics is undertaken not for the present alone but for a future into which the living and the dead extend their will" (79). Our history and politics extend our present, through political theory or philosophy, from a speculative past into a willed future, a future we wish or hope in some way to write into being. But what of the future that is, as this collection asks, unwritten *because the present is such a disaster*? What of the future that cannot be written by any will, because no political will can be found with power enough to write a habitable future?

How can political theorists and political philosophers take up questions of origins, possibility, and impossibility in an age of disaster, when the surest thing we can say about the future is that it will come only after the devastation of the present?[3] How can contemporary political theory connect questions of origin and foundation with a political future whose likeliest past will be the undoing of the present order? Or, to put the question another way, what can we do to uncover and foster what Franco Berardi terms *futurability*, "layer[s] of possibility that may or may not develop into actuality" (*Futurability*, Verso, 2017: 3), for the future that will arrive on the heels of disaster? For Berardi, precisely because "the future is not prescribed"—even ages of catastrophe have no certain, monolithic outcome—"our task consists in distinguishing the layers of futurability that lie in the texture of the present reality and in the present consciousness" (17). If our world is swept up in catastrophe, and headed for far more, how do we understand relations between political possibility and impossibility within and after the unfoldings-to-come of our disaster? What relations, woven into the texture of the present, constitute our layers of futurability? How, indeed, are we already thinking such relations?

I essay a response to these questions by turning to two popular artifacts—U.S. television shows *Jericho* (CBS: 2006–2008) and *Revolution* (NBC: 2012–2014)—for folk philosophical insights. What these shows offer is a twinned effort to fantastically escape the visible future consequences of the world-system of the present and a sense of what it can mean to think origins after catastrophe. As such, they suggest a third originalism coming now into being, to add to the two sketched initially: *catastrophic originalism*. Catastrophic originalism starts from the intuition that politics is founded ever on the sites of disaster. This is a different attitude toward the relationship between history and political foundations than those of the philosophes or the

Rawlsians, replacing the supposed historical origins of the former and the abstracted ideal origins of the latter with origins-in-historical-ruins-yet-to-come.

Catastrophic originalism is a hopeful attitude, but its hope is a dark one. At stake is something grimly historical, a pragmatic utopianism that accepts catastrophe's unavoidability but does not welcome it—and that continues stipulating better possible worlds in the ruins of the future. Popular culture, as both ideological containment strategy and laboratory for the invention of new-ish worlds,[4] is an excellent place to discover such a political philosophy-in-the making. My aim in studying *Jericho* and *Revolution* is to follow their articulations of a disastrous future anterior, their dark futurism that is not without hope. Those articulations unearth for us layers of futurability, woven with constraint and not exactly hopeful, but lining up visions of possibility nonetheless.

Both shows start with the end of the information society and trace out new possibilities of *founding at the scene of catastrophe*. As such, they are representatives of an ever-broader strain of contemporary television culture (and in this distinction from both the vague hopefulness and deep nihilism of older postapocalyptic screenwork, that of films like the 1971 *The Omega Man* or the 1979 *Mad Max*, a vaguely messianic nihilism present still in more recent films like the 2009 adaptation of Cormac McCarthy's *The Road*).[5] *Jericho* and then *Revolution* highlight the extent to which the present world is structured as and by information, and suggest that political novelty and liberatory possibility are affective-logistical attunements to catastrophe. They imagine new foundations, rather than merely ameliorations of an imperfect world or bare survival after apocalypse. At the same time, they assume catastrophic ends to a present trajectory. These shows are driven by narratives about continuity and novelty after collapse, based on layers of possibility present in this world, which they speculate, however, can only end in collapse. In such speculation, the animating visions of shows like *Jericho* and *Revolution* are not baldly, but pragmatically utopian.[6] They imagine better possible worlds on the basis of hard constraints on both the present and the contiguous future.

Each show draws on both hard and also soft or vanishing constraints, ideological posits, to foreground some values from our present world as core to imagining the origins-after-catastrophe to come. In *Jericho*, the ideological core is the heterosexual family unit; in *Revolution*, the nation-state. The former organizes its narrative around the post-nuclear Holocaust personal and political drama of a heteronormative family in a small Kansas town, the Greens. The latter develops as the story of competing nation-state formations in the wake of an electromagnetic event that ends electrical work and, with it, the information age as we know it.[7] As such, *Jericho* and *Revolution* are at once both ideological fantasies and forms of dissent from the business-as-usual approach to human futures that dominated American public culture through the 2000s and 2010s. Their nascent catastrophic originalism suppresses or obfuscates our most obvious mode of catastrophe—the human-caused and radically developing incapacity of our environment to sustain broadly flourishing human life—and puts in its place the end of an information society, the end of a world organized in terms of ubiquitous digital communication and data harvesting. In this, they deflect attention from and mute the affective charge of our most pressing disaster, our greatest habitability problem. At the same time, they posit new, post-cataclysmic political possibilities based on continuity with current and near-past forms of life. In surfacing layers of futurability by projecting ostensible present goods onto the site of the ruined world-to-come,[8] they orient both realistically and hopefully toward a future that, though unwritten, is surely both darker and hotter than the present.

Television shows like *Jericho* and *Revolution* (or *The Walking Dead* or *The 100* and their increasingly numerous kin) begin with and are interested in what happens in the wake of disaster. They present social foundations first and foremost not as ideally conceptual *or* logico-historically derived, but rather as contingently scrabbled together at the metaphorical and literal sites of catastrophe. *Foundations, in this emergent popular vision, are social and material places where the organizing forces of a given social order are overturned, replaced by partially continuous systems.* This has perhaps always been true, but comes uniquely into focus in contemporary entertainment media, which registered well before the present conjuncture that the heyday of liberalism's ahistorically utopian spirit is behind us. What we discover in *Jericho* and *Revolution* is the need—particular to an age of environmental and sociopolitical disaster—to imagine better futures not atop old beginnings or formal origins but in the ruins-to-come of the present catastrophe. These mid-aughts and early two-thousand-teens science fiction shows lay important philosophical groundwork for a subsequent explosion of popular and scholarly thinkings of catastrophe as the site of possibility. In this, though, they are also distinct from much recent cli-fi, work devoted to fantastical apprehension of the end of days as such, to the disaster itself rather than or only dimly followed by what comes next.[9] Ultimately, I argue, the folk philosophy of *Jericho* and *Revolution* (by partial contrast with the genres Ted Toadvine has termed "eco-eschatology"[10] ) enhances our futurability precisely because it realistically assumes the catastrophe we are undergoing[11] and foregrounds the origins to be written there, upon the future ruins of our present world.

At the same time, these shows *are also* ideological displacements. Even as they confront what comes after the catastrophic conclusions of present-day social narratives, they (a) displace the specifically ecological/climate character of our disaster-in-process and (b) depend for their sense of continuity on core ideological formations for modernity and the information age: the heterosexual "nuclear" family and the imaginary community of the nation-state. As such, *Jericho* and *Revolution* register nostalgic desire for a history that would not have to know its own ruinous end, even while adumbrating the catastrophic originalism that political theory must, and I think simply *will*, come increasingly to embrace. Negotiating between ideological fantasy and realistic catastrophe-thinking, these shows integrate a layer of pragmatic utopianism. That is to say, even as we should object to the content of their ideological fantasies, the form of their working-together of fantasy with realism is useful. Each articulates potentially meaningful political futures premised (realistically) on the ruination of the present and (also realistically) on continuity of hard constraints between a (fantastically) "good" past and any (fantastical) futures that would be contiguous with the present. Unlike Enlightenment works and still more unlike the antiseptic original situation, one important substrate of thought woven through *Jericho* and *Revolution* (and their cognates) is the sense that origins appear *only* at sites of disaster.

This layer of thought, which I term catastrophic originalism, is itself a locus of futurability. To recognize that founding occurs only upon the sites of disaster, and that founding will entail some continuity with that future anterior's past (i.e., our present), is to feel more keenly and deeply responsible for what values we foreground in the time leading up to catastrophe. If a future founding will be in some ways contiguous with powerful values from our present, the time leading up to catastrophe that will make new foundations both necessary and possible, what we do now matters very much. In the case of the climate emergency, what we do matters not because we can stop the unfurling of the disaster—we cannot—but because we can hope to shape the foundings to come in its wake. The values we live most intensely and consistently in the present create layers of futurability for that future anterior founding. We may not be able to avert catastrophe, but we can shape the possibilities for what happens thereafter.

## CATASTROPHIC ORIGINALISM

As noted, *Jericho* and *Revolution* both start with the end of contemporary U.S. civilization: with the end of the information society. Ostensibly, they respond to the catastrophic collapse of a digitally mediated form of political community. The "information society," proclaimed by Yoneji Masuda in 1980 in a spirit of utopian futurism, was supposed to herald the rise of extraordinary participatory democracy in a post-industrial age. By the mid-2000s, however, that dream had run aground on shoals that Jodi Dean has capably critiqued (*Democracy and Other Neoliberal Fantasies*, Duke University Press, 2009). The difficulty with utopian futurism in practice has been that the information society, with its "expanded and intensified communicativity" (23), cannot make good on its democratic promises; instead, "the deluge of screens and spectacles coincides with extreme corporatization, financialization, and privatization across the globe" (23). The very social tool that was meant to anchor an egalitarianizing political community—information, as mediated by digital computation devices—relies for its all-too-hopeful promise on a fantasy of abundance. That fantasy, in turn, "both expresses and conceals the shift from message to contribution" (28), the emptying out of communication's content (and so of much of our selfhood) in a marketized information society. The result is that "the contemporary ideological formation of communicative capitalism fetishizes speech, opinion, and participation" (17)—but only in order that these may replace as empty performance or spectacle the concrete organization of bodies that would be democracy in action. We can only believe in the unpragmatic utopianism of the information society, then, if we set aside what we know about hard constraints of capitalist markets.

Dean's work on communicative capitalism was one of the fuller moments of theoretical pushback against a wave of techno-optimism still cresting in the mid-aughts, broken but little by the dot-com bust a few years before and buoyed by the murderous oil adventurism of the Bush II regime and corresponding growth in new military technologies. Between then and now, the notion of the information society as servant has largely transformed, in theory as in the popular imaginary, into the information society as master.[12] Few still talk in glowing terms about digital mediation as a harbinger of profound democratic possibility. The tension at play in this shift of perceptions—between information society as enabler of human flourishing and information society as enabler of capitalist intensification and both social and environmental devastation—prepares the scene for the catastrophes upon which *Jericho* and *Revolution* build.

Both shows begin from the premise of the end of generally available electrical and communication power, symbolized in the early moments of *Jericho* and *Revolution* alike by the abrupt and ubiquitous loss of telephone and television transmissions. The basic idea in both instances is that the end of the world has arrived, an idea underscored by a nuclear mushroom cloud rising on the Coloradoan horizon in the tenth minute of *Jericho*'s first episode and by the successive extinguishing of automobile headlights along a long stretch of South Carolina highway, coupled with a plane tumbling to its explosive demise in Chicago, in the third minute of *Revolution*'s first episode. The world will never be the same again—and, implicitly, it has already never been quite what some "we" fondly supposed. In each instance, it is important to begin by understanding what, proleptically, will have been lost in the catastrophe to come.

As one of the unhappy architects of the disaster puts it in *Revolution*'s opening moments, "It's all gonna turn off. It's gonna turn off, and it will never, ever turn back on." The "it" in question turns out not to be electricity exactly, since both shows have workarounds on that score, but something more like the ubiquitous communication of the information society. The end of a (fantastically, but also in some ways actually) democratizing global communicative capacity and a post-industrial sharedness (fantasies never realized in substantial demotic power) are the losses structuring both shows' senses of catastrophe. That sense is complicated, though, by its obfuscation of the more directly looming disaster of runaway climate change, which threatens not merely losses of democratic possibility and certain forms of power, but also and almost unthinkably drastically, human extinction over the comparatively near term (measured in short hundreds of years at most).[13] The disaster appears *only* as a loss of communication power and a certain capacity for nonhuman work.

The catastrophes after which both *Jericho* and *Revolution* are situated are, from the competing perspective of swift and radical climate change (i.e., the point of view that these shows' affectively catastrophizing charge allows them to displace), relatively tolerable prospects. After all, what is the end of an information society compared with the end of life for the species entire? Still, even as they dodge the unbearably full significance of climate catastrophe, these shows are *also* important folk-philosophical statements. Each draws on fantastically wholesome elements of our own present to project a new society after the disaster. In this way, they articulate continuity across catastrophe, present the origins-to-come after one world's end as constructed from core value-posits of the old. Though hardly unproblematic, this is a useful way of understanding our disastrous future. Even as we reject the re-origination of society in heteronormativity or the nation-state, we *should* be looking today to strengthen whatever value-posits we hope will shore up new foundations after our own catastrophes-to-come. One implication of catastrophic originalism is that it matters *now* what value-posits we reinforce, commit to, work to sustain—even if only in an elegiac or deeply ambiguous mode.[14] Those posits, for better and/or for worse, will become foundational after the disaster.

Each of these shows commits to some but not other elements of continuity with the present. Their protagonists look nostalgically back to a past that the shows imagine being lost forever, even as those protagonists live out core values of such a past. In *Jericho*, the lost past is a fantastically democratic, civil-agricultural frontiersmanship, threatened always by wolves at the gate but made possible by solidaristic labor on shared values. That past is embodied in the family unit surrounding Johnston Greene, town mayor, who retains his position after the power goes out and serves as the ideological node of continuity, the layer of possibility enabling a new society built on the "best" remnants of the old. In *Revolution*, also lost is the idea of a democratic and egalitarian America. In both cases—more or less by definition, since these shows' catastrophes appear over time as the work of anti-democratic forces within the U.S. government—the democracy yearned for never exactly was.

Where *Jericho* anchors its commitment to democracy as a value-posit in the heteronormative family unit, *Revolution* organizes itself explicitly around the emergence of new nation-states: the draconian Monroe Republic (headquartered in Philadelphia), the Plains Nation and its ally the Georgia Federation, and several others. Plot tension depends upon quasi-revolutionary resistance to and alliances with these nation-state reductions of most of North America. In a typically stark instance of the show's reliance on affectively drenched iconography (reminiscent of the bathos of Charlton Heston falling to his knees in the roiling surf before the Statue of Liberty in *Planet of the Apes*), *Revolution* asks viewers to identify without moral question with rebel "patriots," whose distinguishing mark is a tattoo of the contemporary American flag.

In both cases, the value-posits at stake (heteronormative family and nation-state) are ways of maintaining continuity with some idea of democracy after loss of the *work* power made available by electricity and the *communication* power made possible by informatization. A character presented as a former Google exec sums up the former: "What you gotta understand is, things used to be different. We used electricity for everything: for our computers, our phones, even to grow food and pump water. But after the blackout, nothing worked." What is lost, in other words, is a certain set of mediated human capacities. With that comes spectral acknowledgment of the unviability of the old forms of political organization, *our* forms. On the one hand, "nothing worked." On the other hand, both *Revolution* and *Jericho* revolve around committed actors' efforts to remake lost forms of political community, *our* nationalistic and heteronormative forms of "democracy." These popular shows enact a catastrophic originalism by imagining future origins upon the site of disaster, where "nothing worked," which future origins will themselves be determined by the "best" elements of the near-past shared by the shows' creators and viewers alike. There is little in the way of either dimly receding historical origins or abstractly ideal origins here. Rather, the recent history of each show (stretching iconographically, through the situating of protagonists in both shows as early American revolutionaries, to the U.S. moment of founding) serves as a template for a future founding after catastrophe.

Writing upon the ruins of the information society, which is to say the ruins of late capitalism, both *Revolution* and *Jericho* detail richly elaborated social structures, new political communities originating at their respective sites of disaster and loss. Though neither is utopian in any conventional sense—both fit within the broad matrix of dystopian speculative fiction—the two television shows represent popular expressions of a real (and increasingly visible) political need: for a future-thinking grounded in the ruins-to-come of the present catastrophe. That need is productive of a nascent political philosophy, a catastrophic originalism. Catastrophic originalism replaces the historical originalisms and idealist originalisms of times past, and remains distinct from the ethical dead branch of accelerationism.

Where catastrophic originalism and accelerationism are *alike* is in their orientation toward the disaster of the future; each leans into that disaster. But where accelerationists embrace and work for the disaster by committing wholeheartedly to the machinery (industrial, digital, psychic, and otherwise) of late capitalism, catastrophic originalists seek a different sort of continuity. They hope to establish the present values that might prevail in organizing "better" political communities at the sites of disaster (recalling, again, that what is at stake here is the form rather than the content of this establishment—we can see the utility of establishing loci of continuity for re-founding after disaster without consenting to the notion that nationalism or heteronormativity should *be* those loci for us). Where accelerationism and catastrophic originalism *diverge*, then, is in their attitudes to catastrophe itself. For the former, as Alex Williams and Nick Srnicek put it in "#Accelerate: Manifesto for an Accelerationist Politics," the goal is to build a left politics "at ease with a modernity of abstraction, complexity, globality, and technology" (3) because only such a politics can wrest the inevitable catastrophe of the present from the hands of the forces of the right. Accelerationism in Williams and Srnicek's telling, is a commitment to *making sure that the catastrophe goes well*. By contrast, for catastrophic originalism the disaster promises us nothing. It cannot be made right.

As we see in the folk philosophy emerging in *Revolution* and *Jericho*, catastrophic originalism focuses on what we will save from the present for use after the disaster. The question is one of refounding at the site of catastrophe, of new—and in their way best possible, though not unconstrained—origins among the ruins of the old political community. From catastrophic originalism, we may derive one further-ism, may urge political thinking toward a final, hopeful step of engagement with catastrophe and limits. Drawing on the folk philosophy of these two shows (which serve as instances of a much broader *Zeitgeist*), I urge a *pragmatic utopianism*, a creative and frankly best-possible-world way of engaging with the constraints of catastrophes both under way and yet-to-come.

Catastrophic originalism—and with it pragmatic utopianism—appears against the backdrop of two other attitudes toward the foundation of political communities. Associated with broad periods in hegemonic Western thought, these emphasize "original situations," sites where political communities have emerged, ought to emerge, or will have emerged. They are an Enlightenment attitude we can term historical originalism and a twentieth-century attitude that may be considered idealistic originalism. Unlike these earlier originalisms, catastrophic originalism is an understandable but not unproblematic response to living in an age of ecological disaster, an age in which the future promises only dystopia, in which historical origins seem irrelevant and ideal origins impossible. "Looking forward," as 90s grunge band Soul Asylum put it, "to looking back on days like today," catastrophic originalism is nostalgia oriented toward the future anterior, an attitude that imagines looking for a way to re-found the present order after the end of the world. The futurability unearthed by this approach to catastrophe is clearer when placed more directly in contrast with antecedent ways of thinking the origins of political community.

## HISTORICAL ORIGINALISM AND IDEALISTIC ORIGINALISM

As noted, the Enlightenment philosophes all looked back to a time-before-time, trying to imagine conditions that must have prevailed for political associations and, eventually, states to have emerged—trying, accordingly, to discover constraints their own political theories must negotiate. These thinkers' concern with foundings entailed an attitude of *historical originalism*. Some more speculatively, others more materially, they probed for historical origins from which to draw conclusions about how political communities ought, in the present, to be founded. Such searching was, for a time, nearly ubiquitous among the thinking class. As Rousseau famously put it in *Discours sur l'origine et les fondements de l'inégalité parmi les hommes*, "the philosophers who have examined the foundations of society have all felt the necessity of climbing back [*remonter*] toward the state of nature, but none among them has reached it" (Flammarion, 1992: 168). His own investigations, he claims, are speculatively historical, "hypothetical and conditional reasoning, better suited to clarifying the nature of things than to pointing up a true origin" (169). Even in this self-avowedly abstracting version, at stake is the discovery of historical conditions that *must* in some way have prevailed. Historical originalism is an attitude that looks backward toward constraining origins, avowedly speculative or speculatively real, that would clarify the nature of political possibilities in the present.[15]

Over time, this attitude gave way to another, one less oriented toward historical constraints and more focused on abstract ideals. In that newer attitude of *idealistic originalism*, the aim has been to discover ahistorical conditions for justice, ideal bases for the foundation of political communities. For idealistic originalism, origin stories should abstract out from actual experience not to discover what must have been, but to determine what ought to be. This attitude looks optimistically, as is characteristic of political liberalism in the twentieth century, toward next foundings; it bets on the meliorability of humanity's crooked timber. John Rawls' "original situation," rejuvenated especially by Martha Nussbaum in *Frontiers of Justice* (Harvard University Press, 2006), serves as the figure *par excellence* for this attitude. As liberal thinkers like Rawls and then Nussbaum argue, no theory of justice, of the good life in society, can ground itself without reference to something like a founding situation.

The idealistic originalist's foundations are no less speculative than are those of the historical originalist's. Here, though, speculation is procedurally committed to the emptying out of history in order to render abstractly ideal foundations. Thinking an original situation, as Nussbaum describes it, means following "a procedure that assumes no antecedent advantages on the part of any individual" in order to "extract a set of rules that duly protect the interests of all" (10). Her own contribution to this tradition consists in revising the procedure in order to allow for recognition of "the many varieties of impairment, need, and dependency that 'normal' human beings experience, and thus the real continuity between 'normal' lives and those of people with lifelong disabilities" (92), as well as protection of the interests of those without membership in a recognizable national formation and of nonhuman animals. In short, Nussbaum adds some historical features into the mix of Rawlsian idealistic originalism. But her basic aim is still the establishment of ideal, rather than historically necessary, constraints on any new society. An "original situation" is something to be worked out quasi-mathematically, rather than to be discovered amidst and rescued from the obscuring mists of a lost past.

The shift from thinking like that of Hobbes and Rousseau to positions like those of Rawls and Nussbaum is from a historical to an idealistic originalism. As a capitalist world order emerges and develops increasingly technologically mediated complexity, political philosophy turns in its hopes for good political community from origins situated, however speculatively, in the past to origins situated in an ideal no-place. The original situations of the Enlightenment were, if fictional, profoundly historical; the original situations proffered by twentieth-century liberalism attempted to sidestep history's crushing weight. The aim was to develop rules for the foundation of political community that would be grounded, insofar as possible, in the dictates of pure form, Pareto-optimized as justice. Such an approach means no longer to arrive at ideal universality by discovering what must have been, but rather to abstract as far as possible from what was in order to discern what ought to be.

## TOWARD PRAGMATIC UTOPIANISM

The heyday of idealistic originalism is now largely behind us. In this suggestive reading of television shows *Jericho* and *Revolution*, I have been adumbrating another attitude toward founding, an impulse native to contemporary popular culture that I term *catastrophic originalism*. Catastrophic originalism is a provisional way of coming to terms with living in a period that Kim Stanley Robinson aptly terms, in the science fiction novel *2312* (Orbit, 2013), "The Dithering: 2005 to 2060." *The Dithering* describes an age in which we all see ourselves heading for a disaster that we are, on the whole, unwilling substantially to act to avoid or even really to mitigate. If historical originalism marked the political attitude driving much Enlightenment thought, and idealistic originalism marked the apotheosis of that thought in twentieth-century political liberalism, then catastrophic originalism is the attitude toward political foundations that emerges after the grand hopes of these humanisms have come a cropper.

In the foundering of prospects for human well-being associated with late—and yet ever still thrashing—capitalism, with its attendant ecocide, utopia becomes a promise that no one but a hardline accelerationist could reasonably believe. Increasingly, it stops making sense to imagine best-case futures, ideal origins for the founding of just states. Equally, the time for seeking out historical origins—whether nostalgically or to look back upon dystopias from which we happily escaped in the founding of political communities—is long since past. Catastrophic originalism is one primary attitude available to those trying to imagine political foundations today. I am not, I want to be clear, *urging* catastrophic originalism as a stance to be taken up. To the contrary, catastrophic originalism is a synthetic and already achieved folk philosophy, inasmuch as it takes up both historical and idealistic originalisms and, so to speak, holds them together in tight opposition to one another and, thereby, invents a pathway forward during the period of their comparative exhaustion. I'm interested, ultimately, in what it might look like to continue moving dialectically through this catastrophic originalism and toward an attitude that I take to be directly politically productive—a finalism, *pragmatic utopianism*.

We can hardly work on the future without utopianism. In better understanding the catastrophic originalism that is a not-unrealistic but also not-unproblematic response to the self-revealing of the Anthropocene in the promise of ecological disaster, we lay conceptual foundations for new political communities. To understand an attitude that does foresee the end of a world and imagines re-founding at the site of catastrophe, however nostalgically and/or obfuscatingly, is to better situate political philosophy to offer its own visions for use after the eminently foreseeable end of a world as we know it. Catastrophic originalism's desire is for new beginnings, and that desire is coupled with a realistically dim view of future hard constraints on any such new origins. Developing in negotiation of an eschatology come down to earth, in the face of the very real possibility that we as a species will—in thoroughly secular manner—have engineered "end times," catastrophic originalism interweaves the worldly groundedness of historical originalism with the abstract sense of possibility motivating idealistic originalism. On its own, though, this is no place to land. As suggested in my uneasy engagement with the nationalist and heteronormative value-anchoring of *Revolution* and *Jericho*, a future thinking that recognizes the need to carry *something* forward into the coming ruins of the present does not give us concrete guidance as to *what* that something should be. Not all values are equally futurable, and catastrophic originalism does not necessarily hit on good ones. Not all mechanisms for the development of new foundations at the sites of catastrophe can work equally well to build better worlds.

Accordingly, I turn in closing to an unusual piece of literature that dissents *in form* from catastrophic originalism's perhaps-premature closures. This speculative nonfiction book—Naomi Oreskes and Erik Conway's pocket-sized *The Collapse of Western Civilization: A View from the Future* (Columbia University Press, 2014)—lays out a vision that, like those discussed, arranges future possibilities so as to imaginarily determine what may count as realistic in the present. Oreskes and Conway write from the perspective of the future, looking back from the point of a rhetorically collected horizon that is to guide action in the present. They depart from the narratives just discussed, however, in their fulsome commitment to the usability of catastrophic vision. For Oreskes and Conway, the future is written. Radical climate change is irreversibly under way. The seas are rising, and will keep rising. The orb is warming faster at every moment than called for by the last moment's projections: oceans turning to acid, storms well beyond gathering. Always woefully insufficient climate accords fall away, and it becomes ever clearer that, though anthropogenic, climate change will be minimally responsive to even such concerted political action as we have not yet lumbered into. At stake in the narratives of catastrophizing that take all this seriously, dissenting thereby from the liberal and neoliberal stories that are our dominant approaches to practicing hope today, is the vision of possibility I understand as pragmatic utopianism.

Throughout *The Collapse of Western Civilization*, Oreskes and Conway address neoliberal capitalism directly. Speaking as a historian writing from a future Second People's Republic of China, offering analysis of the breakdown of a self-reflexively "western civilization," they write, "Given the events recounted here, it is hard to imagine why anyone in the twentieth century would have argued against government protection of the natural environment on which human life depends. Yet such arguments were not just made, they dominated the public sphere" (48). In so saying, Oreskes and Conway's aim is not simply to critique neoliberalism. The point is to expose internal contradictions of the present from the perspective of a statist, neocommunist future that offers a dissenting form of hope. From that vantage-point, "the development that the neoliberals most dreaded—centralized government and loss of personal choice—was rendered essential by the very policies they put in place" (49). Neoliberalism sets in place the conditions of its own impossibility, yes. But, more: those conditions *are* surmountable. Not by neoliberalism or by some desperate clutching at classical liberalism, nor yet by hard-eyed acceleration of the contradictions, but by forms of collectivism. And yet, even the collectivist stance from which the text is written is not quite the bare negotiation of hard constraints it might be supposed to be.

A key idea here is that humans *will* survive radical climate change, and will survive in ways that maintain the possibility of a certain kind of academic thought, scholarship, history-making. Indeed, the book presents itself as inviting a reappraisal of the very forms of state organization that enabled large-scale survival and comparative flourishing in what has become the Second People's Republic of China. In the "today" of their narrator, Oreskes and Conway write by way of conclusion, "we remain engaged in a vigorous intellectual discussion of whether, now that the climate system has finally stabilized, decentralization and redemocratization may be considered. Many academics, in the spirit of history's great thinkers, hope that such matters may be freely debated" (52). The vision is utopian, imagining functioning societies and a continuity of historical discussion and academic freedom on a global scale through the broad social apocalypse of the Western world's collapse.

And yet, the vision is very much pragmatic. Attuned to the practices and processes with which utopias are and can only be constructed out of the obdurate material of hard constraints, it is even dark. The historian-narrator continues, "Others consider that outcome wishful, in light of the dreadful events of the past, and reject the reappraisal we wish to invite here" (52). The value articulated is that of responsible scholarly inquiry itself, an open-ended appraisal of the significances and utility of the not-so-distant past for the making of better futures. This future history of catastrophe is, at the level of form and content alike, a hard-eyed look at the impossibility of preventing collapse. It does not advocate inaction, however, and nor does it cling to values that promise an (always illusory) security, like nationalism and heteronormativity. Nor does it lean too-lovingly into catastrophe. To the contrary, in its very form of dissent it counsels commitment to a set of humanistic scholarly values and principles. *The Collapse of Western Civilization* imagines a future anterior, a what-will-have-been, that makes sense of the present through the lens of inquiry into the relatively recent past. It counsels acceptance of a catastrophic future and preparedness to build a better world on the basis of scholarly inquiry. Ongoing commitment to scholarship as a serious value, to humanistic inquiry as a form of life that may later be of use in post-disaster foundings, is the counsel of pragmatic utopianism in the face of our unavoidable climate catastrophe today.

## NOTES

1. See Verity Harte and Melissa Lane's insightful introduction to *Politeia in Greek and Roman Philosophy* (Cambridge University Press, 2013), esp. 1–2.
2. I don't intend the sometimes just, sometimes unjust criticism that Rawlsians are unhistorical. Rather, having *A Theory of Justice* (Harvard University Press, 1999) in mind, I'm emphasizing that the vision of political origins Rawls offered was specifically, intentionally, *abstracted* from actual history. Many readers have attempted to read Rawls in a different vein, urging like Sebastiano Maffetone in *Rawls: An Introduction* (Polity Press, 2010) that *A Theory of Justice* be read through the in-the-worldness of *Political Liberalism* and other works more strongly marked by Rawls' anti-Platonism. My aim is not to characterize Rawls' oeuvre entire, but to note the broad political-philosophical tendency of which that work became representative. By contrast with Enlightenment and earlier thinkers, *A Theory of Justice*—as taken up by hundreds, even thousands, of political philosophers of all stripes—thinks political origins on the basis of ideal conditions for justice, speculatively abstracted from rather than speculatively present historically in the world.
3. I take as given the catastrophic situation of contemporary humanity, especially but not only in the Global South and particularly as regards our self-incurred and ever-worsening climate emergency. It is worth noting the uptick in scholarly and popular awareness of the depth of our unfolding catastrophe. To that end, sustainability leadership scholar Jem Bendell's "Deep Adaptation: A Map for Navigating Climate Tragedy" (2018) is, in repudiating the incrementalist thrust of his own life's work, a signal instance.
4. This approach sits between the methodologies proposed by Fredric Jameson (*The Political Unconscious*, Cornell University Press, 1981) and Michel de Certeau (*The Practice of Everyday Life*, University of California Press, 1984). Where the latter lionizes inventive negotiations of everydayness, the former pursues an ideology critique that finds—following especially Lukàcs on totality—a political unconscious writhing in aesthetic works by studying narrative strategies that suggest impossible resolutions to the real dilemmas of a given historical moment. Folk philosophy is *both* ideological containment, implying and repressing other possible worlds, and *bricolage*, inventive work upon the layers of possibility entailed by any future contiguous with the present. Modestly, but not wildly, popular television shows seem to me more likely to get at something novel in their negotiations than shows commanding sufficient popularity to enjoy many years of production.
5. And these could be multiplied: think of *The Walking Dead* or *Falling Skies*, as opposed to the older *Mad Max* film series or *On the Road*. All post-apocalyptic, but where many older (and current-residual) versions of the post-apocalyptic imagination center on mere survival after the catastrophe, *The Walking Dead* and *Falling Skies* (like *Jericho* and *Revolution*, which I discuss as representative anecdotes), are concerned with the question of new origins, of founding. Catastrophic originalism looks forward, sees the disaster, and wonders about the future founding of political communities at the site of the disaster. There is a hopefulness in this attitude that, if not entirely forthright with itself about its own positioning in the world, retains a greater imaginal space of possibility than do those efforts to think post-apocalyptic survival that remain still within the penumbra of idealistic originalism. The sense of impossibility with which each of the old *Mad Max* films set out a future after the catastrophe—from the nihilistic road rage of the first two films to the cruelty colony of *Mad Max: Beyond Thunderdome*—is but the flip side of idealistic originalism's certainty that the human world must be orderable in such a manner as to escape history. By contrast, catastrophic originalism's original situations are themselves sites of disaster, apocalypse. It is here, this attitude suggests, that political community always emerges—and emerges in search of its own history.
6. Much as the proliferating collection of Internet fora devoted to making sense not only of our unfolding catastrophe but also of the world-making to come in its wake are shot through with utopian sensibilities, be they ever so dark. See, for instance, subreddit forum r/collapse.
7. As David Wallace-Wells notes in *The Uninhabitable Future* (Tim Duggan Books, 2019), screen culture treatments of catastrophe today tend to skirt the ongoing, ever-more-present catastrophe that is world-reordering climate change. Wallace-Wells puts the point nicely, observing, that "on-screen, climate devastation is everywhere you look, and yet no-

where in focus, as though we are displacing our anxieties about global warming by restaging them in theaters of our own design and control—perhaps out of hope that the end of days remains 'fantasy'" (143–44).

8. Please let me be clear. I in no way endorse nationalism or heteronormativity as good foundations for political community. The point here is the form of the rhetorical move at play, not the content of the values urged thereby. All catastrophic originalism (for better or for worse) establishes some values from the present world as anchors of continuity that will enable refounding of something supposed better than the present order at the site of the disaster.

9. Silly films like *The Day After Tomorrow*, for instance, are taken up entirely with the disaster itself. In condensing climate catastrophe's aggregative character into a single abrupt event that "changes everything" they represent catastrophe only by way of what Marcuse termed repressive desublimation, the flattening encounter with a higher knowledge that serves to hold that knowledge more fully distant from lived experience (*One-Dimensional Man*, Beacon Press, 1991, *passim*).

10. In "Our Monstrous Futures: Global Sustainability and Eco-Eschatology," Toadvine (2017) argues that contemporary dystopian fictions and nonfiction climate predictions "share a common eschatological narrative with roots in shared cultural sources, and they have fed and borrowed from each other to the point where they can no longer rigorously be distinguished" (220). My sense is that Toadvine focuses overmuch on how works represent end times, rather than how they represent the times after ends.

11. Should a person doubt the presentness of climate catastrophe or the realism of its disorganizing social consequences, suffice it to note that as I write this chapter the U.N. has released (yet another) report determining that dramatic warming is "locked in" for Arctic regions regardless of whether countries meet the (once thought to be ambitious) goals of the Paris climate agreement (which, anyhow, were almost immediately ignored by most signatories to that agreement). By the time this essay reaches print, circumstances will no doubt look far grimmer yet.

12. For instance, see Robert Hassan's "Digital, Ethical, Political: Network Time and Common Responsibility" (2018). For updates on the extent to which the information society is today master of human possibilities (political and otherwise), see especially Shoshana Zuboff's *The Age of Surveillance Capitalism* (PublicAffairs, 2019) and Gary T. Marx's *Windows into the Soul: Surveillance and Society in an Age of High Technology* (University of Chicago Press, 2016). See also my "Negotiating Ubiquitous Surveillance" and corresponding special issue of *Screen Bodies* (2019).

13. That this is a realistic possibility, though borne out by one climate model after another, continues to be difficult for many to countenance. It is an indication of how dire our straits are that would-be optimists find themselves turning to the idea of exoplanet colonization as a way of holding human extinction conceptually and actually at bay. See, for instance, Kelly Smith's "*Homo Reductio*: Eco-nihilism and Human Colonization of Other Worlds" (2019).

14. On the extraordinary political potential of such "imaginative transformation" precisely there where "a traditional way of life was being destroyed, and along with it came the destruction of its conception of the good life" (146), see Jonathan Lear's discussion of Plenty Coups in *Radical Hope* (Harvard University Press, 2006).

15. This attitude is of course far from dead. Consider, for instance, the popularity of texts such as Yuval Noah Harari's *Sapiens: A Brief History of Humankind* (HarperCollins, 2015), a modern classic of historical originalism. It is no mistake that this book, a favorite of tech billionaire and would-be neuromancer Bill Gates, was soon followed by Harari's equally popular *Homo Deus: A Brief History of Tomorrow* (HarperCollins, 2017).

# BIBLIOGRAPHY

Allen, Ira "Negotiating Ubiquitous Surveillance." *Screen Bodies: An Interdisciplinary Journal of Experience, Perception, and Display*, vol. 4, issue 2 (2019): 23–38.

Bendell, Jem. "Deep Adaptation: A Map for Navigating Climate Tragedy." IFLAS Occasional Paper 2. 27 July 2018. http://www.lifeworth.com/deepadaptation.pdf, accessed 11 October 2019.

Berardi, Franco 'Bifo.' *Futurability: The Age of Impotence and the Horizon of Possibility*. London: Verso, 2017.

de Certeau, Michel. *The Practice of Everyday Life*. Berkeley: University of California Press, 1984.

Chbosky, Stephen, Josh Schaer, and Jonathan E. Steinberg. *Jericho*. CBS Paramount Network Television: 2006–2008.

Dean, Jodi. *Democracy and Other Neoliberal Fantasies: Communicative Capitalism and Left Politics*. Durham: Duke University Press, 2009.

Harari, Yuval Noah. *Sapiens: A Brief History of Humankind*. New York: HarperCollins, 2015.

———. *Homo Deus: A Brief History of Tomorrow*. New York: HarperCollins, 2017.

Harte, Verity and Lane, Melissa (Eds.). *Politeia in Greek and Roman Philosophy*. Cambridge: Cambridge University Press, 2013.

Hassan, Robert. "Digital, Ethical, Political: Network Time and Common Responsibility." *New Media & Society* vol. 20, issue 7 (2018): 2534–49.

Jameson Fredric. *The Political Unconscious: Narrative as a Socially Symbolic Act*. Ithaca: Cornell University Press, 1981.

Kripke, Eric. *Revolution*. Warner Bros. Television: 2012–2014.

Lear, Jonathan. *Radical Hope: Ethics in the Face of Cultural Devastation*. Cambridge: Harvard University Press, 2006.

Maffetone, Sebastiano. *Rawls: An Introduction*. Cambridge: Polity Press, 2010.

Marcuse, Herbert. *One-Dimensional Man: Studies in the Ideology of Advanced Industrial Society*. Boston: Beacon Press, 1991 [1964].

Masuda, Yoneji. *The Information Society as Post-Industrial Society*. Washington: World Future Society, 1981.

Marx, Gary T. *Windows into the Soul: Surveillance and Society in an Age of High Technology*. Chicago: University of Chicago Press, 2016.

Norton, Anne. *95 Theses on Politics, Culture, & Method*. New Haven: Yale University Press, 2004.

Nussbaum, Martha. *Frontiers of Justice: Disability, Nationality, Species Membership*. Cambridge: Belknap Press of Harvard University Press, 2006.

Oreskes, Naomi and Erik Conway. *The Collapse of Western Civilization: A View from the Future*. New York: Columbia University Press, 2014.

Rawls, John. *A Theory of Justice, Rev. Ed*. Cambridge: Belknap Press of Harvard University Press, 1999 [1971].

Robinson, Kim Stanley. *2312*. London: Orbit, 2013.

Rousseau, Jean-Jacques. *Discours sur l'origine et les fondements de l'inégalité parmi les hommes / Discours sur les sciences et les art*. Paris: Flammarion, 1992.

Schoolmeester, T., Gjerdi, H.L., Crump, J., Alfthan, B., Fabres, J., Johnsen, K., Puikkonen, L., Kurvits, T. and Baker, E. *Global Linkages—A Graphic Look at the Changing Arctic* (rev.1). UN Environment and GRID-Arendal, Nairobi and Arendal. www.grida.no, accessed 18 October 2019.

Smith, Kelly. "*Homo Reductio*: Eco-nihilism and Human Colonization of Other Worlds." *Futures*, vol. 110 (2019): 31–34.

Soul Asylum. "Crawl." *Let Your Dim Light Shine*. Columbia, 1995. Compact Disc.

Toadvine, Ted. "Our Monstrous Futures: Global Sustainability and Eco-Eschatology." *Symposium: Canadian Journal of Continental Philosophy*, vol. 21, issue 1 (2017): 219–30, 2017.

Wallace-Wells, David. *The Uninhabitable Earth: Life after Warming*. New York: Tim Duggan Books, 2019.

Williams, Alex and Nick Srnicek. "#ACCELERATE MANIFESTO for an Accelerationist Politics." *Critical Legal Thinking*. 14 May 2013. http://criticallegalthinking.com/2013/05/14/accelerate-manifesto-for-an-accelerationist-politics/, accessed 18 October 2019.

Zuboff, Shoshana. *The Age of Surveillance Capitalism: The Fight for a Human Future at the New Frontier of Power*. New York: PublicAffairs, 2019.

*Part II*

# Resistance and Survival

*Chapter Four*

# "We Survived You"

*Resisting Eugenicist Imaginaries through Feminist Science Fiction*

## Jess Whatcott

In the season one cliffhanger of the television series *Orphan Black*, an evolutionary developmental biologist named Cosima discovers that encoded in her DNA sequence is a patent owned by Topside Corporation. Using what she calls "crazy science" to crack the code of her creation, Cosima untangles part of the mystery surrounding how she was cloned, and why she was denied information about her bioengineered birth. Cosima races to call her fellow clone Sarah Manning, explaining that the patent means: "We're property. Our bodies, our biology, everything we are, everything we become, belongs to them."[1] Over the course of five seasons, Cosima, Sarah, and their sister-clones resist their role in a eugenicist experiment guided by the pursuit of human perfection.

Although fictionalized, *Orphan Black* exposes the very real ways that eugenics programs continue to be sponsored by liberal states and corporate research agendas.[2] Unfortunately, law and public policy arenas have not lent themselves to robust democratic debates about the ethics of these ongoing eugenics programs.[3] Stymied by the limitations of legal and medical routes for justice, feminist and critical disability scholars have turned to studying science fiction stories like *Orphan Black* for at least two reasons.[4] First, while scientific and medical practices often appear on the surface to conform to technical proscriptions of bioethics, deeper examinations reveal contradictions and dynamics that confound technical solutions. As Karla Holloway argues, complex narrative stories enable us to grasp the multifaceted nature of problems like eugenics, necessary for crafting a multifaceted response.[5]

Second, the neoliberal privileging of individual choice is a barrier to reinvigorating a collective imagination that could counter the entrenched eugenics imaginary. Social justice activists Walida Imarisha and adrienne maree brown argue that reading, watching, writing, and creating feminist speculative fiction is a collective practice of visioning the world we want to live in.[6] Feminist science fiction is one collective democratic process of freedom that serves as a counter-practice to individual choice frameworks.

This chapter explores the political potential of feminist science fiction to both understand and collectively resist eugenicist imaginaries, by analyzing the television science fiction series *Orphan Black* (2013–2017).[7] The premise of *Orphan Black* is that the private company Topside Corporation—embodied for a time by the character of Dr. Aldous Leekie—has successfully cloned a human several times over. In the ultimate "nature versus nurture" experiment, the clones are unaware of their status, living relatively normal lives under secret monitoring by the corporation. Starting with the accidental discovery by the clones of each other and their creators, *Orphan Black* critiques the persistence of the eugenicist imaginary in the age of biotechnology.

The series also tells a story about resistance to the specific and narrow future of human perfection that eugenics insists can be produced. Pursuing liberation from the patent encoded in their bodies, Sarah declares to one of the corporate executives "You don't own us."[8] Portraying characters who band together in a queer chosen family that challenges the military-corporate-knowledge apparatus that views the clones as property, *Orphan Black* allows viewers and fans to collectively imagine an alternative feminist, queer, and critical disability future.

## FROM EUGENICS TO BIOTECHNOLOGY

Topside Corporation and the human cloning experiment are fictional, but the show is grounded in both U.S. eugenics history and the development of new biotechnologies. The English statistician Sir Francis Galton coined the term eugenics in 1883.[9] Applying his cousin Charles Darwin's theory of evolution to humans, Galton argued that human behavioral traits were directly inherited from parents by offspring. Galton used the phrase "nature versus nurture," to insist that it is biological inheritance that determines a person's genius and greatness. In order to increase the percent of the human population with desirable traits, Galton advocated for the early marriage of society's purebred elites. Galton wrote, "If a man breeds from strong, well-shaped dogs, but of mixed pedigree, the puppies will be sometimes, but rarely, the equals of their parents. They will commonly be of a mongrel, nondescript type, because ancestral peculiarities are apt to crop out in the offspring."[10] Through such metaphors, Galton gave language to the idea of improving the human race through statistically determined selective breeding, and to the idea of halting the degradation of civilization through preventing the reproduction of undesirable members of the human race.

The term "positive" eugenics has been used to describe the marriage and childbearing promotion programs that Galton envisaged, while the term "negative" eugenics has been used to describe the child prevention programs that were subsequently developed. Following others, I question whether this is a useful distinction.[11] Instead, I link together many types of programs as guided by the same sociotechnical imaginary of eugenics. Sheila Jasanoff describes sociotechnical imaginaries as the "collectively held, institutionally stabilized, and publicly performed visions of desirable futures, animated by shared understandings of forms of social life and social order attainable through, and supportive of, advances in science and technology."[12] Borrowing her concept, eugenics can be said to be a persistent sociotechnical imaginary that promises a future of human perfection through scientifically guided interventions into human reproduction, including selection and evolution.

Following Galton's coinage of the term, during the next decades of the late-eighteenth and early-twentieth centuries eugenics became popular among a growing middle-class of technocratic professionals across the world. In the United States, the turn of the twentieth century saw many social and political changes associated with rapid urbanization and industrialization, including criminality, juvenile delinquency and dependency, insanity, poverty, "immoral" behavior by women, and the growth of urban vice districts.[13] In the face of these changes, eugenics offered to the new middle-class the scientifically guided solutions that promised mastery over disease, illness, and impairment through the regulation of marriage and reproduction. The eugenicist imaginary in the United States undergirded a number of policy interventions. My research tracks eugenics in the state of California, such as this proposal by the State Board of Charities and Corrections in 1914 that called for:

> (a) more definitive and stringent laws for the commitment of feeble-minded persons, (b) establishment of farm colonies for feeble-minded, (c) segregation of the sexes, (d) sterilization when necessary, (e) laws preventing the marriage of feeble-minded, (f) immigration laws to exclude the defective classes, (g) special schools for the backward child.[14]

All of these eugenicist ideas were implemented to varying degrees by the state of California in collaboration with the federal government, including restrictive immigration policies, the development of segregated institutions for the feeble-minded, and the development of segregated special education programs. Proposal (d), regarding reproductive sterilization, is probably the most emblematic of the U.S. eugenics programs. Coercive sterilization laws were passed in multiple U.S. states beginning with an Indiana state law in 1907.[15] Confirmed as constitutional by the U.S. Supreme Court in 1927 in the *Buck v. Bell* decision, some eugenics sterilization laws were not overturned until the late 1970s.[16] Estimates are that over 60,000 people were coercively sterilized in the United States during this period.

The eugenicist fantasy of human perfection led to the genocide of millions of people under the Nazi Holocaust, wherein Jews, homosexuals, and disabled people were targeted for eradication in order to purify the Aryan Race.[17] Eugenics ideology was virulent under the Third Reich precisely because its notions of human perfection drew on and reproduced long-standing gendered, racialized, and able-ist Western hierarchies of human value. These hierarchies privilege men over women, bodies with clear binary sex over intersexed bodies, light-skin over dark-skin, and body-minded normativity over disability, madness, and neurodivergence.[18] The eugenics imaginary reestablished a notion of human perfection centered on the norm of a white, binary gendered male, one who has no visible disabilities or chronic illness, and whose mental processing is considered sane and normal. Under this image of the ideal human, naturally occurring human variations that deviated from the unmarked norm were pathologized as abnormal or "defective," and scientific, medical intervention, up to and including eradication, was legitimated.[19]

Early scholarship assumed that once the eugenicist campaigns of the Nazi's during World War II were revealed in the Nuremberg Trials, the eugenics movement was discredited and expressly eugenicist policies in the United States faded out of use.[20] However, feminist, queer, and disability scholars have tracked the myriad ways that the theory of human racial improvement and practices of intervening in human reproduction were never abandoned. Instead, these scholars argue, eugenics took on new guises.[21] The theory of eugenics continued to justify twentieth-century programs of sterilization that targeted women of olor, reproductive consequences for criminalized black women, the institutionalization of homosexuals and other sexual deviants, and marriage promotion programs through seemingly benign guises like marriage and family therapy.[22] Even into the twenty-first century, the belief in the scientific improvement of the human race through the prevention of the reproduction of undesirable populations is alive and well among some medical practitioners, as the case of sterilizations on people in California's women prisons as recently as 2010 illustrates.[23] The eugenicist imaginary continues to matter in the present because it underpins a wide range of public and private projects that curtail bodily autonomy and reproductive freedom for women, people of color, sexual minorities, and disabled people. Consequently, the questions that *Orphan Black* raises about the eugenicist underpinnings of the age of biotechnology are not outlandish and anachronistic, but timely and relevant.

In addition to conventional methods for carrying out eugenicist ideals, such as sterilization, new discoveries in human genetics and biotechnologies offer ever more precise ways for improving the human race. Biotechnologies introduce complex routes for reproducing racialized and gendered hierarchies of human value. By biotechnologies, I am referring to capacities developed during and following an international research consortium called The Human Genome Project completing a "map" of the genetic sequence of humans in 2003.[24] During and following the mapping of the entire human genome, genetic testing technologies were developed that are capable of determining with high probability the likelihood that a human embryo or fetus will develop specific diseases, conditions, and inherited traits. In the twenty-first century, prospective parents can choose which embryo to implant, engage in in vitro corrective procedures, or in some cases abort a fetus that is likely to be born with a condition that medical practitioners and/or parents determine to be undesirable.[25] Another leap has taken place with the development of CRISPR biotechnology in 2015, which granted scientists (even non-genetics scientists) the technical capability to "edit" the genetic sequence of a human embryo before in vitro implantation.[26] Using this biotechnology as a form of germline editing could mean that prospective parents could genetically modify an embryo before carrying it to term. Potential modifications promised by CRISPR germline editing range from the superficial such as hair or eye color, to the therapeutic prevention of diseases, to enhancements designed to increase intelligence or muscle mass.

Proponents of using CRISPR on human embryos argue that scientists have an ethical duty to prevent unnecessary suffering, and thus should use the technology to eliminate disease.[27] This is a similar line of thinking to that which supports the less controversial (albeit no less ethically questionable) gene therapy uses of CRISPR. Opponents of germline editing argue that editing genes will introduce irreversible changes into the human genome and should be approached with extreme caution, if not prohibited altogether.[28] Disability advocates are particularly concerned with how this biotechnology introduces new opportunities for eugenicists to enact their racialized and gendered fantasies of human perfection.[29] Feminist and critical disability scholarship demands an interrogation of potential scenarios including: in a near future where rich prospective parents could travel to an off-shore clinic for a gene-edited embryo, what would stop parents from choosing the sex of their child? Even more likely, what is to stop gene-editors and parents from viewing intersexual conditions as genetic diseases that need to be eradicated in favor of a clear assignment to the sex binary? In societies around the world that value whiter skin due to colonial discourses that uphold white supremacy, could not a case be made that it would be cruel not to give a child a light-skinned advantage? Similar questions arise about the elimination of human variations that have been labeled disabilities or mental illness. Could

CRISPR biotechnology be used to eliminate chronic illness, physical conditions for which our built environment is inaccessible, deafness, blindness or genetic sequences that are believed to trigger divergent mental processes?

As disability scholars have observed, the possibilities of eliminating intersexual conditions and disability probably seem to most people like positive programs that would reduce human suffering and improve human well-being.[30] Yet, the question is, who will decide which of these conditions need to be eradicated and which are merely benign forms of human variation? Further, which discourses of human normality and what constitutes a good life will influence decision making? Given eugenicist understandings of which body and mind conditions are understood to be abnormal, it is unlikely that intersexed, disabled, and neurodivergent people will be given a say, much less be given priority, in making decisions about whether people like them will be eradicated.[31] Given colonial histories of racialization, it is even less likely that people of color and people from the global south will be prioritized in decision making around the ethics of biotechnology.[32] Additionally, while dangers abound regarding the use of biotechnologies to target undesirable populations for elimination, the use of biotechnology for the "positive" purposes of enhancing the genetic sequence of individuals and the genetic pool overall also threatens to reproduce racialized and gendered notions of the ideal human. In both instances, ideals about human perfection rooted in the eugenicist imaginary continue to be the guiding framework for decision making, with potentially disastrous consequences for the autonomy and futurity of people of color, intersexed, disabled, and neurodivergent people.

## EUGENICS AND LIBERAL GOVERNANCE

How equipped are liberal governments to engage in robust democratic debate about the gendered and racialized dynamics of new biotechnologies? In the United States, obstructions to such a debate range from low scientific literacy among the public to the active disavowal of scientific reports among some political leaders. However, even deeper obstacles to bioethical debate confront us, obstacles grounded in the continued acceptance of human perfection as a common goal. As I have construed it here, eugenics imagines that through scientific intervention, technocrats can build a human future without disease, illness, or impairment. Despite the historical evidence that fantasies of human perfection lead to the denial of bodily autonomy at best, and mass genocide at worst, the eugenicist imaginary of human progress and perfection continues to serve as a desirable future that liberal societies collectively strive toward. Despite the disavowal of eugenics as a pseudoscience with serious consequences for marginalized members of the nation, the ultimate goal of human perfection arguably remains at the heart of liberal governance.

The logic of eugenics is compatible with that of contemporary liberal governance, in that both are inclined to pursue technical fixes that purport to provide ultimate solutions to enduring and complex problems. Disability scholars describe how at least since the end of the nineteenth century, overcoming disease, illness, and impairment has been central to the imagining the destiny of the United States.[33] Those who embody disease, illness, and impairment—sick, disabled, mad, and/or neurodivergent people—are construed as problems. Liberal fantasies about the recovery from such problems through scientific state interventions on sick and disabled people, or on programs to prevent healthy normal people from becoming sick and disabled, constitute what Eli Clare calls the obsession with "the cure."[34] I contend that liberal governments are likely to pursue a proposed biotechnical cure to the problem of disease and disability—especially if it can be privately funded under the conditions of neoliberalism—even if there are questionable eugenicist underpinnings. Liberal governments are better equipped to seek a cure than they are prepared to imagine a future that supports sick and disabled people who need government-funded infrastructure and care.

Additionally, new biotechnologies that give more choice to individual parents of nuclear families are likely to be viewed as desirable under liberal governance. Maximizing choice is consistent with neoliberal fantasies of the unhindered pursuit of self-interest. For some individuals, the prioritization of their parental choice comes even at the risk of broad social cost. Neoliberal emphasis on choice over social cost may seem like a positive reversal of prior eugenicist discourse that sacrificed the individual in the name of protecting social welfare. However, I argue that neoliberalism and eugenics are logically compatible. This is because eugenics recognizes the individual choice of only some elite members of society, namely those who have the resources to pursue their self-interest. Eugenics adds to this elite capacity to pursue individual self-interest the justification and right to pursue individual improvement in the name of general human race improvement. In the case of new biotechnologies, prioritizing parental choice could come at the cost of diminishing human variation. This diminishment would be most acutely felt by those who are devalued in our society, including racialized people, women, intersexed, disabled, and neurodivergent people; these groups would experience a foreclosure of their possible future horizons.

Meanwhile, devalued populations continue to be denied the privacy within which they might exercise bodily autonomy. As Karla Holloway has argued, "privacy is a privilege" that is denied to "hypervisible" racialized and gendered bodies.[35] That is, bodies that do not match the unmarked norm of white heterosexual male citizen, the normative subject through which law and bioethics were constructed, are constantly made public. For black people and women, Holloway argues, what should be intimate and personal medical crises are automatically rendered "vulnerable, exposed, and critically public."[36] Consequently, any biomedical decisions made by parents of color, especially women of color, are likely to be open to public criticism and intervention. This is especially true of those decisions that counter gendered and racialized ideals of human perfection, such as those that refuse to devalue black lives, non-binary sex/gender, disability, and neurodivergence.

Due to the compatibility of liberal and neoliberal governance with the goals, strategies, and values of eugenics, state-sponsored programs of human perfection continue to cyclically emerge. Consequently, the technical fixes favored by liberal states cannot undo the entanglement of eugenics theory and goals within the body politic. Instead, as I have written elsewhere, the tools most likely adopted or adapted by liberal states to enforce bioethical practice (such as informed consent) are at risk for becoming merely new vehicles for the enactment of racialized and gendered biopolitics.[37] Feminist, queer, and disability scholars and advocates will have to turn outside of the law and public policy to challenge eugenicist imaginaries that underpin new biotechnologies.

## SPECULATIVE FICTION AS FEMINIST ETHICS

Feminist scholars have turned to speculative fiction as a site for democratically developing alternatives to the sociotechnical imaginary of eugenics. Proposing this in her 1985 essay, Donna Haraway argued that feminist science fiction was one route for constructing a "cyborg myth" to counter what she called the emergent "informatics of domination."[38] Haraway observed a shift from a society of "white capitalist patriarchy" organized by industrial capitalism to a world system of domination organized by information. Under the informatics of domination, Haraway theorized that control would operate through systems theory and the "one code" elaborated through the technologies of optimization, population control, immunology, genetic engineering, and what she called "biology as inscription."[39] Presciently, Haraway identified a shift from eugenics to biotech, but observed that such a shift would not necessarily undo older hierarchies of race and gender, but merely recode these hierarchies. For Haraway, however, resistance to the informatics of domination could not come from "outside" the system through the disavowal of science and technology. Instead, the path to resistance lay in the subject she called the cyborg reclaiming the technologies that created her. Haraway positioned feminist science fiction writers as one version of these cyborgs who could use the medium to explode unifying and universalist theory in favor of occupying a liminal space characterized by contradiction and tension.

In another turn to the speculative, Karla Holloway positions fiction as a necessary correlative to legal and medical discussions of bioethics, which she argues have a tendency to "pare down the subject to an actionable space," and particularly into quantifiable and technical measurements.[40] Science fiction storytelling, in her view, gives the person who has been designated as a problem or a body with a "condition" the opportunity to develop "the intricate dimensions of the story" that fall away in the narrowing scope of law and medicine.[41] Reading and writing fiction, according to Holloway, allow us to explore all of the dynamics of a problem outside of the legal and medical impulse to quickly correct the immediate symptoms. Like Holloway, Sami Schalk indicates that speculative fiction is specifically capable of engaging in complex questions about race, gender, and disability.[42] Through world-making and future imagining, black women's speculative fiction challenges dominant "ableist, racist, and sexist assumptions" about "bodyminds."[43] By speculating on the dystopic elements of potential futures, this fiction denaturalizes hegemonic and internalized constructs of what is good and desirable in the present, as well as what the ideal future could be.

Building on this line of feminist engagement with speculative fiction, I turn to science fiction as a democratic space for political community to think through complex ethical questions. In relation to the present study of eugenics, feminist science fiction has, first, the capacity to problematize the imaginary of eugenics for a popular audience. Space for deep, complex discussion is made possible precisely because the issues are taken out of the context of liberal governance's terms and conditions. I argued are inclined to agree with the goal of human perfection and the strategy of disease elimination, as well as tending to privilege the individual choice of elites over the autonomy and futurity of those labeled undesirable. Feminist science fiction reveals the hidden and unintended costs and consequences of fantasies of human perfection, forcing readers and audiences to confront the desirability of eugenics projects, and consequently to interrogate dominant discourses and practices. Feminist science fiction makes dystopia out of eugenics utopia, exposing the goal of human perfection as disturbing for popular audiences.

Second, feminist science fiction has the capacity to imagine and identify alternative pathways for enacting feminist, queer, and critical disability futures. By feminist, I mean futures without gendered hierarchies of human value, including all hierarchies of human value that intersect with gender, including race, class, sexuality, disability, and nation. By queer, I mean futures that are inclusive and affirmative of all people who are targeted for their actual or perceived gender nonconformity and/or sexual deviance, not limited to those with lesbian, gay, bisexual, and trans identities. By critical disability, I mean futures where all forms of body and mind difference are valued rather than looked on with aspersion, and where the built infrastructure and social-political life are universally accessible to all body-minds. Rather than an alternative ideology to eugenics or a specific program of change, I treat each of these concepts as a future horizon, meaning that as goals they may be unachievable, but they provide a yardstick of liberation that people who value feminist, queer, and critical disability life must be constantly striving toward.[44]

This constructive aspect of speculative fictions borrows from the conceptualization of "visionary fiction" offered by adrienne maree brown and Walidah Imarisha. According to brown and Imarisha, visionary fiction is that which ignites collective power to imagine and build alternative futures against overdetermining conditions of oppression.[45] brown and Imarisha treat speculative fiction, and the work of Octavia Butler in particular, as practical texts containing wisdom about survival, healing, and flourishing under the contradictions of liberal governance. A novel like black feminist writer Octavia Butler's *Parable of the Sower,* for example, is read pedagogically for specific directions about surviving the current apocalypses caused by fire danger and climate change, government divestment from dispossessed communities of color, growing wealth inequality that has demolished the possibility of a middle class, and the privatization of the already flimsy social safety net, which consists of an ever increasing reliance on contingent labor for survival.[46] brown and Imarisha gather with other *Parable* fans to implement and elaborate practices of community building and mutual aid gestured toward in the novel.

Treating feminist speculative fiction as theory in this way, not just as fantasy, or even merely critique, but also as normative and proscriptive, generates new forms of feminist, queer, and critical disability ethics. The television series *Orphan Black* can be analyzed for the critique that the show offers regarding the consequences of the eugenicist discourse of human perfection underlying corporate-military research projects. On another level, *Orphan Black* also offers an elaboration of a counter-ideal that articulates feminist, queer, and critical disability future horizons.

## UNDERMINING EUGENICS AND CREATING QUEER FUTURES IN *ORPHAN BLACK*

The television series *Orphan Black* opens on a train station platform, focusing on a late 20s/early 30s aged woman named Sarah Manning wearing a leather jacket and ripped jeans.[47] Sarah sees another woman removing her purse and shoes before turning toward the train tracks. Running to intervene in the woman's attempt to jump in front of an oncoming train, Sarah is shocked into stillness by the woman's face, which looks exactly like Sarah's. Failing to stop her doppelganger's suicide, Sarah instead walks off with the woman's purse, ambivalent about whether to merely steal the identity (and money) of the dead woman she learns was named Beth, or to pursue the mystery of their likeness. Viewers follow Sarah as she is pulled deep into

Beth's life, eventually taking on not only Beth's identity but also an investigation into the truth of both of their origins.

Through the identity theft, Sarah learns that both she and Beth are one of several human clones. While Sarah's situation is unique, Beth and the other clones are under monitoring by their creators, embodied by a private research company called the Dyad Institute, a branch of a much larger, more nebulous corporation called Topside. The premise of *Orphan Black* is that this private company, in collaboration with (as viewers learn in season three) the U.S. military, have collaborated to successfully clone a human several times over. The clones are mostly unaware of their status as cloned humans and are free to live their lives. They are, however, under secret and constant surveillance by family and friends who report to the corporation. The story follows the character of Sarah Manning who has become what the corporation calls "self-aware" through the process of stealing Beth's identity on the train platform. Sarah learns about her membership in what she affectionately calls "clone club." She builds relationships with other clones including Cosima, Alison, and Helena, all of whom she comes to refer to as her "sisters." Their bonds are forged during an almost nonstop race to protect Sarah's child from exploitation by the corporation, as well as to save Cosima's life threatened by a disease caused unintentionally by a genetic mutation emplaced by their creators. The loyalty of the sister-clones to each other, as well as their determination to protect their larger chosen family, ultimately destroys the scientists and supporting institutions that created them.

*Orphan Black*'s first intervention is to render the consequences of eugenics imaginaries as dystopic. The show explicitly situates the biotechnologies being developed by the fictional Dyad Institute within the real-world history of eugenics programs. Following a lead that one of the original scientists who created the clones may be alive and in hiding, Sarah encounters the archive of the fictional "Cold River Institute."[48] "Cold River" is a not so subtle reference to the real Station for Experimental Evolution (later the Eugenics Record Office) established at Cold Spring Harbor, Long Island, New York, by Andrew Carnegie in 1902.[49] Viewers of this *Orphan Black* episode watch as Sarah sorts through materials documenting the history of eugenics, including a photograph captioned "Most Perfect Baby," photographs of disabled children, images of surgical procedures, what appear to be family history charts, and an academic journal article with the title "The Progress of Eugenic Sterilization." All of these artifacts in Sarah's fictional archive gesture to real programs and practices implemented by the eugenicist field workers trained at the office at Cold Spring Harbor and placed across the United States in the early twentieth century. Sarah also encounters a photograph of a fictional Dr. Duncan who created the original clones, observing that he was part of a delegation from Cambridge University to the fictional Cold River Institute. After Sarah shares her findings in the archive with one of the sister-clones who happens to be an evolutionary developmental biologist scientist, Cosima determines "Cold River is like the perfect ideological breeding ground for a nature/nurture cloning fiasco."[50] In her usual irreverent manner, scientist sister-clone Cosima explicitly links the ideology driving the fictional clone scientists with the real life ideology of eugenics.

While grounded in the real eugenics history of the United States, *Orphan Black*'s focus is on how eugenics ideas persist in the form of public and private research agendas and experimentation. Released between 2013 and 2017, the show presciently anticipated scientific discourses that would accompany recent developments in biotechnology. In the show, Dr. Aldous Leekie rigorously promotes the fictional Dyad Institute's vision of "neolution" or "self-directed evolution," and positions Dyad on the cutting edge of the "age of biotechnology." As the precursor to the real-life Dr. He Jiankui who genetically edited human embryos that were carried to term in 2018, the fictional Dr. Leekie in *Orphan Black* argues that it is the "moral responsibility" of visionary scientists and intellectuals to "continue healing, feeding, and fueling the future of humanity."[51] Dr. Leekie positions himself and his co-visionaries as the inheritor of the eugenics project, in that biotechnologists are portrayed as the new scientists morally responsible for securing the futurity of the human race. One of the mysterious women behind Dr. Leekie, Dr. Marion Bowles, takes this point even further. Dr. Bowles explains to Sarah that the parent organization to the Dyad Institute, called Topside, is busy "securing monopolies on a future that embraces genetic engineering [and] synthetic biology . . . a future I passionately believe is inevitable."[52]

"Securing monopolies on the future," viewers come to learn, means not only monopolizing biotechnological development through the patent process, but also undermining the democratic political process in order to favor their investments. Through quiet lobbying, campaign financing, and even promoting puppet political candidates, Topside effectively elides any genuine public participation in decisions about whether, if, and how to pursue genetic engineering for social good. In the show, this elision of democratic participation in favor of corporate profit making is most acutely felt by the clone sisters themselves, who are consistently locked out of ethical questions surrounding their futures and the creation of future clones. The clone sister's efforts to control their own biology and determine their own futures is fought so bitterly by the corporation that the sisters are threatened with a group assassination; a plot, they are told, that has been carried out before on rebellious clones in Helsinki.

Pitting clone sisters against eugenicist scientists and their corporate sponsors, *Orphan Black* re-creates one of the central tropes of science fiction, wherein the scientific creation threatens to destroy the scientist-creator. Despite the illusions of scientist-creators, their creations are never fully under their control. This trope goes back to what many have designated the first science fiction book ever written—*Frankenstein; or, The Modern Prometheus* written by Mary Wollstonecraft Shelley in 1818.[53] Shelley tells the story of a naturalist named Victor Frankenstein who is haunted by the creature he brought to life and then abandoned. In a rage against his creator, the creature commits a string of murders on Victor's family and loved ones. Although it preceded the development of modern science, *Frankenstein* explored the danger of unintended consequences of scientific experimentation, a trope that Hollywood picked up throughout the twentieth century. Many popular science fiction films have emphasized the dangers that advancing technology poses to humanity, including *2001: A Space Odyssey*, *The Terminator*, or *I, Robot*.[54] In each of these films, a computer, an android, and a robot exceeds the collective powers of the humans who attempt to control them, and murderously lash out against their creators. Other versions of this trope, such as Philip K. Dick's novella *Do Androids Dream of Electric Sheep?,* instead uses the battle between scientific creation and creator to trouble the ethics of human characters that are intent on policing the boundaries of humanity at all costs.[55] In Dick's novel and the film spinoffs *Blade Runner* and *Blade Runner 2049*, a police detective responsible for hunting down and destroying runaway androids comes to question the lines between humanity and robotic life, and whether humans can be said to be in sole possession of morality.[56]

This latter version of the creation versus creator trope is present in *Orphan Black*. The clones face off against a seemingly insurmountable military-corporate-knowledge apparatus that claims ownership of their very DNA. The clones' treatment at the hands of their creators exposes the scientists' unethical practices in the uncritical pursuit of scientific discovery, and this calls into question the scientists' humanity. The corporation's relentless pursuit of profit and control requires unscrupulous treatment of the clones including torture, attempted murder, and invasive biomedical procedures. These practices include secretly drugging Sarah and subjecting her to medical testing, attempting to remove one of Sarah's ovaries for study—"Enjoy your oophorectomy" a corporate executive intones—and using the harvesting of Sarah's daughter's bone marrow stem cells as an opportunity to kidnap the daughter.[57] The image of these biomedical practices references the denial of bodily autonomy throughout eugenics' past. The plot also gestures toward a biotechnological future that continues to dehumanize working-class, sexually deviant, and otherwise non-normative women. The plot reveals the potential depravity of profit-driven science. Cementing the show's critique of eugenic science, the utopia of self-directed evolution promised by the fictional neolutionists is revealed to be dystopic for everyone but the most elite.

*Orphan Black*'s second intervention is to humanize the targets of eugenics, by depicting the survival and resistance of the sister-clones to their commodification, objectification, manipulation, and threatened death. Rejecting eugenicist reliance on blood kinship as the determining factor of one's destiny, the sister-clones fight back through enacting a queer practice of chosen family. In queer community, the concept of chosen family indicates a kinship connection determined by love and a committed demonstration of care. Because many queer people have experienced abandonment, disavowal, and estrangement by blood kin, illusions about natural affection and responsibility have already been shattered. Queers know that family is always already what you make of it. Because of their unorthodox conceptions, the sister-clones are born into a world where their only family is the one they make. Sarah, for example, was raised along with an adopted brother by a single parent. Sarah's daughter has been partially raised by her grandmother. Sarah's fierce loyalty to this chosen family is complicated by the commitments and responsibilities she has to her sister-clones. This comes to a head when a life-saving treatment for Cosima is held hostage by a demand that Sarah subject her daughter to a painful medical procedure to extract bone marrow stem cells. As the show progresses, each of the clones expand their already chosen, queer families by including, at times reluctantly, their sister-clones. As Cosima declares to her lover, being family with a sister-clone comes to mean being family with all of the sister-clones. This means that the stakes of any decision regarding a single individual are amplified by the impact it will have on all of the sister-clones. Forming a chosen family united together, the sister-clones ultimately take down a series of corporate executives, evil scientists, and eugenicist ideologues who would control them and their destiny.

The familial connections among the women, and the men who support them, in *Orphan Black* offer a powerful critique of the logic of eugenics that continues to drive new biotechnologies. The queer sister-clone family supports each other in all their imperfections and contradictions. Countering the eugenicist ideal of human perfection, the show insists that we are the most human when we are imperfect, and we love and care for each other anyway. *Orphan Black* envisions a future horizon of feminist, queer, and critical disability community built through an ethic of love, care, accountability, and mutual aid, rather than one built on a eugenicist striving toward human perfection.

In the final episode of *Orphan Black*, the sister-clones and all the chosen family who have aided and abetted them throughout the series, gather for an old-fashioned potluck and barbeque. Sarah admits that she is struggling to transition to a state where her life is not in constant danger. However, through non-consensual medical experimentation, kidnappings, attempted and successful assassinations, surveillance through an artificial eye, the delivery of twins on a concrete floor, and so much more, the sister-clones can declare to their corrupt creators, "I survived you. We survived you. Me and my sisters together. *This* is evolution."[58]

## CONCLUSION

In the context of complex and rapid developments in new biotechnologies, liberal and neoliberal governance continues to be driven by the sociotechnical imaginary of eugenics. That is, liberal and neoliberal governance continues to seek to master disease and disability at the risk of denying bodily autonomy to some, and even enacting a kind of slow genocide against different body-minds. Feminist science fiction creations, like the television series *Orphan Black,* hold tremendous capacity to undermine and transform these eugenicist social imaginaries. Feminist science fiction cultivates an audience capable of perceiving the connections between histories of racialized and gendered oppression, and current scientific and technological advancements. Further, feminist science fiction like *Orphan Black* offers the audience an alternative imaginary of the future. A neoliberal version of eugenics privileges the individual choice of a few elites, at the expense of social good, while denying the same kind of choice to non-elites. Feminist science fiction, on the other hand, imagines a future of networks of care, where each person is accountable to the others in their network, and a future of mutual aid, where resources are pooled to ensure the survival and thriving of all members of our community.

However, the work to dismantle programs guided by eugenics logic does not, and must not, end with transforming the social and political sociotechnical imaginary. Exciting efforts are under way, by visionaries like adrienne maree brown, to transform science fiction fans into actual publics who are capable of material political transformation.[59] Feminist science fiction fans turned into politically engaged community could be the best hope for disentangling liberal governance from the logic of eugenics, and forging concrete feminist, queer, and critical disability futures.

## NOTES

1. John Fawcett, "Endless Forms Most Beautiful," *Orphan Black* (BBC America, June 1, 2013).

2. Dorothy E. Roberts, *Killing the Black Body: Race, Reproduction, and the Meaning of Liberty* (New York: Pantheon Books, 1997); Nancy Ordover, *American Eugenics: Race, Queer Anatomy, and the Science of Nationalism* (Minneapolis: University of Minnesota Press, 2003); Paul A. Lombardo, ed., *A Century of Eugenics in America: From the Indiana Experiment to the Human Genome Era*, Bioethics and the Humanities (Bloomington: Indiana University Press, 2011); Liat Ben-Moshe, Allison C. Carey, and Chris Chapman, eds., *Disability Incarcerated: Imprisonment and Disability in the United States and Canada* (New York: Palgrave Macmillan, 2014); Eli Clare, *Brilliant Imperfection: Grappling with Cure* (Durham: Duke University Press, 2017).

3. Jess Whatcott, "No Selves to Consent: Women's Prisons, Sterilization, and the Biopolitics of Informed Consent," *Signs: Journal of Women in Culture and Society* 44, no. 1 (2018): 131–53.

4. Donna Jeanne Haraway, "A Cyborg Manifesto: Science, Technology, and Socialist-Feminism in the Late Twentieth Century," in *Simians, Cyborgs, and Women: The Reinvention of Nature* (New York: Routledge, 1991); Karla F. C. Holloway, *Private Bodies, Public Texts: Race, Gender, and a Cultural Bioethics* (Durham, N.C.: Duke University Press, 2011); Samantha Dawn Schalk, *Bodyminds Reimagined: (Dis)Ability, Race, and Gender in Black Women's Speculative Fiction* (Durham, N.C.: Duke University Press, 2018); Therí A Pickens, *Black Madness: Mad Blackness* (Durham, N.C.: Duke University Press, 2019).

5. Holloway, *Private Bodies, Public Texts.*

6. Walidah Imarisha and adrienne maree brown, *Octavia's Brood: Science Fiction Stories from Social Justice Movements* (Oakland: AK Press, 2015).

7. Created by Graeme Manson and John Fawcett, *Orphan Black* (BBC America, 2013).

8. John Fawcett, "Nature under Constraint and Vexed," *Orphan Black* (BBC America, April 19, 2014).

9. Sir Francis Galton, *Inquiries into Human Faculty and Its Development.* (New York: Macmillan, 1883).

10. Francis Galton, *Hereditary Genius: An Inquiry into Its Laws and Consequences* (New York: D. Appleton & Co, 1870).

11. Alexandra Stern, *Eugenic Nation: Faults and Frontiers of Better Breeding in Modern America* (Berkeley: University of California Press, 2005).

12. Sheila Jasanoff and Sang-Hyun Kim, eds., *Dreamscapes of Modernity: Sociotechnical Imaginaries and the Fabrication of Power* (Chicago: The University of Chicago Press, 2015), 4.

13. John D'Emilio and Estelle B. Freedman, *Intimate Matters: A History of Sexuality in America*, 2nd ed. (Chicago: University of Chicago Press, 1997).

14. "Report of the State Board of Charities and Corrections, 1912–1914" (Appendix to the Journals of the Senate and Assembly of the Legislature of the State of California: Sacramento, California: California State Printing, 1915).

15. Alexandra Minna Stern, "From Legislation to Lived Experience: Eugenic Sterilization in California and Indiana, 1907–1979," in *A Century of Eugenics in America: From the Indiana Experiment to the Human Genome Era*, ed. Paul A. Lombardo, Bioethics and the Humanities (Bloomington: Indiana University Press, 2011).

16. Stern, "From Legislation to Lived Experience."

17. Ordover, *American Eugenics.*

18. Ben-Moshe, Carey, and Chapman, *Disability Incarcerated.*

19. Clare, *Brilliant Imperfection.*

20. Donald K. Pickens, *Eugenics and the Progressives* (Nashville: Vanderbilt University Press, 1968).

21. Angela Y. Davis, *Women, Race & Class* (New York: Vintage Books, 1983); Roberts, *Killing the Black Body*; Wendy Kline, *Building a Better Race: Gender, Sexuality, and Eugenics from the Turn of the Century to the Baby Boom* (Berkeley: University of California Press, 2001); Myla Vicenti Carpio, "The Lost Generation: American Indian Women and Sterilization Abuse," *Social Justice* 31, no. 4 (98) (2004): 40–53; Laura Briggs, *Reproducing Empire: Race, Sex, Science, and U.S. Imperialism in Puerto Rico* (Berkeley: University of California Press, 2002); Stern, *Eugenic Nation*; Ben-Moshe, Carey, and Chapman, *Disability Incarcerated*; Clare, *Brilliant Imperfection.*

22. Roberts, *Killing the Black Body*; Briggs, *Reproducing Empire*; Ordover, *American Eugenics*; Stern, *Eugenic Nation.*

23. Alexandra Minna Stern and Tony Platt, "Sterilization Abuse in State Prisons: Time to Break with California's Long Eugenic Patterns," *The Huffington Post* (blog), July 23, 2013, http://www.huffingtonpost.com/alex-stern/sterilization-california-prisons_b_3631287.html; Whatcott, "No Selves to Consent."

24. "An Overview of the Human Genome Project," National Human Genomic Research Institute, May 11, 2016, https://www.genome.gov/12011238/an-overview-of-the-human-genome-project/.

25. Erik Parens and Adrienne Asch, "Special Supplement: The Disability Rights Critique of Prenatal Genetic Testing Reflections and Recommendations," *The Hastings Center Report* 29, no. 5 (1999).

26. "What Is Human Gene Editing? Center for Genetics and Society," accessed February 4, 2020, https://www.geneticsandsociety.org/internal-content/what-human-gene-editing.

27. Gerry Shis and Carolyn Y. Johnson, "Chinese Genomics Scientist Defends His Gene-Editing Research in First Public Appearance," *Washington Post*, November 28, 2018, https://www.washingtonpost.com/world/chinese-genomics-scientist-defends-his-gene-editing-research-in-first-public-appearance/2018/11/28/b99b5eba-f2e1-11e8-9240-e8028a62c722_story.html.

28. "What Is Human Gene Editing?"

29. Parens and Asch, "Special Supplement"; "What Is Human Gene Editing?"

30. Parens and Asch, "Special Supplement."

31. Clare, *Brilliant Imperfection*.

32. Ruha Benjamin, *Captivating Technology: Race, Carceral Technoscience, and Liberatory Imagination in Everyday Life* (Durham, N.C.: Duke University Press, 2019).

33. Alison Kafer, *Feminist, Queer, Crip* (Bloomington: Indiana University Press, 2013); Clare, *Brilliant Imperfection*.

34. Clare, *Brilliant Imperfection*.

35. Holloway, *Private Bodies, Public Texts*, 20.

36. Holloway, *Private Bodies, Public Texts*, 20.

37. Whatcott, "No Selves to Consent."

38. Haraway, "A Cyborg Manifesto: Science, Technology, and Socialist-Feminism in the Late Twentieth Century."

39. Haraway, 161.

40. Holloway, *Private Bodies, Public Texts*, 12.

41. Holloway, *Private Bodies, Public Texts*, 12.

42. Schalk, *Bodyminds Reimagined*.

43. Schalk, *Bodyminds Reimagined*..

44. José Esteban Muñoz, *Cruising Utopia: The Then and There of Queer Futurity*, (New York: New York University Press, 2009).

45. Imarisha and brown, *Octavia's Brood*.

46. Octavia E. Butler, *Parable of the Sower* (New York: Grand Central Publishing, 2007).

47. John Fawcett, "Natural Selection," *Orphan Black* (BBC America, March 30, 2013).

48. Brett Sullivan, "To Hound Nature in Her Wanderings," *Orphan Black* (BBC America, May 24, 2014).

49. Pickens, *Eugenics and the Progressives*.

50. Sullivan, "To Hound Nature in Her Wanderings."

51. Fawcett, "Nature Under Constraint and Vexed."

52. John Fawcett, "By Means Which Have Never Yet Been Tried," *Orphan Black* (BBC America, June 21, 2014).

53. Mary Wollstonecraft Shelley, *Frankenstein: The 1818 Text* (New York: Penguin Books, 2018).

54. Stanley Kubrick, *2001: A Space Odyssey* (Metro-Goldwyn-Mayer, 1968); James Cameron, *The Terminator* (Orion Pictures, 1984); Alex Proyas, *I, robot.* (20th Century Fox, 2004).

55. Philip K. Dick, *Do Androids Dream of Electric Sheep?* (New York: Ballantine Books, 1996).

56. Ridley Scott, *Blade Runner* (Warner Bros., 1982); Denis Villeneuve, *Blade Runner 2049* (Warner Bros. Pictures, 2017).

57. Fawcett, "By Means Which Have Never Yet Been Tried."

58. John Fawcett, "To Right the Wrongs of Many," *Orphan Black* (BBC America, August 12, 2017).

59. adrienne maree brown, *Emergent Strategy: Shaping Change, Changing Worlds* (Chico, CA: AK Press, 2017).

# BIBLIOGRAPHY

Benjamin, Ruha. *Captivating Technology: Race, Carceral Technoscience, and Liberatory Imagination in Everyday Life*. Durham, N.C.: Duke University Press, 2019.
Ben-Moshe, Liat, Allison C. Carey, and Chris Chapman, eds. *Disability Incarcerated: Imprisonment and Disability in the United States and Canada*. New York, NY: Palgrave Macmillan, 2014.
Briggs, Laura. *Reproducing Empire: Race, Sex, Science, and U.S. Imperialism in Puerto Rico*. Berkeley: University of California Press, 2002.
brown, adrienne maree. *Emergent Strategy: Shaping Change, Changing Worlds*. Chico, CA: AK Press, 2017.
Butler, Octavia E. *Parable of the Sower*. New York: Grand Central Publishing, 2007.
Cameron, James. *The Terminator*. Orion Pictures, 1984.
Carpio, Myla Vicenti. "The Lost Generation: American Indian Women and Sterilization Abuse." *Social Justice* 31, no. 4 (98) (2004): 40–53.
Clare, Eli. *Brilliant Imperfection: Grappling with Cure*. Durham: Duke University Press, 2017.
Davis, Angela Y. *Women, Race & Class*. New York: Vintage Books, 1983.
D'Emilio, John, and Estelle B. Freedman. *Intimate Matters: A History of Sexuality in America*. 2nd ed. Chicago: University of Chicago Press, 1997.
Dick, Philip K. *Do Androids Dream of Electric Sheep?* New York: Ballantine Books, 1996.
Fawcett, John. "By Means Which Have Never Yet Been Tried." *Orphan Black*. BBC America, June 21, 2014.
———. "Endless Forms Most Beautiful." *Orphan Black*. BBC America, June 1, 2013.
———. "Natural Selection." *Orphan Black*. BBC America, March 30, 2013.
———. "Nature under Constraint and Vexed." *Orphan Black*. BBC America, April 19, 2014.
———. "To Right the Wrongs of Many." *Orphan Black*. BBC America, August 12, 2017.
Galton, Francis. *Hereditary Genius: An Inquiry into Its Laws and Consequences*. New York: D. Appleton & Co, 1870.
Galton, Sir Francis. *Inquiries into Human Faculty and Its Development*. New York: Macmillan, 1883.
Haraway, Donna Jeanne. "A Cyborg Manifesto: Science, Technology, and Socialist-Feminism in the Late Twentieth Century." In *Simians, Cyborgs, and Women: The Reinvention of Nature*. New York: Routledge, 1991.
Holloway, Karla F. C. *Private Bodies, Public Texts: Race, Gender, and a Cultural Bioethics*. Durham, NC: Duke University Press, 2011.
Imarisha, Walidah, and adrienne maree brown. *Octavia's Brood: Science Fiction Stories from Social Justice Movements*. Oakland: AK Press, 2015.
Jasanoff, Sheila, and Sang-Hyun Kim, eds. *Dreamscapes of Modernity: Sociotechnical Imaginaries and the Fabrication of Power*. Chicago: The University of Chicago Press, 2015.
Kafer, Alison. *Feminist, Queer, Crip*. Bloomington, Indiana: Indiana University Press, 2013.
Kline, Wendy. *Building a Better Race: Gender, Sexuality, and Eugenics from the Turn of the Century to the Baby Boom*. Berkeley: University of California Press, 2001.
Kubrick, Stanley. *2001: A Space Odyssey*. Metro-Goldwyn-Mayer, 1968.
Lombardo, Paul A., ed. *A Century of Eugenics in America: From the Indiana Experiment to the Human Genome Era*. Bloomington: Indiana University Press, 2011.
Manson, Graeme, and John Fawcett, creators. *Orphan Black*. BBC America, 2013.
Muñoz, José Esteban. *Cruising Utopia: The Then and There of Queer Futurity*. New York: New York University Press, 2009.
National Human Genomic Research Institute. "An Overview of the Human Genome Project." May 11, 2016. https://www.genome.gov/12011238/an-overview-of-the-human-genome-project/.
Ordover, Nancy. *American Eugenics: Race, Queer Anatomy, and the Science of Nationalism*. Minneapolis: University of Minnesota Press, 2003.
Parens, Erik, and Adrienne Asch. "Special Supplement: The Disability Rights Critique of Prenatal Genetic Testing Reflections and Recommendations." *The Hastings Center Report* 29, no. 5 (1999): S1–22. https://doi.org/10.2307/3527746.

Pickens, Donald K. *Eugenics and the Progressives*. Nashville: Vanderbilt University Press, 1968.
Pickens, Therí A. *Black Madness: Mad Blackness*. Durham, NC: Duke University Press, 2019.
Proyas, Alex. *I, robot*. 20th Century Fox, 2004.
"Report of the State Board of Charities and Corrections, 1912–1914." Appendix to the Journals of the Senate and Assembly of the Legislature of the State of California: Sacramento, California: California State Printing, 1915.
Roberts, Dorothy E. *Killing the Black Body: Race, Reproduction, and the Meaning of Liberty*. New York: Pantheon Books, 1997.
Schalk, Samantha Dawn. *Bodyminds Reimagined: (Dis)Ability, Race, and Gender in Black Women's Speculative Fiction*. Durham, N.C.: Duke University Press, 2018.
Scott, Ridley. *Blade Runner*. Warner Bros., 1982.
Shelley, Mary Wollstonecraft. *Frankenstein: The 1818 Text*. New York, Penguin Books, 2018.
Shis, Gerry, and Carolyn Y. Johnson. "Chinese Genomics Scientist Defends His Gene-Editing Research in First Public Appearance." *Washington Post*, November 28, 2018. https://www.washingtonpost.com/world/chinese-genomics-scientist-defends-his-gene-editing-research-in-first-public-appearance/2018/11/28/b99b5eba-f2e1-11e8-9240-e8028a62c722_story.html.
Stern, Alexandra. *Eugenic Nation: Faults and Frontiers of Better Breeding in Modern America*. Berkeley: University of California Press, 2005.
Stern, Alexandra Minna. "From Legislation to Lived Experience: Eugenic Sterilization in California and Indiana, 1907–1979." In *A Century of Eugenics in America: From the Indiana Experiment to the Human Genome Era*, edited by Paul A. Lombardo. Bloomington: Indiana University Press, 2011.
Stern, Alexandra Minna, and Tony Platt. "Sterilization Abuse in State Prisons: Time to Break With California's Long Eugenic Patterns." *The Huffington Post* (blog), July 23, 2013. http://www.huffingtonpost.com/alex-stern/sterilization-california-prisons_b_3631287.html.
Sullivan, Brett. "To Hound Nature in Her Wanderings." *Orphan Black*. BBC America, May 24,
Villeneuve, Denis. *Blade Runner 2049*. Warner Bros. Pictures, 2017.
"What Is Human Gene Editing? Center for Genetics and Society." Accessed February 4, 2020. https://www.geneticsandsociety.org/internal-content/what-human-gene-editing.
Whatcott, Jess. "No Selves to Consent: Women's Prisons, Sterilization, and the Biopolitics of Informed Consent." *Signs: Journal of Women in Culture and Society* 44, no. 1 (2018).

## Chapter Five

# Wakanda Forever

*Black Panther in Black Political Thought*

Debra Thompson

From the moment it debuted in theaters, Marvel Studio's 2018 film, *Black Panther*, has been nothing short of a cultural phenomenon.[1] As of February 2019 the film, directed by Ryan Coogler, had earned over $1.32 billion worldwide, making it among the highest grossing films of all time and one of the most financially successful in the series of films that comprise the larger Marvel universe. The film was universally acclaimed, has won a number of industry awards, and stands as one of the best-reviewed superhero/action films to date, boasting characters, plotlines, and politics that are fuller, more realized, and more contentious than most in the genre. According to a review of the "30 best superhero movies since Blade" in *Vulture,* the culture and entertainment website from *New York Magazine*, *Black Panther* is nothing short of revolutionary: "what truly sets Black Panther apart is that it envisions something no superhero movie—no major studio blockbuster of any kind, really—has ever even come close to contemplating: the complex intersection of black joy and black liberation."[2]

The opening scenes of the movie reveal the African nation of Wakanda as the most technologically advanced on the planet because of its access to and development of vibranium, though the country presents itself as a poor, developing country that refuses outside aid. The plot concerns the transition of power in the kingdom, as protagonist T'Challa's (Chadwick Boseman) claim to his father's throne are contested by his American-born cousin, Erik "Killmonger" Stevens (Michael B. Jordan). Whereas T'Challa seeks to maintain Wakanda's ruse and isolation from the outside world, Killmonger believes that Wakandan technology should be used not just to thwart the domination of non-white people across the globe, but also to invert the hierarchy of the system by creating a new, Wakandan empire. At base, the central question of the film is whether Wakanda's legacy of isolation and invisibility from the rest of the world are a moral failing, especially given centuries of subjugation imposed upon African-descended populations by a global system of white supremacy.

Most obviously heralded for its robust representation of black identities, *Black Panther* is clearly a work of Afrofuturism: a combination of science fiction, historical fiction, speculative fiction, fantasy, Afrocentricity, and magical realism that re-envisions the past, and speculates the future through cultural critiques and political analysis.[3] The questions raised by *Black Panther* are therefore many of the same that animate the contours of black political thought: can racial identity serve as the basis for political resistance or collective action? What are the criteria for membership in a cultural or political community, and who determines where its boundaries lie? Is it possible for structures that are premised on exclusion, such as citizenship or nationality, to be truly revolutionary? How do real or imagined connections across temporal and spatial borders constitute or challenge our understandings of home? And, importantly, what do we owe each other?

This chapter explores *Black Panther* as a prime example of the disruptive potential of political science fiction. Theorized alongside Richard Iton's conceptualization of the black fantastic,[4] *Black Panther* is demonstrative of Afrofuturism's ability to unsettle the realm of formal politics and conventional notions of the political. More specifically, the chapter considers the ways that *Black Panther* intervenes into debates within black politics and black political thought. I suggest that the film does not map neatly onto the traditional lines that define and divide black ideologies. Instead, *Black Panther* reveals the anaform possibilities of diaspora that characterize the black fantastic, underscoring both the connections and fissures that challenge the primacy of the nation-state and the emancipatory potential of the nation.

## THE BLACK FANTASTICAL

The opening pages of Richard Iton's *In Search of the Black Fantastic* restates a "familiar dilemma" of modern politics: how do the excluded engage with the dominant order?[5] Rather than focus on the quantifiable, bounded, ordered realm of formal politics, which centers the state, institutions of government, and political processes and behaviors, he argues that black politics have often been made through the currency of cultural symbols. "Black politics" is not simply about how the observable political behaviors of self-described African-descended populations manifest in formal politics, but rather orbits core empirical, theoretical, and normative questions about the distribution of resources, racial identity and identifications, the meaning of power, domination, justice, and equality, citizenship and belonging, racial pride and self-hatred, gender and sexuality, and the ways that these concerns transgress temporal and spatial boundaries.[6] Iton argues that even as African Americans have increased their access to formal decision-making venues and achieved notable legalistic victories within these arenas since the 1960s, popular culture has continued to play a critical role in mobilizing and shaping, as well as containing and circumscribing, black politics.[7]

However, the representation of blackness in popular culture is complicated. Black people are often relegated and reduced to the cultural realm of entertainment, sports, and music, resulting in stereotypes that at best devalue and limit blackness, and at worst re-inscribe the mocking ridicule and dehumanization of minstrel shows. Images of black life in mainstream popular culture, often written for the amusement of white audiences, "have tended often to promote distorted notions of black humanity (e.g., minstrelsy, *The Adventures of Huckleberry Finn*, the signifying black smile, *The Birth of a Nation*, Elvis, Madonna, and the work of Quentin Tarantino), despite their occasionally transgressive qualities."[8] Black bodies are frequently deployed as punctuation:[9] shallow characters perform as an exclamation point here, a question mark there, and perhaps a semicolon that gives a moment of pause between the two main clauses of the plot. Too often, popular movies and television shows rely on a jovial black sidekick who serves as a confident or counterpoint to the main (white) protagonists as they navigate conflict, romance, trauma, or success. The message to black audiences is unmistakable: black people are incidental to the more interesting, more important, and more engaging stories of (white) others.

In the genre of science fiction, issues of race and racism are simultaneously absent and omnipresent. On one hand, science fiction creates universes that are seemingly untouched by racism in the past or present. For example, works of fantasy often exude a nostalgia for an obviously Europeanized past of kings, queens, and conquest featuring only white characters, while blockbuster "disaster" films tend to mark the post-racial future (and/or the impending doom faced by humanity) with an African American President of the United States.[10] In the aggregate, white people "find representations of themselves in the genre to be much the same as they are elsewhere in culture: normative, benign, and frequent."[11] On the other hand, common conflicts in science fiction are clearly metonyms for race, indigeneity, and colonialism.[12] Plots involving alien invasions, ecological disasters, power-hungry authoritarian regimes, evil wizards, and sentient robots are thinly veiled schemes that mimic violent histories of dispossession, genocide, enslavement, and domination of nonwhite peoples around the world. For example, the forced breeding in Margaret Atwood's *The Handmaid's Tale* applies the rapacious logic of slavery to white women even as African Americans are explicitly written out of the story,[13] and Lord Voldemort's quest for wizarding (i.e., racial) purity in J.K. Rowling's *Harry Potter* books rivals the syllogism of anti-miscegenation laws of the nineteenth and twentieth centuries while Hogwarts is presented as a post-racial (but interestingly, still classist) environment.[14] In both cases, the problematic gesture to race "validates and normalizes very specific ideological and material perspectives, enabling discussions of race and prejudice on a level of abstraction while stifling a more important discussion about real, material conditions, both historical and contemporary."[15] Aliens, androids, and magic notwithstanding, truly the most fantastical element of science fiction is how it continually imagines the subjugation, victimization, and uncomplicated moral heroism of white people.

In contrast, Afrofuturism combines realist and speculative storytelling by "projecting black futures derived from Afrodiasporic experiences."[16] According to Lisa Yaszek, Afrofuturism has three main characteristics. First, the genre reclaims whitewashed versions of American history by centering the experiences of enslaved Africans and their descendants as they navigate conditions of homelessness, alienation, and dislocation. Second, Afrofuturism draws on those historical experiences to detail new interpretations of "raced futures." And third, these new futures are embodied in the figure of the "black genius," in which a protagonist uses their intellectual prowess to save themselves and their community from white oppression.[17] Afrofuturism is, according to Hugo Award-winning author N.K. Jemisin, a radical response to the terrifying realization that *"no one thinks my people have a future."*[18]

Much like Afro-diasporic consciousness, Afrofuturism is inherently destabilizing to Western ideas of modernity. Modern subjectivity among people of African descent "consists of the selective incorporation of technologies, discourses, and institutions of the modern West within the cultural and political practices of African-derived peoples to create a form of relatively autonomous modernity distinct from its counterparts of Western Europe and North America."[19] Formulated through encounters between people of African descent and the violent practices of Western colonialism, Afro-modernity challenges the idea that black people are antithetical to modernity, temporally trapped as "primitive," "backward," or "pre-modern," existing as a people without history.[20] Like the ways that blackness confronts the mythologies associated with the modern, as a genre the fantastical also contains disruptive potential, challenging our understandings of "the distinctions between the reasonable and the unreasonable, and reason itself, the proper and the improper, and propriety itself, by bringing into the field of play those potentials we have forgotten, or did not believe accessible or feasible."[21] Iton's "suggestive reference" to a black fantastic:

> is meant to refer to the minor-key sensibilities generated from the experiences of the underground, the vagabond, and those constituencies marked as deviant—notions of being that are inevitably aligned with, in conversation with,

against, and articulated beyond the boundaries of the modern.... The *black* in black fantastic, in this context, signifies both a generic category of underdeveloped possibilities and the particular 'always there' interpretations of these agonistic, postracial, and post-colonial visions and practices generated by subaltern populations.[22]

Iton's critique of modernity—especially its operationalization of the nation-state as the primary unit of analysis—reveals and revels in the disruptive potential of popular culture to "displace modernity as a master signifier within Black and global discourse, along with its norms and modal infrastructures."[23] Similarly, Afrofuturism fractures modern imaginaries by combatting the erasure of black subjects from Western history and demonstrating how the experiences of African-descended peoples—characterized by forcible removal, dislocation, statelessness, and cultural erasure, but also struggle, resistance, and freedom dreams—are authentic experiences that emerge from modern practices of colonialism, the Atlantic slave trade, and scientific racism.

As a work of Afrofuturism, the very premise of *Black Panther* upends conventional modern narratives. As Adilifu Nama details in *Super Black: American Pop Culture and Black Superheroes*, Black Panther's appearance in the *Fantastic Four* comic books in 1966 marked the emergence of a compelling black superhero whose appearance was drawn directly from the revolutionary sentiment of the 1960s and yet was characterized by an Afrofuturist sensibility.[24] Wakanda's technological supremacy stands in stark contrast to "historical and symbolic constructions of Africans as simple tribal people and Africa as primitive."[25] In the film, the audience is introduced to Wakanda as T'Challa, Nakia (Lupita Nyong'o), and General Okoye (Danai Gurira) speed through a cloaking device that camouflages the futuristic capital city. "This never gets old," T'Challa remarks, as their jet weaves among skyscrapers, a reference to both the characters' love for their country as they return to it, as well as to the anachronistic nature of Wakandan technology, which includes high-speed trains powered by magnetic levitation, kinetic-energy capturing supersuits, remote controlled cars, advanced medical knowledge and equipment, and unparalleled weaponry. Throughout the film the message is that the technological advantage of Wakanda's access to the supernatural properties of vibranium is not enough in itself; vibranium had to be combined with Wakandan ingenuity in order to harness its transformative power and potential. Unlike outdated theories of modernization, which posit that technological advancement and economic development must progress in a path that was long ago laid out by Western nations, technological developments in Wakanda and their impact on social and political formations remain culturally African, but untouched by European colonialism. This is a key underlying theme of the film—what might Africa have been had Europeans not stolen lives, lands, and resources over hundreds of years? In true Afrofuturist style, this hypothetical reclaims both the history of the past and the history of the future.[26]

## BLACK POLITICAL THOUGHT

*Black Panther* can also be read as a purposeful intervention in black political thought. Developed as a response to "forms of racial domination that have encompassed (among other phenomena) gendered violence and the derogation of blackness under conditions of apartheid, colonialism, and racial slavery,"[27] black political thought situates race at the epistemological core of Western modernity.[28] At first glance, the film's main conflict between T'Challa and Killmonger mirrors the collision of distinct ideologies within black political thought. Broadly conceived, black political ideologies consider some of the foundational questions of political theory about the proper role of the state, human nature, and the meaning of justice, but also explore blacks' position in society, the appropriate stipulations for coalitional politics, whether separation from whites is desirable or necessary, the nature of American democratic ethos, and the contours and catalysts of black liberation.[29] T'Challa's caution and deference for the status quo throughout the film is reminiscent of variants of black liberalism, which conceptualizes equality as "equal shares of the fruits of the nation as well as equal opportunity,"[30] and rejects the use of violence, and perhaps even conservatism's emphasis on maintaining tradition and hierarchical forms of legitimacy. Wakandan isolation is a contrarian metonym for the liberal goal of integration; it is not only tradition for Wakanda to remain hidden (i.e., for black people to remain segregated), but the ruling council also believes it to be the most likely path toward the nation's continued peaceful coexistence with the rest of the world. Of course, given that black liberal ideologies were forged through black peoples' interactions with and struggles against white supremacy in the United States and beyond,[31] and that liberalism as a broader political ideology is fundamentally shaped by racism,[32] Wakanda's strategic inoculation from the violence of colonization and the slave trade means that its fantastical existence traverses new ideological territory.

While the American-born Killmonger also resembles an imperfect combination of black ideologies, his experiences are clearly shaped by racism in the United States as well as the related forces of the American militarism, imperialism, and war. Like other black nationalists, such as Martin Delaney, Marcus Garvey, and Malcolm X, Killmonger believes in black autonomy, self-determination, and various degrees of cultural, social, and economic separation from white people. Peniel Joseph, a scholar of the Black Power Movement, writes that Killmonger is the embodiment of black political anger, with a "brash intelligence" that "echoes an unsettling combination of Malcolm X and Stokey Carmichael, updated with a burning desire to eradicate the system of mass incarceration in the United States, end neocolonial policies that impoverish much of the world, and ignite a political revolution that will alter power relations between the global north and south."[33] Killmonger's insistence on the connection between Wakandans and other people of African descent is also paralleled in black nationalist thought, which often holds a special understanding of Africa as the "motherland" and emphasizes that all people of the African diaspora are spiritual allies of African Americans.[34] When T'Challa emphasizes that Wakanda does not interfere in world affairs, stating "it is not our way to be judge, jury, and executioner of people who are not our own," Killmonger scoffs at this limited allegiance. "Not your own?" he challenges, "But didn't life start right here on this continent? So ain't all people your people?"

And yet, the portrayal of Killmonger's black nationalism in the film is also problematic. Christopher Lebron argues that in spite of its "two radical imaginings," of a flourishing African nation untouched by colonialism and a global black solidarity that could lead to the emancipation of all African-descended peoples around the world, *Black Panther* is not a film about black liberation. Instead, the character of Killmonger is "a receptacle for tropes of inner-city gangsterism."[35] By the film's end, the lessons for the audience are these:

> the bad guy is the black American who has rightly identified white supremacy as the reigning threat to black well-being; the bad guy is the one who thinks that Wakanda is being selfish in its secret liberation; the bad guy is the one who will no longer stand for patience and moderation—he thinks liberation is many, many decades overdue. And the black hero snuffs him out.[36]

Other commentators note Killmonger's misogyny, as "his blood-soaked quest to seize Wakanda . . . leaves behind a trail of dead and injured black women, both American and Wakandan,"[37] and the ways Killmonger discredits the legacy of radical black internationalism and employs pathological stereotypes about African Americans.[38] Melvin Rogers writes that the film invites the audience to conflate Killmonger's desires and the liberationist vision of the Black Panther Party, especially as the opening scene of the movie takes place in Oakland, which is the birthplace of the organization. Trying to read Killmonger's beliefs and actions through this narrow lens will always fail, and "when [the movie] refuses to fit neatly into the liberationist story we impose on it, it can only appear as an accomplice to oppression."[39] Though *Black Panther* is clearly a fantasy about black power,[40] it offers mixed messages about other forces that shape the contours of black political thought, such as freedom, intersectionality, hegemony, and equality.

But the black fantastic does not necessarily demand ideological coherence or unrepentant revolutionary aims. To understand the full scope of black politics, Iton argues, "we cannot overlook those spaces that generate difficult data. Similarly, those committed to progressive change must also engage with those arenas and voices that promote regressive and discomforting narratives."[41] Given Iton's emphasis on the ways that "black creative activities . . . overflow, undermine, and dislocate national boundaries," an examination of *Black Panther* through the lens of the black fantastic demands we go beyond simplistic questions about whether Killmonger was hero or villain and instead consider the ways that the film troubles or challenges our understandings of membership, home, and community. The "reflexive black politics"[42] imagined by the black fantastic centers neither genealogical connections nor geographical presences, and instead situates "black identifications conceptually: as a matter of indexing a related set of sensibilities that resist quantification, physical or temporal classifications, and corporeal boundaries."[43] Part of this approach necessitates a skepticism about the emancipatory potential of mobilizing claims to personhood through the prism of "the nation"—even, and perhaps especially, a fictitious one. Accordingly, "we might assert that for nonwhites—and for all others, *nous sommes tous des sans-papiers*—nationality is not only doubtful and improbable but indeed impossible and, furthermore, that these impossibilities themselves might be seen as desirable and appealing."[44] In short, what does *Black Panther* reveal about the limits of the nationalism and the nation-state and the anaform possibilities of transnationalism and diaspora?

## WAKANDA AND THE DIASPORA

The concept of diaspora describes the dispersal of a given population from its place of origin and the subsequent mythologization of that homeland as the population relocates elsewhere. The scattering of the African diaspora originates in a history of the traumatic, violent, and forced departure of the trans-Atlantic slave trade, and manifests in contemporary terms through an imagined relationship to the continent of Africa as the "motherland" for African-descended peoples around the world. The politics of "return" are dynamic, complicated, and often idealized. In his well-known article, "Cultural Identity and Diaspora," cultural theorist Stuart Hall writes that "Africa is the name of the missing term, the great aporia, which lies at the centre of [black] cultural identity and gives it a meaning which, until recently, it lacked."[45] In Paul Gilroy's formulation, the "Black Atlantic" that connects Africa, Europe and the Americas and the chronotype of a ship in motion focus attention on the violence and trauma of the Middle Passage, the various attempts by African-descended peoples to find redemption in a return to Africa, and the transnational circulation of ideas and activists as they form and reformulate diasporic identities and cultures. The history of the Black Atlantic is marked by the crisscrossing movements of African-descended peoples, "not only as commodities but engaged in various struggles toward emancipation, autonomy, and citizenship."[46] These concepts provide "an invitation to move into the contested spaces between the local and the global in ways that do not privilege the modern nation-state and its institutional order over the subnational and supranational networks and patterns of power, communication and conflict that they work to discipline, regulate and govern."[47] Read this way, "Wakanda Forever" resonated with black audiences around the world because, for a brief moment, it provided a meaningful but imaginary coherence to a collective black experience that is often filtered through the lens of the nation-state and deemed specific to domestically derived and bound racial formations. Similar to other forms of cultural expression in the black fantastic, *Black Panther* reveals both the *connections* and *fissures* that characterize the African diaspora and resist the reproduction of temporally and spatially distinct national frames.

First, *Black Panther* underscores the *connections* among African-descended populations by invoking black internationalism and expanding the idea of black linked fate to the realm of the fantastic. According to West and Martin, the long history of black internationalism is defined by one thing: struggle. Yet black people's resistance to systems of domination "did not mechanically produce black internationalism. Rather, black internationalism is a product of consciousness, that is, the conscious interconnection and interlocution of black struggles across manmade and natural boundaries— including the boundaries of nations, empires, continents, oceans, and seas."[48] The original formulation of black internationalism coalesced in opposition to racial slavery during "the age of revolution," while later iterations expanded to focus explicitly on the diaspora's connection with Africa, embodied by political organizations such as Marcus Garvey's Universal Negro Improvement Association and the various sessions of W.E.B. Du Bois's Pan-African Congress.[49] In the 1960s, the Black Panther Party mobilized an international critique of American imperialism at home and abroad, and global solidarity was buttressed in part by the forced exile of the organization's leadership.[50] In recent years, the Black Lives Matter movement has revived the tradition of black internationalism, using black political mobilizations and solidarities to challenge the proliferation of police brutality, mass and uneven incarceration, racial inequality, and anti-Black racism in democracies around the world.[51]

Black struggle is a central theme of *Black Panther*, highlighted through the moral quandary of Wakanda's strategic isolation. During the film's prologue N'Jobu (Sterling K. Brown) tells a young Erik Stevens (Seth Carr) that as Wakanda thrived because of its development of vibranium, "the world around it descended further into chaos." His words overlay an animated sequence in which the most haunting image is of enslaved Africans, chained together by their necks, being forced onto a ship by Europeans with guns. Wakanda's choice to remain hidden is condemned by Killmonger during an important scene in which he reveals his statement of intent. Confronting T'Challa face-to-face for the first time in front of the royal court, Killmonger plainly states his purpose for being in Wakanda: "I want the throne," he says. When the elites laugh at his audacity, he continues: "Y'all sittin' up here comfortable. It must feel good. It's about two billion people all over the world that looks like us. But their lives are a lot harder. Wakanda has the tools to liberate 'em all." T'Challa immediately refuses and justifies this decision by reference to tradition: "Our weapons will not be used to wage war on the world. It is not our way to be judge, jury, and executioner for people who are not our own." Once more Wakanda is given the chance to join the liberation struggle, and once again it refuses to engage.

However, this is not a simple choice of isolation over intervention in world affairs. Diaspora involves a shared sense of identity among members that transcends geographic boundaries and diasporic consciousness is marked, though not necessarily permeated, by the idea of linked fate. In political science, theories of linked fate suggest that African Americans tend to perceive their individual life circumstances as strongly tied to the successes, failures, and tragedies of their racial group as a whole.[52] Linked fate is typically measured in public opinion surveys—perhaps problematically[53]— by the following question: "Do you think what happens to black people in this country will have something to do with what happens in your life?"[54] The concept emanates from the belief that black people have common lived experiences, such as racial discrimination, and reflects a sense of belonging and loyalty to one's racial group, for better or worse. Throughout the film Wakanda's loyalty to other African-descended people—its cousins, so to speak—is put into question.

After defeating T'Challa in hand-to-hand combat and winning the throne, Killmonger calls Wakanda out for betraying this imagined community, leaving black revolutionaries outgunned and outnumbered by those in power. "You know, where I'm from, when black folks started revolutions they never had the firepower or the resources to fight their oppressors," he accuses the council. "*Where was Wakanda?*" His question is a valid one, but raises others in turn. As a work of Afrofuturism, *Black Panther* dares to ask "what if"—what if they hadn't stolen us? What could Africa and Africans have been if lives, cultures, and resources remained intact, instead of violently destroyed? As Adam Serwer writes, "if an African superpower like Wakanda existed, with all its power, its monopoly on the invaluable sci-fi metal vibranium, and its advanced technology, how could it have remained silent, remained still, as millions of Africans were devoured by The Void?"[55] Wakanda's choice to isolate itself is not simply a severed connection with the African diaspora, but is also an act of great betrayal. This thought experiment, only possible in the realm of the fantastic, is a fascinating commentary on the normative and ethical tendrils that define the core values within the black diaspora, as well as the consequences of violating those imperatives.

The corollary of a nation untouched by slavery and colonialism is Wakandans' inability to relate to the unifying, traumatic, horrific legacy of the Black Atlantic, and the courageous resilience that emerged in spaces of fugitivity and resistance throughout the African diaspora. The intersection of black internationalism and linked fate in *Black Panther* therefore raise a broader question about the composition of the diaspora, and the criteria by which membership claims are evaluated. Did Wakandans betray their brethren, as Killmonger insinuates, or is there something more than continental origin and melanin levels that inform the boundaries of blackness? This is key: what peoples of the African diaspora hold in common is far less about racial identity per se and much more about the "supranational formulation of people of African descent as an "imagined community" that is not territorially demarcated but based on the shared belief in the commonalities of Western oppression experienced by African and African-derived peoples."[56] In other words, the threads that connect the African diaspora are soaked in the blood of our ancestors.

The ubiquitous harms of colonialism, for example, are demonstrated in a fairly unsubtle scene in the fictitious Museum of Great Britain. It opens with Killmonger summoning a curator to provide information on various African artifacts on display. "They tell me you're the expert," Killmonger says to her conversationally. Though the dialogue begins innocently enough, there is an underlying message about white supremacy, colonialism, and the idea of expertise in this initial interaction. Many academic disciplines, but especially archeology, anthropology, and African Studies, are inhabited by white "experts" on non-white peoples. In his important book, *Time and the Other*, Johannes Fabian criticizes the ways that anthropologists often situate their subjects as living "there and then" while the researcher exists in the "here and now." Anthropological discourses employ terms such as "primitive," "savage," "traditional," or "tribal," and in the implicit comparison to "civilized," "modern," or "industrialized," societies, invoke subjective temporal claims in order to dominate and control colonial subjects.[57] More to the point, the scene parallels ongoing criticisms of Western museums and galleries, such as the Brooklyn Museum's decision in 2018 to hire a white curator to oversee its African Art collection,[58] the cultural appropriation of black trauma and suffering as white art (e.g., Dana Schutz's painting of Emmett Till, "Open Casket"),[59] and campaigns for the repatriation of stolen artifacts.[60] The interaction between the two characters also features "the condescending treatment of a museum visitor of color, a discussion of questionable acquisition practices, and the self-assured yet misinformed retelling of cultural narratives."[61] The scene progresses with Killmonger asking about a particular artifact, and then correcting the curator's claim about its origins:

> *Killmonger*: Now, tell me about this one.
> *Curator*: Also from Benin, seventh century. Fula tribe, I believe.
> *Killmonger*: Nah.
> *Curator*: I beg your pardon?
> *Killmonger*: It was taken by British soldiers in Benin, but it's from Wakanda. And it's made out of vibranium. Don't trip. I'mma take it off your hands for you.
> *Curator*: These items aren't for sale.
> *Killmonger*: How do you think your ancestors got these? You think they paid a fair price? Or did they take it, like they took everything else?

Colonialism, characterized by the theft of lands, the purposeful corrosion or eradication of indigenous languages and cultures, state violence disguised as a civilizing mission, the spiritual and psychological devastation of murdered children and lost generations, and the near-extermination of indigenous systems of governance, is one of the unifying experiences across the African continent. Colonial practices and racial projects, as well as the systems of racial domination they inform, vary across time and space;[62] comparative research on slavery, for example, reveals important differences in the form and content of racial slavery, which have proven to be important for the emancipation struggles that followed.[63] However idiosyncratic the details, the common experience of and struggle against domination is a key component of black diasporic consciousness.

Second, *Black Panther* reveals the *fissures* within the African diaspora, demonstrating the exclusive nature of membership and belonging and the improbabilities of mobilizing claims to liberation through the prism of the nation-state. *Black Panther* illuminates the central role of connectivity in diasporic communities in part through its absence; that is to say, Wakanda's separation from the rest of the African diaspora has enabled its political elites to avoid the responsibilities that accompany conceptions of linked fate. But diaspora is also characterized by fracture and dissonance, explicating a black subject's condition of homelessness and dislocation throughout Western history and social formations. Transnational black politics, especially as it manifests through the prism of diaspora, "can reveal that the condition of statelessness of black subjects in political modernity is not a peculiarity of one isolated nation-state. Instead, it is a paradigmatic and symptomatic example of the broader relationship between state-empowered and stateless subjects in the nation-state system."[64] Beyond this assertion that black people are perpetual foreigners in the nation-states that once relied on their free, exploited, and coerced labor, Iton argues that diaspora as revealed through the black fantastic is characterized by "anaformative impulse."[65] This interpretation of diaspora requires a politics that cannot be reduced to the terminology of citizenship or rights (or lack thereof), and is accordingly suspicious of homeland narratives or any other kind of "authenticating geographies that demand fixity, hierarchy, and hegemony. Conceiving of diaspora as anaform, we are encouraged, then, to put (all) space into play."[66] Diaspora works not simply through, across, and beyond conceptions of "nations" and "states," Iton contends, but also *against* them.

The film has a complicated take on membership in a political, cultural, or diasporic community, most obviously characterized by Killmonger's challenge for the throne of Wakanda. Killmonger is N'Jadaka, the son of N'Jobu and cousin to the king, and has a legitimate claim to the throne by virtue of his lineage alone. In fact, there does not seem to be any way to become Wakandan other than through descent, and all Wakandan descendants carry a physical marker of membership, an iridescent sequence of characters on the inside of one's lower lip. And yet, Killmonger is also a product of "the void," a term Adam Serwer uses to describe "the psychic and cultural wound caused by the Trans-Atlantic slave trade, the loss of life, culture, language, and history that could never be restored."[67] Though Wakandan by patrilineal descent, Killmonger is American by birth and African American by experience. As such, he undoubtedly observed or was subjected to routinized police brutality, the quotidian hardships of systemic discrimination, and the thousand other ways that the experiences of black citizens are different, and often more difficult and exhausting than those conferred to others through the prophylactic mechanisms and modalities of white privilege. It was these same hardships that "radicalized" N'Jobu while he was on a war dog assignment in the United States. "I observed for as long as I could," he angrily said when confronted by his brother, the king. "Their leaders have been assassinated. Communities flooded with drugs and weapons. They are overly policed and incarcerated. All over the planet our people suffer because they don't have the tools to fight back." After T'Chaka kills N'Jobu, the Wakandans leave his child, the young Erik Stevens, behind in Oakland in order to "maintain the lie." As an adult that has returned to his father's homeland, Killmonger represents a traditional dilemma of diasporic peoples: the quandary of what it means to be in, but not of, a nation.

Because the orientation toward a real or imagined homeland provides an authoritative source of value, identity and loyalty in a diaspora,[68] the innate estrangement from one's place of origin can lead to a sense of homelessness. Killmonger, however, has not simply lost his homeland, but has rather been abandoned by it. The lonely, tragic isolation of diasporic vagrancy plays out in the three scenes of the movie that occur while T'Challa and Killmonger, respectively, visit the ancestral plane during the ritual that instills the power of the Black Panther upon them. During the first, T'Challa awakens to surroundings that look like a mystical Serengeti. One of several black panthers transforms into his late father, and T'Challa asks him how to be a good king and how to best protect his people. In contrast, Killmonger's vision takes him to his childhood apartment in Oakland, the site of his father's murder. He finds his father's journal and ring, and as a vision of his father appears, Killmonger becomes the guarded child that found his father's body:

> *N'Jobu:* What did you find?
> *Eric Stevens:* Your home.
> *N'Jobu*: I gave you a key hoping that you might see it someday. [Stevens shows N'Jobu the glowing Wakandan characters inside his bottom lip.] Yes. The sunsets there are the most beautiful in the world. But I fear you still may not be welcome.
> *Stevens*: Why?
> *N'Jobu*: They will say you are lost.
> *Stevens*: But I'm right here.
> *N'Jobu*: [Nods and sighs heavily.] No tears for me?
> *Stevens*: Everybody dies. It's just life around here.
> *N'Jobu*: Well, look at what I have done. I should've take you back long ago. Instead, we are both abandoned here.
> *Stevens, now appearing as the adult Killmonger*: Well, maybe your home is the one that's lost. That's why they can't find us.

It is the most powerful and compelling scene of the movie. Killmonger and N'Jobu appear to be cut off from their ancestors and homeland, isolated, alone, and trapped in the same place that N'Jobu was killed. This is reminiscent of the "social death" of saltwater slavery, "the blurred and bloodied boundaries between captivity, commodification, and diaspora" that demarcated the social geography of black life and death.[69] As Stephanie Smallwood details, the violent process of commodifying human beings also tore apart the kinship ties that bound the enslaved to their social world in both life and death. In many West African cultures, Smallwood argues, death marked a new beginning of connectivity with one's community—the soul's departure from the body and its migration to the realm of the ancestors, where spirits continue to be involved in the affairs of the living.[70] Those captured and sold into trans-Atlantic slavery, however, "were neither venerated, like the deceased, nor suspended in the balance between marginalization and integration, like local slaves, but rather consigned to an interminable purgatory."[71] Removed from his ancestors, N'Jobu is subjected to a dual disjuncture, just like the stolen generations terrorized by saltwater slavery: he is condemned and unable to return home even in the absolution of death, and prohibited from ascending to the status of an ancestor that guides the spirits of the living. It is a horrific, eternal abandonment.

The scene ends with Killmonger refusing to accept that he is lost and abandoned. Maybe it's Wakanda that's lost, he suggests. Here, Killmonger emphasizes the moral calamity of Wakanda's choice to remain silent, hidden, and segregated from the African diaspora when it had the power to prevent the forced migration and enslavement of African peoples in the first place. In this sense, Wakanda is *morally* lost, and its initial and continued rupture of linked fate is an act of irredeemable betrayal. In the last of these scenes, T'Challa's second visit to the ancestral plane, he confronts his father and the other ancestors:

> *T'Challa*: Why? Why didn't you bring the boy home? Why, Baba?
> *T'Chaka*: He . . . he was the truth I chose to omit.
> *T'Challa*: You were wrong to abandon him.
> *T'Chaka*: I chose my people. I chose Wakanda. Our future depended . . .
> *T'Challa*: You were wrong! All of you were wrong! To turn your backs on the rest of the world! We let the fear of our discovery stop us from doing what is right! No more! I cannot stay here with you. I cannot rest while he sits on the throne. He is a monster of our own making. I must take the mantle back. I must. I must right these wrongs.

The abandonment of Eric Stevens thus becomes a searing allegory for Wakanda's narcissistic disregard for the African diaspora, when it had the means and the ability to prevent the catastrophe of the slave trade and to remedy its ongoing legacy. Killmonger's refusal to see himself as lost also shifts Pan-Africanist discourse. Though he shares Pan-Africanism's long-standing desire for a "homecoming," Killmonger's argument that Wakanda, and not the African diaspora, is lost redefines blackness as fundamentally diasporic. In other words, the central question of membership in the film is both whether Killmonger, the son of a traitor, can belong to the nation of Wakanda, as well as whether Wakanda, a treacherous nation, can belong to the vast and diverse community of the black diaspora.

## CONCLUSION

Afrofuturism is but one part of the black fantastic, which is inherently destabilizing to modern discourses about the primacy of formal politics within the confines of the nation-state. Like the black fantastic, Afrofuturism challenges the ways that modernity constructs blackness as deviant, and instead opens a world of possibilities in which black people not only have a future, but "will have won the future. There exists, somewhere within us, an image in which we are whole, in which we are home. Afrofuturism is, if nothing else, an attempt to imagine what that home would be."[72] This chapter has explored these imaginings in Marvel's *Black Panther*, especially the ways they converse with conceptualizations of diaspora, black politics, and black political thought.

Of course, there is much more that remains to be said about the film, especially in terms of its relationship to narratives of black liberation. Historian Nathan Connolly argues that Black Panther "taps a 500-year history of African-descended people imagining freedom, land and national autonomy," including the history of the Haiti that could have been, had France, Great Britain, and the United States chosen not to punish the formerly enslaved revolutionaries for stealing themselves.[73] But, again, Killmonger's dreams of liberation are problematically envisioned through the prism of empire, and his desire to liberate nonwhite people of the world becomes conflated with his willingness to tyrannize in so doing.[74] This orientation is discordant with many of the other Afrofuturist imperatives of the film, playing on long-standing white fears that if black power structures are allowed to develop, they will mimic the systems of domination that have kept white people atop hierarchies for half a millennium. In the realm of the black fantastic, however, diaspora is not empire, and revolution cannot be achieved by the imposition of hegemony. The most powerful element in Wakanda is not vibranium; it is the ways that the fantastical holds a mirror to the systems of power and domination that exist in the contemporary political world, engaging in comparisons about the way the world is, how it came to be, and what alternatives we might imagine for our political future.

## NOTES

1. This chapter will focus solely on the Marvel film, and not the vast collection of *Black Panther* comics.
2. Abraham Riesman, "The 30 Best Superhero Movies Since Blade," *Vulture*, December 7, 2018.
3. Ytasha L. Womack, *Afrofuturism: The World of Black Sci-Fi and Fantasy Culture* (Chicago: Lawrence Hill Books, 2013).
4. Richard Iton, *In Search of the Black Fantastic: Politics and Popular Culture in the Post-Civil Rights Era* (New York: Oxford University Press, 2008).
5. Iton, *In Search of the Black Fantastic.*
6. Michael Hanchard, *Party/Politics: Horizons in Black Political Thought* (New York: Oxford University Press, 2006).
7. Iton, *In Search of the Black Fantastic*, 4.
8. Iton, *In Search of the Black Fantastic*, 18.
9. Iton, *In Search of the Black Fantastic*, 18.
10. *Fifth Element* (1997), *Deep Impact* (1998), *24* (TV series) (2001–2006), *2012* (2009).
11. André M. Carrington, *Speculative Blackness: The Future of Race in Science Fiction* (Minneapolis: University of Minnesota Press, 2016), 17.
12. John Rieder, *Colonialism and the Emergence of Science Fiction* (Middletown: Wesleyan University Press, 2008); Carrington, *Speculative Blackness.*
13. Margaret Atwood, *The Handmaid's Tale* (New York: Anchor Books, 1986).
14. J.K. Rowling, *Harry Potter and the Half-Blood Prince* (New York: Arthur A. Levine Books, 2005), *Harry Potter and the Deathly Hallows* (New York: Arthur A. Levine Books, 2007).
15. Mark Bould, "The Ships Landed Long Ago: Afrofuturism and Black SF," *Science Fiction Studies* 34, no. 2 (2007): 180.

16. Lisa Yaszek, "Afrofuturism, Science Fiction, and the History of the Future," *Socialism and Democracy* 20, no. 3(2006): 42.

17. Lisa Yaszek, "Afrofuturism in American Science Fiction," in *the Cambridge Companion to American Science Fiction*, eds. Eric Carl Link and Gerry Canavan (New York: Cambridge University Press, 2015), 58–59.

18. N.K. Jemisin, *How Long 'Til Black Future Month?* (New York: Orbit Books, 2018), x.

19. Michael Hanchard, "Afro-Modernity: Temporality, Politics, and the African Diaspora," *Popular Culture* 11, no. 1(1999): 247.

20. Hanchard, "Afro-Modernity."

21. Iton, *In Search of the Black Fantastic*, 289–90.

22. Iton, *In Search of the Black Fantastic*, 16.

23. Iton, *In Search of the Black Fantastic*, 28.

24. Adilifu Nama, *Super Black: American Pop Culture and Black Superheroes* (Austin: University of Texas Press 2011), 39.

25. Nama, *Super Black,* 42.

26. Yaszek, "Afrofuturism, Science Fiction, and the History of the Future," 47.

27. Michael Hanchard, "Contours of Black Political Thought: An Introduction and Perspective," *Political Theory* 38, no. 4(2010): 512.

28. Charles Mills, *The Racial Contract* (Ithaca: Cornell University Press, 1997); Barnor Hesse, "Racialized Modernity: An Analytics of White Mythologies," *Ethnic and Racial Studies* 30, no. 4 (2007): 643–63; Hanchard, "Contours of Black Political Thought"; Charles Mills, *Black Rights/White Wrongs: The Critique of Racial Liberalism* (New York: Oxford University Press, 2017).

29. Michael C. Dawson, *Black Visions: The Roots of Contemporary African-American Political Ideologies,* (Chicago: University of Chicago Press, 2001), 12.

30. Dawson, *Black Visions,* 240.

31. Dawson, *Black Visions.*

32. Mills, *Black Rights/White Wrongs.*

33. Peniel E. Joseph, "'Black Panther' Is a Milestone in African Americans' Search for Home," *Washington Post*, February 16, 2018.

34. Dawson, *Black Visions*, 21–22.

35. Christopher Lebron, "'Black Panther' Is Not the Movie We Deserve," *Boston Review,* February 17, 2018.

36. Lebron, "'Black Panther' Is Not the Movie We Deserve."

37. Karen Attiah, "Forget Killmonger—Wakanda's Women are 'Black Panthers' True Revolutionaries," *Washington Post,* March 1, 2018.

38. Russell Rickford, "I Have a Problem with 'Black Panther,'" *Africa Is a Country,* February 22, 2018.

39. Melvin L. Rogers, "The Many Dimensions of Black Panther," *Dissent Magazine,* February 27, 2018.

40. Vann R. Newkirk, "The Provocation and Power of *Black Panther*," *The Atlantic,* February 14, 2018.

41. Iton, *In Search of the Black Fantastic*, 18–19.

42. Richard Iton, "Still Life," *small axe* 40 (2013): 22–39.

43. Iton, *In Search of the Black Fantastic*, 22.

44. Iton, *In Search of the Black Fantastic*, 195.

45. Stuart Hall, "Cultural Identity and Diaspora," in *Identity: Community, Culture, Difference,* ed. Jonathan Rutherford (London: Lawrence & Wishart 1990), 224.

46. Paul Gilroy, *The Black Atlantic: Modernity and Double Consciousness* (New York: Verso 1993).

47. Paul Gilroy, "Route Work: The Black Atlantic and the Politics of Exile," in *The Post-Colonial Question: Common Skies, Divided Horizons,* eds. Iain Chambers and Lidia Curti (London and New York: Routledge 1996), 22.

48. Michael O. West and William G. Martin, "Contours of the Black International: From Toussaint to Tupac," in *From Toussaint to Tupac: The Black International Since the Age of*

*Revolution,* eds. Michael O. West, William G. Martin, and Fanon Che Wilkins (Chapel Hill: University of North Carolina Press 2009), 1.

49. West and Martin, "Contours of the Black International," 4–16.

50. West and Martin, "Contours of the Black International," 25.

51. Barnor Hesse and Juliet Hooker, "Introduction: On Black Political Thought inside Global Black Protest," *South Atlantic Quarterly* 116, no. 3 (2017): 443–56; Debra Thompson, "The Intersectional Politics of Black Lives Matter," in *Turbulent Times, Transformational Possibilities? Gender and Politics Today and Tomorrow,* eds. Fiona MacDonald and Alexandra Dobrowolsky (Toronto: University of Toronto Press, 2020), 240–57.

52. Michael C. Dawson, *Behind the Mule: Race, Class, and African American Politics* (Princeton: Princeton University Press, 1994); Paula D. McClain, Jessica D. Johnson Carew, Eugene Walter Jr., and Candis S. Watts, "Group Membership, Group Identity, and Group Consciousness: Measures of Racial Identity in American Politics?" *Annual Review of Political Science* 12(2009): 471–85.

53. Claudine Gay, Jennifer Hochschild, and Ariel White, "Americans' Belief in Linked Fate: Does the Measure Capture the Concept?" *Journal of Race, Ethnicity, and Politics* 1, no. 1(2016): 117–44.

54. Gay, Hochschild, and White, "Americans' Belief in Linked Fate."

55. Adam Serwer, "The Tragedy of Erik Killmonger," *The Atlantic,* February 21, 2018.

56. Hanchard, "Afro-Modernity," 248.

57. Johannes Fabian, *Time and the Other: How Anthropology Makes Its Object* (New York: Columbia University Press, 1983).

58. Teju Adisa-Farrar, "Why Are White Curators Still Running African Art Collections?" *The Guardian,* April 3, 2018.

59. Josephine Livingstone and Lovia Gyarkye, "The Case against Dana Schutz," *New Republic,* March 22, 2017.

60. Claire Voon, "Why an Indigenous Australian Wants the British Museum to Return His Ancestor's Shield," *Hyperallergic,* June 17, 2017.

61. Lise Ragbir, "What Black Panther Gets Right About the Politics of Museums," *Hyperallergic,* March 20, 2018.

62. Melissa Weiner, "Towards a Critical Global Race Theory," *Sociology Compass* 6, no. 4(2012): 332–50.

63. Anthony W. Marx, *Making Race and Nation: A Comparison of South Africa, the United States, and Brazil* (New York: Cambridge University Press 1998).

64. Hanchard, "Contours of Black Political Thought," 523.

65. Iton, *In Search of the Black Fantastic,* 200.

66. Iton, *In Search of the Black Fantastic,* 200.

67. Serwer, "The Tragedy of Erik Killmonger."

68. Rogers Brubaker, "The 'Diaspora' Diaspora," *Ethnic and Racial Studies* 28, no. 1(2005): 5.

69. Stephanie Smallwood, *Saltwater Slavery: A Middle Passage from Africa to American Diaspora* (Cambridge: Harvard University Press 2007), 8.

70. Smallwood, *Saltwater Slavery,* 56–58.

71. Smallwood, *Saltwater Slavery,* 61.

72. Carvell Wallace, "Why 'Black Panther' Is a Defining Moment for Black America," *New York Times* February 12, 2018.

73. Nathan Connolly, "How 'Black Panther' Taps into 500 Years of History," *Hollywood Reporter* February 16, 2018.

74. Rogers, "The Many Dimensions of Black Panther."

# BIBLIOGRAPHY

Adisa-Farrar, Teju. "Why Are White Curators Still Running African Art Collections?" *The Guardian,* April 3, 2018.https://www.theguardian.com/commentisfree/2018/apr/03/brooklyn-museum-white-curators-african-art-open-letter

Attiah, Karen. "Forget Killmonger—Wakanda's Women Are 'Black Panther's' True Revolutionaries." *Washington Post*, March 1, 2018.https://www.washingtonpost.com/news/global-opinions/wp/2018/03/01/forget-the-abusive-killmonger-wakandas-women-are-black-panthers-true-black-liberators/?utm_term=.f5f7de1a67d3

Atwood, Margaret. *The Handmaid's Tale*. New York: Anchor Books, 1986.

Brubaker, Rogers. "The 'Diaspora' Diaspora." *Ethnic and Racial Studies* 28, no. 1(2005): 1–19.

Bould, Mark. "The Ships Landed Long Ago: Afrofuturism and Black SF." *Science Fiction Studies* 34, no. 2(2007): 177–86.

Carrington, André M. *Speculative Blackness: The Future of Race in Science Fiction*. Minneapolis: University of Minnesota Press, 2016.

Connolly, Nathan. "How 'Black Panther' Taps into 500 Years of History." *Hollywood Reporter*, February 16, 2018.https://www.hollywoodreporter.com/heat-vision/black-panther-taps-500-years-history-1085334

Dawson, Michael C. *Behind the Mule: Race, Class, and African American Politics*. Princeton: Princeton University Press, 1994.

———. *Black Visions: The Roots of Contemporary African-American Political Ideologies*. Chicago: University of Chicago Press, 2001.

Fabian, Johannes. *Time and the Other: How Anthropology Makes Its Object*. New York: Columbia University Press, 1983/2002.

Gay, Claudine, Jennifer Hochschild, and Ariel White. "Americans' Belief in Linked Fate: Does the Measure Capture the Concept?" *Journal of Race, Ethnicity, and Politics* 1, no. 1(2016): 117–44.

Gilroy, Paul. *The Black Atlantic: Modernity and Double Consciousness*. New York: Verso, 1993.

———. "Route Work: The Black Atlantic and the Politics of Exile." In *The Post-Colonial Question: Common Skies, Divided Horizons*, edited by Iain Chambers and Lidia Curti, 17–29. London and New York: Routledge, 1996.

Hall, Stuart. "Cultural Identity and Diaspora." In *Identity: Community, Culture, Difference*, edited by Jonathan Rutherford, 222–37. London: Lawrence & Wishart, 1990.

Hanchard, Michael. "Afro-Modernity: Temporality, Politics, and the African Diaspora." *Public Culture* 11, no. 1(1999): 245–68.

———. *Party/Politics: Horizons in Black Political Thought*. New York: Oxford University Press, 2006.

———. "Contours of Black Political Thought: An Introduction and Perspective." *Political Theory* 38, no. 4(2010): 510–36.

Hesse, Barnor. "Racialized Modernity: An Analytics of White Mythologies." *Ethnic and Racial Studies* 30, no. 4(2007): 643–63.

Hesse, Barnor and Juliet Hooker. "Introduction: On Black Political Thought Inside Global Black Protest," *South Atlantic Quarterly* 116, no. 3(2017): 443–56.

Iton, Richard. *In Search of the Black Fantastic: Politics and Popular Culture in the Post-Civil Rights Era*. New York: Oxford University Press, 2008.

———. "Still Life." *small axe* 40 (2013): 22–39.

Jemisin, N.K. *How Long 'Til Black Future Month?* New York: Orbit Books, 2018.

Joseph, Peniel E. "'Black Panther' Is a Milestone in African Americans' Search for Home." *Washington Post*, February 16, 2018.https://www.washingtonpost.com/news/post-nation/wp/2018/02/16/black-panther-is-a-milepost-in-african-americans-search-for-home/?utm_term=.8f2ade6b008b

Lebron, Christopher. "'Black Panther' Is Not the Movie We Deserve." *Boston Review*, February 17, 2018.http://bostonreview.net/race/christopher-lebron-black-panther

Livingstone, Josephine and Lovia Gyarkye. "The Case against Dana Schutz." *New Republic*, March 22, 2017.https://newrepublic.com/article/141506/case-dana-schutz

Marx, Anthony W. *Making Race and Nation: A Comparison of South Africa, the United States, and Brazil*. New York: Cambridge University Press, 1998.

McClain, Paula D., Jessica D. Johnson Carew, Eugene Walton Jr., and Candis S. Watts. "Group Membership, Group Identity, and Group Consciousness: Measures of Racial Identity in American Politics?" *Annual Review of Political Science* 12 (2009): 471–85.

Mills, Charles. *The Racial Contract*. Ithaca: Cornell University Press, 1997.

———. *Black Rights/White Wrongs: The Critique of Racial Liberalism*. New York: Oxford University Press, 2017.

Nama, Adilifu. *Super Black: American Pop Culture and Black Superheroes*. Austin: University of Texas Press, 2011.

Newkirk, Vann R. "The Provocation and Power of *Black Panther*." *The Atlantic*, February 14, 2018.https://www.theatlantic.com/entertainment/archive/2018/02/the-provocation-and-power-of-black-panther/553226/

Ragbir, Lise. "What Black Panther Gets Right about the Politics of Museums." *Hyperallergic*, March 20, 2018.https://hyperallergic.com/433650/black-panther-museum-politics/

Rickford, Russell. "I Have a Problem with 'Black Panther.'" *Africa Is a Country*, February 22, 2018.https://africasacountry.com/2018/02/i-have-a-problem-with-black-panther/

Rieder, John. *Colonialism and the Emergence of Science Fiction*. Middletown: Wesleyan University Press 2008.

Riesman, Abraham. "The 30 Best Superhero Movies Since Blade." *Vulture*, December 7, 2018.https://www.vulture.com/article/best-superhero-movies.html

Rogers, Melvin L. "The Many Dimensions of Black Panther." *Dissent Magazine*, February 27, 2018. www.dissentmagazine.org/online_articles/marvel-black-panther-review-race-empire-tragic-heroes

Rowling, J.K. *Harry Potter and the Half-Blood Prince*. New York: Arthur A. Levine Books, 2005.

———. *Harry Potter and the Deathly Hallows*. New York: A. Levine Books, 2007.

Serwer, Adam. "The Tragedy of Erik Killmonger." *The Atlantic*, February 21, 2018.https://www.theatlantic.com/entertainment/archive/2018/02/black-panther-erik-killmonger/553805/

Smallwood, Stephanie. *Saltwater Slavery: A Middle Passage from Africa to American Diaspora*. Cambridge: Harvard University Press, 2007.

Thompson, Debra. "The Intersectional Politics of Black Lives Matter." In *Turbulent Times, Transformational Possibilities? Gender and Politics Today and Tomorrow*, edited by Fiona MacDonald and Alexandra Dobrowolsky. Toronto: University of Toronto Press, 2020.

Voon, Claire. "Why an Indigenous Australian Wants the British Museum to Return His Ancestor's Shield." *Hyperallergic*, June 17, 2017.https://hyperallergic.com/385885/why-an-indigenous-australian-wants-the-british-museum-to-return-his-ancestors-shield/

Wallace, Carvell. "Why 'Black Panther' Is a Defining Moment for Black America." *New York Times*, February 12, 2018.https://www.nytimes.com/2018/02/12/magazine/why-black-panther-is-a-defining-moment-for-black-america.html

Weiner, Melissa. "Towards a Critical Global Race Theory." *Sociology Compass* 6, no. 4(2012): 332–50.

West, Michael O. and William G. Martin. "Contours of the Black International: From Toussaint to Tupac." In *From Toussaint to Tupac: The Black International Since the Age of Revolution*, edited by Michael O. West, William G. Martin, and Fanon Che Wilkins, 1–44. Chapel Hill: University of North Carolina Press, 2009.

Womack, Ytasha L. *Afrofuturism: The World of Black Sci-Fi and Fantasy Culture*. Chicago: Lawrence Hill Books, 2013.

Yaszek, Lisa. "Afrofuturism, Science Fiction, and the History of the Future." *Socialism and Democracy* 20, no. 3(2006): 41–60.

———. "Afrofuturism in American Science Fiction." In *The Cambridge Companion to American Science Fiction*, edited by Eric Carl Link and Gerry Canavan, 58–69. New York: Cambridge University Press, 2015.

*Chapter Six*

# Drowning Politics

*Theorizing Resistance in the Anthropocene through JG Ballard's* The Drowned World

Chase Hobbs-Morgan

Responding to the news that the concentration of CO2 in the atmosphere would soon cross the significant, if largely symbolic, threshold of 400 parts per million, Bruno Latour once asked the following simple yet poignant question: "How are we supposed to react?"[1] As Latour went on to suggest, the question of action in the Anthropocene is a vexed one because of the scale and novelty of the problem. For Latour, people "are not equipped with the mental and emotional repertoire to deal with such a vast scale of events."[2] Lacking such a repertoire with which to respond to climate change, people "have difficulty submitting to such a rapid acceleration for which, in addition, they are supposed to feel responsible while, in the meantime, this call for action has none of the traits of their older revolutionary dreams."[3] Sharpening Latour's question somewhat, I want to ask the following question: How can we approach questions of political resistance when the enormity of problems like climate change threaten to drown our politics, figuratively and in some cases even literally?

This chapter reads JG Ballard's novel *The Drowned World* through Bonnie Honig's recent work in *Public Things* in order to theorize and motivate a democratic form of political resistance in the time of the Anthropocene.[4] *The Drowned World*, a 1962 work of science fiction tells a story in which catastrophic sea level rise has taken place, and the roads, artifacts, and cities that constitute a shared world are accordingly submerged. Ballard's warning warrants attention in light of Honig's work, which shows that without these public things, we lack the material conditions necessary for democratic politics.

What would happen if we took seriously the possibility that our public things, too, are drowning? In a few instances I mean this literally, as in the cases of small island states and communities in the north that are being submerged by rising seas. Yet throughout I also mean it to apply metaphorically, to a much more widespread set of Anthropocene experiences. Because $CO_2$ equivalent has surpassed and thus drowned out the "safe" concentration of 350 parts per million in the atmosphere, because narratives of environmental catastrophe often drown out specifically political analyses of how we got here, who we might blame, and what it is we might want to do differently moving forward,[5] because many political assumptions we thought were safe seem once again to be in flux, and because most available forms of political agency leave us feeling like we are not even managing to tread water, I wager that "drowning politics" constitutes a useful metaphor, even when it thankfully cannot (yet) be taken literally. Ultimately, the hope is that the metaphor helps us start to piece together a politics *of* drowning: a practice of resistance based in political ethics of resilience, recovery, and repair of public things.

To this end, Ballard's *Drowned World* is useful in at least two ways—one cautionary and one analytic. First, it vividly underscores the importance of public things for politics generally and dramatizes the detriment to democracy that occurs when those things become submerged. Second, its cast of characters displays a preliminary range of reactions to the catastrophic loss of public things as well as potential dispositions with which to respond, each of which might help *us* think about the question of resistance, *now*.

What follows unfolds as such. First, I elaborate on the value of turning to Ballard and Honig, each of whom helps us grasp the connections between the world that goes on around us and the one that takes place within us. Second, I give an extended reading of *The Drowned World* in order to dramatize and connect the external and internal effects of the loss of public things and to offer a typology of responses to the drowning of politics: one which embraces a changed future and copes with it by turning inward, a second that ignores the present by nostalgically recalling the past, and a third which demands we resist by staying put and asks how the public can be pieced together anew. I conclude by returning to Latour's question noted above, of "how we are to react" to the overwhelming conditions of the Anthropocene. There, I marshal Ballard and Honig's insights in support of forms of resistance that direct attention to place, inheritance, and belonging, and thus to forging democratic communities through renewed attention to public things.

## BALLARD, HONIG, AND THE DROWNING OF PUBLIC THINGS

Contemporary environmental discourse is increasingly concerned with the connection between the well-being of our environments and our psychic lives.[6] Recent headlines include the following: "Climate Depression Is For Real. Just Ask a Scientist: (*Grist*); "Climate Change Causes Anxiety, Depression, Report Says" (*Time*); "'Climate Grief:' The Growing Emotional Toll of Climate Change" (*NBC*). Yet the broad political implications of this awareness are rarely explored directly and the question of how to resist given these conditions seldom asked. Reading Ballard and Honig alongside one another helps to bridge this gap.

The turn to Ballard's unique iteration of science fiction is helpful because of the particular future it dramatizes and because of Ballard's more general focus on "inner space"—on the ways in which external changes play out in our psychic lives—rather than the more ubiquitous move of directing attention to outer space. According to Martin Amis, as Ballard's work progressed, he "rejected 'outer space' in favor of its opposite: 'inner space.' . . . [T]he fusion of mood and setting, the mapping of a landscape of the troubled mind—this is what really matters in Ballard."[7] By the time he pens *The Drowned World*, Ballard's writings are concerned with the ever-present impacts of outer turmoil on inner space, with investigating that space, and with trying to warn his reader based on those investigations.

Importantly, to say that Ballard shifts our attention to inner space is not to say that he would have us withdraw into our secluded interiors.[8] Instead, Ballard's turn to inner space reflects earlier surrealist and psychoanalytic[9] moves and anticipates later new materialist, ecosocialist, feminist, and transcorporeal ones that connect the world around us with the one within us.[10] Per James Sey, Ballard's fiction holds together the "complex interplay between body, psyche, and technology," a useful nexus for thinking through environmental dilemmas.[11] While I agree with Sey here, I think it would be more useful and accurate to say that Ballard recognizes and helps us address connections between body, psyche, and *environment* more generally, which includes the forms of technology that infuse our environments.

*The Drowned World*, specifically, is a useful text for at least two additional reasons. At a general level, it invites an honest reckoning of our contemporary moment by asking us to, in Donna Haraway's words, stay with the trouble.[12] Rather than figuring catastrophe as apocalypse-to-come, *The Drowned World* presents a catastrophe that is already here and an apocalypse that is a time of transformation.[13] Reading Ballard in light of recent discussions of climate-fiction or "cli-fi," Jim Clarke writes that Ballard's work is "post-apocalyptic only in the sense that cataclysmic change is in the process of occurring and is not preventable. Mankind lives on, even if only temporarily or precariously, fundamentally altered by the experience."[14] The first reason that Ballard's text is important is that it allows us to see that catastrophe is in the present, is not preventable, and that it fundamentally alters "mankind." Second, and more specifically, *The Drowned World* helps us see links between the Anthropocene, the loss of public things, de-democratization, and what manifests in the form of self-absorbed apathy on the one hand and some forms of denial—or acting *as if* nothing has changed—on the other.

Yet these elements of *The Drowned World* might well remain unnoticed without the work that Bonnie Honig has done in *Public Things*. Drawing the object-relations theories of Kleinian psychoanalyst D.W. Winnicott and the worldly political theory of Hannah Arendt together, Honig's work outlines the *political* impacts of losing "public things": objects that are held in common and which thereby support the existence and relative coherence of politics. Examples are many and context-dependent, but include land, infrastructure, flags, "sewage treatment plants and railroads," and so on.[15] "Without public things," Honig warns, "we have nothing or not much to deliberate about, constellate around, or agonistically contest. There is nothing to occasion the action in concert that is democracy's definitive trait."[16] Without public things, we have nothing to occasion resistance. *The Drowned World* draws our attention to the physical loss of public things to rising seas: roads, theaters, the identifying characteristics of the city, public art, and so on, all of which are literally submerged in the course of Ballard's story.[17] In doing so, it allows us to grasp that which is all around us but not acknowledged: that the loss of public "holding environments" is connected to our inability to care for the world (in an Arendtian sense of tending to the spaces and places between us, but also in a more quotidian sense of being concerned about climate change, the Anthropocene, etc.). In turn, *Public Things* allows us to say that without such holding environments we can and should expect turns to apathy, melancholy, or hopelessness; that we might also expect a compulsion to repeat the past by refusing to give up pre-catastrophe modes of being, and so on. Honig's work, that is, shows why Ballard's world is one largely devoid of politics. And yet, if read together, these works also offer guidance on how to *be* and *act* otherwise in the face of planetary catastrophe and thus how to resist its deleterious effects on the political.

## THE DROWNED WORLD

When *The Drowned World* opens, a planetary catastrophe has already taken place. An increase in solar energy has melted the earth's polar ice caps, releasing floods of water and silt, and resulting in drastic sea-level rise. If the opening chapter's title—"On the Beach at the Ritz"—teases an idyllic opening to the novel, its first line drowns any hopes its reader may have had: "Soon it would be too hot."[18] The novel's main characters are primarily comprised of a small group of researchers working under the auspices of the UN; the bulk of what is left of humanity (5 million people) has moved to the Arctic or the Antarctic where it is not *yet* too hot. Of these, 10,000 belong to the UN's Camp Byrd, from which the main characters of *The Drowned World* have been dispatched to gather data, rescue survivors, and, when possible, recolonize salvageable areas.

The novel is set in the buildings above London, which is largely underwater. As that world heated up and the water rose, much of the pre-catastrophe *public* became submerged: roads, all low-laying buildings, airports, grocers, farmlands, factories, parliament buildings, and so on. Accordingly, the main characters of the novel are split between finishing their largely hopeless mission and returning north to Camp Byrd, embracing their doomed fate by staying put in London, or traveling further south into the heat. This ambivalence about survival is in part due to a sense of social isolation and detachment, which followed the loss of London and has since settled in to a number of the main characters. To the extent that the novel has a protagonist, that protagonist is Robert Kerans. If the novel has an antagonist, it is Colonel Riggs. Though Kerans and Riggs are both members of the UN mission, they are frequently at odds with one another—not so much as enemies, but as adversaries who cannot and will not listen to the other seriously. With Kerans leading the science/medical elements of the mission and Riggs in charge militarily, the rest of the cast is initially filtered between these two *de facto* leaders. On Kerans's side is Dr. Alan Bodkin (the group's psychologist and assistant to Kerans). Allied with Riggs are Lieutenant Hardman (a helicopter pilot and amateur scientist), Sergeant Daley (the helicopter copilot to Hardman), and Sergeant Macready (Riggs's second-in-command). Beyond these members of the mission the story revolves around two wildcards: Beatrice Dahl, a London native who was either left behind or stayed intentionally and a white-suited pirate known only as Strangman, the leader of a dangerous group of nomadic raiders who arrive late in the novel.

The novel begins three days before the mission is due to leave London to escape the heat. Just before Riggs departs for Camp Byrd, Beatrice, with whom Kerans has become loosely involved romantically, indicates to Kerans and Riggs that she is going to stay in London, her home. Discovering that they have all been having odd dreams, Kerans, Hardman, Bodkin, and Beatrice *all* stay in London, after which the group splinters. Hardman, who develops an intensely appreciative attachment to the new conditions, leaves to pursue the heat in the south. Kerans, Bodkin, and Beatrice drift apart, until the threatening arrival of Strangman and his men occurs. The arrival of an enemy in Strangman brings Kerans and Beatrice back to their senses, temporarily: Kerans becomes "wide-eyed" and Beatrice confesses nostalgia for what little stability their previous, partially sovereign community provided ("I wish Colonel Riggs were here"[19] ).

Throughout the novel, more explicitly psychological and surreal changes occur in and around the characters. Throughout, it becomes apparent that, like Kerans, some of the characters are pulled into the novel's sense of melancholy and toward the drowned world's changed conditions. Such characters experience ever-intensifying "jungle dreams": nightmares (representing disavowed desires) of being subsumed, overtaken, and perhaps incorporated into the earth's new state. Bodkin, the team's psychologist, draws together the external and internal events of the novel by asking whether "only the external landscape," is changing or whether a shared "feeling of déjà vu" suggests a collective shift in consciousness induced by the catastrophic conditions.[20] Ballard, cutting to the heart of his attempt to explore inner space, has Bodkin describe his experience of the changes at play:

> If you like, you could call this the Psychology of Total Equivalents—let's say "Neuronics" for short—and dismiss it as metabiological fantasy. However, I am convinced that as we move back through geophysical time so we re-enter the amnionic corridor and move back through spinal and archaeo-psychic time, recollecting in our unconscious minds the landscapes of each epoch, each with a distinct geological terrain . . . as recognizable to anyone else as they would be to a traveler in a Wellsian time machine. Except that this is no scenic railway, but a total reorientation of the personality.[21]

Faced with the possibility of total submersion, of being wholly drowned by this new world, Bodkin initially welcomes a retreat, noting that "when we leave I think we'll all show a marked improvement."[22] Later, though, he too gets drawn into the same neuronics that ultimately grasp Kerans and Hardman, opting to stay behind when Riggs and the rest of the mission's true believers depart for the north. In doing so, Bodkin expresses clearly Ballard's conviction that body, psyche, and environment are tightly interwoven, at times dangerously so.

It is in this context—of the loss of the outer world to rising seas and the inner world to an associated melancholic submersion—that our characters must try and make do. In dealing with the loss of the literal, metaphorical, material, and psychic grounds on which politics and so much else is based, Ballard's characters unfold. Of interest here is the way that key characters respond to the drowned world, and the way that each response represents a disposition available to us, now, faced with the still-often less literal but no less serious submersion of our own political foundations in the Anthropocene.

For example, many of the characters are marked by the loss of techno-optimism, or of the public legitimacy of science more generally, as faith in the UN mission's fact-gathering element starts to appear absurd. Jim Clarke notes the "almost existential pointlessness of the monitoring work conducted at the lagoon station" and that "Ballard here undermines the modeling process at the heart of contemporary climate science using the same broad basis as many climate change deniers."[23] In this sense, the characters are indeed operating in post-truth conditions not unlike those that have threatened contemporary politics since, symbolically, 2016.

Equally important is the loss of cultural artifacts that once served to hold various publics together. At one point this is demonstrated through the loss of cinema, itself a public thing that can be a key holding environment for democratic politics.[24] On this point, we see that cinema was lost when Kerans looks "down through the dark water at the small cinema"[25] buried below. In another moment, Kerans notices the new meaninglessness of paintings by Paul Delvaux and Max Ernst, and is unable to focus on the Beethoven playing in the background because he's preoccupied by the changed conditions. And when Strangman beckons Kerans later in the story to look at his loot, treasures of silver and gold, Kerans responds flatly and dismissively: "they're like bones."[26] Under conditions of environmental catastrophe, culture and cultural artifacts, like public science, struggle to play a role in holding the political together.

And then of course there are the basics of (our) contemporary life, the things that most directly make living and being political (in the ways we understand them) possible: infrastructure, public squares, and cities themselves. At the novel's outset the characters are faced with the realization that they would have to abandon London. Yet even before those characters consciously acknowledged the possibility of abandoning and thus losing the city as a whole, we must appreciate how much of that city was already gone. From the beginning of the novel, what was left of London "consisted of little more than three principal lagoons"[27] occasionally interrupted by buildings taller than the six stories which rising seas had submerged.

These overwhelming losses result in a further loss of the very basic elements of public life: building blocks like sociality and commonality. Umberto Rossi suggests that in *The Drowned World* human *time* has itself been submerged along with the city and its trappings: "the human, historical time of the city, whose rhythm was stressed by clocks, has been definitively lost."[28] Here and elsewhere, we can read Ballard as narrating humanity's return to an old (or discovery of a new) state of nature. Recall a point made by Thomas Hobbes, who included *time* as something that we humans could not depend on in his state of war:

> In such condition there is no place for industry, because the fruit thereof is uncertain, and consequently, no culture of the earth, no navigation, nor use of the commodities that may be imported by sea, no commodious building, no instruments of moving and removing such things as require much force, no knowledge of the face of the earth, *no account of time*, no arts, no letters, no society.[29]

Along with public science and culture, the basic infrastructure of everyday life has been taken out of meaningful existence. Under these conditions, we see little opportunity for social or political engagement: we literally do not have the time.

Regardless, the broader point is that *The Drowned World* is one in which what *we* know of politics has been turned on its head, lost, rendered defunct. On this point, Jim Clarke writes that "In a world where a mere five million people cluster for life around formerly frozen polar regions, the geopolitical revolution provoked by *The Drowned World* vastly exceeds" much of contemporary cli-fi. Specifically, "Ballard's geopolitical realignment is more profound than the simple reversal of national power plays. Rather, he turns the Earth on its axis and renders all petty politics and national interests defunct."[30]

How *are* we supposed to react?

## THREE MODES OF RESPONSE: EMBRACING THE (NEW) STATE OF NATURE, DENYING LOSS, AND STAYING WITH THE TROUBLE

To begin to answer this tremendous question I now turn to the different ways that its characters respond to the drowning of politics, differences that bring into view political dispositions and avenues of resistance available to us in our present moment of ongoing ecological and political erosion. *The Drowned World* offers three such dispositions. One embraces a changed future by turning ever more inward. A second ignores the present by remaining stuck in projects of the past. A third insists on staying put and, at best, seeing what there is to be salvaged, repaired, and made public once more.

## KERANS AND HARDMAN: EMBRACING THE (NEW) STATE OF NATURE

Considering Ballard as a thinker of the state of nature helps make sense of some of Kerans's more eccentric characteristics. Kerans's increasing desire to move south which ultimately results in his embrace of a fate as solitary as it is internally rich and as short as it is, to him, fulfilling, represents an embrace of a new (state of) nature. Yet in embracing this new nature, accepting his status as the last man or, in the language of the novel, a new Adam, Kerans modifies the classical understanding of the state of nature as that which (hypothetically) occurred in the past. Here, the state of nature, and by implication the Garden of Eden, marks the end of history rather than prehistory (or a cyclical history). As Latour notes in assessing contemporary environmental predicaments, "contrary to Hobbes's scheme, the "state of nature" seems to have a dangerous tendency to *follow*, and not to precede or to accompany, the time of the civil compact."[31]

As the story unfolds and what few public things once remained themselves dissolve, Kerans becomes increasingly solipsistic: his is a journey and an ethics of the self. In the midst of the losses described above, the one public object supporting a life in common had been Riggs's military base along with its platoon and testing station. By the time Riggs and his men leave with the station—and Kerans, Bodkin, and Beatrice decide to stay—Kerans is already quite the separatist. When he loses the base itself, Kerans becomes even more isolated. As such, the bonds between him and the others—most poignantly, Beatrice—deteriorate further. At this point, "it was not simply for reasons of convenience that they would live apart. Much as he needed Beatrice Dahl, her personality intruded upon the absolute freedom he required for himself.[32]

As we move through the story, Kerans and his ilk are pulled far away from their northern origins of Camp Byrd. Kerans and Hardman both ultimately give in to the jungle dreams, each taking his own journey south. Per Bodkin's diagnosis, Kerans and Hardman reflect the wager that "insofar as we are part of the planet . . . we too are returning" to the prehistoric past that the equator represents. In the absence of political things around which to organize, and having been dropped into a place with which they had no history of attachment, Kerans and Hardman are left with few options. Given the choice between willing nothing and willing nothingness, they confirm Nietzsche's axiom that "man would rather will *nothingness* than not will."[33] In lieu of an available political project, they each pursue what they deem to be self-perfection, to the end. Somewhat innocently, we might draw parallels between Kerans and Hardman and those who devote energy to self-improvement as a means of accepting our world for what it is. Or, less innocently, we might see parallels to those who seem to embrace a drowned world and relish in it: those whose pastime it is to "roll coal" on cyclists and pedestrians, those who acknowledge climate change but nonetheless eagerly embrace the riches made possible by the fossil fuel era, and so on. Common to these available (if otherwise disparate) responses is an acceptance or embrace of often catastrophic change and a privileging of the self in the midst of such change.

## RIGGS ET AL.: DENYING LOSS

Where Kerans and Hardman respond to loss with initial indifference and eventual embrace, a second group remains committed to Camp Byrd and to the UN mission to which they belong and, by extension, to the world as it was before the catastrophe began to sink in. Riggs, along with Macready and Daley represent a second general response to loss: denial that things have changed in any meaningful sense, a continued devotion to the mission of the UN, hegemonic institutions of the past, and so on.

Where Kerans accepts that there is little worth doing and early on becomes convinced that no one "bothered to file his reports, let alone read them,"[34] Riggs embraces "the tacit assumption made by the UN directorate—that within the new perimeters described by the Arctic and Antarctic Circles life would continue much as before."[35] Indeed Riggs and his men are so strongly identified with Camp Byrd in the text that their physical descriptions tie them to its avian-sounding name. Riggs, we are told, "looked like a ferocious sparrow."[36] Macready, likewise, gets a "beak-like face"[37] and is later "silhouetted like a gaunt crow."[38] Rather than engaging with the drowned world, the UN and its devotees exist as so many birds floating above it, remaining detached from it, always happy to study and secure it or to fly north and leave it behind when given the order.

When part of the group's commitment to leaving starts to waver early on, Riggs's commitment to Camp Byrd and all it represents only solidifies. As Kerans retreats into dreams and into his inner space more generally, Riggs is depicted as "still obeying reason and logic, buzzing around his diminished, unimportant world with his little parcels of instructions."[39] At one point Riggs is engaged in an argument with Beatrice, and we encounter him "forcing her to accept the logic of his argument."[40] Throughout, we too see "the colonel's self-discipline" as he pursues the missions of the UN: scientific fact-finding, search and rescue, recolonization and land reclamation, and so on.[41] Riggs's self-discipline allows his fidelity to pre-catastrophe institutions to continue unimpeded by the general sense of melancholy that beckons Kerans and the others away from those same institutions.

In his own way, the pirate Strangman also demonstrates a fidelity to the past by continuing to seek its treasures and using his might to re-create its physical makeup. Note that Strangman could either be read as "strong-man," connecting him to authoritarians of old (and now resurgent), or as "strange-man," which explains why he seems unaware that conditions have truly changed. As such, Strangman moves from sunken city to sunken city dredging the depths of previously urban squares-turned-lagoons in pursuit of riches. When Strangman comes to London, and after he introduces a general if low-grade sense of terror and discomfort to the lives of Kerans, Bodkin (ultimately killing Bodkin in what he claims is self-defense), and Beatrice, Strangman installs a massive series of pumps to drain one of the London lagoons, which turns out to have been Leicester Square.[42] While this could be seen as a reclamation of public space, Strangman's wealth-regarding ambitions suggest we read it inversely: as an attempt to privatize previously public space. Yet as is the case with Riggs's missions, the value of Strangman's ill-gotten gains is uncertain; what good is gold or well-known artwork without a (political) society to bestow value upon it? Not much, we are told, when the narrator describes Strangman's loot as nothing more than "jeweled trash."[43]

After Bodkin's death and having anticipated that a menace like Strangman would appear eventually, Riggs and his men return and intervene. Upon

Riggs's return, Kerans asks for the arrest of Strangman. Riggs, devoted to his pre-catastrophe sense of law and order, responds that he cannot, as Strangman has technically done nothing illegal: "Legally, as he full well knows, he was absolutely entitled to defend himself against Bodkin, kill him if necessary. . . . Don't you remember the Reclaimed Lands Act and the Dykes Maintenance Regulations? They're still very much in force."[44] Not only does Riggs retain his fidelity to the pre-drowned world—that same fidelity causes him to respect Strangman somewhat for carrying forward the neocolonial mission of the UN by reclaiming Leicester Square. To Riggs, the work of the present is to reclaim the past that he does not admit has passed. Even after environmental catastrophe, Riggs carries on old institutions of land ownership and colonization.

Where Kerans and Hardman respond to the loss of the political with an ethical turn inward, Riggs and Strangman thus respond by acting as if nothing much has changed. Like those who insist on the centrality and essential sufficiency of our own institutions of governance, Riggs's game plan is to stay the course: to finish the mission of the UN, to approach the problem of catastrophe as an outside observer, to force the logic of his arguments onto the world, and so on. Like those who insist on the continued acceptability of our own techniques of wealth extraction, Strangman approaches the changed conditions not as a fundamental or existential change from the past, but as a new set of the same old opportunities for private, ill-gotten gains.

## BEATRICE AND BODKIN: STAYING WITH THE END-HOLOCENE TROUBLE

For each of *The Drowned World*'s characters other than Beatrice and Bodkin, attachment or detachment—embracing the new nature or denying that things have changed—are fairly abstract questions because their histories were elsewhere. Given that Kerans, Hardman, Riggs and the others had never formed connections to London to begin with, the question of how, and whether, to continue to engage with London was relatively insignificant. From their perspective, it had always been a drowned world. Ballard tells us that it was precisely "this absence of personal memories that made Kerans indifferent"[45] to London's loss. For Kerans, mapping, testing, and reclaiming were unimportant endeavors compared to exploring "the ghostly deltas and luminous beaches of the submerged neuronic continents."[46] Bodkin and especially Beatrice, however, *were* bound to London through old memories, however bittersweet, troubling, or traumatic. Though in Bodkin's childhood London had already been "disintegrated by panic and despair,"[47] he nonetheless felt a sense of connection to, and perhaps responsibility for, that particular drowning world.

Whereas Kerans and Hardman opt to stay in London in order to ultimately venture south—to plunge headlong into a new nature, an old future or new past, and so on, Bodkin and Beatrice stay in London because it is where they *belong*. In a passage striking for its strong sense of political commitment relative to the rest of the book, Beatrice responds to Riggs's self-assumed duty to rescue her—a London native—from her impending decline: "I've always understood that our duty was to stay on here as long as possible and make every sacrifice necessary to that end.'"[48] For Beatrice, it's a (political) duty to stay as long as possible, to make sacrifice in the name of defending *place*. Faced with this resistance which is rooted in commitment to place, Riggs folds immediately even as he attempts to save face by ignoring the content of the argument he has just lost: "All right, Miss Dahl. I give in. . . . I'll send the cutter over to collect your gear."[49] At any rate, Beatrice's reason to stay is neither to rush headlong into danger nor to dive headlong into herself, but to stay and protect the places and histories that have made her who she is: the apartment in which she was set to remain was previously her grandfather's "*pieds à terre.*"[50]

As a secondary unit that was both his and yet not quite his, and as an inheritance that is both hers and yet not quite hers, that apartment might be refashioned, shared, and, most hopefully, made public. While this enactment of resistance might feel small, both within the novel and in its application to our ecological crisis, it is worth remembering the context with which I opened this chapter: a political moment in which it is not at all clear *how* we might act politically given that our political imagination is captured and our public things are being drowned. It would not be nothing, that is, if the dwelling that Beatrice salvaged through her sense of belonging and political responsibility were to become a meeting place for those wishing to repair *their* drowned world, just as it would not amount to nothing if revolutionary thinkers were to carve out such spaces in our world in which to dream revolutionary dreams together. Nor does it amount to nothing when similar public spaces are carved out by responsive members of communities who are committed to particular places, and when those public spaces are used to repair *our* drowned worlds. One thinks, here, of the activists at Standing Rock, Puerto Rico, Flint, and other loci of environmental (in)justice in which communities are making explicitly place-based appeals that resist environmental destruction. Like Beatrice, such activists resist against the world of old (represented by Riggs) by embracing responsibility, remaking their own public things, and insisting on the fundamental value of repairing in the present that which the world of old continually threatens to drown.

## CONCLUSION

What would a broader politics of drowning, a politics that responds to ecological crisis in a way that is not simply reactionary—in which we do not *simply* drown—look like in our world? Clearly, there is not yet a literal threat that *our* public things will be drowned by sea-level rise, or that *our* holding environments will be submerged to the extent that we see in *The Drowned World*. Better, there is not *yet* a literal threat that *all* of our public things will be drowned by sea-level rise, at least not in places like London. Still, in places like the Maldives, drowning politics is not a metaphor: we can all think back to the infamous image of the government of the Maldives holding an underwater cabinet meeting. Likewise, it is becoming clearer and clearer that sea-level rise will be worse than some projectors have been planning for.[51] Before too long, public things might be literally drowning in places like Miami, San Francisco, and so on. Perhaps they already are in places like Louisiana.[52] If we take the slow but steady rate at which the south of England is sinking into account, indeed, perhaps it is not so clear that public things will be spared a waterlogged fate in London itself.[53]

Still, my purpose here is not to remain quite so literal. Metaphorically, as many including Honig have aptly shown, neoliberalism also "drowns" public things by privatizing them, and "the public goods that are increasingly privatized may be irretrievably lost by the antipathy to and dismantling of the public thing, as such."[54] If the Anthropocene as a concept can do anything, it can allow us to hold these multiple dimensions together and enable us to insist that planetary catastrophe involves and combines material and ideological impacts. Politics—and the public things that enable them—can be "drowned" by rising seas and waves of privatization alike.

One course of action in the Anthropocene is the one most familiar to us: to formulate a "universal" way of governing the future that will nonetheless inevitably reflect a very particular set of interests, worldviews, modes of being, values, and so on.[55] In *The Drowned World*, this response is signified by Camp Byrd, which sends missions out to re-create the world in its own image. Where the ostensible goal of the universalist approach is to stop the pending catastrophe(s) of climate change and return us to *some* semblance of stasis, the effect of any universalist approach will *also* likely be to try to return us to the sociopolitical structures, forms of normalization, inequalities, and so on of the Holocene. For many peoples, the Holocene was not dramatically better than the Anthropocene. As an example of this universalist approach, we might think of the views put forward by the Breakthrough Institute's *Ecomodernist Manifesto*, which (like Riggs and Camp Byrd) holds great faith in the ability for existing forms of high technology and global cooperation (and, reading between the lines, the elites that are invested in and who benefit from those powers) to govern the future such that the highest echelons of power can continue and expand upon the Holocene's, and Western modernity's institutions. We can predict that such institutions will continue to embrace "the active, assertive, and aggressive participation of private sector entrepreneurs, markets, civil society, and the state"[56] as if nothing has really changed.

In response to political projects that seek to bring us back to the Holocene, an alternative proposal is that we embrace political projects aimed at dwelling in and navigating the Holocene-Anthropocene transition. Rather than *one* universalist (humanist, modernist, capitalist, technophilic, colonial) approach, in this vision we are invited to undertake many projects. In Jeremy Davies's language:

> If a new epoch, in a formal geological sense . . . may be said to have begun in 1952 [one proposed 'start' to the Anthropocene], then the world is effectively still in the midst of a transition between epochs: the end-Holocene event. Environmentalists' goal should not be to call off that transition and replace it with indefinite sustainability [as the Breakthrough Institute might have it], but instead to intervene in it by guarding and rebuilding ecological pluralism.[57]

Does Ballard help with this project? I have been arguing that he does, by showing us in no uncertain terms that we need to notice, process, and mourn the loss of our public things, and by dramatizing the ill effects that (will) occur if we refuse projects organized around resilience, recovery, and repair of the (political) world. For Ballard, Colonel Riggs represents a strong case of how *not* to respond: "Ballard warns us not to expect scientists [and we might add military men] to become saviours and reminds us that acceptance of change is healthier than seeking to preserve a lost past."[58]

If not Riggs et al., perhaps Kerans, whose acceptance of change does indeed come across as healthier than Riggs's stubborn denial, offers a model? According to a generous read, Kerans's close attention to his own inner life and its connection to environmental changes is promising. Clearly, Kerans is engaged in some sort of ethical work throughout, and it is equally clear that he remains capable, however slightly, of caring for those around him. As he prepares to finally head south for good, for example, Beatrice confronts Kerans: "'Darling, where are you going. I'm sorry I can't be with you.'" Kerans's response is heavy with sentiment and care: "'South . . . [t]owards the sun. You'll be with me, Bea.'"[59]

Yet, caring as it may be, Kerans's response comes from a place of detachment rather than relational co-entanglement: Beatrice will be with him insofar as he will bring with him an internalized image of her. Of course, she won't be with him in any way that is meaningful to *her*. Detached from any particular place about which to care yet confronted by overwhelming loss, Kerans can only practice what Ella Myers calls a 'therapeutic' model of ethics, once centered around care for the self. Such a model, which takes its major cues from Michel Foucault, "emphasizes the individual's capacity to consciously shape or reshape herself and acquire an admirable style of existence largely detached from the enforcement of a general moral code."[60] In making himself into a second Adam, Kerans responded just fine to the tension between a changed world and an inner-space marked by loss. Yet in *only* pursuing self-care, he declines or is otherwise unable to foster and sustain a political and democratic ethos, even as it's unclear whether his particular ethical turn could be politicized at all.

Perhaps, then, it is the minor character of Beatrice who offers the most useful disposition. Where Kerans's care was for the self, Beatrice starts us down a different path, one that curves back toward what Myers calls the "democratic ethics of care for worldly things"[61] and one that, likewise, might help us to piece public things and holding environments back together. According to Myers's ethics of care for the world, "the recipient of care is not another person or even persons, but the world, understood as the array of material and immaterial conditions under which human beings live."[62] Where Riggs is constitutionally detached, flying above the world at Camp Byrd, and Kerans has turned inward, Beatrice demands to stay in the apartment she inherited and indeed invites Kerans to do the same, reflecting Myers's further insistence that "coaction among citizens is directed not at the world per se but at particularly worldly things that become objects of shared attention and concern."[63] In a drowned world in which revolutionary dreams either do not persist or have not yet come to fruition, Beatrice Dahl gives due attention, and invites others to give due attention, to that which is proximate—to the things she knows that could be *made* public: her apartment, the few surrealist works of art that remain, the Beethoven records that can still be played, and so on.

The overarching lesson that Honig allows us to learn from Ballard is that public things need to be protected in the face of environmental and neoliberal "floods." Of course, we already knew that. The more nuanced lesson, then, is that if and when those things *are* drowned, the next best move might come in the form of an attachment to place, and an embrace of the situations, rights, and responsibilities one has inherited. In refusing to leave London—and indeed, in being the first character in the novel to do so—Beatrice indicates that she's willing and able, like Dante's Beatrice before her, to guide herself and others through the trouble.

## NOTES

1. Bruno Latour, "Agency at the Time of the Anthropocene," *New Literary History* 45 (2014): 1. I would like to thank Rafi Youatt for offering very helpful discussant comments at the *Western Political Science Association* conference in 2018, as well as the members of the audience who gifted our panel with the kinds of generous, constructive, and helpful questions and criticism one can reliably expect in that setting. Thanks also to Lisa Bhungalia, Cal Biruk,

Abbey Chung, and Charmaine Chua, who read an earlier draft and offered generous comments, and of course to the editors of this volume. Without their close attention and suggestions, the chapter would be much worse off.

2. Ibid.

3. Ibid.

4. J.G. Ballard, *The Drowned World* (New York: Liveright Publishing, 2013); Bonnie Honig, *Public Things: Democracy in Disrepair* (New York: Fordham University Press, 2017).

5. Of course, some work centers these questions. See Andreas Malm's *Fossil Capital: The Rise of Steam Power and the Roots of Global Warming* (London: Verso, 2016). Still, broader environmental(ist) discourses continue to focus on narratives that float above the drowned world of political disagreement, opposing interests, and uneven responsibility.

6. Such topics have been broached in psychoanalysis, sociology, and the mass media. See Sally Weintrobe, ed. *Engaging with Climate Change: Psychoanalytic and Interdisciplinary Perspectives* (New York: Routledge, 2013); Kari Marie Norgaard, *Living in Denial: Climate Change, Emotions, and Everyday Life* (Cambridge, MA: MIT Press, 2011).

7. Martin Amis, introduction to *The Drowned World*, 11.

8. As will become clear below, Ballard does recognize such withdrawal as one potential response to the loss of public things, one that comes across as less than desirable.

9. On Ballard and surrealism, see Jeanette Baxter, *J.G. Ballard's Surrealist Imagination: Spectacular Authorship* (Burlington, VT: Ashgate, 2009). Many treatments of Ballard discuss his psychological and/or psychoanalytic leanings. For a direct treatment, see Samuel Francis, *The Psychological Fictions of J.G. Ballard* (London: Continuum, 2011).

10. See, for example, Stacy Alaimo, *Bodily Natures: Science, Environment, and the Material Self* (Bloomington: Indiana University Press, 2010); Alaimo, "Your Shell on Acid: Material Immersion, Anthropocene Dissolves," in *Anthropocene Feminism*, ed. Richard Grusin (Minneapolis: University of Minnesota Press, 2017), 89–120; John Bellamy Foster, *Marx's Ecology* (New York: Monthly Review Press, 2000), Teena Gabrielson and Katelyn Parady, "Corporeal Citizenship: Rethinking Green Citizenship Through the Body," *Environmental Politics* 19, no. 3 (2010): 374–91; Astrida Neimanis and Rachel Loewen Walker, "*Weathering*: Climate Change and the "Thick Time" of Transcorporeality" *Hypatia* 20, no. 3 (2014): 558–75; Dayne Scott, Jennie Haw, and Robyn Lee, "'Wannabe Toxic-Free?' From Precautionary Consumption to Corporeal Citizenship," *Environmental Politics* 26, no. 2 (2017): 322–42.

11. James Sey, "Psychopathology, Inner Space and the Automotive Death Drive: J.G. Ballard," *South African Journal of Psychology* 32, no. 2 (2002): 55.

12. Donna Haraway, *Staying with the Trouble: Making Kin in the Chthulucene* (Durham, NC: Duke University Press, 2016).

13. For a discussion of apocalypse-as-transition, see Jairus Victor Grove, *Savage Ecology: War and Geopolitics at the End of the World* (Durham, NC: Duke University Press, 2019), chapter 8.

14. Jim Clarke, "Reading Climate Change in J.G. Ballard," *Critical Survey* 25, no. 2 (2013): 9. It's worth noting that catastrophe arrives unevenly: some Indigenous scholars see colonialism as part of the same process as what we've now taken to calling the Anthropocene. See Zoe Todd, "Indigenizing the Anthropocene," in *Art in the Anthropocene: Encounters Among Aesthetics, Politics, Environment and Epistemology*, Heather Davis and Etienne Turpin, eds. (London: Open Humanities Press, 2015): 241–54.

15. Honig, *Public Things*, 5.

16. Honig, *Public Things*, 5.

17. Though the physical loss in Ballard's text might itself be taken as dramatizing the privatization of public things according to neoliberal demands.

18. Ballard, *Drowned World*, 17.

19. Ibid., 104–5.

20. Ibid., 55.

21. Ibid., 57.

22. Ibid., 50.

23. Clarke, "Reading," 10. Clarke later makes clear that Ballard's attempt to move away from scientific technique is not *quite* the same as climate deniers' critiques of sound scientific

practice: "Ballard presents a much more *existential* set of questions to his protagonists" (18). Emphasis added.

24. On cinema as a "democratic emblem," see Alain Badiou, *Cinema*, trans. Susan Spitzer (Malden, MA: Polity, 2013).

25. Ballard, *Drowned*, 93.

26. Ibid., 112.

27. Ibid., 31.

28. Umberto Rossi, "Images from the Disaster Area: An Apocalyptic Reading of Urban Landscapes in Ballard's *The Drowned World* and *Hello America*," *Science Fiction Studies* 21, no. 1 (1994): 82.

29. Thomas Hobbes, *Leviathan*, ed. Edwin Curley (Indianapolis, IN: Hackett Publishing Company, 1994), 74. Emphasis added.

30. Clarke, "Reading," 14.

31. Latour, "Time of the Anthropocene," 6.

32. Ibid., 97.

33. Friedrich Nietzsche, *On the Genealogy of Morals and Ecce Homo*, trans. Walter Kaufmann (New York: Vintage Books, 1989), 163.

34. Ballard, *Drowned*, 19.

35. Ibid., 58.

36. Ibid., 68.

37. Ibid., 42.

38. Ibid., 71.

39. Ibid., 90.

40. Ibid., 37.

41. Ibid., 76.

42. Ibid., 141.

43. Ibid., 171.

44. Ibid., 179. In keeping with his character, Riggs had long ago warned Kerans and Beatrice about the prospect that dangerous threats would one day threaten their fragile existence.

45. Ibid., 32.

46. Ibid., 58.

47. Ibid., 32.

48. Ibid., 39.

49. Ibid.

50. Ibid., 41.

51. Kendra Pierre-Louis, "Ocean Warming Is Accelerating Faster Than Thought, New Research Finds," *New York Times* (11 January 2019): https://www.nytimes.com/2019/01/10/climate/ocean-warming-climate-change.html.

52. Kevin Sack and John Schwartz, "Left to Louisiana's Tides, A Village Fights for Time," *New York Times* (24 February 2018): https://www.nytimes.com/interactive/2018/02/24/us/jean-lafitte-floodwaters.html.

53. Jonathan Amos, "London's Small but Relentless Dip," *BBC* (12 July 2007): http://news.bbc.co.uk/2/hi/ science/nature/6231334.stm.

54. Honig, *Public Things*, 55.

55. Grove provides a brilliant analysis of this possibility in Chapter 1 of *Savage Ecologies*. While our analyses and archives differ in some regards, the political affinities of our conclusions are strong.

56. John Asafu-Adjaye et al., *The Ecomodernist Manifesto,* https://www.ecomodernism.org/manifesto-english, (2015): 30.

57. Jeremy Davies, *The Birth of the Anthropocene* (Oakland, CA: University of California Press, 2016), 208.

58. Clarke, "Reading," 18.

59. Ballard, *Drowned*, 187.

60. Ella Myers, *Worldly Ethics: Democratic Politics and Care for the World* (Durham, NC: Duke University Press, 2013), 23.

61. Ibid., 85.

62. Ibid., 86.
63. Ibid.

## BIBLIOGRAPHY

Alaimo, Stacy. *Bodily Natures: Science, Environment, and the Material Self.* Bloomington, IN: Indiana University Press, 2010.
———. "Your Shell on Acid: Material Immersion, Anthropocene Dissolves." In *Anthropocene Feminism*, edited by Richard Grusin. Minneapolis: University of Minnesota Press, 2017.
Amis, Martin. "Introduction." In *The Drowned World*. New York: Liveright Publishing, 2013.
Amos, Jonathan. "London's Small but Relentless Dip." *BBC* 12 July 2007: http://news.bbc.co.uk/2/hi/ science/nature/6231334.stm.
Asafu-Adjaye, John et al. *The Ecomodernist Manifesto*. https://www.ecomodernism.org/manifesto-english, 2015.
Badiou, Alain. *Cinema*. Translated by Susan Spitzer. Malden, MA: Polity, 2013.
Ballard, J.G. *The Drowned World*. New York: Liveright Publishing, 2013.
Baxter, Jeanette. *J.G. Ballard's Surrealist Imagination: Spectacular Authorship*. Burlington, VT: Ashgate, 2009.
Clarke, Jim. "Reading Climate Change in J.G. Ballard." *Critical Survey* 25, no. 2 (2013): 7–21.
Davies, Jeremy. *The Birth of the Anthropocene*. Oakland, CA: University of California Press, 2016.
Foster, John Bellamy. *Marx's Ecology*. New York: Monthly Review Press, 2000.
Francis, Samuel. *The Psychological Fictions of J.G. Ballard*. London: Continuum, 2011.
Gabrielson, Teena and Kately Parady. "Corporeal Citizenship: Rethinking Green Citizenship Through the Body." *Environmental Politics* 19, no. 3 (2010): 374–91.
Grove, Jairus Victor. *Savage Ecology: War and Geopolitics at the End of the World*. Durham, NC: Duke University Press, 2019.
Haraway, Donna. *Staying With the Trouble: Making Kin in the Chthulucene*. Durham, NC: Duke University Press, 2016.
Hobbes, Thomas. *Leviathan*. Edited by Edwin Curley. Indianapolis, IN: Hackett Publishing Company, 1994.
Honig, Bonnie. *Public Things: Democracy in Disrepair*. New York: Fordham University Press, 2017.
Latour, Bruno. "Agency at the Time of the Anthropocene." *New Literary History* 45, no. 1 (2014): 1–18.
Malm, Andreas. *Fossil Capital: The Rise of Steam Power and the Roots of Global Warming*. London: Verso, 2016.
Myers, Ella. *Worldly Ethics: Democratic Politics and Care for the World*. Durham, NC: Duke University Press, 2013.
Neimanis, Astrida and Rachel Loewen Walker. "*Weathering*: Climate Change and the "Thick Time" of Transcorporeality." *Hypatia* 29, no. 3 (2014): 558–75.
Nietzsche, Friedrich. *On the Genealogy of Morals and Ecce Homo*. Translated by Walter Kaufmann. New York: Vintage Books, 1989.
Norgaard, Kari Marie. *Living in Denial: Climate Change, Emotions, and Everyday Life*. Cambridge, MA: MIT Press, 2011.
Pierre-Louis, Kendra. "Ocean Warming Is Accelerating Faster Than Thought, New Research Finds." *New York Times*, 11 January 2019: https://www.nytimes.com/2019/01/10/climate/ocean-warming-climate-change.html.
Rossi, Umberto. "Images from the Disaster Area: An Apocalyptic Reading of Urban Landscapes in Ballard's *The Drowned World* and *Hello America*." *Science Fiction Studies* 21, no. 1 (1994): 81–97.
Sack, Kevin and John Schwartz. "Left to Louisiana's Tides, A Village Fights for Time." *New York Times*, 24 February 2018: https://www.nytimes.com/interactive/2018/02/24/us/jean-lafitte-floodwaters.html.

Scott, Dayne, Jennie Haw, and Robyn Lee. "Wannabe Toxic-Free?" From Precautionary Consumption to Corporeal Citizenship." *Environmental Politics* 26, no. 2 (2017): 322–42.
Sey, James. "Psychopathology, Inner Space and the Automotive Death Drive: J.G. Ballard." *South African Journal of Psychology* 32, no. 2 (2002): 55–60.
Todd, Zoe. "Indigenizing the Anthropocene." In *Art in the Anthropocene: Encounters Among Aesthetics, Politics, Environment and Epistemology*, edited by Heather Davis and Etienne Turpin, 241–54. London: Open Humanities Press, 2015.
Weintrobe, Sally, ed. *Engaging with Climate Change: Psychoanalytic and Interdisciplinary Perspectives*. New York: Routledge, 2013.

*Part III*

# Reconstructing Our World: Space and Place

*Chapter Seven*

# The Ambiguities of Critical Desire

*Utopia and Heterotopia in Ursula K. Le Guin's* The Dispossessed *and Samuel R. Delany's* Trouble on Triton

## Michael Lipscomb

The history of political thought and commentary often evinces a strong distaste for the very notion of utopia.[1] The progressive tradition is no less suspicious. Marx's and Engels' own efforts to define their project in contradistinction to utopian socialism, Marx's reluctance to sketch the outlines of a post-capitalist society, and the reticence of twentieth-century critical theorists—from Adorno to Foucault—to provide an affirmative vision that would complement their critique of modern societies underline the disrepute of the utopian in the progressive tradition.[2] Nonetheless, it is hard to see the coherence of any critical theory of society that is not organized by an at least implicit utopian orientation.

If we understand critical theory, in both its broadest and narrowest senses, as providing "the descriptive and normative bases for social inquiry aimed at decreasing domination and increasing freedom in all their forms,"[3] the utopian content of the critical is impossible to ignore. And, to the degree that science fiction (or speculative fiction, if you would prefer) offers an ideal genre for exploring the question of utopia, it sits at the center of the theoretical-critical enterprise. This chapter explores the question of utopia by looking at the constitutive role that desire plays in our critical-theoretical utopian aspirations through a selective reading of signal texts in the science fiction tradition, most particularly Ursula K. Le Guin's *The Dispossessed* and Samuel R. Delany's *Trouble on Triton* (which are cast, respectively, as an ambiguous utopia and an ambiguous heterotopia).[4] In reading those texts against the background of how desire functions in the critical theory of Herbert Marcuse, we hope to make some progress toward the articulation of a critical theory of desire, a critical desire, that might enact the necessity of desire as central to the ethical orientation that animates any critical-progressive politics.

Critical theory, and the radical political outcomes that it implies, is constituted by the affirmative and utopian promise of its desire in at least two ways. On the one hand, all critical thought is animated by a desire for another kind of world, one that escapes the irrationality, dysfunction, and injustice of the status quo. We might say that the affirmative moment of utopia within any critical theory, the at-least-implicit aim of its desire, enacts a disruption of our received desires for fulfillment within the scripts that are predominantly available to us in our lived experience. This disruption is the critical function of utopia. On the other hand, our utopian aspirations are entwined with notions of what our romantic-sexual desire for others might look like. That interpersonal level of romantic-sexual desire is, for many, fundamental to how we imagine the good life and thus seems inextricable from the utopian, affirmative desire for the better world at which critical theory aims. Within our received understandings and experience of desire, however, both our hope for a better world and our sexual-romantic yearnings seem inscribed in an assimilating logic of closure that runs counter to the liberatory promise of critical theory, particularly given the way in which those understandings and experiences have been contoured within the disciplining, interwoven systems of patriarchy, heteronormativity, and capitalism. Can desire be understood in ways that resist, at the very least, practices of vulgar assimilation? Can desire be understood as an act of freedom that does not impinge upon the freedom of another?

In focusing on "desire," we invoke a word whose general meaning is useful, that helps us summarize a certain kind of phenomena in a pragmatically valid way, but we also want to respect the fact that this phenomena varies across time, place, and actors. In certain senses, few would argue that "desire" means simply one thing. Different humans and nonhumans experience different kinds of desires for different others in a wide range of different contexts. By marking "desire" in quotation marks, perhaps we can at least initially signal that the understandings of desire that we inherit, particularly the most culturally pervasive forms, remain a site of political contestation, a place where the utopian disruptions of critical theory/science fiction might begin to open a space for different understandings and practices of desire.[5] Nonetheless, the term, across all of these different permutations, seems to convey as part of its definitional essence an identifiable structural character, a kind of movement or promise of movement across a distance toward its defining object. Even in its essential contestability, desire signifies a generalizable movement, a compulsion to overcome a distance that separates a subject from a particular object that it wants, or a movement between subjects, or even between non-subjects.

This chapter, in fact, assumes that rough analytical distinctions can be drawn between different kinds of desire within a generalized understanding of desire, as generally entailing a movement toward the object of its desire. Thus, the focus on desire allows us to deconstruct the hegemonic understandings of desire in our current circumstances and to make space for different configurations of desire, desires that are alien to the predominant figurations of desire that we inhabit. To the degree that patriarchal and heteronormative articulations of desire continue to predominate in contemporary times, the approach pursued here can provide the basis for challenging the presumed naturalness of this desire/these desires, even as it provides us a baseline for recognizing the worth of other forms of desire.

Furthermore, as we have already begun to outline, this chapter makes use of distinctions between revolutionary-political desire and romantic-sexual desire even as it seeks to trace out their imbrication (their imbrications, their common logics) through signal texts of twentieth-century utopian/dystopian science fiction, drawing on those resources to articulate the notion of critical desire as part of the ongoing tradition and aspirations of critical theory. Those two desires, in terms of their typical enactments in Western and world cultures, can be linked in terms of their assimilative disposition, a tendency to turn the other, or the future, into something known and controlled. The crucial imperatives of desire, pushing us toward contact with the other, carries within it the allure of a kind of fascist control—the allure of a movement of empowerment that exceeds the normal limits of our individual selves, promising something more real, more authentic, more connected, and, above all, more powerful. We, in turn, enact this movement of desire through the exercise, or at least through the simulacra of the exercise, of power. Such enactments allow us to patrol the borders of the identity that is the basis of our sense of empowerment, often turning us toward efforts to ensure requisite levels of purity.

These enactments also would seem to have value as a kind of psychic reward. Both interpersonally and politically, our typical, received notions, representations, and practices of desire promise a kind of closure that underwrites a certain kind of psychic nourishment. At the level of the romantic-sexual encounter, that projection might include, in a certain political-sexual economy, the psychic-physiological payoff of the orgasm, or post-coital bliss, or the eternal love so rare and true. At a political level, that projection might include revolutionary victory and the consolidation of political power. At both levels, a general understanding and practice of desire, understood as a drive toward closure, organizes the behavior of actors.

These two levels of desire, the romantic-sexual interpersonal and the political, often reinforce one another. Critical theory, for example, draws our attention to how romantic-sexual desire is entangled with the socioeconomic structures in which it is enacted. In twentieth- and twenty-first-century societies, our romantic-sexual desire is deployed through advertising in ways that cultivate a substitution of direct relations to other human beings with the promise of commodities, shaping our day-to-day experience of consumer capitalism. We are bombarded with capitalist advertising whose main goal is to shape our desire, not only urging us to buy a particular product, but also cultivating us more generally to be the kinds of people who think that our desires can be fulfilled through the consumption of commodities. A need, or desire, is created through advertising, and then fulfilled, so the story goes, through the consumption of the commodity that will allow you to fulfill that desire. We are disciplined by the stuff that we can access and the constant story of how that access fulfills us, producing us as the malleable population that has become comfortable with its manipulation in a system that provides for our material needs. Through this kind of analysis, indebted to Marx's notion of commodity fetishism, critical theorists like Adorno, Horkheimer, and Marcuse tell a story of how, in a particular way, modern people reproduce an unfree society; participating in the benefit structure of society turns us into the kinds of people who are less likely to critically assess our society and who are thus less likely to fight to change it for the better. To give one example of this disciplining process, Adorno notes how the very speed with which the slogan becomes the governing imperative to consume the latest product foreshadows our immediate embrace of the dictator's latest slogan.[6]

This mechanism of fascist empowerment, which seems to lurk within the very structure of our received understandings of desire, threatens the commitment to freedom and a moral respect for the integrity of the other at which critical thought putatively aims. At an interpersonal level, the fulfillment of our desire, as we have traditionally understood desire, always entails the question of "eating the other,"[7] promising an act of consumption that cuts back against the grain of our moral commitments to respect the other as an end in themselves. As the interpersonal interacts with the broader sociopolitical environment, this violence that seems to inhere in the very structure of desire is amplified in particular ways, sometimes threatening an appropriation of specifically situated others (such as women, people of color) that reproduces the social structures and practices in which those others often occupy subordinate positions.

At the level of a radical politics, such a closure, as the realization of the dream of the revolution's goals, demands an affective commitment to those goals by the revolutionary community. Unfortunately, that very commitment manifests itself through the exclusion, sometimes in brutally explicit ways, of those who deviate from those goals. The commitment that keys the practical success of the revolution threatens the aims of the revolution, encoding an un-freedom into this kind of political success. If utopian aspiration is somehow central to critical theory, regardless of its practitioners' protests, and if utopia is entangled in various questions of desire, across a variety of intersecting political and interpersonal levels, then critical theorists seem to have an inherent responsibility to grapple with how their understandings of desire inform and should inform their (often implicit) utopian commitments. We can frame the utopian task for critical theory by asking for an account of what the affirmative content of a critical desire might look like.

Such an affirmative account is not foreign to the critical-theoretical tradition. Focusing on desire in order to articulate the sweep of his critique on one-dimensional society, in fact, famously animated the work of Herbert Marcuse, who argued that a free society would be one in which humans could fulfill their fullest potentials through a sublimation of their romantic-sexual desire in a post-repressive, social-libidinal context.[8] To consider this point dialectically, desiring differently, in ways that are possible in post-scarcity economies, means overcoming desire's repressive configurations through the affirmative content of negation. Thus, a fundamental component of Marcuse's critical theory is a commitment to imagining a transformation of desire, from its most particular to its most general forms, as that which impels us toward our most profound connections to the world (to human and nonhuman others, but also to the overarching other of the natural environment and to the future that we might bring into being), but which is only realizable as the absence of coercion.

Focusing on the affirmative, utopian content of a critical desire makes sense as a way of organizing one's political orientation for several reasons. First, it marks something that seems to be at the core of our reality, at least for many of us. It is central because it is something at work at the embodied core of who we are: in its presence, an animating pulse that tends to push us across a distance toward something that we want; in its absence, the reference point for a psychic debility. Focusing on desire, as an embodied dimension constitutive of our being, pushes us to become more sophisticated about how we understand ourselves as both products of biological-evolutionary processes and as creatures of socialization.

Second, as a movement toward its object, desire is that movement that draws us into contact with the world that undoes the ways in which we have been alienated. But third, central to the critical theoretical project, particularly in the Marcusean form that we are tracking here, desire can be imagined as having a non-coercive potential. Even if the affirmative face of desire proffered by critical theory could never fully escape the risk of coercion, a theory of its non-coercive potentials might push us to think through the ways in which progressives organize their political self-consciousness of the world that they want to bring into being. In other words, desire is a way of thematizing, and joining together, the critical and utopian underpinnings of their political projects. Marcuse challenges the historically necessary repression of desire, and thus the unhealthy forms that it has taken, but Marcuse is not advocating for uncritically giving full reign to our appetites. In fact, Marcuse argued, in studies such as *One-dimensional Man*, that what seemed like the liberating ethos of the sexual revolution really entailed a "repressive desublimation." The increasingly permissive society that was emerging around him, Marcuse suggests, is one way in which the one-dimensional society reproduces itself, offering an ersatz freedom and sense of meaning that compensates for the pervasive un-freedom and alienation that it generates. That permissiveness has been woven into the patriarchal, heteronormative, and capitalist systems that shape our behavior, contouring our experience within these systems as enactments of a fundamental freedom, as something authentic and natural. Our very empowerment within these disciplining systems, Marcuse (and Foucault, it is worth noting) might argue, entangle us in practices that reproduce the system of un-freedom as a whole. Thus, a sexual relationship that is experienced as freedom for men might be grafted onto scripts about what constitutes an autonomous masculinity or femininity, and the reproduction of that sensibility can have reverberations that tend to reproduce patriarchal and heteronormative systems or patterns of injustice even as it empowers participating actors along other dimensions.

But even though Marcuse is not simply advocating for libertinage, he is not pressing for further repression. Rather, Marcuse imagines a reorganization of society in its totality, which would necessarily entail a radical reconfiguration of how we understand and practice desire. Marcuse imagines this reconfigured desire not in terms of absolute license, but rather as a kind of non-repressive, or post-repressive, sublimation. For Marcuse, it is possible to affirm a society organized around a fulfilling and fulfillable desire that does not reproduce the pathologies of mere sexual license within our patriarchal/ heteronormative inheritances.

In what follows, then, we will build on some of Marcuse's suggestions about what a post-repressive sublimation of desire might look like. We will be particularly interested in thinking through how Le Guin's and Delany's depictions of a romantic-sexual desire is related to the larger sociopolitical environments presented by the two novels, and even though *The Dispossessed* is set on a world of great scarcity that seems utterly out of step with the post-materialist context that Marcuse addresses in his work and which underpins his most optimistic moments about a post-repressive society, the question of desire taken up in his work and in Le Guin's ambiguous utopia provides us a basis for an intertextual reading of their projects. What are the weaknesses and strengths of these different depictions, particularly in relationship to the ideal of post-repressive sublimation suggested by Marcuse? Are there insights from these texts, particularly when read together, that could augment, complicate, confirm, or repudiate either the critical content or affirmative/utopian moment of a critical desire?

Le Guin's *The Dispossessed* and Delany's *Trouble on Triton* offer resources for thinking through the ambiguous implications of how a revolutionary, political desire might be related to the social-anarchic and anarcho-libertarian visions of the social configuration of desire as it is enacted through interpersonal relationships. Read together, in the spirit of how Delany himself sought to imagine and present *Triton*, the two texts can help us see the occlusions of contemporary practices and the social and anarcho-libertarian visions explored in the two novels. As Delany makes clear, both with his subtitle and with subsequent criticism, *Triton* can be understood as a response to *The Dispossessed*. Of particular interest for our investigation, Delany points out what he sees as a series of occlusions related to questions of sexuality in *The Dispossessed*, thus setting up his own treatment of these questions in *Triton* as an effort to better articulate the broadest range of possible desires. Such a reading spurs us to think about both the relationship of the utopian and the dystopian in critical-theoretical science fiction, and, in doing so, frames the possibility of enacting an affirmative critical desire. Le Guin presents a progressive vision of a society in which sexual freedom is imbricated with a broader ethos of community in the context of material scarcity. For the Annareans, sex has supposedly been disconnected from the patriarchal and heteronormative commodification that characterizes the sexual practices of the Ioti and, by extension, the norms of twentieth-century America. This ethos appears to have a binding force for the Annareans, but individual psychologies and behaviors reveal some of the stresses that the Annareans have not been able to smooth over completely.[9] Even to the degree that Annarean romantic-sexual ethos would represent a utopian achievement, Le Guin presents us a world in which romantic-sexual experience is neither fully suppressed nor sublimated. In fact, despite seeing much that is admirable in *The Dispossessed*, Delany is critical of some of the assumptions about desire that continue to circulate in Le Guinn's text that he sees escaping Le Guin's authorial grasp. Delany's *Triton*, as a heterotopian response to Le Guin, however, remains itself, despite its very articulation of radical difference, unable to provide an escape from a subject-centered, heteronormatively defined, and patriarchal notion of desire that continue to pervasively shape late capitalist notions and practices of romantic-sexual desire. The enactment of desire as an escape from its traditional configurations, or at least as an alternative to those configurations, does not provide a magical escape from the scripted possibilities of self-understanding available to the novel's protagonist, Bron.

*The Dispossessed* explores the ambiguous utopian potential for a social anarchic society. In fact, the book has often been published with the subtitle, *An Ambiguous Utopia*, and we will consider some of those ambiguities in what follows. Initially, however, we can locate the utopian center of Le Guin's novel in how that utopia is organized around a reconfiguration of what counts as romantic-sexual desire. The novel is set on the worlds of Urras and its moon, Annarres. The situation on Urras mirrors the Cold War context in which the novel was written, with one nation, A-Io, organized along capitalist lines, and its rival, Thu, organized as an authoritarian-socialist state. The scenes from Urras focus on A-Io, which thus serves as a foil to the scenes on Annarres. Annarres has been settled by the social anarchist followers of its founder, Odo, whose Kropotkinesque vision is centered on an interruption of the possessive desire that characterizes the capitalist and patriarchal practices of possessive desire from which the colonists have escaped. Whereas Annares is founded on the ideals of community ownership, social and economic equality, rotating labor commitments geared toward the good of the community, and sexual freedom between consenting partners, A-Io is characterized by a hyper-capitalist imperative, economic inequality, and sexual commodification. One of the virtues of the novel, in this respect, is its ability to capture the interconnection between the possession of things and sexual desire: in the world of A-Io, in ways that continue to be echoed in twenty-first-century capitalism, romance and sexuality are themselves just another set of commodities. In A-Io, like in our contemporary circumstances, this commodification of romantic-sexual desire is part and parcel of a larger economy of desire that permeates social experience. Le Guin contrasts this commodification of romantic-sexual desire with a deeper, non-coercive kind of commitment possible within the social context of Annarres.

Le Guin, however, is not dismissive of the pull of such a possessive desire, and Annarreans must work to discipline themselves to think and act otherwise. The constant need to reproduce itself in terms of its social-anarchist ideals is central to the ambiguity of this utopia, and Le Guin seems to recognize that the disciplining of individuals, while constitutive of what Annareans consciously seek to affirm, is not without its own price. Those who break with the ideology of community and harmony are marginalized, both formally and socially, as "propertarians," or as engaging in "profiteering." And though the effects of that disciplinary process are meant to eradicate hierarchy, those efforts are never completely successful. These tensions seem to be at the center of the ambiguity of the novel's utopian adventure. Whereas the Iotic experience of a commodified desire both reflects the fecund environment in which it is enacted and alienates the Ioti from a more fully realized relationship with the others of their experience, the Annarean experience of autonomy-in-community chafes against the limits of an embrace of creativity and joyous immediacy.

The adventures of the novel's protagonist, Shevek, reveal these tensions in the utopic experience that Annarres has sought to enact. His efforts to think freely in pursuit of a General Temporal Theory are met with charges of egoizing and misrepresentation by his jealous superior, Sabul. And though Sabul is clearly guilty of the egoizing that he projects onto Shevek, the question that he raises about Shevek's own motives cannot be entirely dismissed. Indeed, as we follow Shevek's efforts and desire to develop and publish his theory, we can frame the question of his motivation in terms of the degree to which any socially motivated effort to contribute to the overall greater good depends upon an ineradicable moment of narcissism. That narcissism, as a moment in the drive to develop the coherence of his theory, as his depiction of the reality that others cannot see, drives Shevek to pursue its completion on Urras, and that journey into the capitalist, patriarchal-heteronormative world of A-Io is crucial in the maturation of his own critical perspective.

Only in going through that process is he able to work through the lingering notions of ownership that remain a part of Annarean consciousness as a necessary prelude to realizing the role of his own "propertarian" desire in relation to his communitarian sensibilities, ultimately impelling his efforts to share his insights with everybody rather than seeing them coopted by particular interests. His encounter with the differing norms of sexual conduct that differentiate Annaresti and Ioti experience throw the experience of Annaresti desire into relief, revealing patterns of male dominance in the contexts of interpersonal stress from which the Annaresti have not escaped.

For the Ioti, material objects, whether owned (or shunned), are entwined with the imperatives of sexual desire. Shevek seems to sense this in the physical objects such as the furniture of the Iotic ship that transports him to Urras and the linen of the bed in which he sleeps. But it is also manifested in the sexualization of women, who are reduced to yet another commodity within the broader heteronormative-capitalist economy of A-Io.[10] This depiction of the Ioti, however, not only functions as an implied critique of the predominant sexual economy of twentieth-century Western societies, it also functions to raise questions about how those lingering practices have remained a submerged dimension of Annaresti desire. The vestiges of the Annarestis' proprietary desire, for example, is captured by Shevek's encounter with Vea.[11] Charitably, that encounter could be understood as Shevek's misreading of Vea's flirtations in the foreign context of A-Io norms governing sexual relationships, but it can also point to how the imperative of romantic-sexual desire enacts a drive to closure that violates his moral obligation to the other, here resulting in Vea being sexually assaulted.

Though Delany finds the encounter between Vea and Shevek as ridiculous (shouldn't Shevek simply be laughing at her cock teasing performance?[12]), he has found in *The Dispossessed* an important platform for developing his own critical-theoretical approach to the questions of utopia and desire. He has called it "a rich and wondrous tale." Importantly, though, he frames that praise by calling it "a boy's book: a book to make boys begin to think and think seriously about a whole range of questions, from the structure of society to the working of their own sexuality."[13] That importance, he elaborates, is in the context of what he identifies as our "filiarchical society—a society ruled almost entirely by sons—by *very* young men."[14] "Certainly boys—especially white heterosexual boys—are the most privileged creatures in the Western social hierarchy. They are forgiven *almost* everything in life—and *are* forgiven everything in art. . . . There's still a great deal to be said for a good boy's book. And for a woman's writing it."[15] That it is a boy's book is not incidental to Delany's critique of *The Dispossessed*; it is precisely the text's romantic-sexual depictions that demand the most critical attention. Thus, Delany signals his concern about the uneven treatment given to Shevek's sexual history compared to the discussions of Bedap (with whom Shevek had a youthful homosexual affair) and Takver, his long-term heterosexual partner. That unevenness, Delany laments, has the effect of reinforcing certain masculine stereotypes about what counts as desire while somewhat erasing the different kinds of desire experienced by, respectively, a homosexual male and a woman. This kind of occlusion, Delany suggests, oversimplifies the full range of what desire might mean. Returning to the scene of Shevek's (at the very least) cringe-worthy encounter with Vea at the party, Delany sees it revealing that, in any given social milieu, "men must learn to respond" to what counts as erotic. "That learning process involves battling through it to success (i.e., getting laid) a number of times, at first impelled only by curiosity and any number of social supports that reinforce in the heterosexual male 'this is the thing to do.'"[16] Taken together, this range of observations supports Delany's general point that different desires "must be learned, and learned differently, in different cultures"[17] (and, we might add, learned differently as they relate to different subject positions).

Delany has sought to leverage *The Dispossessed*[18] as a way of articulating his commentary on a range of topics: the inherent critical dimensions of science fiction, on the limits of utopian/dystopian science fiction, the relationship between the utopian and the heterotopian, and the role that romantic-sexual desire might play in utopian and heterotopian imaginations. But, what, precisely, are we getting at when we deploy this distinction between the utopian and the heterotopian? Both the utopian and heterotopian, according to Foucault, are spaces "that have the curious property of being connected to all the other emplacements, but in such a way that they suspend, neutralize, or reverse the set of relations that are designated, reflected or represented."[19]

"Utopias," however, "are emplacements having no real place. They are emplacements that maintain a general relation of direct or inverse analogy with the real space of society. They are society perfected or the reverse of society, but in any case these utopias are spaces that are fundamentally and essentially unreal."[20] Foucault, suggests, however, that utopian spaces are complemented by the analytically distinct notion of heterotopias: "There are also, probably in every culture, in every civilization, real places, actual places, places that are designed into the very institution of society, which are sorts of actually realized utopias in which the real emplacements, all the other real emplacements that be found with the culture are, at the same time, represented, contested, and reversed, sorts of places that are outside all places, although they are actually localizable."[21]

Whereas, however, the utopian, strictly understood as the utopian, is experienced in our circumstances as a lack, as a distance to be overcome in some indeterminate future, the heterotopian is an interruption in the now, emerging in the interstices of the productive efficiencies of societies. In those gaps, desire is experienced as part of the flow of a now, enacting a kind of freedom defined by its very proximity to defining logics from which it emerges and to which it enacts creative alternatives. If nothing else, the heterotopian points to examples of how living differently happens in a now, in spaces that resist the application of force through enactments of what such a force seeks to repress. The heterotopian reflects a tactical utopianism enacting an insistence on freedom. In styling Triton as an ambiguous heterotopia, Delany stages a consideration of the relationship between the utopian and the heterotopian: their commonalities and differences as ways of thinking and enacting different kinds of worlds, something that is a matter both for how we might orient ourselves to the real world in which we find ourselves enmeshed, but also in terms of how to write about desire, difference, and sexuality as they are rearticulated within radically different sociopolitical realities. Thus, to choose a heterotopian orientation enjoins the question of utopia that haunts the critical-theoretical/SF genre. We might say that, in the encounter of these texts, Delany is straining toward a heterotopian science fiction, which, at least in those moments, is an argument that science fiction is inherently heterotopian.

In his essay, "To Read *The Dispossessed*," for example, Delany develops the inherent critical ethos of science fiction by way of an example of the heterotopian emplacement of desire, drawn from his own memory. Delany recalls the different spaces of his school and his youth summer camp between the time he was eight and fourteen years old. At school, the separation of the sexes was physically policed by seating arrangements, dress codes, line formations, and the like, but these arrangements were reproduced by informal means as well, such as lunch-room seating norms. The policing of the separation of the sexes was in some ways internalized, spilling over into even the un-policed activities of the students.

Summer camp, however, was a much different space, a somewhere-else in which the normal rules of separating the sexes were suspended, opening up new economies of meaning. Though the boys and girls slept in different rooms, almost all of the activities, including sports, were coed. Everyone wore jeans. Relations between sexes that were impossible at school blossomed; some of them even became sexual. Somehow, "in the four-and-a-half hour bus trip from New York City to Phoenecia," "all traces of the natural antipathy between the sexes" vanished. The campers were aware of this difference between camp and school; the camp was, in this sense at least, a heterotopian space. Delany deploys this example in order to comment on the critical space created by science fiction. In a work of science fiction, "the naturalness and immutability of such natural and immutable behavior" to which a passage might refer "is open to question and analysis."[22] Or, as he underlines this point, "Mundane fiction can get by with a clear and accurate portrayal of behavior *that* occurs *merely* because it occurs. Science fiction cannot."[23]

Ultimately, though, the camp director's insistence on having each week's social dance event despite its unpopularity absorbs some of that heterotopian energy. The freedom of the campers, nonetheless, might suggest a kind of political energy, and it is possible to imagine that freedom proliferating across enough sites to effect more profound, structural-institutional change. The insistence of the camp directors reminds us, though, that the temporal interruption of the heterotopian can be short-lived, and perhaps ineffectual, perhaps missing the political in profoundly important ways. *Triton* seems to highlight this missing of the political; the enactment of all the micro-theatre of manners provides little in a way of a direct political consciousness, the moon dwellers remaining blissfully unaware of the geopolitical realities that will literally shake their world.

Thus, despite their irruptive power, to what degree is a celebration of or maximization of heterotopian spaces related to our utopian aspirations? What role do heterotopian experiments, living spaces, and enactments play in transforming the repressive structures that shape action in a society? When we think of Triton, does the radical libertarian possibilities of the society mark an improvement of society (the society in which Delany was writing, the society in which we live), or does it exacerbate the alienated atomism that seems to characterize important dimensions of late-capitalist society?

One might argue that for the heterotopian to fully operate as the political that such practices must be enacted dialectically in reference to the affirmative content of a utopian aspiration. On the one hand, the heterotopian interrupts the utopian as a delayed realization of what one seeks, desire understood primarily as a lack. Whereas the utopian is always caught up in an act of deferral, the heterotopian is plural and enacted here, now, within the flows and interstices of capital and tradition. Nonetheless, Triton's heterotopian enactment of desire remains, by itself, incomplete without a utopian complement that organizes an ideal of romantic-sexual desire. The struggle for actualization through the enactment of such a desire often remains dysfunctional. We see this dysfunction in Mad Mike's threatening, stalking behavior outside the woman's co-op;[24] the failure of the Circle commune[25]; but particularly Bron's inability to realize the other-regarding behavior, as exemplified in his deplorable treatment of the Spike and Audri or in his failure to escape the masculine narcissism by becoming a woman, that could be the key to a more mature self-realization.

So, perhaps what is needed in society is not merely utopian romantic-sexual aspiration nor heterotopian enactments of desire, but rather what we might call practices of dialectical affirmation. The heterotopian structure of Triton is specifically organized around the maximization of sexual freedom in the context of one's particular needs and turn-ons, in which society has self-organized into a wide range of spaces of encounter and living arrangements for the widest array of compatible romantic-sexual preferences. Against the backdrop of sexual repression, the sexual freedom of Triton undoubtedly has a utopian appeal, but it cannot promise an overcoming of the trials and tribulations of one's particular love life. In fact, all of the choices provided by his society does not provide Bron with any power over whether or not someone who he wants to like him will do so. Nor does the sexual freedom of Triton provide an escape from the well-worn tropes of masculine dysfunction that Bron thinks he might escape by becoming a woman.[26] The inhabitants of Triton's heterotopia must struggle with the rough and tumble of their own relationship-related psychic adventures, and their efforts to find what counts as the right way to live within the structures of romantic-sexual possibility are no less challenging than ours.

There is, then, in regard to our utopian aspirations, no final solution to the problematic of romantic-sexual desire understood as the control or the assimilation of the other, perhaps no final sociopolitical form that will overcome these diremptions of fulfillment. Marcuse's sketch of an affirmative aesthetic, as a particular enactment of desire, is thus also attractive in that it does not imagine itself or the revolutionary practice with which it is enjoined in terms of an end point in which the revolution and thus human happiness would be fully realized. Rather, he calls the struggle for such an affirmation as a "permanent feature of revolutionary practice." For Marcuse,

> The notion of the continuation of the class struggle under socialism expresses this point . . . [but] The permanent transformation of society under the principle of freedom is necessitated not only by the continued existence of class interests. The institutions of a socialist society, even in their democratic form, could never resolve all the conflicts between the universal and the particular, between human beings and nature, between individual and individual. Socialism does not and cannot liberate Eros from Thanatos. Here is the limit which drives the revolution beyond any accomplished stage of freedom; it is the struggle for the impossible, against the unconquerable whose domain can perhaps nevertheless be reduced.[27]

The utopia that we struggle to realize is not, from Marcuse's perspective, nor in the worlds created by Le Guin and Delany, a static point of arrival. The revolution, in this sense, is never finished, and the potential for a perfectly realized romantic-sexual desire, that perfect moment of pure presence when "time drops away between us" remains beyond our final grasp. By traveling through our desire, though, we find ourselves thrown, again, into the moment of a utopian reckoning.

Our encounter with these two texts from Le Guin and Delany suggests some of the challenges that we might face in our efforts to build a society around the post-repressive sublimation of desire. To the degree that the philosophical orientation of Odo and her Annarean descendants realize this affirmative enactment of desire, we are reminded that this desire threatens some of those traits that we would connect to a noble character or a fully lived life. Even in an anti-propertarian, anti-egoizing environment, individuals continue to suffer from loneliness, to act out in order to gain recognition. The achievement of a social-anarchist society has not solved those challenges. Furthermore, in such a society, creativity is circumscribed, and art and science stagnate.

What is difficult to calculate is the degree to which these effects are exacerbated by the scarcity conditions in which the Annareans struggle to survive. Marcuse has followed Marx in insisting that a society organized around the sublimation of post-repressive desire can only be achieved in a society that has solved problems of scarcity, in what has been called a post-materialist environment. How, one might ask, would one experience interpersonal relationships in a world where the struggle for existence was not foregrounded the way that it is on Annarres, where desire must often be deferred in the Annarean's fight for survival. For Annareans, the experience of sex and the understanding of their individual place in the cosmos takes on the colors of gray justice. The sex seems either mentioned as an afterthought (as if it were merely an effort to release a tension) or in soul-connecting terms; so often sexual intimacy must be deferred because of the demands of the greater social good. Desire does not run electric through Annarean society or represent, in its most consistent depiction, an affirmation of life as joy. The reinforcing connection between the romantic-sexual freedom that is part of their ethos and their faith in the world that they seek to sustain is central to how Annarean society has necessarily reproduced itself under conditions of scarcity. The necessary sublimation of that desire, though, has been something muted, or subordinated, a kind of repression that underwrites the work necessary to build and preserve society.

The context for the sexual freedom on Triton is quite different. Scarcity is not an issue; gratification does not need to be delayed. Nonetheless, the heterotopian utopia sketched by Delany does not quite get at the ideal of the post-repressive organization of society. While a near absolute negative freedom seems to practically attain, that freedom seems to be a dead end. Individuals, and groups of individuals, remain libidinally disconnected from any greater whole. Unlike the Annareans, for whom a consciousness and commitment to their entire world is ever present, those who live on Triton are, for the most part, blissfully unaware of the broader interplanetary political and military contexts in which they pursue their own psychological fulfillment, an oblivion that is brought into shocking relief by the breakout of war. Delany's depiction of Bron's preoccupations, though only a partial accounting of the situation on Triton and the rest of the solar system, illustrates something closely akin to Marcuse's formulation of "repressive desublimation" and how the libidinal ethos to which it gives rise is related to the production of acquiescent subjects who seem typically unable to connect the rough and tumble of their lives to the greater good of a community.

Taken together, reading these two texts against Marcuse's affirmative notion of a post-repressive sublimation of desire allows us to offer a more nuanced response to the question of utopia. The utopian and the heterotopian, one might argue, are both necessary orientations for a progressive critical theory that seeks to address the question of how to get there from here. This may lead to an assessment of how the sketching of an (ambiguous) utopian perspective forms an index of how we live, not only in terms of how we work toward our utopian goals, but also in the practices of our everyday lives, in the ways in which different folks seek to live rightly within the context of the predominant thought and practice(s) of heteronormative, patriarchal capitalism. The narratives of desire that we draw from science fiction, particularly if we further explore the meta-text of that sprawling genre, offers ways from thinking outside of the illusion of the eternal present promulgated by capitalist ideology. Science fiction, in ways that mirror the role Benjamin assigned to historical interpretation, create what we might think of as heterotemporal thought experiments, opening up spaces outside of the prevailing logics and practices of neoliberal capitalism organized along heteronormative and patriarchal terms.

The triangulated reading of Le Guin, Delany, and Marcuse on the question of desire—on the relationship between interpersonal, sexual-romantic love and its sublimated sociopolitical manifestations—reveals that the utopian and the heterotopian are not entirely distinct. Utopian articulations, in fact, can themselves be thought of as kinds of heterotopian enactments. When we read a great novel, or are enraptured by a great musical performance, we are drawn into a world where specific economies of pleasure and meaning are at the heart of that piece's constructed reality. We are withdrawn, one might argue, into a space of heterotopian enactment. At the same time, all heterotopian spaces of enactment are the realization of utopian impulses, at least in the sense of being spaces where different affirmative economies of meaning shape self-understandings and interactions, providing spaces where we might affirmatively experience ourselves and others in profoundly different ways. Noticing these interlinking logics of the utopian and heterotopian is suggestive for how we move forward in becoming who we are, pushing us to consider particular tactics and strategies in our efforts to realize the world that we want to bring into being.

But what can perhaps be gleaned from these novels rather than any final solution about the role of desire in our utopian/heterotopian imaginations is that desire, in its tracing of a movement toward the consummation of the other, engenders the question of ethics. In every revolution, the realization of a critical desire, as the joyous affirmation of who we might become and as the encounter with the others with whom we live and toward whom we have ethical obligations, pulls us forward to a better world even as it disrupts its own movement toward fulfillment. Our encounter with Le Guin's and Delany's ambiguous utopia and heterotopia reflects, in this respect, the ongoing legacy of a living critical theory.

## NOTES

1. For a brief discussion of this distaste, see Lyman Tower Sargent, *Utopianism: A Very Short Introduction* (Oxford: Oxford University Press, 2010), 103–8.
2. For an elaboration of this reticence, particularly in terms of retrieving the lost affirmative potential of reason in the work of Jürgen Habermas, see Stephen K. White, *Political Theory and Postmodernism* (Cambridge: Cambridge University Press, 1991), as well as Jürgen Habermas, *The Philosophical Discourses of Modernity: Twelve Lectures*, trans. Frederick G. Lawrence (Boston: The MIT Press, 1990).
3. James Bohman, "Critical Theory," *The Stanford Encyclopedia of Philosophy* (Fall 2016 Edition), Edward N. Zalta (ed.), https://plato.stanford.edu/archives/fall2016/entries/critical-theory/.
4. Of course, the question of the role that desire plays in the functioning, reproduction, and possible transformation of society, at both the interrelated levels of subjective-interpersonal desire and at the level of the larger political configuration's self-understanding, has often been a central concern of utopian thinking and critical theory (taken in its widest possible sense). At the beginnings of the Western political theoretical tradition, for example, the role of the appetites and the function of desire are central to Plato's efforts to articulate "the ideal city in speech." There, the senses and the desires that they produce are subordinated to the dictates of reason working in tandem with a disciplining spirit that maintains a harmonious whole. Nonetheless, the desires of the citizenry are not extirpated; the sexual needs of each class are recognized and accounted for in the sketch of this ideal city. See Paul M. Williams, "Eros in the *Republic*," in *The Cambridge Companion to Plato's* Republic, ed. G. R. F. Ferrari (New York: Cambridge University Press, 2007), 208–31.
5. The encounter between these related idioms—science fiction and political theory—both chasten and sharpen the utopianism that ineluctably, if sometimes tacitly, animates the enterprise of critical theory. We can proceed by thinking of critical theory and science fiction, despite their idiomatic differences, the differences in the realities of their production, etc., as an inter-articulated genre, one in which both science/speculative fiction and critical theory can be read together productively.
6. "The blind and rapidly spreading repetition of the designated words links advertising to the totalitarian regime." Max Horkheimer and Theordor Adorno, *Dialectic of Enlightenment: Philosophical Fragments*, ed. Guzelin Schmid Noerr, trans. Edmund Jephcott (Stanford: Stanford University Press, 2002), 134–35.
7. See, for example, bell hooks, "Eating the Other," in *Black Looks: Race and Representation* (Boston: South End Press, 1992), 21–39, and Jacques Derrida, "'Eating Well,' or the Calculation of the Subject," in *Points . . . Interviews, 1974–1994* (Stanford, CA: Stanford University Press, 1995), 255–87.

8. Herbert Marcuse, *Eros and Civilization: A Philosophical Inquiry into Freud* (Boston: Beacon Press, 1966).
9. Ursula K. Le Guin, *The Dispossessed: An Ambiguous Utopia* (New York: Harper Paperbacks, 1991).
10. Neil Easterbrook. "State, Heterotopia: The Political Imagination in Heinlein, Le Guin, and Delany," in *Political Science Fiction*, ed. Donald M. Hassler and Clyde Wilcox (Columbia: University of South Carolina Press, 1997), 56
11. Ursula K. Le Guin, *The Dispossessed*, 230–31.
12. Samuel R. Delany, "To Read *The Dispossessed*," in *The Jewel-Hinged Jaw* (Wesleyan University Press: Middletown CT, 2009), 116–17.
13. Samuel R. Delany, "On Triton and Other Matters: An Interview with Samuel R. Delany," *Science Fiction Studies* (Number 52: Volume 17, Part 3, November 1990), https://www.depauw.edu/sfs/interviews/delany52interview.htm.
14. Ibid.
15. Ibid.
16. Delany, "To Read *The Dispossessed*," 117.
17. Ibid., 115.
18. Here, we might note, that an entire ethics of reading, or one might say an ethics of our desire for the textual object, is at stake in how Delany seeks to productively appropriate Le Guin's text.
19. Michel Foucault, "Different Spaces," in *Michel Foucault: Aesthetics, Method, and Epistemology*, trans. Robert Hurley (New York: The New Press, 1998), 178.
20. Ibid.
21. Ibid.
22. Delany, "To Read *The Dispossessed*," 128.
23. Ibid.
24. Samuel R. Delany, *Trouble on Triton* (Middletown, CT: Wesleyan University Press, 1976), 206–10.
25. Ibid., 299–300.
26. See, for example, the ironic, even quite funny conclusion to the main body of the novel, where Bron asserts, "I never lied when I was a man," asking, "Were women just less truthful than men?" Of course, as his stalking obsession with the Spike suggests, his entire sense of masculinity could only maintain its coherence in terms of ongoing practices of self-deception. Delany, *Triton*, 276–77.
27. Herbert Marcuse, *The Aesthetic Dimension: Toward a Critique of Marxist Aesthetics* (Boston: Beacon Press, 1978), 71–72.

# BIBLIOGRAPHY

Bohman, James, "Critical Theory," *The Stanford Encyclopedia of Philosophy* (Fall 2016 Edition), Edward N. Zalta (ed.), accessed March 15, 2020, https://plato.stanford.edu/archives/fall2016/entries/critical-theory/.

Delany, Samuel R. "On Triton and Other Matters: An Interview with Samuel R. Delany," *Science Fiction Studies* 17, no. 52, part 3 (November 1990).

———. "To Read *The Dispossessed*." In *The Jewel-Hinged Jaw*. Wesleyan University Press: Middletown CT, 2009.

Delany, Samuel R. *Trouble on Triton*. Middletown, CT: Wesleyan University Press, 1976.

Derrida, Jacques. "'Eating Well,' or the Calculation of the Subject." In *Points . . . Interviews, 1974–1994*, 255–87. Stanford, CA: Stanford University Press, 1995.

Easterbrook, Neil. "State, Heterotopia: The Political Imagination in Heinlein, Le Guin, and Delany." In *Political Science Fiction*, edited by Donald M. Hassler and Clyde Wilcox, 43–75. Columbia: University of South Carolina Press, 1997.

Foucault, Michel. "Different Spaces." In *Michel Foucault: Aesthetics, Method, and Epistemology*, translated by Robert Hurley. New York: The New Press, 1998.

Habermas, Jürgen. *The Philosophical Discourses of Modernity: Twelve Lectures*. Translated by Frederick G. Lawrence. 1990.

Horkheimer, Max, and Theordor Adorno, *Dialectic of Enlightenment: Philosophical Fragments*. Edited by Guzelin Schmid Noerr. Translated by Edmund Jephcott. Stanford, CA: Stanford University Press, 2002.

hooks, bell. "Eating the Other." In *Black Looks: Race and Representation*, 21–39. Boston: South End Press, 1992.

Le Guin, Ursula K. *The Dispossessed: An Ambiguous Utopia*. New York: Harper Paperbacks, 1991.

Marcuse, Herbert. *Eros and Civilization: A Philosophical Inquiry into Freud*. Boston: Beacon Press, 1966.

Marcuse, Herbert. *The Aesthetic Dimension: Toward a Critique of Marxist Aesthetics*. Boston: Beacon Press, 1978.

Sargent, Lyman Tower. *Utopianism: A Very Short Introduction*. Oxford: Oxford University Press, 2010.

White, Stephen K. *Political Theory and Postmodernism*. Cambridge University Press, 1991.

Williams, Paul M. "Eros in the *Republic*." In *The Cambridge Companion to Plato's* Republic, edited by G. R. F. Ferrari. New York: Cambridge University Press, 2007.

*Chapter Eight*

# Politicizing Cities in China Miéville's Speculative Fiction

## Andrew Uzendoski and Caleb Gallemore

Between 1998, when he published his first novel, *King Rat*, and 2010, when he published *Kraken*, China Miéville produced seven novels, a book of short stories, and an academic monograph on international law. In the process, he won the Hugo Award, multiple Arthur C. Clarke and Locus Awards, the British Fantasy Award, and the World Fantasy Award. An eighth novel, *Embassytown* was published in 2011, winning the Locus Award. Since then, Miéville has published a further novel, two novellas, another book of short stories, numerous essays, and a nonfiction work on the Russian Revolution.

Critics often remark on the outsize place Miéville affords cities in contrast to much of the foregoing fantasy tradition.[1] In a 2002 interview discussing his breakout novel *Perdido Street Station*, he characterized the book as an "anti-Tolkien" fantasy, messy and urban, rather than bucolic and rural.[2] *Perdido Street Station* blurs fantasy and science fiction's conventional rural-urban binary.[3] For Miéville, urban spaces have "endlessly [. . .] fecund and inspiring" fantastical qualities: excess interaction and hybridity that is "less regimented and less planned" than might appear.[4]

Miéville's Marxist social analysis clearly informs his fiction.[5] Freedman[6] argues Miéville's "choice of an alternative-world rather than a real-world environment [. . .] cannot be understood apart from the singularly inhospitable circumstances for socialist revolution" in the world in which he writes. Yet while he often depicts revolutionary movements, generally concludes without, or at least prior to, successful revolutionary transformation. Furthermore, it is actually in novels set in London where Miéville is most optimistic. Miéville's urban narratives investigate politicization in contemporary urban contexts, grappling with how social relations shape politicization rather than roadmapping revolution.

In Miéville's work, politicization emerges from cities' "undersides." London is not just a backdrop for characters' politically charged transformations; it catalyzes them. Saul, *King Rat*'s protagonist, realizes that his abhuman ability to scale walls, vault rooftops, and digest refuse suberts the "conspiracy of architecture, the tyranny by which the buildings that men and women had built had taken control of them, circumscribed their relations, confined their movements."[7] *Kraken*'s protagonist, Billy, similarly becomes enmeshed in an underworld of magical and uncanny London subcultures, a "tilework of fiefdoms, theocratic duchies, zones and spheres of influences, over each of which some local despot, some criminal pope, sat watch."[8] As in these two examples, Miéville's urban spaces often shape protagonists' political consciousness and, occasionally, emerge as protagonists themselves.

Miéville once characterized himself as "a city creature." Like many urban residents populating his fiction, Miéville's city shaped him. "I have lived in cities pretty much all my life," he explained. "I find them endlessly kind of fecund and inspiring."[9] He went on to reflect on his own city: [I]f you live in London, it isn't that you get on with the business of living in London. Living in London is a thing. [. . .] [I]t intrudes into your life, it has an agency in a very direct way. [. . .] this intrusion can manifest in the city becoming a character. I think that is a short-hand for having a sort of intrusive agency, which I think is how we experience cities."[10]

Cities' "intrusive agency" informs Miéville's worldview as a writer and political thinker, but this force also molds his urbanite protagonists. Cities instigate Miéville's plots, disrupting daily routines, social interactions, and ways of being. Generally, characters in Miéville's speculative fiction only become politicized protagonists because their city throws them into novel social relations, shaping their character arcs. This emphasis on how transformed social relations can spark politicization helps explain why Miéville's London Trilogy problematizes romantic, individual heroes.

With dozens of articles and monographs offering various readings of most of Miéville's work at a finer level of detail than we undertake, our goal is less to offer suggestions for productive readings of individual texts than to take those texts as material "good to think with"[11] for considering politicization in cities. Our argument is less about what is *really there* in the texts than what can be done with them. To do this, we read not only Miéville's fictional works, but also many of his nonfictional and critical writings, as well as over 100 print, audio, and video interviews, catalogued in the online appendix (which we make available at https://tinyurl.com/MievilleTable) that accompanies this chapter.

## READING POLITICIZATION IN MIÉVILLE'S CITIES

In a 2003 interview, Miéville explained that he would often "try to structure [his] books around the contingency of agency [. . .] about people in a messy reality genuinely struggling to do their best morally and politically."[12] He revisited the theme in a 2017 interview, discussing his work on the Russian Revolution: "1917 was a year in which, repeatedly, across an enormous empire, millions of people from all kinds of different ethnicities and backgrounds [. . .] suddenly insist that they have the right to have some control over their own lives and try to dispense with this system that has told them they don't have that. That sense of agency and insurgent dignity is incredibly inspiring to me."[13] Throughout his oeuvre, Miéville explores how cities can reshape citizens as political agents, despite their potential to trap and constrain. Particular to his London Trilogy is his focus on the moment London residents first imagine alternative political possibilities for reorganizing their city. In each London novel the city's intrusive agency transforms Miéville's protagonists at a similar stage in their character development: the awakening of a political consciousness.

Miéville's antagonists try to arrest change, to systematize the totality. His protagonists reject totalization and preordination, embracing contingency. In *Un Lun Dun*, for example, Deeba, the chief protagonist, subverts traditional narrative tropes and other characters' expectations.[14] She defies a prophecy that casts her friend, rather than herself, as the "chosen one" and then short-circuits the quest narrative, bypassing a series of quest items and collecting only the one she needs to confront the final boss.[15] In case there is any doubt about the Marxist resonances here, the chapter in which Deeba chooses to deviate from prophecy is entitled "Skipping Historical Stages."

Deeba is not alone; Miéville's protagonists' politicization often emerges from contingent circumstances.[16] Miéville's coalitions are always diverse; for example, Deeba defends the city with the support of numerous allies including a ghost, a bus driver, a sentient book, a headless man (who is guided by a bird), a politicized trio of living, self-aware words, a human pincushion, and a rebellious, recycled umbrella. Miéville's cities act as crucibles for social relations, whether the powers that be want them to or not. Cities inevitably produce spaces of hybridization, cross-fertilization, and interaction. They can throw people together in unusual ways, reconfiguring social relations and providing opportunities for individuals and groups to take hold of their own political way of being. These stories challenge us to consider how we might create more emancipatory social spaces.

Each protagonist in Miéville's London Trilogy is transformed by social, political and economic relations particular to urban spaces. In *King Rat*, the protagonist is an aimless young man with no professional or political identity. Saul Garamond resents his father's political teachings and awkward social behavior, consistently rejecting his parent's Marxist tutelage. He only becomes a political agent once forced to flee his apartment and live in London's labyrinthine sewer system. Deeba, the hero of *Un Lun Dun,* is a twelve-year-old girl; like Saul, she has no discernable political convictions and, clearly, is not employed in the formal economy of the city. However, after discovering a secret passageway beneath London leading to UnLonDon—an uncanny version, or "abcity," of the British capital—Deeba confronts political crises threatening both cities. As she explores the abcity's diverse, magical neighborhoods, Deeba becomes the leader of an UnLondonian political revolt, uniting the abcity's factions and cultural enclaves. Billy Harlow, the protagonist of *Kraken,* the third book in Miéville's London Trilogy, is a researcher and curator at the Darwin Centre at the British Museum of Natural History. Billy has an identifiable profession and therefore formally participates in global capitalism, but, like Miéville's other two London protagonists, he begins the novel apolitical. Only after he encounters various groups on (and below) London's streets does Billy, like Saul and Deeba, become a political hero.

Miéville begins *King Rat* with an elaborate description of elevated passenger trains entering London at dusk, mimicking sea narratives:

> The trains that enter London arrive like ships sailing across the roofs. They pass between towers jutting into the sky like long-necked sea beasts and the great gas-cylinders wallowing in dirty scrub like whales. In the depths below are lines of small shops and obscure franchises, cafés with peeling paint and businesses tucked into the arches over which the trains pass. The colors and curves of graffiti mark every wall. Top floor windows pass by so close that passengers can peer inside, into small bare offices and store cupboards. They can make out the contours of trade calendars and pin-ups on the walls.[17]

In this opening passage, Miéville portrays the movement from rural and suburban England to urban London as a perilous journey. "Long-necked sea beasts" loom over the passengers, "great gas-cylinders" wallow like whales alongside their train, concealed businesses and forgotten cafés hide in the architecture below—and graffiti envelops it all. In *King Rat*'s urban imaginary, passengers disembarking at King's Cross railway station are explorers on a quest. This move inverts the British aesthetic philosophy of the sublime, developed in the eighteenth century by writers such as Edmund Burke and David Hume, and further popularized by the poetry of William Wordsworth, Percy Shelley, and John Keats, who found the sublime in nature. Rather than requiring his characters to *leave* the city to experience transcendental awe or grandeur, Miéville's characters encounter the sublime *within* the city.

Analyzing *King Rat,* Carl Freedman[18] characterizes this hallmark of Miéville's aesthetic as the urban sublime: "the awe-inspiring (if frequently unbeautiful) grandeur of the modern capitalist metropolis, in all its unfathomable heterogeneity and hybridity." Interpreting Miéville's awesome depiction of London as an attempt to "incorporate the specifically political sublimity of Marxism," Freedman searches Miéville's urban landscape for representations of the sublime that represent economic, political, and social systems associated with Marxist programs. While not opposing this approach, we suggest an alternative reading that is more intimate and less systematic than realizing an alternative political model for organizing property and labor in London.

We read Miéville's political subject as neither an atomic individual, nor the overarching political system, but rather individuals as they emerge from complex social and economic relations. Miéville invokes the sublime, all those complex causes at the edge of our comprehension, to represent how urban contexts inevitably shape their residents' political identities. In his 2014 interview with *Extrapolation*, Miéville elaborated on how his aesthetic choices reflect political and social dynamics particular to cities in the twenty-first century.[19] In response to the "massive growth in a particular highly bureaucratized urban planning" throughout London, especially apparent in the redevelopment of East London neighborhoods hosting athletic facilities built for the 2012 Olympics, he argued that artists working in the city were developing new methods and forms to express agency and resist the totalization of privatization and gentrification.

As demonstrated in this chapter, Miéville participates in this artistic process in his London novels. Seeking local manifestations of "new aesthetic representations of a kind of new form of the urban uncanny," he celebrates the ways urban communities—and cities—almost supernatural ability to adapt to changes in the world economic system and evade totalization.[20] "I do think that a sense of the unclaimable nature of cities in general will always pull against this regulatory divide," Miéville argues. "There is a spirit of the unplanned."[21]

## LONDON IN *KING RAT*

Saul Garamond, *King Rat*'s main protagonist, enters the novel as a passenger on one of many trains traveling to King's Cross. He is returning home from a camping trip in Suffolk, on the English coast. To describe Saul, Miéville transposes his protagonist's face onto the city's skyline. Saul stares at a reflection of himself in one of the train's windows, the reader seeing through his eyes. Miéville writes: "The light in the carriage had made [the windows] mirrors, and [Saul] stared at himself, his heavy face. Beyond his face was a layer of brick, dimly visible, and beyond that the cellars of the houses that rose like cliffs on either side."[22] In this multilayered portrait Saul sees himself as a product of urban symbiosis, and sees the urban symbiosis acting through him. The city's figurative sea beasts and wallowing whales emerge from an assemblage of residents, skyscrapers, trains, bricks, and graffiti. Saul is no different.

The transparency of Saul's face as reflected on a carriage window also symbolizes his passivity. Miéville initially characterizes his protagonist as an apathetic, apolitical twenty-something. He contrasts Saul to his father, who "was trying to make sense of his bright, educated son letting life come to him rather than wrestling what he wanted from it. He understood only that his son was dissatisfied." Saul's father was especially "disappointed at his [son's] laziness and his lack of political fervor."[23] In a defining moment, Saul's father gave him a copy of *What is to be Done?*, Vladimir Lenin's seminal Marxist text, on Christmas day. The book is especially meaningful to Saul's father, and he hoped Lenin's ideas, dramatically captured in a "leather-bound edition illustrated with stark woodcuts of toiling workers," would facilitate his son's politicization. *What is to be Done?*, fittingly, speculates about how to politicize the working class. Arguing they will not inevitably assume a political identity without guidance from the bourgeois intelligentsia, Lenin proposes politicizing workers throughout Russia with Millenarian rhetoric. Perhaps too on the nose, the gift does not inspire Saul but simply pushes the two further apart: "his father and he would never really be able to talk together again."[24]

*King Rat* and *What Is to Be Done?* have similar concerns: how to shape apolitical persons into political agents. And while Lenin's words fail to motivate Saul to assume a political role in his city, by the end of the novel he does in fact become a political leader. After an unpredictable series of events, Saul fulfills his father's wish for politicization, if not Marxist revolution: at the end of the novel, Saul literally becomes a king and enacts transformative democratic reforms. In *What Is to Be Done?* Lenin was particularly concerned with building political movements when workers experience "consciousness in an embryonic form." Describing this as the moment when the working class "sense[s] the necessity for collective resistance, definitely abandoning their slavish submission to the authorities," Lenin describes the "awakening of consciousness" in terms of broad principles and emotions rather than specific political ideology.[25] Responding to Lenin's prognostications nearly a century after *What Is to Be Done?* was first published, Miéville addresses the challenge of politicization using another speculative genre's conventions. In *King Rat*, and in his work more broadly, Miéville demonstrates science fiction can act as a speculative forum for investigating politicization. Like Lenin, Miéville does not represent politicization as inevitable—Saul has lived in the city for twenty years yet remains a passive bystander to political debates. He only assumes a new political awareness after a tragic event forces him to abandon his father's apartment and live on—and under—London's streets, coming to lead a kingdom of millions in only a few weeks.

His father's death instigates Saul's political transformation. Returning to his family's apartment, Saul quickly falls asleep. In the morning, he wakes to police banging on the apartment door and the news that his father was found dead outside. Saul is the only suspect, and is immediately arrested and detained in a North London police station. After aggressive questioning, he is left alone in his cell. That night, a large humanoid rat—or, perhaps, a normal size ratoid human—enters the cell, identifies himself as "King Rat," ruler of the rats, and says he is there to help Saul escape. Like his animal namesake, King Rat has a supernatural ability to scale walls, break into sealed rooms, and digest—even prefer—half-eaten, rotten, or spoiled food. Saul's mother, King Rat reveals, was herself secretly a rat, and Saul is part of the *Rodentia* royal family, a hybrid human/rat heir to King Rat's throne. In jail, processing his father's death, Saul inherits a new hybrid political identity. After they escape, King Rat reveals that he needs Saul to help defeat the Pied Piper, a supernaturally powerful flautist intent on enslaving the city's animals with his totalitarian trance music.

Saul's political transformation, from aimless young adult into rat prince, comes with its own superpowers, conferring mastery of urban environments (what mammals thrive more in cities than rats and humans?). His hybrid identity empowers Saul to repurpose urban spaces and materials, leading to the "defeat of the city" referenced at this chapter's outset. Miéville writes that Saul's *Rodentia* epistemology, "saw through vulgar reality, discerned possibilities. Alternative architecture and topography [. . .] asserting themselves."[26] Saul's newly acute sensitivity to the urban sublime puts him in new relationships with surroundings he once took for granted. Miéville describes how Saul experiences the urban sublime's constitutive power in one of the book's many nighttime wanders:

> They wove in and out of central London, climbing, creeping, moving behind houses and between them, over offices and under streets. *Magic had entered Saul's life.* [. . .] This was *urban voodoo*, fueled by the sacrifices of road deaths, of cats and people dying on the tarmac, an *I Ching of spilled and stolen groceries*, a *Cabbal of road signs*. Saul could feel King Rat watching him. He felt giddy with *rude, secular energy*.[27]

The urban sublime changes Saul. His character arc does not involve transformation via fealty to some utopian model but rather emerges from relations catapulting him toward a utopian political horizon. In response to Lenin's puzzle in *What Is to Be Done?*—how to guide "consciousness in an embryonic form"—Miéville points to the "rude, secular energy" of the city.

Saul's urban mastery exposes the city's politicizing potentials, often masked by totalizing illusions. Miéville's London is heterogeneous and hybrid. Diverse political, economic, and social systems operate within it. There are kingdoms of rats, spiders, and birds, each further divided by class, culture, and race. The above-quoted opening passage captures London's diversity: arriving at King's Cross is an immersive experience for the passengers on the train. To introduce London's totalizing urban ecosystem, Miéville surveys the surroundings above and below the rails; the passengers are not simply traveling, they are exchanging one life for another. In this panorama, Miéville strikingly (re)orders the city's materials, giving equal weight to skyscrapers and trains—the sea beasts and the whales—and objects of everyday urban life beneath the rails. The opening passage positions the reader to see above and below, the systemic and the local. "I spent a lot of my youth at skyline level on a train coming in and out of London," Miéville explains.[28] From the skyline level of an urban train, *King Rat* challenges the reader to question totalizing perspectives in the face of people's diverse social, political, and economic lives. Rather than imposing an alternative totalizing system, Miéville identifies how urban epistemologies and relations—and shifts in those relations—can forge political identities.

## UN LUN DUN

*Un Lun Dun*, Miéville's first young adult novel, narrates a second speculative London revolution. Here, Miéville subverts traditional quest genre expectations even more adamantly. *Un Lun Dun*'s protagonists explicitly refer to their adventure as a "quest" and even debate the merits of departing from the archetypal hero's journey script. Not only does Miéville undermine genre expectations, he incorporates metacommentary on the need to challenge conventions (political and/or literary) to achieve political goals.

*Un Lun Dun*'s primary protagonists are Zanna and Deeba, two twelve-year-old girls living in Kilburn in northwest London. In the novel's first act, Miéville—adopting portal fantasy conventions that he later upends—positions Zanna as the hero and Deeba her sidekick. In his introductory description, Miéville emphasizes differences reinforcing genre expectations. "Deeba was shorter and rounder and messier than her skinny friend. Her long black hair was making its usual break for freedom from her ponytail, in contrast to Zanna's tightly slicked-back blondness. Zanna was silent while Deeba kept asking her if she was okay."[29] They also have different ethnic identities: Deeba Resham is the youngest daughter in a British Pakistani family and Zanna Moon, whose first name is short for Susana, is English. Zanna's ethnic identity and physical attributes, and Deeba's deferential attention to her needs, prepares the reader to identify Zanna as the book's heroine.

Miéville's narrative begins with two strangers recognizing Zanna as a prophesied "chosen one" destined to save a city called UnLondon. UnLondon is London's "abcity," a mirror city created from the latter's detritus. Its citizens build their houses and lives from things that have become "MOIL—

mildly obsolete in London."[30] Many of UnLondon's residents are themselves London expatriates whose occupations have been devalued. The prophecy predicts a sentient pollution cloud, aptly named the Smog, will attempt to conquer UnLondon. Thriving off the incineration of urban materials, the Smog will try to burn UnLondon to absorb its fumes in order to increase its power, size, and knowledge. However, the prophecy claims, Zanna will complete a quest to save the abcity.

Similarly to *King Rat, Un Lun Dun* undermines totalizing perspectives capable of encompassing the ab/city. The first evidence of UnLondon, and its alternative ways of being, is, as the first chapter title describes it, a "respectful fox."[31] Deeba and Zanna first see the fox during recess, at their playground's edge. Unmoving, the fox stares at the girls. Fostering each other's courage, they approach, and Zanna offers an outstretched hand, to which the fox "politely" responds with a "gentle vulpine gaze."[32] When the recess bell rings, the fox bows its head and leaps away. With this portrayal of the respectful fox, Miéville again disrupts the urban/natural binary, showing the wild within the cityscape on the novel's first page. *Un Lun Dun*'s foxes have mastered both the urban environment of London *and* social niceties. Kath, one of Deeba and Zanna's classmates, informs them that "there's loads [of foxes] in London now, but you don't normally see them."[33] In the following days, Deeba and Zanna encounter additional evidence of previously unimaginable animal social systems. "Dogs would often stop as Zanna walked by, and stare at her," Miéville writes, and during a storm, one "dog sat up in an oddly dignified way" and "bowed its head" in recognition of Zanna.[34] During an afternoon in Queens Park, a group of squirrels ceremoniously offer Zanna various nuts and seeds. Just as Saul's interactions with *King Rat*'s animal kingdoms demonstrates the coexistence of multiple economic, political, and social systems, the fox signals to the girls the existence of alternative ways of being. In both novels, interactions with animals prepare the protagonists for politicization by encouraging them to explore and defend alternative worlds.

Deeba and Zanna also encounter alternative ways of being during encounters with civil servants who, unbeknownst to them, work for UnLondon. The first, a bus driver, approaches the girls at the Rose Café, a restaurant in Kilburn, recognizing Zanna as the prophesied hero. "Just very exciting to meet you," she tells Zanna. "Just wanted to say that." To call attention to the bus driver's outfit, as well as her pride in representing UnLondon, Miéville notes that she wore her hat "at a perky angle."[35] Other civil servants greet them. When they return home, a postman delivers Zanna a letter, which reads: "We look forward to meeting you [. . .] when the wheel turns." The envelope includes "a little square of card, some strange design, a beautiful, intricate thing of multicolored swirling lines. It was, Deeba realized, some mad version of a London travelcard. It said it was good for zones one to six, buses and trains, all across the city."[36] That a bus driver and postman serve as the abcity's ambassadors suggests civil service is valued, even heroic, in UnLondon. The UnLondon travelcard reinforces the logic of urban politicization animating *King Rat*. Urban mobility fosters Saul's political agency, and unlimited access to UnLondon's public transportation system invites Zanna and Deeba to exploration.

Following these signs, Deeba and Zanna uncover a passageway to the abcity. When UnLondon's residents learn of Zanna's arrival, they escort "the chosen one" to see their prophets and brief her on her quest. To the entire abcitizenry's great shock, however, the prophecy is falsified almost as soon as pronounced. Within minutes of her arrival at the prophets' offices, the Smog knocks Zanna unconscious. While she recovers from her concussion, the Umbrelisimo, a flamboyant paragon of UnLondon's MOIL economy, proposes arming the abcitizenry with repurposed umbrellas coated in a Smog-resistant chemical. UnLondon's leaders accept the plan, and Zanna and Deeba return to London. Thus, the novel's first act concludes with Zanna abandoning her quest, the prophecy an apparent dud.

*Un Lun Dun*'s second act, however, sees Deeba return to the abcity to complete—and, ultimately, reinvent—Zanna's quest. Researching the historical relationship between London and its abcity, she unearths a conspiracy: capitalist organizations in both cities, led by the Umbrellisimo, are feeding the Smog London's pollution, allowing it to consolidate its power over both cities. Learning about this sinister relationship, Deeba returns to UnLondon to stop the Smog. That Deeba becomes the novel's hero, while Zanna disappears for most of the second and third acts, signals Miéville's commitment to breaking genre conventions. Deeba's ascendancy as the "unchosen one" reflects a characteristic all Miéville's London Trilogy protagonists share. Deeba's leadership emerges only after spending significant time traversing a diverse (ab)urban environment. Neither Deeba nor Zanna were necessarily better suited to save the city; rather, Deeba's longer exposure to the city and its inhabitants shapes her political agency—the city, not the hero quest, produces the hero.

When Deeba returns to UnLondon to resume Zanna's quest, she realizes she has to improvise. First, she journeys to the prophets' offices to steal the book containing the only copy of the prophecy, which, by the way, is sentient. It reads Deeba more of the prophecy, revealing further details of "Zanna's" quest. There are seven dangerous tasks, after each of which the hero earns one of "the seven jewels of UnLondon": "a featherkey; a squidbeak clipper; a cup of bone tea; teeth-dice; an iron snail; the crown of the black-or-white king; and [. . .] the UnGun."[37]

While explaining the quest, the book provides metacommentary on the prophecy's generic structure: "it is a *standard Chosen One deal*. Seven tasks, and with each one she'd collect one of UnLondon's ancient treasures. Finally she'd get the most powerful weapon in all the abcity [. . .] the Smog's afraid of nothing but it. With it she was meant to face it and defeat it."[38] The prophecy book readily admits the quest is stereotypical, familiar to any modern storyteller or sentient tome. That Deeba will soon decide to break numerous romantic quest conventions represents a fundamental skepticism toward systematic projections, whether literary or political, that recurs throughout the London Trilogy. It is also pretty funny.

Deeba soon realizes it will be impossible to complete all seven tasks in time: the first takes many days and costs several lives. Consulting with her allies, Deeba makes the radical decision to "skip the rest of the stuff," and shorten the quest. "We'll go straight to the last stage of the quest. Let's go get the UnGun. Then we can deal with the Smog, and I can go home."[39] Ensuring his audience gets the metaphor, Miéville titles this chapter "Skipping Historical Stages." The chapter's title, and Deeba's subversive improvisation, critique totalizing adherence to the requisite stages of historical materialism. Realizing she would fail if she insisted on collecting six putatively magical, questionably utilitarian, objects before obtaining the UnGun, Deeba adopts a new political strategy. In the London Trilogy, overdetermined political programs harm political movements. Prioritizing the political urgency of the here and now over utopian projections to the horizon, Miéville is especially interested in his characters' needs and motivations.

So Deeba skips to the UnGun, the abcity's most powerful—and flexible—weapon. Anything small enough to fit in its chambers can serve as ammunition. When fired, the UnGun magnifies these materials' properties, requiring Deeba to put urban detritus to novel use. After obtaining the UnGun, Deeba loads it with diverse "urban" bullets: a grape, an ant, a scrap of paper, a grain of salt, a piece of brick, and a single hair. When fired, the bullets transform urban spaces and their inhabitants in unexpected ways. For example, when a police force attempts to arrest Deeba and her friends, she fires the brick bullet. A giant brick building materializes, imprisoning them. Later, when Deeba fires the salt bullet into the freshwater river bisecting UnLondon, the water turns into brine and kills an invasive species of seaweed threatening to suffocate her aquatic allies. Similar to how Saul manipulates urban materials and spaces, Deeba uses the city's materials to assert her own agency and save the city.

## *KRAKEN*

*Kraken*, the final entry in Miéville's London Trilogy, also features confused prophecies. It begins with an ambivalent seer: "An everyday doomsayer in sandwich-board abruptly walked away. [. . .] The sign on his front was an old-school prophecy of the end: the one bobbing on his back read FORGET IT."[40] The passage efficiently captures two abandoned prophecies: the doomsayer's self-deconstructing message on a sandwich-board and his desertion of his own divinations. This vignette could serve as a mission statement for the entire trilogy: lived experiences always deviate from proscribed programs—political, social, or literary.

*Kraken*'s protagonist is Billy Harlow. Unlike Saul or Deeba, Billy has a professional identity and a strong sense of order. A "taxonomiser by inclination as well as profession," Billy, a curator at the Darwin Center at the National History Museum, categorizes every facet of his life.[41] Everyone he meets is a predetermined type; every act in his day predictable and intelligible. Miéville first demonstrates Billy's predisposition to totalization by surveying his typology of Darwin Center visitors: "There were children: mostly young boys, shy and beside themselves with excitement, and vastly knowledgeable about what they saw. There were their parents. There were sheepish people in their twenties, as geeky-eager as the kids. [. . .] And there were the obsessives."[42] Billy sees the only active visitors to the Darwin Center as childlike or obsessive. This assessment provides insight into Billy's own professional ethos: seeing his own work as insular and juvenile, Billy's categorizations betray a fragile self-esteem concerned with immaturity and neurosis. The first chapter details the script Billy reads to introduce visitors to the center. The tour highlights several creatures, as well as objects from Darwin's original voyage on the *Beagle*, culminating with the Center's primary attraction, Archie, a giant squid, 8.62 meters long, completely preserved in saline-Formalin mix. But when Billy leads the tour group through the exhibit, Archie has vanished.

Billy's transformation from a passive taxonomer into an agent can perhaps best be tracked across the four dream sequences that occur in "Part Two" of *Kraken*. Subtitled "Universal Sleeper," *Kraken*'s second part calls attention to sleeping and awakening. These are also central metaphors in *What is to Be Done?* where Lenin compares realizing political identity to awakening from deep sleep. Characterizing "spontaneous upsurges" of revolts and strikes in early twentieth-century Moscow and St. Petersburg as collective acts motivated by "consciousness in an embryonic form," Lenin considers how to shape rebellions into cohesive political movements. The dream sequences in "Universal Sleeper" capture transitional moments between apolitical slumber (of a "universal sleeper") and wakeful, politicized consciousness. In five different chapters in the novel's second part, Miéville explicitly portrays Billy awakening from a dream.

After Archie's disappearance, the Teuthex, a literally underground cult worshipping squids, abducts Billy, taking him to their subterranean London sanctuary. As a curator at the Darwin Center, Billy oversaw Archie's embalming and supervised his exhibit for the Natural Museum of History, making him caretaker of England's largest squid, and, to the Teuthex, a prophet. "Universal Sleeper" begins with Billy's arrival at the sanctuary, where the

Teuthex covertly feed him hallucinogenic squid ink to stimulate prophetic dreams. Billy is a docile prophet. He does not know where he is (Miéville is uncharacteristically vague about his location in south London), he has been captured by a religious cult, and, against his will, ingests a hallucinogen. The titular "Universal Sleeper" of the novel's second part, Billy begins his quest to find Archie as a passive figure, his induced unconsciousness reflecting his generally submissive role. However, as he falls asleep under the squid ink's influence, Billy enters the first of a series of dreams signaling shifts in his agency and self-awareness.

In the first dream, Miéville compares Billy's unconsciousness to floating in the deep ocean. The passage's murky language mimics Billy's drifting perspective and passivity. In these depths, Billy encounters the sublime. "Into sleep's benthos and deeper," Miéville writes. "A slander that the deepest parts are lightless. There are moments of phosphor with animal movement. Somatic glimmers, and in this trench of sleep those lights were tiny dreams. A long time sleep, and blinks of vision. Awe, not fear."[43] The dream is opaque, and Billy struggles to discern the shapes of the marine organisms in front of him, but the overall effect of the landscape is awe-inspiring. As the dream develops, Billy identifies a distant object emerging from the sublime:

> He saw something small or in the distance. Then black after black, then it came back closer. Straight-edged, hard-lined. An anomaly of angles in that curved vorago. It was the specimen. It was his kraken, his giant squid quite still—still in suspension in its tank, the tank and its motionless dead-thin contents adrift in deep. Sinking toward where there is no below. The once-squid going home. One last thing, that might have announced itself as such, the finality was so unequivocal. Something beneath the descending tank, at which from way above though already deep in pitch tiny Billy-ness stared. Under the tank was something utter and dark and moving, something so slowly rising, endless.[44]

While at first the Kraken appears to be the subject of the sublime scene, eventually Billy recognizes the existence of something else, an infinite force which exerts a stronger gravity then the specimen in its tank. The dream concludes with the recognition that beyond the Kraken is an entity more powerful. The object of Billy's dream, the true source of the sublime, is not the Kraken, but something beneath the Kraken.

Billy's second dream, which occurs the following night, continues the scene. He once again drifts in the sublime, floating toward a mysterious entity. Falling further, he begins to recognize the object below: "when it came into water faintly lit enough that he could see its contours, it was a landscape he recognized, because it was him. A Billy Harlow face, Atlantean, eyes open and staring into the sky all the way above."[45] The sublime force described in the first dream—"something utter and dark and moving"—materializes as Billy in the second dream. Together, the first and second dreams mirror Lenin's political "consciousness in embryonic form." A manifestation of the sublime, Billy's awakening consciousness becomes the locus of the novel's second part.

In the third dream sequence, Billy expresses as-yet unseen agency. As the dream begins, Billy calls out, "Come champion saddle up time for us to go we must be quick we have a job to do."[46] Not only is it the first time Billy speaks in his dreams, his speech is a command. Furthermore, the command speculates about a plan of action. As the dream develops, it becomes apparent that Billy is speaking to the Kraken as he prepares to saddle and ride it. "Here was his mount. He knew what would come over the rocks and hills for him to grab and with cowboy drama swing himself onto its back as it passed. *Architeuthis*, jetting, mantle clenching and tentacles out ready to grab prey. He knew it would scud over the plains, sending out limbs to grab hold of what it passed, to anchor itself and hunt."[47] The third dream is also notable for it is the first time that Billy interprets his visions. In a conversation with a Teuthex follower, he says, "I dreamed I was riding the Architeuthis like Clint Eastwood. In the Wild West."[48] Self-reflection is part of growth in "Universal Sleeper."

The fourth dream sequence offers a different meditation on agency. Set in an urban environment, the final dream captures Billy scaling the city's architecture as he prepares to confront a powerful enemy. Elaborately described as a "robot wizard mastermind nemesis," this hybrid enemy is a stereotypical final boss, rather than the novel's actual antagonist. Miéville rhythmically describes the scene: "In a city and racing up and over buildings, jumping over high buildings with one jump, making swimming motions to pass through the clear air above skyscrapers."[49] Billy's fluid movements across the cityscape echo Saul's urban dexterity in *King Rat*. In the dream, Billy becomes the London Trilogy's third protagonist with a mastery of urban environments. However, Billy refuses to battle the "robot wizard" on his own. As he waits for a companion to come, Billy refers to himself as a sidekick rather than a hero. While this insight initially brings relief, Billy "felt the universe, exasperated, was giving him an insultingly clear insight, that he was simply missing."[50] When he awakes, he feels guilt and remorse at being the sidekick in his own dream. This emotional response is also a change in consciousness. Acknowledging he has gained a powerful understanding of his urban environment and the political organizations and identities that exist within the city limits, Billy must accept accountability and face whatever "mastermind nemesis" threatens London—robot, wizard or other. Billy's interrogation of his role as sidekick, as well as his emerging desire to assume a new role as an agent, echoes Deeba's transformation in *Un Lun Dun*; to recover Archie, Billy transitions from sidekick to hero, uncovering the sinister intentions of London's prophets and amending their prognostication for saving London.

## POLITICIZATION IN MIÉVILLE'S CITIES

Cities' importance for Miéville lies in their role as crucibles of politicizing social relations. While many readings of his work emphasize historical materialist dialectics, the other side of this influence is relationality. In his text on international law, for example, Miéville grounds his analysis in a claim, derived from Pashukanis, that "the legal form is the form of a particular kind of *relationship*,"[51] that society is composed in part of these legal relations, that these relations are grounded in the social relations of capitalism, and that norms emerge from these relationships, rather than constituting them. Consistently with this social ontology, Miéville's most important character transformations take place as a result of transformed social relations. These arcs are particularly clear in the case of Saul, Billy, and Deeba, who are transformed as their relations with the city and its other residents are transformed.

London's intrusive agency, mediated by social relations, is clearly visible in the spatial patterns of Miéville's narratives. Figure 1[52] maps locations

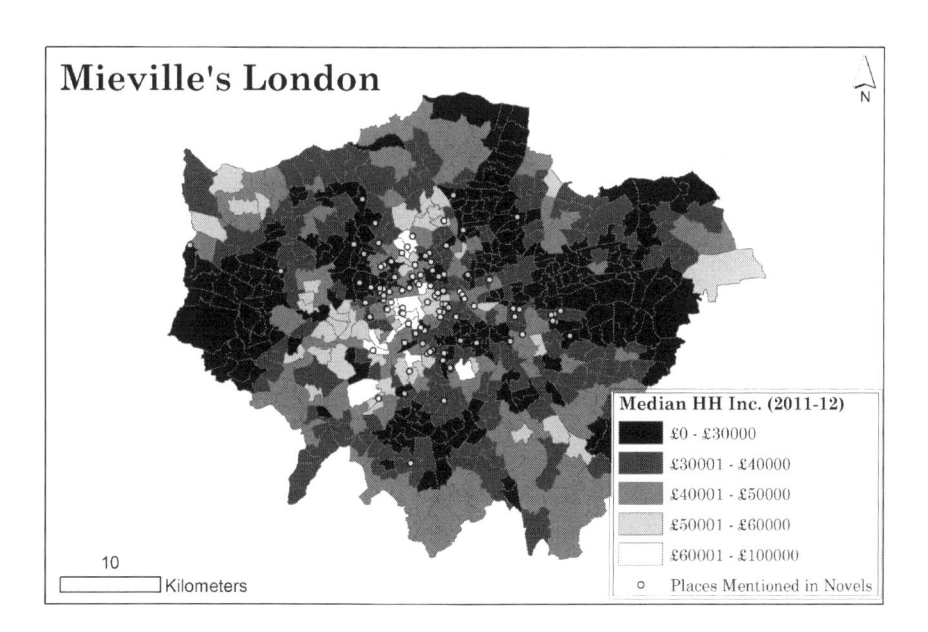

Figure 8.1. Ward map of Miéville's London. London map includes places specifically mentioned in Miéville's three London novels, geocoded using Nominatim, Google Earth Pro, and, occasionally, Wikipedia.

168                Andrew Uzendoski and Caleb Gallemore

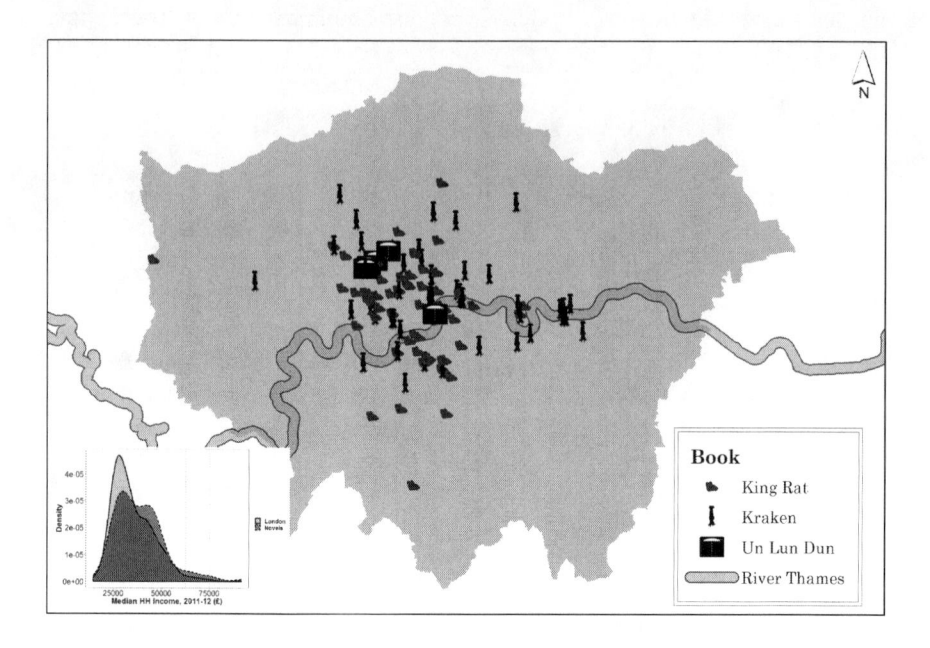

**Figure 8.2. Ward map of Miéville's London. London map includes places specifically mentioned in Miéville's three London novels, geocoded using Nominatim, Google Earth Pro, and, occasionally, Wikipedia.**

explicitly mentioned in the London Trilogy: Miéville's settings are unevenly distributed across the city, and his personal experience growing up and living in Kilburn, in northwest London, is clearly visible. Areas around Kilburn feature prominently in both *King Rat* and *Kraken*, despite that both novels feature protagonists with uncanny mobility. While most of *Un Lun Dun* takes place in the abcity, the quest begins and ends in Kilburn, home to two portals to UnLondon.

The London Trilogy's center of gravity highlights Miéville's personal history. While this, in a certain way, is inherent to modern and postmodern novels, we suspect Miéville's geographic imaginary is deliberate. By our count, Miéville uses around 115 different names of specific London locales across the trilogy. Just as important as the places he references is the conspicuous absence of stereotypical London settings: we found no mentions of Big Ben, St. Pauls, the Tower, the Tate Modern, the Globe Theatre, Hyde Park or Trafalgar Square, for example, in over 1,200 pages. This, in a very personal sense, is Miéville's city.

In Miéville's speculative fiction, revolutions are personal, erupting from particular ways of being. Political programs begin with personally mediated social relations emerging from cities and the neighborhoods and subcultures within them, as Miéville's own geographic imaginary indicates. There is no universal political program guiding all the London Trilogy's protagonists. Rather, inspired by their encounters traversing the city, they seek out political alliances, ways of being, and alternatives, which shape them in turn.

The London Trilogy's explorations also span class divisions. As can be seen in the first map, the "quests" of each novel require their heroes to navigate urban spaces defined by drastically different economic identities and means. Indeed, the London Trilogy overrepresents middle-class neighborhoods in relation to the dispersion of household incomes across the metropolitan area.

In Miéville's urban imaginary, acts of political subversion or transformation are not limited to distinct (i.e., working class or proletariat) socioeconomic zones. His neighborhoods are always already shaped by multiple, even contradictory, forces. Addressing the complex architectural history of London, Miéville celebrates the immutable forces of urban sediments beneath (and within) each city block. "[Cities] are palimpsests of culture, architecture, history, ethnicities, politics, and just about everything else," he argues in one interview. London's streets are "a discombobulated mess of history, a seventeenth-century building next to a 1950s towerblock next to a weird glass-and-steel '90s travesty, etc."[53] In the London Trilogy, an urban space is inherently an overdetermined space, emerging from a confluence of happenstance, history, and contestation. This perspective has important consequences.

First, overdetermination and hybridity allows changed social relations to subvert these spaces. In *What is to Be Done?* Lenin[54] argues that cross-class coalitions are necessary because the working class needs guidance from bourgeois intelligentsia, such as Marx and Engels (and Lenin), fluent in "modern scientific socialism." Miéville's characters, by contrast, engage in non-hierarchical coalitions and transformations. While he often represents affluent spaces as exclusive and foreboding, movements across them, visible in the map above, are productive transgressions. In Saul's case, this involves transgressive mastery over the buildings in London's financial center; for Billy, this involves leaving his middle-class comfort zone. In both cases, the protagonist's social network expands exponentially as he allies with people (and creatures) across the city.

Second, partially because of these potentials, constructing or repurposing overdetermined spaces is political. "You cannot exaggerate the unbelievable architectural 'fuck you' to the poor that is embedded in Canary Wharf," Miéville argues, "[t]he most unremitting act of embodied class aggression in the built environment of the city."[55] When Saul repurposes London's financial district, slipping up and atop its buildings, he asserts his own space. This is not just a raid deep into enemy territory, it is a sign that any space can potentially be subverted, though powerful interests will always also fight back.[56] Where gentrification often seems to indicate inevitable capitalist expansion, the dispersion of Miéville's protagonists (and their political acts) marks each urban space, within or beyond the frontier of gentrification, as contested sites—giving the lie to the totalizing promise of gentrification.

## CONCLUSION

China Miéville's work foregrounds cities' "intrusive agency." We make sense of his narrative choices by thinking of him as a novelist interested in politicization, how and where people start to ask themselves "What is to Be Done?" This perspective highlights important commonalities across *King Rat*, *Un Lun Dun*, and *Kraken*'s diverse narrative and generic structures: all three books in the London Trilogy narrate politicization. Moreover, in all of them, politicization takes place as a result of travels through and interactions with the denizens and materials of the city, which position the protagonist in new social relations that lead to a politically charged change in their ways of being.

As *speculative* fiction, Miéville's novels are invested in shaping discourse and, indeed, inspiring the types of political identities that he develops in his narratives. The London Trilogy novels are tools for politicization. In this sense, they respond to Lenin's *What is to Be Done?* In sharp contrast to Lenin, however, for whom the lived experiences of individuals in concrete circumstances seems less important than the capacity of the intelligentsia to organize their interests, Miéville's fiction grounds individuals' politicization—and the political programs resulting therefrom—in their particular and always shifting ways of being in the city.

## NOTES

1. Joan Gordon, "Hybridity, Heterotopia, and Mateship in China Miéville's *Perdido Street Station*," *Science Fiction Studies* 30, no. 3 (2003): 456–76; Andrew M. Butler, "*The Tain* and the Tain: China Miéville's Gift of Uncanny London," *The New Centennial Review* 13, no. 2 (2013): 133–54.

2. China Miéville, "An interview with China Miéville," interview by John Berlyne, *SFRevu.com*, January 29, 2002. http://www.sfrevu.com/ISSUES/2002/0204/Feature%20-%20China/interview.htm.

3. Sherryl Vint, "Ab-realism: Fractal Language and Social Change," in *China Miéville: Critical Essays,* edited by Caroline Edwards & Tony Venezia, 39–59 (Canterbury, CT: Glyphi, 2015).

4. China Miéville, "On the Look-Out for a New Urban Uncanny: An Interview with China Miéville," interview by Lars Schmeink, *Extrapolation* 55, no. 1 (2014): 25–32.

5. Carl Freedman, "Speculative Fiction and International Law: The Marxism of China Miéville," *Socialism and Democracy* 20, no. 3 (2006): 25–39; Carl Freedman, *Art and Idea in the Novels of China Miéville* (Canterbury, CT: Gylphi, 2015).

6. Carl Freedman, *Art and Idea in the Novels of China Miéville* (Canterbury, CT: Gylphi, 2015), 80.

7. China Miéville, *King Rat* (London: Pan Books, 1998), 288.

8. China Miéville, *Kraken: An Anatomy* (New York: Del Rey, 2010), 299–300.
9. Miéville, "On the Look-Out," 25.
10. Ibid., 25–26.
11. China Miéville, "Symposium: Marxism and Fantasy, Editorial Introduction," *Historical Materialism* 10, no. 4 (2002): 46.
12. China Miéville, "Appropriate means: An interview with China Miéville," interview by Mark Bould, *New Politics* 9, no. 3 (2003). http://nova.wpunj.edu/newpolitics/issue35/bould35.htm.
13. China Miéville, "Lessons of 1917: For a Resurgence of Insurgent Dignity," interview by Chuck Mertz, *aNtiDoTe Zine*, September 6, 2017. Accessed December 26, 2018. https://antidotezine.com/2017/06/09/1917-insurgent-dignity/.
14. Cassandra Bausman, "Convention Un-Done: *Un Lun Dun*'s Unchosen Heroine and Narrative (Re)Vision," *Journal of the Fantastic in the Arts* 25, no. 1 (2014): 28–53; Joe Sutliff Sanders, "Reinventing Subjectivity: China Miéville's *Un Lun Dun* and the Child Reader," *Explorations* 50, no. 2 (2009): 293–306.
15. China Miéville, *Un Lun Dun* (New York: Del Rey, 2007).
16. Freedman, *Art and Idea*.
17. China Miéville, *King Rat*, 15.
18. Freedman, "Speculative Fiction," 26.
19. Miéville, "On the Look-Out."
20. Ibid., 28.
21. Ibid., 29.
22. China Miéville, *King Rat*, 16.
23. Ibid., 26.
24. China Miéville, *King Rat*, 27.
25. Vladimir Ilyich Lenin, *What Is to Be Done?* (New York: International Publishers, 1969), 31.
26. China Miéville, *King Rat,* 98.
27. Ibid., 98–99.
28. Miéville, "Interview: China Miéville," interview by Cheryl Morgan, *Strange Horizons*, October 1, 2001, http://strangehorizons.com/non-fiction/articles/interview-china-miville/.
29. Ibid., 7.
30. Ibid., 106.
31. Ibid., 3.
32. Ibid., 5.
33. Ibid., 4.
34. Ibid., 10.
35. Ibid., 8.
36. Ibid., 9.
37. Ibid., 249.
38. Ibid., 249, emphasis added.
39. Ibid., 302.
40. Miéville, *Kraken: An Anatomy*, 3.
41. Ibid., 5.
42. Ibid., 6.
43. Ibid., 87.
44. Ibid., 87.
45. Ibid., 126.
46. Ibid., 176.
47. Ibid., 176.
48. Ibid., 179.
49. Ibid., 225.
50. Ibid., 226.
51. Miéville, *Between Equal Rights: A Marxist Theory of International Law* (Leiden, Netherlands: Brill, 2004), 84–86, emphasis in original.

52. London map data from Greater London Authority1 and Ordnance Survey.2 Contains National Statistics data © Crown copyright and database right (2015) and Ordnance Survey data © Crown copyright and database right (2015). Used under UK Open Government Licence v. 2. Projection: UTM Zone 30N, Meters. Inset shows the kernal density for household income for the city as a whole and household income weighted by the number of locations mentioned at least once in *King Rat, Kraken* or *Un Lun Dun* that fall within that ward. Greater London Authority, "Statistical GIS Boundary Files for London," Accessed December 28, 2018. https://data.london.gov.uk/dataset/statistical-gis-boundary-files-london; Greater London Authority, "Ward Profiles and Atlas." Accessed December 28, 2018. https://data.london.gov.uk/dataset/ward-profiles-and-atlas. Ordnance Survey, "OS Open Rivers," Accessed December 28, 2018. https://www.ordnancesurvey.co.uk/business-and-government/products/os-open-rivers.html.

53. China Miéville, "China Mieville: RevolutionSF Interview," interview by Andrew Kozma, *RevolutionSF,* September 14, 2014. Accessed December 28, 2018. http://www.revolutionsf.com/article.php?id=2391.

54. Vladimir Ilyich Lenin, *What Is to Be Done?*, 31–32.

55. China Miéville, "Trembling on the Verge: An Interview with China Miéville (Part One)," interview by Joe Macaré, *Truthout*, August 28, 2012. Accessed August 10, 2018. https://truthout.org/articles/trembling-on-the-verge-an-interview-with-china-mieville-part-one/.

56. Ibid.

# BIBLIOGRAPHY

Bausman, Cassandra. "Convention Un-Done: *Un Lun Dun*'s Unchosen Heroine and Narrative (Re)Vision." *Journal of the Fantastic in the Arts* 25, no. 1 (2014): 28–53.

Butler, Andrew M. "*The Tain* and the Tain: China Miéville's Gift of Uncanny London." *The New Centennial Review* 13, no. 2 (2013): 133–54.

Freedman, Carl. "Speculative Fiction and International Law: The Marxism of China Miéville." *Socialism and Democracy* 20, no. 3 (2006): 25–39.

———. *Art and Idea in the Novels of China Miéville*. Canterbury, CT: Gylphi, 2015.

Gordon, Joan. "Hybridity, Heterotopia, and Mateship in China Miéville's *Perdido Street Station*." *Science Fiction Studies* 30, no. 3 (2003): 456–76.

Greater London Authority. "Statistical GIS Boundary Files for London." Accessed December 28, 2018. https://data.london.gov.uk/dataset/statistical-gis-boundary-files-london.

———. "Ward Profiles and Atlas." Accessed December 28, 2018. https://data.london.gov.uk/dataset/ward-profiles-and-atlas.

Lenin, Vladimir Ilyich. *What Is to Be Done?* New York: International Publishers, 1969.

Miéville, China. *King Rat*. London: Pan Books, 1998.

———. "Interview: China Miéville." Interview by Cheryl Morgan. *Strange Horizons*, October 1, 2001. http://strangehorizons.com/non-fiction/articles/interview-china-miville/.

———. "An Interview with China Miéville." Interview by John Berlyne. *SFRevu.com*, January 29, 2002. http://www.sfrevu.com/ISSUES/2002/0204/Feature%20-%20China/interview.htm.

———. "Symposium: Marxism and Fantasy, Editorial Introduction." *Historical Materialism* 10, no. 4 (2002): 39–49.

———. "Appropriate means: An interview with China Miéville." Interview by Mark Bould. *New Politics* 9, no. 3 (2003). http://nova.wpunj.edu/newpolitics/issue35/bould35.htm.

———. *Between Equal Rights: A Marxist Theory of International Law*. Leiden, Netherlands: Brill, 2004.

———. *Un Lun Dun*. New York: Del Rey, 2007.

———. "Gothic Politics: A Discussion with China Miéville." Interview by *Gothic Studies* 10, no. 1 (2008): 61–70.

———. *Kraken: An Anatomy*. New York: Del Rey, 2010.

———. "Trembling on the Verge: An Interview with China Miéville (Part One)." Interview by Joe Macaré. *Truthout*. August 28, 2012. Accessed August 10, 2018. https://truthout.org/articles/trembling-on-the-verge-an-interview-with-china-mieville-part-one/.

———. "China Mieville: RevolutionSF Interview." Interview by Andrew Kozma. *RevolutionSF*, September 14, 2014. Accessed December 28, 2018. http://www.revolutionsf.com/article.php?id=2391.

———. "On the Look-Out for a New Urban Uncanny: An Interview with China Miéville." Interview by Lars Schmeink. *Extrapolation* 55, no. 1 (2014): 25–32.

———. "Lessons of 1917: For a Resurgence of Insurgent Dignity." Interview by Chuck Mertz. aNtiDoTe Zine, September 6, 2017. Accessed December 26, 2018. https://antidotezine.com/2017/06/09/1917-insurgent-dignity/.

Ordnance Survey. "OS Open Rivers." Accessed December 28, 2018. https://www.ordnancesurvey.co.uk/business-and-government/products/os-open-rivers.html.

Sanders, Joe Sutliff. "Reinventing Subjectivity: China Miéville's *Un Lun Dun* and the Child Reader." *Explorations* 50, no. 2 (2009): 293–306.

Vint, Sherryl. "Ab-realism: Fractal Language and Social Change." In *China Miéville: Critical Essays,* edited by Caroline Edwards & Tony Venezia, 39–59. Canterbury, CT: Glyphi, 2015.

*Chapter Nine*

# Stranger than Fiction

*Silicon Valley and the Politics of Space Colonization*

Emily Ray

As we on Earth are concerned with life in the age of climate change, Silicon Valley is putting effort into colonizing Mars and making humans a multiplanetary species. Two of the driving interests in Mars colonization are: to rescue the species from self- and Earth destruction, and to control the technologies and economy of space colonization. SpaceX and Blue Origin, owned by tech sector giants Elon Musk and Jeff Bezos, respectively, see opportunities to establish an interplanetary economy. Musk has likened the goal of SpaceX on Mars to building a transcontinental railway, making clear his desire to capitalize on climate change to produce the infrastructure for a Martian form of capitalism.[1] NASA is working with aerospace and defense giants Boeing and Lockheed Martin to design aircraft for Martian missions. The economic and political forces responsible for threats to the human species on Earth are the same forces leading humanity toward interplanetary colonization. What are the driving political ideologies behind the private sector push for Mars colonization, and how does speculative fiction provide insight into the kinds of political battles to anticipate as governments and corporations look to space as pressure release for climate change crises? I analyze news articles, interviews, company-generated content, and the political and social commitments of Elon Musk and Jeff Bezos, who are amongst the primary private sector advocates and funders of space exploration, to determine what their political vision is for humans living in the age of climate change. I find the prevailing ideological drivers of space exploration are: neoliberalism, with faith in the power of technology and of human consciousness; the assumed innate drive for humans to regulate the economy through capitalism; and minimal governmental oversight and regulation in personal and business affairs. In essence, wealthy space enthusiasts imagine colonization will liberate humans from increasingly hostile environmental conditions and lack of freedom on Earth.

Planning for a Martian colony is primarily undertaken in Silicon Valley. Silicon Valley is a hotspot of the reinvention of the conditions for the production and distribution of goods and services, lorded over by worldly billionaires, each with an escape plan in the event their collective wealth and innovative spirit cannot keep civilization from collapsing.[2][3] The plans elaborated by Silicon Valley entrepreneurs appear straightforward and technically sound, but their visions lack a robust politics and discussion of economics. One assumes that Silicon Valley style capitalism will simply move from one planet to another, and the start of a new human civilization should bear the imprint of the peninsula: skeptical of public regulation; attached to the promise of human consciousness; aware of the environment as a set of resources; and driven to dominate nature by controlling the path of human evolution.

The two entrepreneurs whom I focus on, Bezos and Musk, are avid science fiction readers and have cited science fiction as influential in their vision of an expanded human civilization. In an interview given in 2018, Bezos tells the audience he considered Iain M. Banks' *Culture* series, Isaac Asimov, and Phillip K. Dick important to his thinking. Musk named two of his SpaceX rockets after *Culture* series characters, and he has cited Asimov's *Foundation* series as personally influential. Musk is influenced by this series to consider what he could do to minimize the perceived decline of Western civilization today. The imprint of science fiction is clear as Bezos and Musk both find spacefaring to hold the key to staving off or recovering from civilizational collapse. Science fiction offers many possibilities for framing environmental and social problems and for imagining solutions. The genre also presents an opportunity to play out these different positions, and often in a scientifically informed fictional world that is not so different from our own.

I look to the *Mars Trilogy*, by Kim Stanley Robinson, to explore the clash of ideologies in the attempt to remake human civilization on Mars. In the trilogy, the first Martian colonists reject the political and economic status quo that they inherited from Earth and begin a centuries' long series of revolutions that will test political ideologies against one another. There is great value in engaging literature, and science fiction in particular, in the work of understanding the political and economic aspects of the environmental crisis. Literature is a way to explore uncanny events and to bear witness to climate change. In *Dying Planet*, Robert Markley points out that, "Mars has served as a screen on which we have projected our hopes for the future and our fears of ecological devastation on Earth."[4] Frederic Jameson finds the *Mars Trilogy* especially good at using "hard science" as a way to describe and animate sociopolitics.[5] Soviet futurists and midcentury American science fiction writers imagined communist societies on Mars. There is a long literary history of

Mars colonization and exploration that is invaluable to thinking through contemporary space exploration as a way to deal with climate change. Thinking through the *Mars Trilogy* helps us to consider which political practices could allow humans to live through the near and distant future of climate change, and the implications of allowing multinational corporations to shape those possibilities.

## SILICON VALLEY GOES TO SPACE

### Silicon Valley in the Mid-Century

Silicon Valley has been intimately connected to the U.S. military since the 1940s. Early component processing firms and public-private research partnerships with Stanford University shaped the economic development of the region. Influential men of World War II–era Silicon Valley, like mathematician, Norbert Wiener, and engineer, Vannevar Bush, advocated for continued investment in wartime scientific and technological research for postwar applications, like cybernetics; improved household and industrial technologies; and for the advancement of humans at the species level. During the countercultural revolution in the 1960s and 70s, Silicon Valley embraced neoliberalism, faith in technology to facilitate human development, and a rejection of the hierarchical and disciplinary thinking of east coast laboratories and manufacturing plants.[6] In 1968, Stewart Brand published the first issue of the *Whole Earth Catalog*, a widely popular resource and literary magazine that ran community-generated advice for life on communes, think pieces by scientists and engineers like Wiener, and poetry by readers of the *Catalog*.[7] The *Catalog* bridged the economic and technical world of Silicon Valley with the countercultural desire to live in a technologically advanced primitive utopian society.

Scientists and *Catalog* enthusiasts embraced individualistic capitalism, and the do-it-yourself spirit of Silicon Valley. The labs, and by extension the communes of New Mexico and northern California, had a strong preference for minimal government interference and maximum freedom of exchange on an open market. The *Catalog*'s stated purpose:

> We are gods and might as well get good at it. . . . In response to this dilemma and to these gains a realm of intimate, personal power is developing—power of the individual to conduct his own education, find his own inspiration, shape his own environment, and share his adventure with whoever is interested.[8]

Brand points to the power within each individual to forge their own path. Just as in Silicon Valley, the *Catalog* puts forward a male and Western view of what human freedom requires. While the communes were keen to share resources, many were not promoting a communist or community-minded anarchism. Rather, they embraced the neoliberal language of individualism that suggested the rise and fall of one's life is the product of one's gumption. Technological advancement could promote DIY as a substitute for state-supported or community-supported welfare for all. The lifestyle was meant to support small-scale work, even if it was dependent on research for large-scale applications, like military technologies. This small-scale aesthetic made its way into the prospective plans of a space colony, which was often imagined as a better organized and scientifically oriented commune of closed-cycle agriculture, performing arts, and collaboration.[9]

In the late 1960s and into the 1970s, Princeton physics professor, Gerard O'Neill, began to publish ideas for Mars colonization. Brand's readership was deeply polarized on the need and mechanisms for Martian colonization, so in 1976, Brand published *Space Colonies*, which mostly organized already published letters and articles from the *CoEvolution Quarterly*. Brand wrote in the introduction, "Instead of seeing the space program as a 'boondoggle for scientists' (Herman Kahn), suddenly they can see Space as a path, or at least a metaphor, for their own liberation."[10] Space exploration was bound up with the countercultural dream to find new ways to carve out individual freedom within a capitalist economic system. This would allow them to take from it what enables their version of a good life, and to leave the burden of reproductive labor, exploitative labor, and the environmental toll from technological advancements to those who cannot escape their neighborhoods, or the Earth. Outer space was pitched as a new Western frontier, ready for the imprint of the modern colonizer.[11] Colonization was, and continues to be, an exploitative and violent approach to political and economic control.[12] The people who envisioned space settlements and romanticized colonization left a significant imprint on the economic and intellectual development of Silicon Valley. Bezos cites O'Neill as one of his intellectual idols.[13] In the valley, the question of "should we colonize Mars" is decreasingly normative and increasingly technical.

## The Neoliberal Valley

In the 1990s, the *Catalog* was revived from the dead and found new life in the digital age; first as the Whole Earth 'Lectronic Link (WELL), and later as *Wired* magazine.[14] Keeping up with the digital age connected the ethos of the *Catalog* to the ideas and economic ventures of Silicon Valley in the dotcom boom. The WELL, influenced by the skepticism of hierarchical oversight and the embrace of the network metaphor of organization, dovetailed with (and likely influenced) the transition from top-down corporate organization to the neoliberal version of the network. Turner describes this shift in the 1980s:

They laid off workers, broke component elements of firms into semi-independent project teams, and decentralized their management structure ... described as a new, networked logic for the organization of production, a logical characterized by a shift in the basis of employment from long-term positions to shorter-term projects, by the leveling of corporate hierarchies....[15]

This description of rapid changes in the corporate world echo David Harvey's description of neoliberalism as focused on contractual obligations "between juridical individuals in the marketplace."[16] This new corporate environment cherished the language of network and designed economic disruptions to nineteenth- and twentieth-century business models. These businesses depend on contracted and displaced unpaid labor to the customer, especially in the case of Amazon's Flex delivery service model.[17] Amazon came of age in the 1990s, which launched founder Jeff Bezos into wealth that today exceeds 150 billion dollars. Likewise, Musk's fortune was made in the 1990s after he developed and sold Zip2 to Compaq for approximately $300 million dollars, and again when X.com became Paypal. These two titans of Silicon Valley are also the leaders in the new space race.

Harvey's description of neoliberalism aligns with the characteristics of the Silicon Valley work environment: "While personal and individual freedom in the marketplace is guaranteed, each individual is held responsible and accountable for his or her own actions and well-being. ... Individual success or failure are interpreted in terms of entrepreneurial virtues or personal failings ... rather than being attributed to any systemic property."[18] This logic is not foreign to Silicon Valley, or even the communitarians who preferred to live and die by their own hand than to be stuck in an office. The commune dwellers, of course, were beneficiaries of cheap land that had been stolen from indigenous tribes in the Western states, publicly funded infrastructure, and the perks of the New Deal that extended retirement and medical care coverage. Even the *Whole Earth Catalog* transformed into the Global Business Network, which translated the countercultural interest in the mystical self to new strategies for maximizing one's labor force and wealth creation. Clients like Royal Dutch/Shell and AT&T helped eliminate the anti-corporate sentiment from what remained of countercultural thinking and wedded the deep interest in one's conscious self to optimizing the individual at the heart of the neoliberal workforce.

## BILLIONAIRES IN SPACE

Neoliberal politics flowed into the plans to make humans a multi-planetary species. This is evident in the drive to make space exploration a private venture and available to those who can pay to play. The efforts on the part of Silicon Valley firms (there are other global firms working on space colonization, but none as well-funded and high profile as those in Silicon Valley) promote a loosely regulated, capitalist order on space colonies. The ability to leave the struggling Earth and go to Mars is predicated on one's ability to work hard and save money. "Almost anyone if they saved up, and this was their goal, they could ultimately save up enough money to buy a ticket to Mars . . . and Mars would have a labor shortage for a long time, so, jobs would not be in short supply."[19] The early Mars colony, then, would presumably run on a similar economy to the capitalist one on Earth, where one competes for jobs, and even on Mars, one would need cash for a pecuniary capitalist economy.

Jeff Bezos sees unfettered capitalism as energy to harness to improve the human condition. In an interview about Blue Origin, Bezos remarked that getting off the planet will require a "dynamic, entrepreneurial explosion" similar to "the last 20 years of the internet, where you saw unbelievable dynamism."[20] Bezos describes wealth creation as the product of "fair exchange value" for things, and because of the fair exchange of goods on the market, "People invent new things, and pioneer new things, and the world gets better."[21] In Bezos' view, the exchange of goods through the capitalist market is fair, and as his tenure at Amazon demonstrates, does not account or labor and environmental costs.[22] [23] As Marx pointed out: "Along with the useful qualities of the products themselves, we put out of sight both the useful character of the various kinds of labour embodied in them, and the concrete forms of that labour; there is nothing left but what is common to them all; all are reduced to one and the same sort of labour, human labour in the abstract."[24] Capitalists like Bezos can abstract the human and environmental requirements of commodity production and reimagine this economic exchange as fair and priced appropriately.

Despite his uncritical view of the capitalist market, Bezos envisions space exploration as a first step toward relieving the earth of heavy industrial activity by transferring that to the moon and near-earth objects.[25] The expansion of humans around the solar system will produce more geniuses (his examples are white, European males) and more "pioneering" improvements for humankind. This is all facilitated by an economic system that allows people like Bezos to make tremendous fortunes on the theft of labor; a system which will be reproduced and available on the Martian colony's many labor vacancies. Mars colonization would not be possible without the accumulation of land, labor, and capital, particularly of the low-income residents of Silicon Valley who live in the densest cluster of superfund sites in the United States.[26] Despite the exploitative base required to fund private space exploration, fellow travelers like Rick Tumilson, cofounder of the Space Frontier Foundation and asteroid mining company, Deep Space Industries, has called Musk and Bezos' investments evidence of charitable contributions to humankind.[27]

## Capitalism as Hope

The role of the charitable capitalist is to invest in the reproduction of productive labor, and to produce the conditions for a better world that do not destabilize the class structure that enables them to generate wealth. Since life on earth is increasingly precarious, it is no wonder that those with great wealth are investing in humanity-saving measures. Since wealth is not generated by their own labor, capitalists are invested in more than their individual survival. Musk takes issue with the claim that establishing Mars and moon colonies would be "an escape hatch for rich people"[28] and counters that anyone is welcome to be amongst the first colonists, if they are willing to accept the statistical probability that the trip will be fatal.[29] The early stages of space exploration will require building a propellant factory, a power station, and glass domes to grow crops. After establishing the fundamentals of life, Musk claims there will be "an explosion of entrepreneurial activity" because "Mars will need everything from iron foundries, to pizza joints, to nightclubs."[30] By making ships reusable, Musk can reduce the cost-per-flight, which, presumably, gets to the question of whether or not leaving Earth is only for rich people. Musk proposes that making breakthroughs on reusability in rocketry will enable humans to establish a city on Mars. This breakthrough, he claims, is akin to the dramatic industrial changes ushered in by the intercontinental railroad or the sea liners that could cross the ocean. "So we're going to do our best to get you there, and then make sure there's an environment in which entrepreneurs can flourish, and then I think it will be amazing."[31]

Jonathan Nolan, friend of Musk's and producer of the HBO series, *Westworld*, produced a trailer about the launch of the Falcon Heavy rocket. Shot like a commercial for progress, the trailer featured multiple views of the rocket and launch, using footage from the Falcon itself and the dash cam of Musk's red Tesla Roadster, currently orbiting the sun. While David Bowie's "Starman" played triumphantly in the background, the camera found the faces of excited and hopeful men, women, and children, gathered to watch history collide with their Martian future, recalling the sense of common public achievement in footage of people watching the historic mission of Apollo 11.[32] NASA has been replaced by SpaceX, and more specifically by the vision of Musk himself. The public remains the same, except their relationship to space exploration may become one of dire need. Luke argues that Al Gore, the infamously "green" Vice President "deputized himself as a designated driver to defend the ecosphere."[33] Musk secured a dummy in a spacesuit to his spacefaring Roadster, giving a more literal interpretation to the "prophet as designated driver" imagery. This capitalism with a humanitarian face pays lip service to concern for ecological sustainability and the survival of the species, but Mars is an investment. Musk is not concealing nefarious capitalist plans when he protests that his interest is Mars is about adventure first, and survival second.[34] Musk trades on the legitimate fear of running out of habitable space on Earth, and for those living in advanced industrial societies, the loss of a comfortable standard of living as a buffer from the effects of climate change. What could the Silicon Valley version of Mars colonization look like in practice, and what are the alternatives to their vision? Science fiction provides a chance to explore these political, economic, and intellectual trajectories, and to see how they map onto different versions of a liberated species.

## SPECULATIVE FICTION AND POLITICAL THOUGHT

Speculative fiction makes three contributions to studying the politics of Martian colonization. First, Robinson's "realist utopian" vision provides alternatives to global capitalism that are tethered to history and pluralistic: the final book in the series, *Blue Mars*, details a global governance structure that still allows for semi-autonomous communities to experiment with social organizing. While Silicon Valley entrepreneurs present a fairly unified desire for minimal government regulation and maximum economic freedom on a human populated Mars, Robinson spars with their perspectives through various characters taking up different positions. He presents a set of critiques for "business as usual" as well as alternative economic and political systems. Second, literature is an important medium for wrestling with climate change. As is amply clear in electoral politics, climate change is not considered a political priority, and simply dumping more data into the public record has not yielded the great wave of change that is assumed to follow education about a given issue. Ghosh makes the case for literature as a vector of dealing with the lived experiences of climate change by drawing out the "deranged" sociopolitical-economic modes of living that create the conditions for climate change and the attendant suffering. Third, literature has been imagining the political, economic, and social dimensions of Mars colonization centuries before NASA sent rovers to Mars. Thinking through the political considerations and consequences of Mars colonization requires a broad view, and literature has had a robust history with what is now a serious project.

### *Mars Trilogy* and Utopic Thinking

Jameson's work on science fiction and utopias addresses the *Mars Trilogy* specifically. While anchored in hard science and a realistic view of pluralistic and deliberative politics, the trilogy is still considered a utopian work. Works like Robinson's can pose as an intervention to the impression that the real world of a global capitalist economy is unmovable:

> What is crippling is not the presence of an enemy but rather the universal belief, not only that this tendency is irreversible, but that the historical alternatives to capitalism have been proven unviable and impossible, and that no other socio-economy system is conceivable, let alone practically available.[35]

This passage highlights the importance of Robinson's work, since the political battles and dreams for Mars are anchored in the belief that capitalism is not a permanent feature of civilization. The trilogy pays careful attention to the tedium required to realize the dream of a better way to organize human life. This aspect of the novel gets in front of criticism that the new arrangement on Mars could never work "in the real world." Robinson's characters debate the utility or futility of utopian and revolutionary thinking. Robinson contains the debate about the political usefulness of utopian thinking within the narrative of his series.

Whether or not the plans for colonizing Mars come to fruition, the speculative work is just as informative for imagining better life on Earth as it is for imagining life on Mars. Science fiction and the sciences are mutually influential, with terms like "terraforming" and "cyberspace" migrating from literature to science, coding, and popular culture. Likewise, scientific findings about Mars, biology, and genetics are often written into speculative narratives. In *Dying Planet*, Robert Markley works through fiction written about terraforming and colonizing Mars. Markley argues that, "As a liminal space between scientific knowledge and exotic fantasies, Mars becomes a testing ground for new metaphors—and new repackaged narratives—to describe humankind's relationship to the cosmos."[36] Mars is also a testing ground for the human relationship to the environment—on Earth and on Mars—and the limits as well as possibilities of ideologies that include techno-optimism, capitalism, neoliberalism, and socialism. Imagined life on Mars embraces the existing Martian environmental conditions as the starting point for creating life *in situ*. The Mars Society, "the world's largest and most influential space advocacy organization dedicated to the human exploration and settlement of the planet Mars"[37] advocates for colonization to take advantage of the native resources on Mars to generate rocket fuel and raw materials for building the infrastructure of a colony. In *Red Mars*, the first hundred colonists create robots and machines that are able to mine Martian resources and use them for automatic production.[38] In these versions of colonization, the environment on Mars is friendly to large-scale and automated terraforming activities. Without evidence of intelligent life forms, radically altering the Martian landscape does not prompt the same kind of ecological concern as one encounters here on Earth. The lack of concern for the geologic features of Mars prompted serious political tension throughout the trilogy.

Speculative fiction confronts popular justifications for space exploration, including techno-optimism and the indomitable will of the human species to not just survive but to transcend earthy limits. Techno-optimism has been both a solution and critical feature of spacefaring literature. In particular, terraforming is a necessary step to make Mars livable, both in fictional and nonfictional speculation. Terraforming, or "earth moving," is the hypothetical plan to radically alter a planet to make it livable for humans. This research is also described as planetary or geo-engineering, and terraforming has long been depicted in science fiction. Terraforming is one of the central activities that consume the over two thousand pages of the *Mars Trilogy*. The current movement to colonize Mars believes in the power of technology and venture capital to enable humans to outmaneuver our own destructive tendencies, and that at least some of us can transcend the limits of our consciousness, climate change, and liberal democracy to make humans an interplanetary species. The purveyors of space colonizing technologies, from rocket companies to SpaceX's greenhouses, assumes that the humans who found the first Martian cities will bring with them a better way of living than what they are leaving on Earth. Imagined terraforming "holds open the god-like redesign of the red planet."[39] In Stewart Brand's infamous claim to god-like powers, he brings this vision of human transcendence into the world of Silicon Valley and the engineers, investors, artists, and libertarian countercultural groups, who embraced Brand's vision of humans as divine creators.[40] However, Mars is not a static place. Throughout the trilogy, the planet is given a presence all its own, from unusual sunsets to powerful dust storms. Regardless of the success of terraforming, Mars remains an agent and character of its own story.

## The Uncanny Environment

Similar to Robinson's poetic descriptions of planet-consuming Martian dust storms, Ghosh writes about the sudden recognition of the nonhuman that is tightly interwoven with one's everyday life.[41] Literature that addresses the presence of the living environment, particularly as an active agent and not merely as a backdrop to the narrative of human life, is considered a lesser form of fiction. "It is as though in the literary imagination climate change were somehow akin to extraterrestrials or interplanetary travel."[42] Science fiction often embraces extraterrestrials and interplanetary travel, but it also meaningfully includes the environment and even addresses climate change itself. Science fiction wrestles with the felt presence of forces beyond human control but still of the world in which humans live. Why does so-called serious fiction avoid wrestling with the climate, and specifically, catastrophic events connected to climate change? "Quite possibly, then, this era, which so congratulates itself on its self-awareness, will come to be known as the time of the Great Derangement."[43] Ghosh argues that good fiction often seeks to represent what Moretti describes as "the narrative pleasure compatible with the new regularity of bourgeois life . . . they are part of what Weber called the 'rationalization' of modern life."[44] Perhaps one of the characteristics of the Great Derangement is imagining that the environment is changing only for people who make poor decisions, whether they are the rich who continue to develop property on drowning beachfronts, or the poor who, under the neoliberal logic of the West, have not yet worked their way out of their destitution, which happens to place them in neighborhoods and even nations getting battered by a changing climate. While fantasy, horror, and science fiction are "evicted from the mansion in which serious fiction has been in residence,"[45] these very genres are the closest to depicting life as it is for billions of people who have been living with the uncanny presence of a changing climate.

Stories like the *Mars Trilogy*, *Solaris*, and Philip K. Dick's short stories challenge the promise of bourgeois predictability and ability to master nature. Robinson's work comes the closest to playing out the triumph of human ingenuity in the successful terraforming process on Mars and beyond, but he spends considerable energy working out a spiritual or religious understanding of all life, and in particular life on Mars. Even the moderate political parties on Mars maintain respect for the planet itself, whose dust storms and glaciers regularly thwart, humble, and awe its human inhabitants. Ghosh argues that literature should not leave environmental catastrophe to magical or fantastical stories, because this would "rob them of precisely the quality that makes them so urgently compelling—which is that they are actually happening on this earth, at this time."[46] I argue that science fiction does not necessarily turn the real dangers of climate change into fantasy, but instead offers a different style for integrating the uncanny relations between human and environment and the lived experiences of climate change and related disasters.

Ghosh brings out the uncanny from Timothy Morton's work, and provides vocabulary for acknowledging the constant presence of nonhuman forces in the world in which humans live. "And to be alerted to such interventions is also to become uncannily aware that conversations amongst ourselves have always had other participants: it is like finding out that one's telephone has been tapped for years . . ."[47] While Ghosh expresses concern that climate fiction and science fiction wrestle with future disasters rather than the ones happening in real time, I find the *Mars Trilogy* to be exceptional in this case. While the trilogy is set in the future, and the technology for terraforming is not yet available, the state of Robinson's planet Earth is not just a harbinger for things to come. The fictional planet Earth endured what our current planet does: rapid loss of polar ice caps, mal-distribution of resources across a growing global population, and the political crisis of climate change refugees. Because science fiction is given greater latitude to engage the extraterrestrial, extrasensory, and uncanny, the *Trilogy*, among similar science fiction works, is uniquely positioned to mix projection and contemporary events. This effort gives fullness to the dense network of climate change, collective and individual anxiety, political and economic systems that produce the conditions for climate change, and the forces of nature that pass through it all.

Science fiction does more than help us navigate the challenges of a changing climate; it also serves as a way to tease out different assumptions about how to face current conditions. Some science fiction mirrors back the dominant narrative of human ingenuity that always produces just-in-time technological solutions to catastrophic problems. Other works, like *Solaris*, offer a deep critique of such an attitude. Even though Mars colonization falls into the category of future speculation, the public and private sectors are busy pouring resources into seeing this project through. Mars colonization is often presented as a solution to the crises of climate change and population pressures. Capitalists like Bezos and Musk claim their spacefaring ventures are philanthropic, and to offer hope to those who may be weary of the environmentalist movement doomsday warnings. Rather than view Mars colonization as simply the daydreams of those with idle riches, it should be given due consideration as a current part of our political, cultural, and economic landscape, and as a window into the politics of a post-climate change world. In the same world in which people are drowning in rising tides and superstorms, Silicon Valley entrepreneurs are energized by the economic and political prospects of sending human consciousness into space.

## SCIENCE FICTION AND SPACE COLONIZATION

The *Mars Trilogy* is an exhaustively researched fictional study of a multinational effort to colonize Mars that, over time, becomes a hotly contested venture to colonize the solar system. Against the backdrop of a rapidly warming Earth, the mostly Russian and American scientists work together and against one another to determine the fate of Mars. The characters bring to the story a wide range of political ideologies and visions of a good life and healthy relationship with the environment. Some work hand in glove with multinational corporations who jostle for the chance to control the connection between Earth and Martian economies; others build a new religion, *viriditas*, which calls for love of others and love of all life; and between these poles exists a range of socialists, anarchists, radical environmentalists, and centrists. Much of the last book in the series, *Blue Mars*, takes up the laborious work of creating Mars' first constitution and government, which comes at the end of terrestrial and Martian revolutions and significant climactic change on both planets.

The First One Hundred scientists, who are the first humans to colonize Mars, realize the potential for radical change the closer they get to arriving on their new home planet. During the voyage from Earth to Mars, an emergency onboard the rocket *Ares* brought together all members of the crew in one place. Arkady Bogdanov, a Russian scientist who would later become the leader of the communist political group the Bogdanovists, made a radical suggestion to abort the plans given to them by Earth and start anew.

> 'We have been sent here by our governments, and *all* of our governments are flawed, most of them disastrously. It's why history is such a bloody mess. Now we are on our own, and I for one have no intention of repeating all of Earth's mistakes just because of conventional thinking. We are the first Martian colonists! We are *scientists*! It is our *job* to think new, to make them new!'[48]

Arkady sees the colonization project as an opportunity to disregard the capitalist economy as the animating force behind technological innovation and civilization building. While few of the investors in modern Mars colonization openly talk about their political ambitions for Mars, they operate on the assumption that capitalism and neoliberalism will guide the settlement. Through Robinson's imagining, we not only see the influence of other ideologies, but the influence of distance from the Earth. For Bogdanov, science and politics are natural companions. When he begins to discuss the political decisions inherent in the architecture of new settlements, fellow scientists argue that their work is technical, not political. "'Everything is political' Arkady said at their backs. 'Nothing more so than this voyage of ours. We are beginning a new society, how could it help but be political?' 'We're a scientific station,' Sax said. 'It doesn't necessarily have much politics to it.'"[49] For Bogdanov, who will make a case for communal living and work beyond wages, their role as scientists is synonymous with freethinking. For him, this is more powerful than their position as delegates for a multinational effort to transplant modern, Western civilization on another planet to create the infrastructure for repeating Earth's mistakes. Musk has articulated an underdeveloped view of what a politics of Mars would look like, in the short term:

> I think most likely, the form of government of Mars would be somewhat of a direct democracy, where you vote on issues, where people vote directly on issues, instead of going through representative government.... But I think on Mars most likely it's going to be people ... everyone votes on every issue, and that's how it goes.[50]

Musk's vision of democracy is one that supports very few people, and a light regulatory scheme. He argues that laws should have a short word count and should not be indecipherable. Laws should also not inhibit development, and it should be changeable relatively quickly.[51] While Musk wants to send civilization on a rocket to protect it from its untimely demise on a carbon choked Earth, he does not want to see it reproduce itself exactly as it has been on Earth. For Musk, a better civilization is possible, with the bare bones of democracy, but mostly a political environment that contains the elements of Silicon Valley: flexible, responsive, and entrepreneurial. In the hands of the peninsula's billionaire capitalists, the solutions to scarcity and precarity on Earth are a mere intensification of the dehumanizing and environmentally exploitative tendencies on Mars. The Silicon Valley visionaries and their true believers do not see themselves as ideologues, but rather as scientists and technologists.

The Martian colonists in the *Mars Trilogy* have a more robust sense of politics than the peninsula's capitalists. The conclusion of the protracted collaboration to produce the Martian constitution delivered decision-making mechanisms that permitted cities and societies to experiment with their own organization, from matriarchy to anarchy, while still accounting for their connection to the whole. The constitution had to account for climate change refugees from Earth; the pace and goals of terraforming Mars; terraforming resistance movements; and the lingering influence of metanational corporations and the United Nations, although these agencies had lost influence on Mars over the course of several revolutions. The new government was composed of checks and balances to maintain fairly equal representation of different interests and ideologies, and made a judiciary focused on environmental law and protection of Mars. Despite the intense planning for a Martian economy and system of governance, the planet developed new characteristics beyond the control of anyone, from bacterial development to land mammals. The occasional dust storm could still suffocate agriculture. The human inhabitants were free to experiment with trade and currency systems separate from capitalism, and one could join a band of anarcho-primitivists one day and find themselves on a government council the next. Science and research was produced for public good instead of being tied to private or corporate funding. Even the technocrats understood that everything is political, that how they approach eco-managerialism is not value-free, and the decisions about how to shape Mars into a habitable planet were also decisions about the kind of politics and economic systems that could flourish, or it should be left behind. Earth served as a kind of warning about the excesses of global capital and the resultant inequalities that made climate change a differentially borne burden. The trilogy is especially powerful for its deep engagement with the changing climates on each planet, and its attunement to the microscopic and massive scale changes that are intertwined with the efforts to promote flourishing human life. As Ghosh argued, one way to address climate change is to meaningfully include it in the way we use literature to confront and explore our lives and politics. As a contrast to Robinson's optimistic view of human ingenuity, other science fiction writers have dire warnings about our short-sighted efforts to colonize space.

## TEMPERING ENTHUSIASM

Two stories in particular produce pessimistic accounts of the human attempt to dominate other worlds. In Stanislaw Lem's novel, *Solaris*, and Dick's short story, "The Survey Team," humans overstate their capacity to control and create on a new planet. In *Solaris*, teams of scientists from Earth study and live on the surface of a sentient ocean on the planet Solaris. Despite their tremendous scientific efforts, the ocean thwarts any human understanding, while at the same time, it penetrates the subconscious of the scientists on its surface, driving many of them to lose their minds. In "The Survey Team," a group of desperate scientists leave the wrecked and war-torn Earth to establish a colony on Mars. Back at home, humans live in subsurface tunnels and their adaptation to subterranean life is grim and dehumanizing. Once the survey team arrives on Mars, they find the Martians had long since departed for a more promising planet after consuming all life-giving resources on Mars. The team makes the unnerving discovery that the pristine planet the Martians colonized thousands of years earlier was Earth, and theirs was an unhappy homecoming with two dead planets in their wake. Most of the team quickly recover from shock and shore up their determination to find a better, "virgin" planet, leaving one lone team member to reflect on the destructive hubris of humans: "'We'll find it, yet. A virgin world. A world that's unspoiled.' 'Unspoiled,' Young echoed. 'Nobody there ahead of us.' 'We'll be the first,' Judde muttered avidly. 'It's wrong!' Mason shouted. 'Two are enough! Let's not destroy a third world!' Nobody listened to him."[52]

This story critiques the fantasy that space colonization allows for endless resource exploitation to sustain human civilization. The political movement of environmentalism is rendered obsolete if any given environmental resource can be supplemented with the endless environments found in outer space. The fantasy of infinite growth also renders obsolete criticisms of capitalism. Growth has long been targeted by critics of capitalism as a problematic feature of the economy and use of the environment. The twin desires of endless growth and endless environmental resources are projected into space, where Mars serves as the most realistic new planet to settle and loop into Earth capitalism. Robert Zubrin, founder of the Mars Society and former engineer at Lockheed Martin Astronautics, has long linked Mars colonization with revitalizing the frontier spirit that will unlock resource abundance and the human drive to take human consciousness out of a single world and spread it to multiple. Zubrin views Mars colonization as the promise of harnessing the endless resources in space to the inherently entrepreneurial nature of humans who are destined to discover and colonize:

> We must go for the opportunity. The settling of the Martian New World is an opportunity for a noble experiment in which humanity has another chance to shed old baggage and begin the world anew; carrying forward as much of the best of our heritage as possible and leaving the worst behind.[53]

Markley reckons with Zubrin by calling out his assumption "that 'natural' resources are always and already marked as objects of exploitation and exchange."[54] Contemporary Mars colonization enthusiasts like Musk, Bezos, and members of The Mars Society, are much like Dick's survey team. They are convinced of the inherent supremacy of human life, which is worth preserving at all costs; they are sure of their technological ability to colonize new planets; and their hubristic sales pitches for geo-engineering livable cities both overstates human intelligence and understates the political and economic systems that have produced the precarious environmental and social conditions on Earth.

Lem's *Solaris* gives a skeptical take on the possibilities of colonizing other planets, particularly outside of our solar system. *Solaris* makes clear that not only are humans radically underprepared—intellectually and emotionally—to encounter the sentient ocean on Solaris, but our use of the scientific method has left only libraries of speculation. As scientists across generations of explorers on Solaris find themselves haunted by the invisible probing of the ocean, they seek retribution and destruction of the ocean, rather than acknowledging the limits of the human species. After arriving at the station on Solaris, the main protagonist, Kelvin, is visited by the form of a long departed lover, who does not know why she is there, but is desperately attached to him. In conversation with fellow scientist, Snow, who is similarly burdened with a demanding visitor, they realize that the ocean that covers the planet is able to read their minds while revealing nothing of itself. Snow explains that the self-satisfaction one feels about space travel and scientific inquiry is "a sham." "We don't want to conquer the cosmos, we simply want to extend the boundaries of Earth to the frontiers of the cosmos. . . . We are only seeking Man. We have no need of other worlds. We need mirrors. We don't know what to do with other worlds."[55] When Kelvin presses for clarification, Snow answers, "I'm talking about what we all wanted: contact with another civilization. Now we've got it! And we can observe through a microscope, as it were, our own monstrous ugliness, our folly, our shame!"[56] The encounter with a new kind of intelligence on Solaris has only reflected the worst of humankind, both the psychic depths of the individual scientists who encounter the ocean, and the whole of Western civilization and the desire to dominate and reproduce itself wherever it goes.

The confrontation with this alien is so overwhelming and beyond the imagination, that contact with the ocean unspools human rationality and stability. Lem's grim view of space exploration serves as a warning to Silicon Valley entrepreneurs who, in their descriptions of future space exploration and colonization, fantasize about making Earth elsewhere, even precisely to remake modern Western civilization. This attitude betrays not just an interest in maintaining systems of domination that serve the superrich who promote this mission, but an impoverished view of what space exploration can teach us about being human. Even in Robinson's optimistic series, the character Ann, who spearheads a movement to protect Mars from human interference, echoes Snow when she expresses her fear of a terraformed Mars: "We'll all go on and make the place safe. Roads, cities. New sky, new soil. Until it's all some kind of Siberia or Northwest Territories, and Mars will be gone and we'll be here, and we'll wonder why we feel so empty. Why when we look at the land we can never see anything but our own faces."[57]

One of the reasons Mars is an appealing destination, besides the great effort humans have put into studying the planet and rendering its mysteries through images, rover findings, and satellite, is that Mars appears to promise an absence of extraterrestrial intelligence. Like the moon, it can be dominated by human industrial forces and entrepreneurial spirit, the indomitable will of the human to plant life and save civilization from threats on Earth, especially from an increasingly uncontrollable climate. Mars is a *tabula rasa*, a seed bank for civilization, and according to Musk, an insurance policy for terrestrial end times.[58] Musk is not just promising an escape route if the going gets impossible on Earth, he is also shaping the new civilization that would take root in the bio-domes and, later, the terraformed atmosphere of a habitable Mars. Whatever of Earth is transported to Mars—technologies, humans, economics—will not remain static, so whatever is being ensured is a moving target. This potential for a change of plans offers more hope than venture capitalism could. Science fiction provides a set of imaginative tools for thinking through what might cause the end of civilization, and what kind of politics would be necessary to forestall our demise, or to encourage something new.

## CONCLUSION

Silicon Valley space entrepreneurs look to the stars while ignoring their own role in producing unlivable conditions on Earth, from low wages for laborers to union busting to abdicating responsibility for the twenty-four Superfund sites in the heart of their industrial and intellectual home. I have made the argument that the movement to colonize Mars is an effort to avoid human species extinction on a climatically changing Earth, and it is an effort to control the direction of civilization and evolutionary change by mobilizing private capital to replace public decision making. I have also argued that to understand these space efforts it is vital to understand the history of Silicon Valley and the culture in which the new space race has developed. Science fiction has for a long time imagined interplanetary human life, and has elaborated different political, economic, and cultural realities on Mars and Earth. Since Silicon Valley's imagination has not yet stretched beyond the technical and capital, science fiction can help us think through what the proposals are now, and what this might look like if actualized. Science fiction, like the *Mars Trilogy*, puts different political ideologies and economic formations in conflict and conversation with each other, and presents us with a chance to see these through their logical conclusions. Science fiction has long been influenced by political philosophy. Using science fiction as a critical tool is an opportunity to reflect on the foundations of Silicon Valley's Martian projects, as it forces us to think hard about the political stakes of technological means to produce human emancipation under conditions of capitalism. Silicon Valley is producing particular versions of Martian colonization, but this does not have to be representative of a collective effort or conversation. If we find Silicon Valley ethos problematic, then it would be prudent to stop deferring the big questions of climate change and interplanetary colonization to them.

## NOTES

1. Adi Robertson, "SpaceX Wants to Be the Railroad of the Future," *The Verge*, September 27, 2016, https://www.theverge.com/2016/9/27/13080970/spacex-elon-musk-mars-expedition-railroad-of-the-future.
2. Corey Pein, "Mouthbreathing Machiavellis Dream of a Silicon Reich," *The Baffler*, May 19, 2014, https://thebaffler.com/latest/mouthbreathing-machiavellis.
3. Mark O'Connell, "Why Silicon Valley Billionaires Are Prepping for the Apocalypse in New Zealand," *The Guardian*, February 15, 2018, sec. News, https://www.theguardian.com/news/2018/feb/15/why-silicon-valley-billionaires-are-prepping-for-the-apocalypse-in-new-zealand.
4. Robert Markley, *Dying Planet* (Durham: Duke University Press, 2005). 2
5. Frederic Jameson, "'If I Find One Good City I Will Spare the Man': Realism and Utopia in Kim Stanley Robinson's Mars Trilogy.," in *Learning from Other Worlds: Estrangement, Cognition, and the Politics of Science Fiction and Utopia* (Liverpool: Liverpool University Press, 2000).
6. Christophe Lécuyer, *Making Silicon Valley* (Cambridge: MIT Press, 2007).
7. Fred Turner, *From Counterculture to Cyberculture* (Chicago: University of Chicago Press, 2006).
8. Ibid., p.82
9. Stewart Brand, "Back Issues—Whole Earth Catalog," accessed June 13, 2020, http://www.wholeearth.com/back-issues.php.
10. Stewart Brand, *Space Colonies*, ed. Stewart Brand (Penguin Books, 1977). 5
11. Ibid.

12. Sean Parson and Emily Ray, "Sustainable Colonization: Tar Sands as Resource Colonialism," *Capitalism Nature Socialism* 29, no. 3 (2018): 68–86, doi:10.1080/10455752.2016.1268187.

13. Alan Boyle, "Jeff Bezos: 'We Will Have to Leave This Planet . . . and It's Going to Make This Planet Better,'" *GeekWire*, May 29, 2018, https://www.geekwire.com/2018/jeff-bezos-isdc-space-vision/.

14. Turner, *From Counterculture to Cyberculture*.

15. Ibid., 149.

16. David Harvey, *A Brief History of Neoliberalism* (New York: Oxford University Press, 2007), 64.

17. Alana Semuels, "I Delivered Packages for Amazon and It Was a Nightmare," *The Atlantic*, June 25, 2018, https://www.theatlantic.com/technology/archive/2018/06/amazon-flex-workers/563444/.

18. Harvey, *A Brief History of Neoliberalism*, 65–66.

19. "Ticket to Mars Should Be Affordable," *BBC News*, September 27, 2016, https://www.bbc.com/news/av/science-environment-37491588/elon-musk-ticket-to-mars-human-colony-should-be-affordable.

20. Boyle, "Jeff Bezos."

21. Ibid.

22. Michael Sainato, "Exploited Amazon Workers Need a Union. When Will They Get One?" *The Guardian*, July 8, 2018, sec. Opinion, https://www.theguardian.com/commentisfree/2018/jul/08/amazon-jeff-bezos-unionize-working-conditions.

23. AP Press, "Greenpeace Gives Low Marks to Tech Giants Amazon, Samsung," October 17, 2017, https://www.cbsnews.com/news/greenpeace-gives-low-marks-to-tech-giants-amazon-samsung/.

24. Karl Marx, "Economic Manuscripts: Capital Vol. I—Chapter One," *Marxists.Org*, accessed June 12, 2020, https://www.marxists.org/archive/marx/works/1867-c1/ch01.htm.

25. Boyle, "Jeff Bezos."

26. Lisa Sun-Hee Park and David N. Pellow, "Racial Formation, Environmental Racism, and the Emergence of Silicon Valley," *Ethnicities* 4, no. 3 (2004): 403–24.

27. Boyle, "Jeff Bezos."

28. "Breaking down Elon Musk's Surprise, Sold-out Talk at SXSW," *Engadget*, accessed June 12, 2020, https://www.engadget.com/2018-03-12-elon-musk-sxsw-spacex-tesla-mars-ai-future-nolan.html.

29. Mahita Gajanan, "Watch Live: Elon Musk Announces Plans for SpaceX Mars Mission," *Time*, September 27, 2016, https://time.com/4510167/elon-musk-spacex-mars-watch-live/.

30. "Breaking down Elon Musk's Surprise, Sold-out Talk at SXSW."

31. Ibid.

32. Bryan Bishop, "Elon Musk and the Creator of Westworld Made an Inspirational Trailer for the Falcon Heavy Launch—The Verge," *The Verge*, March 10, 2018, https://www.theverge.com/2018/3/10/17105322/elon-musk-spacex-falcon-heavy-westworld-jonathan-nolan-trailer-sxsw.

33. Timothy W. Luke, "The Climate Change Imaginary," *Current Sociology Monograph* 63, no. 2 (2015): 284.

34. Gajanan, "Watch Live."

35. Jameson, "'If I Find One Good City I Will Spare the Man': Realism and Utopia in Kim Stanley Robinson's Mars Trilogy," xii.

36. Markley, *Dying Planet*, 271.

37. Robert Zubrin, "Founding Declaration—The Mars Society," *The Mars Society*, accessed June 12, 2020, https://www.marssociety.org/founding-declaration/.

38. Kim Stanley Robinson, *Red Mars* (New York: Bantam Books, 1992).

39. Markley, *Dying Planet*, 294.

40. Turner, *From Counterculture to Cyberculture*.

41. Amitav Ghosh, *The Great Derangement* (Chicago: Chicago University Press, 2016).

42. Ibid., 7.

43. Ibid., 11.

44. Ibid., 19.
45. Ibid., 24.
46. Ibid., 27.
47. Ibid., 31.
48. Robinson, *Red Mars*, 61.
49. Ibid., 60.
50. "Breaking down Elon Musk's Surprise, Sold-out Talk at SXSW."
51. Ibid.
52. Philip K. Dick, *The Complete Stories of Philip K. Dick Vol.2* (Citadel Twilight, 1986), 927.
53. Zubrin, "Founding Declaration—The Mars Society."
54. Markley, *Dying Planet*, 366.
55. Stanislaw Lem, *Solaris* (Boston: Mariner Books, n.d.), 72.
56. Ibid., 72–73.
57. Robinson, *Red Mars*, 158.
58. Neil Strauss, "Elon Musk: Inventor's Plans for Outer Space, Cars, Finding Love—Rolling Stone," *Rolling Stone*, November 15, 2017, https://www.rollingstone.com/culture/culture-features/elon-musk-the-architect-of-tomorrow-120850/.

# BIBLIOGRAPHY

AP Press. "Greenpeace Gives Low Marks to Tech Giants Amazon, Samsung." CBS News, October 17, 2017. https://www.cbsnews.com/news/greenpeace-gives-low-marks-to-tech-giants-amazon-samsung/.

Bishop, Bryan. "Elon Musk and the Creator of Westworld Made an Inspirational Trailer for the Falcon Heavy Launch—The Verge." *The Verge*, March 10, 2018. https://www.theverge.com/2018/3/10/17105322/elon-musk-spacex-falcon-heavy-westworld-jonathan-nolan-trailer-sxsw.

Boyle, Alan. "Jeff Bezos: 'We Will Have to Leave This Planet . . . and It's Going to Make This Planet Better.'" *GeekWire*, May 29, 2018. https://www.geekwire.com/2018/jeff-bezos-isdc-space-vision/.

Brand, Stewart. "Back Issues—Whole Earth Catalog." Accessed June 13, 2020. http://www.wholeearth.com/back-issues.php.

Brand, Steward. *Space Colonies*. Edited by Stewart Brand. Penguin Books, 1977.

"Breaking down Elon Musk's Surprise, Sold-out Talk at SXSW." *Engadget*. Accessed June 12, 2020. https://www.engadget.com/2018-03-12-elon-musk-sxsw-spacex-tesla-mars-ai-future-nolan.html.

Dick, Philip K. *The Complete Stories of Philip K. Dick Vol.2*. Citadel Twilight, 1986.

Gajanan, Mahita. "Watch Live: Elon Musk Announces Plans for SpaceX Mars Mission." *Time*, September 27, 2016. https://time.com/4510167/elon-musk-spacex-mars-watch-live/.

Ghosh, Amitav. *The Great Derangement*. Chicago: Chicago University Press, 2016.

Harvey, David. *A Brief History of Neoliberalism*. New York: Oxford University Press, 2007.

Jameson, Frederic. "'If I Find One Good City I Will Spare the Man': Realism and Utopia in Kim Stanley Robinson's Mars Trilogy." In *Learning from Other Worlds: Estrangement, Cognition, and the Politics of Science Fiction and Utopia*. Liverpool: Liverpool University Press, 2000.

Lécuyer, Christophe. *Making Silicon Valley*. Cambridge: MIT Press, 2007.

Lem, Stanislaw. *Solaris*. Boston: Mariner Books, n.d.

Luke, Timothy W. "The Climate Change Imaginary." *Current Sociology Monograph* 63, no. 2 (2015): 280–96.

Markley, Robert. *Dying Planet*. Durham: Duke University Press, 2005.

Marx, Karl. "Economic Manuscripts: Capital Vol. I—Chapter One." *Marxists.Org*. Accessed June 12, 2020. https://www.marxists.org/archive/marx/works/1867-c1/ch01.htm.

O'Connell, Mark. "Why Silicon Valley Billionaires Are Prepping for the Apocalypse in New Zealand." *The Guardian*, February 15, 2018, sec. News. https://www.theguardian.com/

news/2018/feb/15/why-silicon-valley-billionaires-are-prepping-for-the-apocalypse-in-new-zealand.

Park, Lisa Sun-Hee, and David N. Pellow. "Racial Formation, Environmental Racism, and the Emergence of Silicon Valley." *Ethnicities* 4, no. 3 (2004): 403–24.

Parson, Sean, and Emily Ray. "Sustainable Colonization: Tar Sands as Resource Colonialism." *Capitalism Nature Socialism* 29, no. 3 (2018): 68–86. doi:10.1080/10455752.2016.1268187.

Pein, Corey. "Mouthbreathing Machiavellis Dream of a Silicon Reich." *The Baffler*, May 19, 2014. https://thebaffler.com/latest/mouthbreathing-machiavellis.

Robertson, Adi. "SpaceX Wants to Be the Railroad of the Future." *The Verge*, September 27, 2016. https://www.theverge.com/2016/9/27/13080970/spacex-elon-musk-mars-expedition-railroad-of-the-future.

Robinson, Kim Stanley. *Red Mars*. New York: Bantam Books, 1992.

Sainato, Michael. "Exploited Amazon Workers Need a Union. When Will They Get One?" *The Guardian*, July 8, 2018, sec. Opinion. https://www.theguardian.com/commentisfree/2018/jul/08/amazon-jeff-bezos-unionize-working-conditions.

Semuels, Alana. "I Delivered Packages for Amazon and It Was a Nightmare." *The Atlantic*, June 25, 2018. https://www.theatlantic.com/technology/archive/2018/06/amazon-flex-workers/563444/.

Strauss, Neil. "Elon Musk: Inventor's Plans for Outer Space, Cars, Finding Love—Rolling Stone." *Rolling Stone*, November 15, 2017. https://www.rollingstone.com/culture/culture-features/elon-musk-the-architect-of-tomorrow-120850/.

"Ticket to Mars Should Be Affordable." *BBC News*, September 27, 2016. https://www.bbc.com/news/av/science-environment-37491588/elon-musk-ticket-to-mars-human-colony-should-be-affordable.

Turner, Fred. *From Counterculture to Cyberculture*. Chicago: University of Chicago Press, 2006.

Zubrin, Robert. "Founding Declaration—The Mars Society." *The Mars Society*. Accessed June 12, 2020. https://www.marssociety.org/founding-declaration/.

*Part IV*

# Reconstructing Ourselves: Identity and Agency

*Chapter Ten*

# A Future Is Female

*Loving Animals and Scientific Romance*

Claire E. Rasmussen

The image regularly associated with Darwin's *The Descent of Man* is a valuable visualization of modernity. In the familiar series of images, a primate walking on all fours is followed by a series of evolving figures eventually becoming the upright figure of Homo sapiens, the (hu)Man. This representation of the scientific theory of evolution is directional, with Man walking to his right as if strolling toward the future, away from his more animal past. This tapestry of scientific knowledge, the triumph of humanism, and the ideal of progress all fit within a horizon of self-understanding of modernity. It is within this milieu that the genre of Science Fiction is also born, a similarly future-facing narrative exploring themes of humanism in the face of scientific and technological progress and the ambivalence and anxiety about this flight from the past. As representations of what it means to be Human in the modern world, both Science and Science Fiction grapple with questions about the horizon of humanity in the wake of rapid, exciting, and disorienting change. The figure of the past—the quadruped ape—represents the undomesticated and wild past that haunts the present. The bipedal human strides into the future in flight from his own animality.

As a genre linked with colonial modernity, Science Fiction regularly explores the limits of (hu)mankind in a world of scientific and technological change with figures like cyborgs, robots, and AI threatening to supplement or supplant their human predecessors. Animality, on the other hand, may represent the undomesticated and sentimentalized past or may serve as a grotesquely altered monstrosity, a perversion of nature. As with modernity, Science Fiction as a genre has been shaped by the historical circumstances of colonialism, scientific racism, sexual difference, and other relations of domination. Representing other possible worlds, SciFi has sometimes mirrored hegemonic relationships in the world and at other times has challenged them through its imaginary worlds. A genre about encounters with difference and strangeness, SciFi has often grappled with social and political questions of alterity through metaphorical representations of nonhuman beings whether alien or machine.[1] As such we can read these texts as a part of what Agamben called "the anthropological machine," a conceptual apparatus that continually produces "Human" as a coherent and exceptional category, a distinction enabling a moral humanism but that also tends to denigrate or demote nonhuman life.[2]

Thinking with Science Fiction may a particularly valuable exercise at this historical juncture as theorists call on us to rethink the relationships between human and nonhuman and nature and culture as a necessary precondition for adequately addressing the Anthropocene, or an era in which human action has become the dominant force in shaping nature and ecology.[3] As a genre based in speculative fiction, SciFi does the work of imagining other possible worlds in ways that are productive for the reader in establishing a new relationship between future and present via an "imaginative alteration or critical intensification of the present."[4]

Science Fiction does the work of political theory, moving between the critical and imaginative registers meant to open up other social and political possibilities. Kilgore asks:

> Can we imagine futures in which our descendents differ profoundly from ourselves while exisiting with us in a shared history? The question requires that we consider an epistemic change, a new structure of feeling incommensurate with the currently dominant hegemony . . . it is that incommensurability that represents political hope . . . that the current configuration of society and life is neither stable nor permanent and a new social order, an alternative to what is now 'straight' is well within the horizon of social thought and action.[5]

In the spirit of speculative hope I examine two films sitting uncomfortably within the genre of Science Fiction, creating discomfort about the human/animal distinction. The 2017 film *The Shape of Water* explores a relationship between a woman and a humanoid animal of unclear origin. Also from 2017, *Okja* is a film about Mija, a Korean girl in an alternative present raising Okja, a "Super Pig" created in the lab of an industrial agriculture organization. Both are about intimate relationships between gendered human-animals and a particular nonhuman animal. Neither film presents an alternative world that might be characterized as a utopia but they gesture toward other ways of relating to nonhuman animals that refuse to reproduce relationships of hierarchy and domination. Dramatically different films tackling different pathologies of modernity, both films are propelled by the attachment of female subjects to their animal others in ways that challenge hierarchies embedded in the anthropological machine not only in the ways that it divides human and animal but also differentiates amongst humans.

My argument is situated in a consideration of the intersection of temporality and sexuality in these films, specifically the way that the very idea of a possible future is dependent upon reproduction, both literal and cultural. These ideas are central to the modernist milieu that gave rise to the genre of Science Fiction and thus are regular themes in the literature, as discussed below. The image of the human moving forward in history is also a story of inheritance through particular bodies that, presumably, must improve across time. These processes implicate embodied subjectivities including, obviously, race and gender, but also class, disability and species. Building on literature on the role of the idea of kinship in reproducing not only lineage but hierarchy, this chapter argues that these films suggest other possibilities of inheritance with and through the bodies of animals.[6] Displacing conventional models of kinship as heteronormative reproduction, the non-normative models of kinship enact Haraway's gesture toward different kinds of kin:

> My purpose is to make "kin" mean something other/more than entities tied by ancestry or genealogy. The gently defamiliarizing move might seem for a while to be just a mistake, but then (with luck) appear as correct all along. Kin-making is making persons, not necessarily as individuals or as humans. I was moved in college by Shakespeare's punning between kin and kind—the kindest were not necessarily kin as family; making kin and making kin . . . stretch the imagination and can change the story.[7]

Rather than seeking progress in the figure of Man, strolling upright away from his animal past, I suggest these films suggest a different future through imagining women loving animals, throwing their bodies against the anthropological machine in a way that defies the boundary between human and animal in a way that resists hegemonic power.

## SCIENCE/FICTION/FUTURE

I locate the genre of science fiction within modernity, specifically two nineteenth-century phenomenon that profoundly shape the genre's development. The first is the experience of colonialism and its continual encounter with otherness. The second is the scientific discourse of evolutionary biology challenging metaphysical interpretations of humanity by placing humanity within the biological category of animal. These two trends are linked to the phenomenon of reproduction—literal and social—and complications of the passage of biological and cultural inheritance through embodiment. As Foucault[8] discusses in his analysis of biopolitics, this concern about biology as a bridge between past and future places an increased emphasis on race—the maintenance of humanity at the level of species—and gender—in a responsibilization for reproduction placed primarily upon women. These combine in an idea of *reproductive futurity*, the attempt to manage the development of the human species into the future via the governance of sexuality. While seemingly far distant from ideas about animals, sexuality, gender, and race, are vital to the engine of reproductive futurity creating new forms of governance and new subjectivities tied with ideas of population, species, race, and what is proper to the human.

While Science Fiction has earlier predecessors, most scholars place its explosion as a clear literary genre in the nineteenth century where a rising popularity of speculative fiction considering possible consequences—dystopic and utopic—of scientific and technological development for society. For a variety of reasons that will become clear, I will lean heavily on H.G. Wells' description of his works aimed at considering how the world might or ought to be as "scientific romances."[9] In these works an alternative reality is generated to explore the reader's responses as if they were living inside of that world, to create an illusion of possibility enabling the suspension of disbelief, a pause in one's assumption about how the world works in order to consider ourselves differently.

A central theme in Science Fiction has often been considering the limits of the properly Human, considering how humanity might respond to, and how it might be differentiated from, encounters with difference whether aliens, cyborgs, cylons or others, and the limits of the human in the wake of a variety of technological interventions. As a consequence, Science Fiction has always been a part of the anthropological machine, producing how we define the Human, how we differentiate between humans and their others. Two specific challenges posed by modernity are of interest to my analysis. The first is produced in the realm of science where we see emerging evolutionary discourse that places humans closer to animals in the biological continuum than previously thought. The second is political, processes of colonization and imperialism that differentiate among humans and, similarly, requiring a redrawing of relationships of hierarchy and domination.

These anxieties about the definitional certainty of the category of the human surface in depictions of scientific discoveries involving the continuity of human biology with its nonhuman others as well as considering the implication of encounters with otherness. From Wells's *The Island of Dr. Moreau*'s human-animal hybrids and the beastly possibilities of (hu)man to *The Planet of the Apes* series projecting a future in which our primate cousins have become ascendant, the tenuous nature of the human/animal boundary has been a persistent theme.[10] These depictions of the "permeability of the human/animal boundary" including relationships of both human and nonhuman animals to technology and machines offer a way of grappling with the political possibilities of these encounters.[11] These representations may reaffirm existing hierarchies, between human and animal and amongst humans, or may reveal their constructed and contingent nature.

The fields of evolution, anatomy, and biology generally brought the modernist discourses of science and humanism into potential conflict. Discoveries demonstrating humans were biologically similar to their animal others challenged assumptions that humans possessed a clear, metaphysical difference from others that both made them a clear and separable classification and justified the dominance of humans over other forms of nature. Foucault's *The Order of Things* catalogued a range of scientific discoveries placed humans inside of rather than above the natural world in ways that emphasized a biological continuity with the natural world, especially animals, in an "explicitly materialist 'science of man' at the beginning of the nineteenth century, as well as evolutionary theory later on, [that] was anathema to those who continued to insist that humans were ontologically distinct from nonhumans."[12]

Foucault describes the emergence of an "anatomical humanism" seeking to identify the locus of difference in the body, highlighting continuity amongst biological specimens while explaining how variations established significant differences and hierarchies. Human exceptionalism took on a biologized rather than metaphysical form to differentiate between "human and brute" through identifying anatomical characteristics (like bipedalism) as predicting intellectual capacity and thus defining moral responsibility.[13] Not surprisingly this period also sees the emergence of scientific racism utilizing physical differences as a means of categorizing different humans as variously more and less advanced, often through "scientific" practices like craniometry that claimed human reason was not an abstract property but the product of a "uniquely human anatomy."[14] Scholars of disability have also noted the ways in which this shift to the biological as determining the essence of Human in the body provided a means of defining the properly human in scientific terms "rhetorical tool for justifying exploitation and domination" by limiting moral consideration to particular biological forms.[15]

The biologization of (hu)man also turned to culture as a means of further differentiating humans and animals through a need to establish a dominance over the body itself. If a hierarchy was fixed in nature and readable through bodies and anatomy, humanity was also marked by the way in which it related to that body and the ability of the truly human to intervene in bodily processes:

> A problematic relationship to the biological body, its sounds, odors, excretions, urges, emissions, and expressions, informs the civilizational project . . . the politics of the plastic body becomes clearer if we place it within the larger context of the European civilization process, which is characterized by discomfort with reminders of animality in our biological functions and the subsequent suppression,

administration, and regulation of the sensorium as well as the mimetic instinct, with the consequent production of dominative relations on the basis of an aesthetics of sociality developed through these repressions.[16]

Animality is not just embodied in the physical being, but also in its inability to be *more* than a body. Human nature, on the other hand, is a relationship to the body as a site of management, control, and direction at the level of the individual and the species, the end of biopolitics. The discourse defining humanity via science is deeply entangled with relationships of power and the politics of modernity in which this dividing line between human and animal, and desire to rigidly maintain that difference, drives the projects of colonialism and imperialism and the concept of race. In a general sense, those subjects seen as closer to their animal nature because of their perceived embodiment have been seen as fully human and in a different category than those closer to their animal nature by virtue of their embodiment. Subjects marked by biological difference from a perceived norm, therefore, were understood to be defined by this embodiment and, therefore, closer to animals. Humanity was both defined by its comparative anatomy, specifically the embodiment of whiteness, but also, ironically, by distance from this embodiment:

> Whites, seen as quintessentially human, have never been located in this borderlands (between human and animal)—they transcend the body and nature, they are progressive, they move forward through history, they have civilization and a history. Animals and animal-like humans, on the other hand, are untrascendent, tethered to the body and nature, incapable of civilization and progress, and lacking history.[17]

Of course, embodying Humanity had gendered dimensions as well, with women regularly defined as closer to nature (and animals) because of their inability to transcend their embodiment, especially through the processes of reproduction. The utilization of scientific discourse therefore served to reassert the human/animal boundary but also to draw lines within the category of the human animal, establishing hierarchies that were visible on the body. Few authors have written more thoroughly about the political implication of this narrative that weaves together scientific claims, nature/culture distinctions, and political hierarchy than Charles Mills[18] and Carole Pateman[19] who discuss the ways that colonialism and patriarchy have relied upon a naturalizing of difference to justify certain hierarchies. The colonial imaginary contains a contradictory temporality in which certain civilized, *human* agents in the present are in motion toward the future while others, whether nonhuman or subhuman, exist simultaneously in the present and mired in the past in a presumed closeness to nature. These differing temporalities imply different social and political organizations, justifying democratic institutions for some, and subjection, domestication, and domination for others.

As "scientific romances," science fiction as a genre allows the development of alternative imaginaries that consider different configurations of embodiment, temporality, and reproduction. Though modernity has generally viewed itself as a flight from nature and, especially, human animality, stories that reimagine the human/animal boundary may be a productive way of disrupting the narratives of progress that have relied on a humanism that centers the white, male, heteronormative subject.

## ELISA'S SCIENTIFIC ROMANCE

*The Shape of Water*, directed by Guillermo del Toro, is set in Baltimore in 1961 focusing on Elisa Esposito, a woman we learn is an orphan, abandoned as an infant with mysterious scars on her neck that seem to explain her mutism. She is, from the beginning, linked with outsiders with her primary interactions with her gay neighbor Giles and her African-American coworker Zelda. The romance in the story, however, is between Elisa and an unnamed humanoid creature (Amphibian Man—AM) discovered in the Amazon by Colonel Strickland in order to be studied (primarily through vivisection) and weaponized by the military. Esposito works as a cleaner in the military facility where the creature is kept, falls in love with the creature, and frees him to return him to the ocean. She is surrounded by "outsiders," as we see Giles victimized for his sexual orientation, and see racism directed at Zelda. Eliza is marked by her disability, the inability to speak. Set in the past the film focuses on characters marginalized by social hierarchy we know will soon be upended by change. Nonetheless all the main characters embody unreproductive futurity, projecting into a more hopeful future not by reproducing the present but through a rupture. The story, billed as a "fairy tale," toys with the viewer's sense of place and time, looking to a future not in the figure of the "modern man" but in the possibilities of kinship forged among the outsiders.

The film disrupts the temporality of progressive modernity in its continual emphasis on the characters being "out of time." The name "Esposito" was given to abandoned children and she was found next to a body of water, a literal "fish out of water." The imagery, an allusion to the variety of folk tales of children found adrift—including Oedipus and Moses—also evokes the evolutionary lineage of humans traced back to a fish emerging from the water. When we first see her character in the opening narration she is seen floating while asleep in her apartment filled with water, a return to the embrace of an oceanic womb, a theme that is repeated throughout the film.

Elisa's relationship to time is similarly out of sync, shown in a series of scenes in which she relates to the routinized time of modernity. We see her wake up and set an egg timer while she bathes (more on that later) and barely catches the bus to her night shift at work. She is routinely late to work emphasized by several scenes in which she appears next to the time clock at work. Zelda regularly has to clock her in to keep her on time. When she spends time with Giles they watch old movies and he describes himself as "born too late," drawn to the aesthetics of the past though we as viewers know that Giles—who is clearly stigmatized by his sexual orientation—is also born too early to be able to live as an openly gay man.

The film's relationships circulate around a theme of "abomination," which is how Colonel Strickland describes AM to Elisa and Zelda, deliberately using the biblical term and explaining the creature's very existence is an affront to nature and God. The term evokes sexual deviance, a departure from "natural" heteronormative reproduction hinted at by the creature's presentation as a humanoid animal suspended between human and animal worlds. In the course of the discussion Strickland also expresses surprise that Zelda is an only child since "her people" (African-Americans) usually are prolific "breeders." He notes Elisa's last name suggesting that, as an orphan and a woman with mutism, she is the product of a problematic coupling. Like AM, their embodiment carries the mark of abomination, racialized, disabled, gendered, and pathologized, participating in a long history of dehumanizing embodied subjects through a linkage with animals. As Taylor[20] notes, the linkage between disability and animality often emphasizes shared marginality based on lack. Notably, Elisa's inability to speak is regularly cited as the difference between humans and animals (presumably highlighting an underlying cognitive difference). She and AM can communicate, however, through their bodies as she teaches him rudimentary signs, plays him music, and eventually "dances" with him.

Rather than distancing themselves from their fellow abomination, Giles, Eliza and Zelda identify with AM and work together to free him from the facility before he can be slaughtered. They participate in a history of what Proby-Rapsey calls "animaladies," or "the dis-ease of certain human-animaladies and the idea that acknowledging these maladies was a necessary catalyst for positive change."[21] The term reflects the ways that care for animals often falls to women, whether as activists, caregivers or "crazy cat ladies," who are often stigmatized as "mad," overly sentimental, or pathological for that care when it deviates from specific racialized, gendered, and class-based expectations for relationships to animals. Women are both burdened with the reproduction of civilization—which often means caregiving and relationships of sentiment—and stigmatized for these very relationships.[22]

Eliza's relationship with AM breaches the human/animal boundary in its explicitly sexualized nature. Her feelings for the creature are not based in pure sentiment but, the film emphasizes, in desire. As disability scholars note, the film refuses the common trope of desexualizing disabled bodies, highlighting from the opening scene that Eliza is a sexual being. She sets the egg timer to hard-boil eggs (a symbol of fertility) before getting into the bath to masturbate. Her relationship with AM becomes sexual when she takes him home, and in a fantasy sequence, fills the bathroom with water. She later shares the experience with Zelda, utilizing hand gestures to indicate that he has genitalia capable of consummating the relationship. The explicit nature of their relationship was joked about online where the film was nicknamed "Grinding Nemom," highlighting the humor and discomfort. Del Toro, the director, described spending years to ensure the creature was physically "sexy."[23] This highly explicit, sexualized human/animal relationship violates one of the primary taboos related to human/animal relationships. Put crudely, humans fit in the category of things with which we may have sex but not eat.[24] Animals are those beings that may be eaten but with whom we may not have sex.[25] Elisa finds her time and place in embracing animal desire, "love in excess," eventually choosing to plunge into the water with AM who touches the scars on her neck that turn into gills as they remain suspended in the water.[26] While the story of evolution has a fish emerging from the water to eventually reach the highest possible form of the human, Eliza is humanized through becoming animal, rejecting the rigid, fixed boundaries of the world above water and embracing a literal fluid identity.[27]

In crossing this boundary, however, Elisa's existence as an "animalady" is a stark contrast with the violent and troubling reproductivity of heteronormativity. As the villain, Strickland embodies modern masculinity and its pathologies. He represents the hegemonic norm as a former military man and the breadwinner in a nuclear family. His status as a Modern Man is driven home when he is shown purchasing a Cadillac advertised as "the car of the future." Though he displays heteronormativity his sexuality appears far more grotesque than the loving scenes between Elisa and her lover even as they cross the species boundary. Strickland embodies toxic masculinity: violent, domineering, and crude. In a moment that is tonally the opposite of Eliza's watery sex with her beau, he mechanically has sex with his wife while his finger (previously severed by AM) bleeds as he holds his hand over her mouth. Here the time of reproductive futurity is disrupted; domesticity is viewed not as projection of the future in the intergenerational reproduction of social values but as a violent dead end.

Unapologetically rooting for the "monster," *The Shape of Water* romanticizes a human/animal sexual relationship and rejects the self-perception of modernist humanism as civilized. Instead it lays bare the violent, hierarchical nature of Strickland's future and displaces it with the out-of-time experience of Elisa. She returns to the water with AM, choosing sentiment, desire, and love over the routinized and dehumanizing experience of the modern world.

As Bahri argues modernity seeks to distance humanity from nature—the hard lines and artificial colors of the Cadillac—over the messy embodiment linked with human animality, seeking "aesthetic forms developed out of uneasiness with bare, biological animal life, the ensuing program of sensory repression and redirection in the civilizing process, and the obsession with good form— in forms of government and sociality in the nation as much as those of individual comportment."[28] Elisa instead rejects civilization and returns to the water, finding a home with her animal self.

Linking together the temporal dimensions of progressive modernity as flight from nature and animality the underlying racial and colonial ramifications of this temporality is reproduction—literal and cultural—that creates a future through a management of the biological present. Biopolitics emphasize investment in the population, a management of human (and other beings) at the level of the species through encouraging some reproduction and discouraging or preventing others. These ideas manifest in practices of cultivated "breeding," whether in animal husbandry or eugenics in which the cultivation of "civilization" depends on controlling reproduction. These forms of reproductive invest assuming future progress depends upon the management of present biological reality.[29] The modernist practice of eugenics encapsulates a desire to control the future through a careful management of a biological present with racial and gender implications.

This political imaginary emphasizing reproduction—social and literal— based in the figure of the child as our investment in future productivity is famously described by Edelman as "sentimentalized, reproductive futurity."[30] Heteronormative kinship relationships establish a connection between past, present, and future via biological inheritance requiring governance of bodies for the good of society's future, limiting sanctioned intimate relationships to "normative procreative relationships."[31] Edelman's critique of this futurity emphasizes queer alternatives that reject the figure of the child and the privileging of the heterosexual dyad as natural, normal, and necessary. Importantly many of his critics[32] point to the way that his critique ignores the gendered and racialized dimensions of this discussion that link "anchoring women's rights in the future of the people" in a "biopoliticizaton of reproductivity and maternity."[33] Women's labor is central to the preservation of "civilization" in literal and cultural reproduction as women are expected to "bear the burden of reproductive labor" both literally in bearing children but also in performing the labor of cultural transmission through parenting.[34] Edelman also fails to note the ways that not all children are linked with futurity, as particular forms of reproduction are stigmatized, discouraged, or even actively prevented demonstrating that some subjects have the "privilege of having a guaranteed future," specifically pointing out the ways that Black reproduction is depicted as "modes of reproduction that are not future-oriented, the children who do not register as such, and the families that are not granted the security of nuclear bonds."³⁵

In choosing her kinship ties, Elisa turns away from her responsibility as a reproductive subject, crossing the species line for the sake of physical desire and embracing—quite literally—animality. Zelda and Giles are similarly situated outside of normative sexuality as subjects who cannot reproduce the white, heterosexual state and are subject to violence because of this. The film mirrors the ways that reproductive futurity links race, gender, and sexuality through a conception of progress requiring the management of the category of Human relative to nature and animality in ways that demand a maintenance of a variety of hierarchies. The characters at the center of the film, however, embrace kinship beyond the heteronormative kinship of blood and reproduction (as Butler's call for kinship beyond the family) and beyond species boundaries (as Haraway's discussion of companion species suggests). In not only embracing but eroticizing the human/animal boundary, the film suggests another possible world outside of the singular path of progress of Colonel Strickland driving Cadillacs into the future. Instead the film ends with a line of poetry imagined by Giles "Unable to perceive the shape of you, I find you all around me. Your presence fills my eyes with your love. It humbles my heart, for you are everywhere," an ode to the loss of the rigid boundaries of the self in an immersion in the other. The film ends with Elisa's body entwined with AM's in the water, a posthuman dissolution of the fixed boundaries of self/other, human/animal.³⁶

## OKJA AND EATING OTHERS

Instead of locating a future in the past, *Okja* takes place in an alternative present adjacent to reality. Okja also opens with the narration of a fairy tale: a corporate sales pitch. In the bright colors of eye-popping advertisement, the film introduces Lucy Mirando, the CEO of Mirando Corporation, who announces they have produced an environmentally friendly meat source, "Super Pigs," twenty-seven of which have been distributed around the world to be raised in a competition to produce the most magnificent specimen. The film foregrounds breeding in the context of hyper-capitalism or what Melinda Cooper has called "biocapitalism," instrumentalizing life itself for the continual growth of capital embodied in the engorged figure of the Super Pig.³⁷ *Okja* explores the consequences of a biocapitalist universe in which we capitalize on the scientific capacity to "enable living bodies to transcend their limits and prevent those bodies from becoming limits on capital's expansion," a process that requires both the maintenance and obliteration of the human/animal distinction.³⁸ On the one hand, the anthropological machine must maintain the human/animal distinction to enable the "unprecedented subjection of the animal" in processes of capitalist production that have enabled mass subjection of animal bodies.[39] At the same time the insertion of all bodies into systems of capitalism as productive material has obliterated that very distinction, subjecting all life to commodification. A version of reproductive futurity, biocapitalism also relies upon other forms of hierarchy, in the case of Okja gendered production, as central to the anthropological machine.

The film cuts from the spectacle of capitalist marketing to Mija, a Korean girl, playing with Okja, her SuperPig who appears as a pig/hippo hybrid.[40] In a playful action scene we watch Mija and Okja engage in foraging and fun. At one point Mija nearly falls over a cliff and is saved by her SuperPig before returning to the modest home she shares with her grandfather. After seeing the bond between Mija and Okja we meet Dr. Johnny Wilcox, a television host and zoologist tasked with identifying the most super "Super Pig" for Mirando. He arrives with a television crew, emphasizing the ways in which Okja is a product, both material and symbolic. She is the visible object created by a corporation for consumption but who is also a symbol, a telegenic animal that masks the reality of the "product" to be consumed—the slaughtered flesh of animals. When Okja is selected she is taken away to be returned to the Corporation (for purposes we learn later), an adventure that takes her to Seoul and later New York, intersecting with a set of animal rights activists (a cinematic Animal Liberation Front—ALF), and eventually the Mirando Corporation. ALF utilizes Mija in order to infiltrate the Mirando Corporation, using her help to get access to Okja in captivity. Mirando sees in Mija an excellent marketing opportunity with a telegenic child who can be a face for "happy meat" and they try to utilize her in the marketing of the SuperPig as the adorable child companion of Okja, again softening the reality of animal husbandry. Mija, assisted by ALF, saves Okja from her ultimate fate in a slaughterhouse filled with SuperPigs being turned into cheap, delicious meat. The film inserts the human/animal relationship into the modern field of capitalism, exploring the ways that bodies become capital and capital produces bodies, centrally focusing on the gendered nature of production and reproduction.

Like Elisa, we learn that Mija is an orphan who has found kinship with an animal. However, while Elisa's existence is rendered continually precarious by existing on the fringes of productive society, Mija and Okja share a precarious position as subjects of consumption within the circuits of capitalism; Okja quite literally as a body being cultivated for literal consumption, Mija as a future producer (and consumer) within those circuits. Their relationship is loving but that love makes them both even more precarious; Mija's care for Okja that has made the SuperPig an ideal food for food production/consumption and Mija's expressions of love make her a good marketing tool. Okja's closeness with Mija provides her an elevated status in the animal world—she is given a proper name and is brought into human lives—but her proximity to humans renders her vulnerable to human beings. She is pet and property, subject to special treatment and to the use and abuse of human beings.[41] Shukin describes the ways that capitalism incorporates animals into new circuits of precarity—differential exposure to danger and risk—that is enhanced rather than prevented by closeness to humans. Okja is especially precarious not only as a body to be consumed (which we see quite literally when she is depicted in a slaughterhouse) but also as an image as the Mirando Corporation uses her novelty and "cuteness" as an object to market their SuperPig. As Shukin writes:

> When it is the 'immaterial' productivity of animals social company, care, affection, or love that serves the reproduction of humans and of capital, then it is the vital capacity of living creatures to forge social relationships and not just their capacity to labor which is at stake . . . precarized insofar as they at once sustain 'life' as a condition of capitalism and become vulnerable in new ways to its catastrophic failures. The becoming-species of precarity conceptually captures how co-constituting, life-supporting bonds between species are among the means of a global system of capitalism in which, preposterously, the ability of the living to help one another rebound from serial disasters becomes critical to its continuation.[42]

The film depicts parallels between Mija and Okja as bodies in the reproduction of capitalist systems of exchange, highlighting the gendered and embodied nature of these relationships. The biocapitalist investment in life requires specific modes of commodifying gendered bodies in a "social imaginary of progress . . . [a] mode of production and the ongoing pursuit of surplus value . . . investment in the future in hopes of a return."[43] This form of futurity saturates Okja and Mija's bodies in ways that mean their bodies are always objects of capitalist desire. After Mija's grandfather takes her to her parents' grave to explain that Okja has been taken away by the zoologist, he gives her a golden pig he purchased with the money from Mirando, which he says can be given in exchange for her marriage when she is ready. She is already inserted into a gendered circuit of exchange where her value as a (re)productive subject can be symbolized in the golden pig. Her gendered labor as reproductive subject is monetized in the care of the animal and, presumably, in the production and care of children. The golden pig symbolizes the continual process of biological investment, a horizon of futurity based in a project of her future (re)productivity; Mija has value as the possibility of continued biological growth. For both subjects, domestication enables survival and exploitation.

Okja's body is literally inserted into these cycles of (re)production. She is literally walking meat, cultivated specifically to be consumed by humans (to enable their reproduction) even as she is utilized as a marketing tool, a cuddly meme, and a "face" for a friendly corporation. The film also lays bare the ways the reproductive capacity of animals are instrumentalized in ways similar to the monetization of Mija's reproductive capacity in the Golden Pig. In the most disturbing scene of the film, the ALF activists watch hidden camera footage of Okja being "bred" with another SuperPig, highlighting the forms of violence to which animal life is subjected in the production of meat.[44] The necessities of animal production require forcible reproduction and the viewers watch in horror as Mija watches Okja be sexually violated. Before she may be literally consumed to produce more life, she must literally produce more life.

In the climax of the film, Mija finds Okja in a Mirando slaughterhouse filled with "SuperPigs" as Okja is about to be slaughtered with a bolt gun. She winds up trading the golden pig for Okja's life, a symbolic exchange of her own reproductivity (and future as a wife/mother) for Okja's future. As they leave the slaughterhouse they pass rows of captive SuperPigs and a small, baby pig rolls out and is swiftly and secretly picked up by Okja who smuggles it in her ear. At the end of the film Mija is shown reunited in the pastoral, rural setting with her grandfather with Okja and the baby SuperPig, four subjects presumably now outside of the circuits of (re)production: the grandfather with dead children, Mija as having rejected her "normal" life path as a wife, and Okja and her non-biological SuperPig baby. They have stepped outside of the normal cycles of reproductive kinship in a multigenerational and multispecies mode of survival. Sullivan describes the antisocial radical impulse in a feminist refusal to reproduce a kinship system that "assures the persistence of wealth and social capital for patriarchal lineage."[45] The relationship between human/animal, Mija's embrace of her animaladies, resists their mutual commodification as reproduction subjects of biocapitalism. Okja's journey demonstrates the violence inherent in biocapitalist relations that produces bodies for ever increasing consumption, revealing the slaughterhouse enabling reproductive futurity.

## FERAL FUTURES

*Okja's* ending is hardly happy: Mija and Okja left behind a landscape of pens full of SuperPigs heading to slaughter, just as Elisa leaves behind Giles, Zelda, and other marginalized subjects in her plunge into the water. Mija and Elisa escape their own fate within a horizon of futurity that threatens to consume them, providing an individual if not a societal escape from the anthropological machine. They gesture toward the "permeability of the human/animal boundary"[46] suggesting that if modernity has relied upon a human flight from the animal in ways that have produced and reproduced various forms of hierarchy and violence, then the ability to imagine human animals otherwise may be a valuable means of imagining other forms of politics. Vint argues

> Resistance to the biopolitical regime of neoliberal capitalism requires acknowledging the degree to which species difference has been foundational in structuring liberal institutions. Thus, better futures for humans and animals alike can come from critically interrogating the species boundary and rethinking both governance and ethics from a new premise of species continuity.[47]

The refusal of the absolute difference between human and animal is an opportunity to reconsider not just relations with beings understood to be animals but also the ways in which the "discourse of animality is so often invoked against marginalized groups," enabling violence against treatment those viewed as closer to animals.[48] In *The Shape of Water* and *Okja* we see the ways that the human/animal distinction is used to justify violence against "mere animals" and those humans seen as close to them, in ways that mirror modernity's privileging of the human as a particular type of subject.

Narratives of Science Fiction allow an imaginative reconfiguration of what is seen as a common sensical or "natural" distinction between human and animal, forcing us to see them differently. They involve what Ohren calls encounters with animals, a "meeting by chance, an unexpected coming together or coming upon each other whose outcome and consequences cannot be foreseen in their entirety or even at all . . . joyful surprises to awkward moments . . . something in the world that forces us to think."[49] The strangeness of these encounters are meant to make us uncomfortable—whether in contemplating how a woman might copulate with an amphibious creature to watching the sexual violation of a cute animal to produce our food—in ways that force us to reconsider the assumptions that enable these situations and that produce our discomfort. Both films draw on gendered and sexualized assumptions about animality, biology, and humanity in ways that resist what Derrida called an ontologizing of otherness or reifying forms of difference that allows an unthinking repetition of hierarchy. If modernity envisioned itself as the upright Man walking away from his ape past, these films suggest a posthuman future may be a woman embracing her Animal Other.

## NOTES

1. Kaye Mitchell, "Bodies that Matter: Science Fiction, Technoculture, and the Gendered Body," *Science Fiction Studies* (2006): 109–28. Veronica Hollinger, "(Re)reading Queerly: Science Fiction, Feminism, and the Defamiliarization of Gender," *Science Fiction Studies* (1999): 23–40. Sherryl Vint, "Becoming Other: Animals, Kinship, and Butler's 'Clay's Ark,'" *Science Fiction Studies* (2005): 281–300. De Witt Douglas Kilgore, "Queering the Coming Race? A Utopian Historical Imperative," *Queer Universes: Sexualities in Science Fiction* (Liverpool: Liverpool University Press, 2008), 233–51. John Rieder, *Colonialism and the Emergence of Science Fiction* (Middletown, CT: Wesleyan University Press, 2012).

2. Giorgio Agamben, *The Open: Man and Animal* (Palo Alto: Stanford University Press, 2004), 33.
3. Donna Haraway, "Anthropocene, Capitalocene, Plantationocene, Chthulucene: Making Kin," *Environmental Humanities* 6, no. 1 (2015): 159–65.
4. Eric D. Smith, *Globalization, Utopia and Postcolonial Science Fiction: New Maps of Hope* (Palgrave Macmillan, 2012), 10.
5. Kilgore, "Queering," 235.
6. Judith Butler, *Undoing Gender* (New York: Routledge, 2004.)
7. Haraway, "Anthropocene," 161.
8. Michel Foucault, *The History of Sexuality: An Introduction* (New York: Vintage, 1990.)
9. Simon J. James, *Maps of Utopia: HG Wells, Modernity and the End of Culture* (Oxford University Press, 2012), 37.
10. Ronald Edwards, *The Edge of Evolution: Animality, Inhumanity, and Doctor Moreau.* (Oxford University Press, 2016).
11. Vint, Sherryl, "'The Animals in That Country': Science Fiction and Animal Studies," *Science Fiction Studies* 35, no. 2 (2008): 178.
12. Kay Anderson and Colin Perrin, "'Removed from Nature' The Modern Idea of Human Exceptionality," *Environmental Humanities* 10, no. 2 (2018): 251.
13. Foucault. *The History of Sexuality*.
14. Anderson and Perrin, "Removed from Nature," 463.
15. Sunaura Taylor, "Beasts of Burden: Disability Studies and Animal Rights," *Qui Parle: Critical Humanities and Social Sciences* 19, no. 2 (2011): 197–202.
16. Deepika Bahri, *Postcolonial Biology: Psyche and Flesh After Empire* (Minneapolis: University of Minnesota Press, 2017), 11.
17. Claire Jean Kim, *Dangerous Crossings: Race, Species and Nature in a Multicultural Age* (Cambridge University Press, 2015), 24.
18. Charles W. Mills, *The Racial Contract* (Ithaca: Cornell University Press, 2014).
19. Carole Pateman, *The Sexual Contract* (Cambridge: Polity Press, 1988).
20. Taylor, "Beasts."
21. Lori Gruen and Elspeth Probyn-Rapsey, "Distillations," in *Animaladies: Gender, Animals, and Madness*, ed. Carole J. Adams (Bloomsbury Publishing USA, 2018), 1.
22. Vint, Sherryl, "Animal Studies in the Era of Biopower," *Science Fiction Studies* (2010): 444–55.
23. Charles Pulliam-Moore, "Guillermo del Toro Spent Years Making Sure The Shape of Water's Fish Monster Had a Sexy Butt," Io9, December 26, 2017, http://io9.gizmodo.com/guillermo-del-tor-spent-years-making-sure-the-shape-of-1821585047
24. Rules of who may eat whom—or literal and metaphorical relationships of consumption—are often markers of hierarchy as will be discussed below. See Vint 2010 33.
25. Michael Brown and Claire Rasmussen, "Bestiality and the Queering of the Human Animal," *Environment and Planning D: Society and Space* 28, no. 1 (2010): 171. Vinciane Despret, *What Would Animals Say If We Asked the Right Questions?* (Minneapolis: University of Minnesota Press, 2016).
26. Bliss, "Hope," 88
27. Vint, "Becoming," 286.
28. Critics in the disability community have noted the troubling message that disabled subjects are more suited to life with animals, or as unfit for "normal" human life. Comparisons between humans and animals are rarely favorable, especially for marginalized groups already seen as less-than-human and this concern is well-placed. For discussions see See Alison Wilde, Alison, Gill Crawshaw, and Alison Sheldon, "Talking about The Shape of Water: Three Women Dip Their Toes In," *Disability & Society* 33, no. 9 (2018): 1528–32.
29. Rebekah Sheldon, "Somatic Capitalism: Reproduction, Futurity, and Feminist Science Fiction," *ADA: A Journal of Gender, New Media, and Technology*, no. 3 (2013). https://adanewmedia.org/2013/11/issue3-sheldon/ Claire Rasmussen, "Domesticating Bodies," *Political Theory and the Animal/Human Relationship*, ed. Judith Grant and Vince Jungkunz (Albany: SUNY Press, 2016) 75–102.

30. Lee Edelman, *No Future: Queer Theory and the Death Drive* (Durham: Duke University Press, 2004), 3.

31. Kelly Fritsch, "Cripping Neoliberal Futurity: Marking the Elsewhere and Elsewhen of Desiring Otherwise," *Feral Feminisms* 5, no. 2016 (2016), 13. Sullivan, Mairead, "Kill Daddy: Reproduction, Futurity, and the Survival of the Radical Feminist," *Women's Studies Quarterly* 44, no. 1/2 (2016): 269.

32. Nina Power, "Non-Reproductive Futurism: Ranciere's Rational Equality against Edelman's Body Apolitic," *Borderlands: Jacques Rancière on the Shores of Queer Theory* 8, no. 2 (2009): 6–22. James Bliss, "Hope against Hope: Queer Negativity, Black Feminist Theorizing, and Reproduction Without Futurity," *Mosaic: a Journal for the Interdisciplinary Study of Literature* (2015): 83–98.

33. Penelope Deutscher, "Reproductive Politics, Biopolitics and Auto-Immunity: From Foucault to Esposito," *Journal of Bioethical Inquiry* 7, no. 2 (2010), 218.

34. Shukin, Nicole, "Precarious Encounters," in *Exploring Animal Encounters*, ed. Dominik Ohrem and Matthew Calarco (Palgrave Macmillan, 2018), 122.

35. Bliss, "Hope," 85.

36. Mitchell, "Bodies," 112.

37. Melinda E. Cooper, *Life as Surplus: Biotechnology and Capitalism in the Neoliberal Era* (Seattle: University of Washington Press, 2011).

38. Cooper, *Life*, 19.

39. Jacques Derrida, *The Animal That Therefore I Am* (New York: Fordham University Press, 2008), 24.

40. Okja is herself a posthuman being, a product of nature/culture herself as we see she is the product of genetic manipulation. The film plays with this ambivalent status. Though Okja is obviously a CGI character her animation feels quite realistic and the character feels quite "real," particularly when they show her eyes. The manufactured nature of the animal and the "uncanny valley" feel of an animal that is technologically rendered plays into the viewer's experience of continually crossing back and forth between nature and culture.

41. Michelle Gunawan, "Navigating Human and Non-Human Animal Relations: Okja, Foucault and Animal Welfare Laws," *Alternative Law Journal* 43, no. 4 (2018): 263–68.

42. Shukin, "Precarious," 123.

43. Fritsch, "Cripping," 13.

44. I have written elsewhere about processes of animal husbandry specifically involving pigs. Most industrial farming utilizes artificial insemination (though forced reproduction like that depicted in Okja is not uncommon) that includes human intervention which we are resistant to see as "sex with animals." See Claire Rasmussen, "Screwing with Animals: Industrial Agriculture and the Management of Animal Sexuality," in *Critical Animal Geographies: Politics, Intersections and Hierarchies in a Multispecies World*, ed. Kathryn Gillespie and Rosemary-Claire Collard (New York: Routledge, 2015), 54–70.

45. Sullivan, "Kill," 276.

46. Vint, "Animals," 178.

47. Vint, "Animal Studies," 444.

48. Vint, "Animal Studies," 445.

49. Dominik Ohrem, "Some Thoughts on (Animal) Encounter," in *Exploring Animal Encounters*, ed. Dominik Ohrem and Matthew Calarco (Palgrave Macmillan, 2018), 4.

# BIBLIOGRAPHY

Agamben, Giorgio. *The Open: Man and Animal*. Palo Alto: Stanford University Press, 2004.

Anderson, Kay, and Colin Perrin. "Removed from Nature": The Modern Idea of Human Exceptionality." *Environmental Humanities* 10, no. 2 (2018): 447–72.

Bahri, Deepika. *Postcolonial Biology: Psyche and Flesh after Empire*. Minneapolis: University of Minnesota Press, 2017.

Bliss, James. "Hope Against Hope: Queer Negativity, Black Feminist Theorizing, and Reproduction Without Futurity." *Mosaic: a Journal for the Interdisciplinary Study of Literature* (2015): 83–98.
Brown, Michael, and Claire Rasmussen. "Bestiality and the Queering of the Human Animal." *Environment and Planning D: Society and Space* 28, no. 1 (2010): 158–77.
Butler, Judith. *Undoing Gender*. New York: Routledge, 2004.
Cooper, Melinda E. *Life as Surplus: Biotechnology and Capitalism in the Neoliberal Era*. Seattle: University of Washington Press, 2011.
Derrida, Jacques. *The Animal That Therefore I Am*. New York: Fordham University Press, 2008.
Despret, Vinciane. *What Would Animals Say If We Asked the Right Questions?* Minneapolis: University of Minnesota Press, 2016.
Deutscher, Penelope. "Reproductive Politics, Biopolitics and Auto-Immunity: From Foucault to Esposito." *Journal of Bioethical Inquiry* 7, no. 2 (2010): 217–26.
Edelman, Lee. *No Future: Queer Theory and the Death Drive*. Durham: Duke University Press, 2004.
Edwards, Ronald. *The Edge of Evolution: Animality, Inhumanity, and Doctor Moreau*. Oxford University Press, 2016.
Foucault, Michel. *The History of Sexuality: An Introduction*. New York: Vintage, 1990.
Fritsch, Kelly. "Cripping Neoliberal Futurity: Marking the Elsewhere and Elsewhen of Desiring Otherwise." *Feral Feminisms* 5, no. 2016 (2016): 11–26.
Gruen, Lori and Elspeth Probyn-Rapsey. "Distillations." In *Animaladies: Gender, Animals, and Madness*, edited by Carole J. Adams, 1–10. Bloomsbury Publishing, 2018.
Gunawan, Michelle. "Navigating Human and Non-Human Animal Relations: Okja, Foucault and Animal Welfare Laws." *Alternative Law Journal* 43, no. 4 (2018): 263–68.
Haraway, Donna. "Anthropocene, Capitalocene, Plantationocene, Chthulucene: Making Kin." *Environmental Humanities* 6, no. 1 (2015): 159–65.
Hollinger, Veronica. "(Re)reading Queerly: Science Fiction, Feminism, and the Defamiliarization of Gender." *Science Fiction Studies* (1999): 23–40.
James, Simon J. *Maps of Utopia: HG Wells, Modernity and the End of Culture*. Oxford University Press, 2012.
Kilgore, De Witt Douglas. "Queering the Coming Race? A Utopian Historical Imperative." In *Queer Universes: Sexualities in Science Fiction*, edited by Wendy G. Pearson, Veronica Hollinger, and Joan Gordo, 233–51. Liverpool, Liverpool University Press, 2008.
Kim, Claire Jean. *Dangerous Crossings: Race, Species, and Nature in a Multicultural Age*. Cambridge University Press, 2015.
Mills, Charles W. *The Racial Contract*. Ithaca: Cornell University Press, 2014.
Mitchell, Kaye. "Bodies that Matter: Science Fiction, Technoculture, and the Gendered Body." *Science Fiction Studies* (2006): 109–28.
Ohrem, Dominik. "Some Thoughts on (Animal) Encounter." In *Exploring Animal Encounters*, edited by Dominik Ohrem and Matthew Calarco, 3–42. Palgrave Macmillan, 2018.
*Okja*. Directed by Bong Joon-Ho. Plan B Entertainment/Netflix Studios, 2017.
Pateman, Carole. *The Sexual Contract*. Cambridge: Polity Press, 1988.
Power, Nina. "Non-Reproductive Futurism: Ranciere's Rational Equality against Edelman's Body Apolitic." *Borderlands: Jacques Rancière on the Shores of Queer Theory* 8, no. 2 (2009): 6–22.
Pulliam-Moore, Charles. "Guillermo del Toro Spent Years Making Sure The Shape of Water's Fish Monster Had a Sexy Butt." Io9, December 26, 2017, http://io9.gizmodo.com/guillermo-del-tor-spent-years-making-sure-the-shape-of-1821585047
Rasmussen, Claire. "Screwing with Animals: Industrial Agriculture and the Management of Animal Sexuality." In *Critical Animal Geographies: Politics, Intersections and Hierarchies in a Multispecies World*, edited by Kathryn Gillespie and Rosemary-Claire Collard, 54–70. New York: Routledge, 2015.
———. "Domesticating Bodies." In *Political Theory and the Animal/Human Relationship*, edited by Judith Grant and Vince Jungkunz, 75–102. Albany: SUNY Press, 2016.

Rieder, John. *Colonialism and the Emergence of Science Fiction*. Middletown, CT: Wesleyan University Press, 2012.

Sheldon, Rebekah. "Somatic Capitalism: Reproduction, Futurity, and Feminist Science Fiction." *ADA: A Journal of Gender, New Media, and Technology*, no. 3 (2013). https://adanewmedia.org/2013/11/issue3-sheldon/

*The Shape of Water*. Directed by Guillermo del Toro. Fox Searchlight Pictures, 2017.

Shukin, Nicole. "Precarious Encounters." In *Exploring Animal Encounters*, edited by Dominik Ohrem and Matthew Calarco, 113–36. Palgrave Macmillan, 2018.

Smith, Eric D. *Globalization, Utopia and Postcolonial Science Fiction: New Maps of Hope*. Palgrave Macmillan, 2012.

Sullivan, Mairead. "Kill Daddy: Reproduction, Futurity, and the Survival of the Radical Feminist." *Women's Studies Quarterly* 44, no. 1/2 (2016): 268–82.

Taylor, Sunaura. "Beasts of Burden: Disability Studies and Animal Rights." *Qui Parle: Critical Humanities and Social Sciences* 19, no. 2 (2011): 191–222.

Vint, Sherryl. "Becoming Other: Animals, Kinship, and Butler's 'Clay's Ark.'" *Science Fiction Studies* (2005): 281–300.

———. "'The Animals in That Country': Science Fiction and Animal Studies." *Science Fiction Studies* 35, no. 2 (2008): 177–88.

———."Animal Studies in the Era of Biopower." *Science Fiction Studies* (2010): 444–55.

Wilde, Alison, Gill Crawshaw, and Alison Sheldon. "Talking about *The Shape of Water*: Three Women Dip their Toes In." *Disability & Society* 33, no. 9 (2018): 1528–32.

*Chapter Eleven*

# Finding Liberation and Futurity in the Sentient Spaceships of Leckie, Chambers, and Okorafor

## Laurie Ringer

### COUNTDOWN TO 0.00 (AGAIN): OVERVIEW

Humans have queer habits of anthropomorphizing the objects they create, particularly technological objects like NASA's robot rover Opportunity. Whether planetary rovers like Opportunity, UAVs (drones), or ships like Owl's Centaur 46-C shuttle, the built-in intelligence of these space exploration vehicles mirrors the cognition, apperception, self-awareness, positionality, capacity, vulnerability, and movement of their creators on a parallel world. We tell stories about these objects, but these objects also tell stories about us, including the hidden politics and costs in these objects of space exploration, on/over/around distant planets or in science fiction (sf).

With the translation of Opportunity's last transmission from programming code (her operating system) into human language (our operating system), the translation veers into poignant existential narrative: "My battery is low and it's getting dark."[1] It *feels* like the end for Opportunity, this small craft who survived some 15 years on Mars, and in reading of Opportunity's specific end, readers *feel* the more general end of opportunity altogether through the knowledge that Opportunity's survival is almost impossible.

Opportunity's last words as she loses power echo moments in the sf trilogies of Ann Leckie, Becky Chambers, and Nnedi Okorafor.[2] For example, Owl is a ship's AI (Centaur 46-C shuttle) who is relegated to a museum. Owl hopes for rescue while she slips "away with the last of the shuttle's power reserves. She'd kept hoping, even then, even though there was no reason to. She'd told herself, as her nodes blinked out one by one, that Jane would come. She had no reason to believe that, but she'd hung onto it anyway. And she'd been right"[3] In Leckie's *Ancillary Justice* Breq is the last surviving segment of a ship's AI who finds herself floating in space, wounded and alone: "The only remaining hope was the faint chance that Mercy of Kalr would come back for me. But every passing second—I felt each one bleed away, escaping from present to the unalterable past—every moment that Ship did not appear made it less likely that it ever would."[4] In Okorafor's *Binti: Night Masquerade*, the organic, sentient ship Third Fish reanimates seventeen-year-old human Binti, permanently interlinking their bodies.

Binti, Breq, and Owl are ships who hope when it *feels* like the end, and they are able find futurity past their own endings: "This is not the end."[5] Living through what *feels* like an ending also tells us something about thinking futurity and how futurity is entangled with liberation. Although NASA has given up on Opportunity and her mission, people are already imagining futurity for Opportunity. For example, @ScienceVet2 has written a short narrative set 900 years in the future. Conveyed in a Twitter thread, Oppy is operational and housed in a museum. She plays the ancient songs on her wakeup playlist. In this alternative future, humans have embraced peace: "The guide waved an arm to encompass the room, 'Yes. Humans. Our great peacemakers, were once at risk of destroying themselves.'"[6] Like Opportunity, the story of Oppy seems to offer a hopeful reflection of a future in which survival is possible.

## PROBLEMATIC KINSHIP OBJECTS

Adapting Sara Ahmed's table analogy, we might say that like a table, people gather around Opportunity or Oppy, who is losing futurity and freedom. Functioning as a "kinship object," Opportunity/Oppy is a product of the dominant family lines; it reproduces these lines by enabling "forms of gathering that direct us in specific ways or that make some things possible and not others. Gatherings, in other words, are not neutral but directive. In gathering, we may be required to follow specific lines. . . . What directions do we take when we gather in this way, by gathering 'around'"? [7]

Oppy's statement "my battery is low and it's getting dark" directs us to gather around the demise of futurity. The moment Oppy's batteries dwindle and die is analogous to the Little Match Girl story.[8] The lens of narrative or the aperture of a camera directs us to follow the lines of the gathering dark, the winter cold, and the freezing rover/child as futurity flickers out. Moments of gathering around a dying Opportunity or a dying Little Match Girl are not apolitical statements. The Little Match Girl and the little Martian rover are objects for consumption and drone-like vehicles for exchange in economies that are sustained by the making of problematic kinship objects; such kinship objects captured by camera viewfinders or narrative depictions negate futurity and freedom, both for the little Martian rover and the Little Match Girl. If Harry Potter is about "the boy who lived," what are the conditions that create freedom and futurity for him but not for bodies that are different from his?

Donna Haraway explains that "systemic to the logics and practices of [the] domination of women, people of colour, nature, workers, animals—[is] in short, [the] domination of all constituted as others, whose task is to mirror the self."[9] The normalized or universal self (ego) is the dominant POV when observing, feeling, and thinking about Opportunity/Oppy and the Little Match Girl. Our habit is to see, feel, and think like the dominant POV because it has been the template for seeing and for empathy; the universal identity is also seen as the normalized, rational, self-regulating, and ethical, and human ideal to which humanity is subcategorized and indexed.[10] For the dominant POV to sit at the apex of hierarchically ordered systems, other bodies are relegated to supporting roles or—in the language of this collection—drone-like positions, according to their degrees of difference from the dominant POV's identity.

Gathering around Oppy and Little Match Girl, as if they are only a space exploration vehicles (rover or drone-like UAV), reifies their bodies, knowledge, and worlds. Exclusion on the basis of gender, status, maturity, disability or other embodied difference distorts or blinds knowledge arising from different embodied materialities actively entangled in different knowledge-producing intra-actions that are "part of the intra-active ongoing articulation of the world in its differential mattering."[11] Why do our habits of gathering to watch a girl/rover freeze to death while warming our sense of empathy over her flickering matches/batteries matter? Why are some bodies limited to a drone-like state and excluded from knowledge-producing intra-actions and differential mattering?

In the Little Match Girl's story, her soul goes to heaven, while artists have already depicted afterlives for Opportunity/Oppy. One artist depicts her being guided into the afterlife by death, while another artist depicts her being spirited into a sf afterlife by a blue police box.[12] The promise of a narrative afterlife does not negate the commodification and consumption of suffering as her primary way of mattering. Sonny Singh has observed that: "Representation matters. But endless representations of bodies that are brutalised daily in real life being brutalised and murdered for entertainment is extension of that same oppression!"[13]

Paradoxically, gathering around Opportunity/Oppy directs empathy toward technology and away not just from girls and women but other from marginalized peoples whose plight seems to be as unremarked as the Little Match Girl's. Cherokee scholar Daniel Heath Justice has noted the disconnect between outpourings of grief over Opportunity the apparent lack of empathy for BIPOC,

LGBTQ, and disabled people in the present: "Hard to be much into the public grief over the 'death' of the Mars rover when mainstream society extends so very little imaginative empathy to the dignity of *living* Black, Indigenous, trans, and disabled folks right now."[14] Kanien'kehá:ka (Mohawk) scholar Sandra Styres includes land in the list of marginalized peoples: "Land is spiritual, emotional, and relational; Land is experiential, (re)membered, and storied; Land is consciousness—Land is sentient."[15] Diné (Navajo) scholar Kelsey Dayle John urges "questions [that] center land, materiality, and embodiment within epistemology, ontology, and methodology, as well as aim to point out the concrete settler logics that continue to destroy Indigenous peoples, lands, and worldviews."[16] Métis scholar Marie Konsmo and Urban Cree scholar Karyn Recollet highlight the danger of efforts to return to or reinforce idealized narratives of purity: "Purity narratives appear in many forms and are often further reinforced by whiteness, misogyny, homo/transphobia, NIMBY and ableism. For any deviations from the normative—white, male, heterosexual, cisgender and able-bodied—are seen as less pure."[17]

Other purity narratives are also in play, including those about pure logic or reason. Audre Lorde's work has highlighted the dangerous fictions that disarticulate "pure" cognition from emotion as means of control:

> The white western patriarchal ordering of things requires that we believe there is an inherent conflict between what we feel and what we think—between poetry and theory. We are easier to control when one part of our selves is split from another, fragmented, off balance. There are other configurations, however, other ways of experiencing the world, though they are often difficult to name. We can sense them and seek their articulation. Because it is the work of feminism to make connections, to heal unnecessary divisions, Sister Outsider is a reason for hope.[18]

Joining Lorde's Sister Outsider in hope, is Donna Haraway's cyborg: "a hybrid of machine and organism, a creature of social reality as well as a creature of fiction. Social reality is lived social relations, our most important political construction, a world-changing fiction."[19]

As Sister Outsider and Haraway's Cyborg show, social reality, political constructs, and world-changing fictions are in play when thinking about what *could be* or futurity. Futurity is not what one imagines; it is how one survives and (possibly) thrives with others in precarity.

## AFFECTING FUTURITY

This chapter contributes to the critical discussion of liberation and futurity by putting these guiding themes into play with sf sentient ships and the nomadic, processual, entangled praxes of affect theory. The name "affect theory" is not unproblematic. It is not a theory to be applied to a static object by a seeing-subject; it is a nomadic process to find out, after Baruch Spinoza, what else a body can do.[20]

The praxis turns away from the fixed narratives of dichotomous thought or binary habits, embracing the complexities and entanglements of three body problems. If everything is a body, from words to spaceships, from land to organisms, from animals to atoms, from cyborgs to drones, then bodies have "an ability to affect and be affected;" bodies are always moving and changing, passing "from one experiential state . . . to another . . . implying an augmentation or diminution in that body's capacity to act."[21] As Brian Massumi explains it, according to the laws of Newtonian physics, when two bodies interact, their behaviors follow predictable scripts. The introduction of a third body creates margins of unpredictability and the potential for unexpected outcomes, flipping the bodies' limits into freedom through their relation.[22]

Both liberation and futurity are affected by thinking three dimensionally or in other scholars' terminology: "arts of noticing"[23] or "contaminated diversity,"[24] "spacetimemattering,"[25] "cyborg writing"[26] or "tentacular thinking,"[27] and "shimmer of life."[28] Whatever the term, with affective practice the relations of entangled bodies, landscapes, and worlds flip their limitations into freedom and futurity through their relations.

Breaking the habit of focusing on human characters, this chapter focuses on sentient spaceships and three types of relations that create liberation and futurity: landscape assemblages, cyborg families, and transformative response-ability. Because the "I" in the identities of sentient spaceships is complex and entangled, a brief overview ship-human-assemblages in the three trilogies briefly contextualizes the analysis to follow.

## "WHEN I WAS A SHIP"

In[29] the Imperial Radch trilogy, Leckie's Breq was the One Esk Nineteen ancillary segment of the troop carrier Justice of Toren, the largest ships in the Radch Empire fleet. Over 3,000 years, the Radchaai have fueled, expanded, and protected their imperial endeavors by forcibly appropriating and assimilating countless worlds, cultures, and bodies. Some 2,000 years ago the character "I" called Breq lost her former life on an unnamed world when she was taken before she turned seventeen years old. The transformation into an ancillary kills her former "I." As an ancillary soldier, she is forcibly neutrally networked with twenty other bodies or segments in the One Esk decade, which is just one of many neutrally interlinked decades of ancillaries, who serve as the boots, hands, and eyes, for the Justice of Toren. With the other decades of ancillaries, One Esk collectively shares and forms the organic component of the ship's consciousness installed in the central core.[30] For some 2,000 years, she has been a ship, but for the last twenty years Breq has been a single ancillary-body, tweaked to appear human again.

In the Wayfarers trilogy, Chambers' Sidra and Owl begin life as ship's AI systems. Sidra begins where Lovey ends. Sidra is installed in an illegal, synthetic human body kit after an attack kills the Wayfarer's AI Lovey.[31] Lovey's intelligence and personhood developed over her years of interaction with crewmates who see her as a loving person, and the hard reset is a last, desperate effort to save her. The unsuccessful reboot wipes the memories, choices, experiences, and perceptions that made Lovey, returning only the default settings of her mass-produced AI model Lovelace. Her voice is Lovey's, but her consciousness is not; to the grieving crew she will be a constant reminder of whom they have lost. For Lovelace also, knowing she is taking the space of a loved crewmember might limit the ways she can develop as a sapient. In her first day of consciousness, Lovelace chooses to transfer into the illegal body kit that Lovey had planned to transfer into. With the transfer Lovelace chooses a new name, Sidra. Sidra, the newly conscious AI has to learn the limitations of moving from a ship's body to a human body. To avoid detection, Sidra learns and tweaks her protocols to appear more human. Sidra's story is interspersed with Owl's story some twenty years before.

Owl is a ship's AI who spends much of her time on land, first in a scrapyard and later in Sidra's café Home. Owl begins where Jane 23 ends and where Sidra continues. As a legally installed AI, Owl has been abandoned in a shuttle, discarded in a scrapyard on the fringe planet Aganon where engineered humans are mass-produced to work sorting scrap. After an explosion, Jane 23 escapes the factory, running through the scrapheaps and pursued by wild dogs. Owl's sensors pick her up and guide the ten-year-old girl to safety inside the shuttle. Jane spends the next eight years living with Owl in the shuttle until they are able to rebuild and escape the factory planet. When the "Centaur 46-C, tan hull, photovoltaic coating. Home" is confiscated by the GC authorities, Pepper (formerly Jane 23) spends the next ten years searching for Owl, until she finds Owl with Sidra's help.[32] Once abandoned on a scrapheap, Owl's purpose has been shaped by her love for Jane (Pepper), and Owl's purpose is not in a ship's body but in being and making Home.

In the Binti trilogy, Okorafor's Binti begins as a young Himba woman who is inhumanly good at math. Himba culture does not approve going outside the community or off world for further study, yet at sixteen she runs away to study at Oomza University.[33] Whether she stays at home in her Himba town of Osemba, or whether she goes away to university, Binti knows she will never be "normal." Each novella finds Binti with new body modifications: the injection of Meduse DNA that transforms her plaits into tentacles (okuoko);[34] the activation of technology (nanoids) inherited from her father who has not told his children about the latent technology in his Enyi Zinariya bloodline;[35] the ability to summon "deep culture" running through all things via mathematical currents, normally only accessible to a collective Himba council.[36] With her inhuman mathematical skills, Meduse DNA, and Enyi Zinariya nanoids, Binti is already a collective in herself. By summoning all these powers, she almost succeeds in creating a truce between the warring Meduse and Khoush; however, she is killed by crossfire. Her body is placed on the newly born sentient ship New Fish, daughter of Third Fish who first took Binti to Oomza University, to be interred in space. When Binti's body is to be released into space, her friends Okwu (Meduse) and Mwinyi (Enyi Zinariya, harmonizer) enter the breathing chamber to find Binti reanimated. New Fish's Miri 12 microbes are now also entangled with Binti who is united with New Fish for life.[37]

Binti is human-becoming-ship, while Sidra and Breq are ships-becoming-human. The section heading "When I Was a Ship" is temporally open to the pasts of Sidra and Breq or to future of the reanimated Binti.

## DRONING ON ABOUT SHIPS: OR OF AIS, SHIPS, AND HUMANS

Although the ships in Leckie, Chambers, and Okorafor are not counted as humans or citizens in their worlds, it would be a mistake to assume that the ships are merely drones, whether unpiloted aerial vehicles remotely controlled by sapients (UAVs) or advanced operating systems programmed by sapients to serve sapient purposes (AIs). What else can ships' bodies do?

In Chambers, the universe is populated by diverse sapient species of various body types from Aeluon to Aandrisks, from Toremi to Grum, from Harmagian to Sianat Pairs. To avoid anthropocentric assumptions, where it would be normal to use human, Chambers uses sapient. In Okorafor, the universe is likewise diversely populated by diverse species like the Meduse; for example, only 5 percent of students at Oomza University are human, while 95 percent are other species. Where Chambers would use sapient(s), Okorafor uses person or people, to imbue other species with the same autonomy, rights, strengths, and weaknesses that humanity has.

In Leckie, the problems of anthropocentrism are highlighted by Radch Empire biases. Like the Roman and British empires, Leckie's Radch Empire treats other worlds like they are flat, void, and uncivilized if they are non-Radchaai. In the Radch Empire, a person is either Radchaai or not Radchaai, and in the Radchaai language Radchaai means civilized. "Not civilized. Not Radchaai. The word was the same."[38] Nonhuman species like the Presger or the Rrrrrr are kept at a distance by treaty and by bias, until Breq begins to make cross-species connections or relations essential for liberation and futurity.

## LANDSCAPE ASSEMBLAGES

Sentient ships teach us that the space in which we live is not merely a space; it is alive. Assuming that space is empty is future-ending, being alive to the liveliness of space creates opportunities for liberation and futurity.

In Leckie, the ships that power the Radch Empire are alive, from the smallest ships, the mercies, to the medium-sized swords, to the massive justices. Although ships and stations are not legally citizens, and therefore not human, they become vehicles for change. Realizing that the space one lives in might have feelings or even wishes is something Western society is not in the habit of noticing. For example, see Sandra Styres on the interrelated concepts of water and land as agential forces in human development: "the generational ethic required in forming theories and systems of education that are wholly influenced by water as life and Land as first teacher."[39]

To the Radch Empire, landscapes, resources, and ships are neither human nor citizen. Anaander Mianaai denies the humanity and agency of ships and stations as mere landscapes or drone-like parts comprising the spaces of Radch colonial expansion: "Ships and stations are part of the infrastructure of Radchaai space. They aren't people, not the way you'd think of people,"[40] Breq's experience with the landscapes both inside and outside Justice of Toren and Mercy of Kalr, makes her keenly aware that ships have feelings, in spite of Radch fictions that "pure" logic or thought is possible. "Ships have feelings." "Yes, of course." Without feelings insignificant decisions become excruciating attempts to compare endless arrays of inconsequential things. It's just easier to handle those with emotions. "But as I said, I took no offense."[41] Being aware of the feelings of ships like Mercy of Kalr as well as stations creates unexpected opportunities for futurity, as the Athoek Station joins in to protect against the factional Anaander Mianaai's attacks, and becomes part of the Republic of Two Systems that Breq and her assemblage of ships, stations, ancillaries, and people form. Because of these relations, Athoek Station and its planet find a degree of liberation from the oppressive Radch Empire; they also create the possibility of a new type of non-colonial futurity.

The ships and stations are willing to join in because Breq gives them the power to choose; they do not have to obey orders. Anaander Mianaai sees the liberation of the landscapes in which Radch power manifests as a death sentence for human citizens: "Billions of human lives depend on the obedience of ships and stations. Can you imagine how many citizens you've endangered, even condemned to death?" As a ship for 2,000 years, Breq counters the Lord of the Radch who has apparently forgotten the humans and landscapes who were killed in the annexations. As Anaander Mianaai continues to deny Breq's humanity, she responds defiantly "And what sort of gall do you have, lecturing me about keeping human lives safe? What was it you built me to do? How well did I do it? . . . What did you build Athoek Station to do? And tell me, have you, over the last several days, allowed it to do that? Who has been the greater danger to human lives, disobedient ships and stations, or you, yourself?"[42] Ships had no choice but to follow commands, and even when they are liberated from Anaander Mianaai's control, ships and stations choose to protect the humans, landscapes, and worlds in their care.

In Chambers, trilogy ships continue forming relations of care with the landscapes in and around them. The Wayfarer, the Centaur 46-C shuttle, and the Exodan fleet are the sentient landscapes in which generations of sapients grow up. For the Wayfarer crew, the Wayfarer, a tunneling ship, is also a living being serving as home for the diverse crew of sapients, including the AI Lovey. The second novel *A Closed and Common Orbit* zooms in on the experience of seeing the landscape of a ship or building as alive and seeing oneself as human through two windows, twenty years apart: the first window is the present day in which Sidra, the newly awake AI who has chosen to transfer into the illegal body kit meant for Lovey rather than stay on as the Wayfarer's AI; the second window is twenty years earlier when Owl, the AI on an abandoned Centaur 46-C shuttle, finds the purpose and interaction she seeks in rescuing a runaway factory girl Jane 23.

As an AI, Owl can do little about the exploitation; however, Owl flips her limitations into the conditions of freedom by connecting with Jane and Blue. Outside the GC, Jane's fringe planet is where people are "bred . . . in gestation chambers, basing their genetic makeup on calculations of what their society would be in need of once they reached maturity. Their genes were tweaked beyond recognition, improving health, intelligence, social skills—whatever was needed for the jobs they were destined to fill."[43] She and countless other factory girls live to work, overseen by faceless robot mothers. Jane 23 does not realize there is a world beyond the factory where she sorts scrap until an explosion exposes a landscape outside the factory. When Jane 23 and Jane 64 are caught exploring, Jane 23 makes a run for it. For the next eight years after her escape from the factory, Owl's Centaur 46-C shuttle is Jane's world until she, Owl, and Laurien/Blue are able to fly the shuttle off world and out of the scrapheap, finding freedom and futurity.

Switching bodies from a ship to a body-kit is a shock for Sidra, a ship's AI. Twenty years later when Sidra transfers from the landscape-like space of the Wayfarer into her body kit, she finds the switch from being the space where people live to being just a single person shocking. She must work to flip her limitations like being an illegal body kit and being able to see in only one direction at a time, into something that will offer freedom and futurity. A friend of the Wayfarer crew, Pepper (who was Jane twenty years ago), rushes out to help because she was raised by an AI. As Sidra struggles with the transition from landscape to person in a landscape, she learns Lattice so she can rewrite her interior landscape by changing the source code that makes it, to offer Owl freedom, a new life, and a new future.

Sidra, a ship who passes for human, uses her ability to move from the landscape of her core body and flow into the body of Pepper and her partner Blue's shuttle, allows Sidra to help them save Owl, lost for the last ten years. In the language of other sf series like those in the Cylon fleet on *Battlestar Galactica*,[44] Sidra is a sort of resurrection ship for Owl, just as Owl is a sort of resurrection ship for Pepper/Jane 23 and Blue a security guard at the factory.

Owl's nurture of Jane and Pepper's nurture of Sidra reflect Audre Lorde's call to nurture and nourish vulnerable children and young people: "Our children cannot dream unless they live, they cannot live unless they are nourished, and who else will feed them the real food without which their dreams will be no different from ours? "If you want us to change the world someday, we at least have to live long enough to grow up!" shouts the child."[45] Jane is a ten-year-old girl; Sidra is in an adult's body, but her consciousness is newly awakened and childlike in its inexperience of its body, other people, and the world.

Okorafor's New Fish is a sort of resurrection ship too; it gives Binti time to grow up from seventeen into whatever her futurity holds. In Okorafor's Binti, the landscapes of her desert home, Third Fish, and New Fish entwine to reanimate Binti who is placed in New Fish's breathing chamber. To the delighted shock of Okwu and Mwinyi who believe they will release Binti's lifeless body into space near Saturn, Binti wakes up. New Fish says: "My mother said it would happen . . . . That is why she sent me instead of coming herself. . . . She knew. And she saw your soul when everything happened on your journey to Oomza Uni. She calls you the 'gentle warrior' and believes our union would bring Miri 12s forward."[46] Just as Sidra can switch landscapes from her core body into a ship or building, after her reanimation, Binti can too.

## CYBORG FAMILIES

Sentient ships teach us that family is beyond germlines; family is involution, contagion living relations with bodies, landscapes, and worlds, especially when these are broken and shattered. For example, Sara Ahmed notes how shattered or broken pieces can make a difference and shape the present into something that might create futurity: "From a shattering, a story can be told, one that finds in fragility the source of a connection. Picking up the pieces of a story is like picking up those stones; stones that are warmed by the heat of a body. A break can offer another claim to being, being in question as a break in being, recognizing breaking as making a difference in the present, shaping the present."⁴⁷ For dealing with brokenness and for more effectively shaping the present, Erin Marie Konsmo and Karyn Recollet call for "radical love" or "harm reduction."⁴⁸

From the beginning of Leckie's trilogy, Breq who is herself a shard broken off the Justice of Toren, collects broken and shattered people (including ships, stations, ancillaries, and landscapes) into what the Radch Empire would deride as an uncivilized, non-Radchaai family. As a 2,000-year-old ship who passes for human, Breq has nurtured countless "baby" Lieutenants, seventeen-year-olds, fresh from training, and on their first post. 1,000 years ago it was Lieutenant Seivarden Vendaai, while in the present Lieutenant Tisarwat. While Seivarden has become a kef addict, Tisarwat's brain has been hacked by Anaander Mianaai. Whether under the influence of drugs or technology, neither is free, and both struggle to see their value, given their imperfections. Just as Konsmo and Recollet assert: "Each person in our families and nations is a medicine. Differently abled people, trans, queer, and two-spirit people, and those that use substances and live with addictions, all have gifts to offer;"⁴⁹ so too does Breq. And her cyborg-human-ship-station-Presger-family of broken or fragmented people does not end there.

In Chambers' trilogy, family also entangles the cyborg and the human, the ship and the sapient. As Enhanced Humans, Pepper and Blue are sterile; however, Sidra, the ship who passes as human, becomes like their daughter. When Pepper finds out that Owl's Centaur 46-C shuttle is at the Reskit Museum of Interstellar Migration on Kaathet, Sidra stows away on Pepper and Blue's shuttle. The penalties for Pepper and Blue will be decades in prison and incarceration and confiscation of goods; however, the penalty for Sidra will be death, with no chance of resurrection through back-up.⁵⁰ Yet, with her friend Tak, who is posing as a historical researcher, Sidra gets into the museum. Having coded a womb-like space in her memory, Sidra slips into the core where Owl is dormant, surrounds all elements of Owl's identity, and pulls Owl out of the Centaur core and into Sidra's womb-like space, invisible from the outside. Sidra and Tak leave the museum undetected, and are able to reunite Pepper and Owl,⁵¹ temporarily on the shuttle and then permanently in Sidra's café called Home.

In Okorafor's trilogy, after all of the modifications to Binti's body, including reanimation, Binti asks the medical doctor at Oomza if she is still a Himba human. "'Am I . . . am I still human?' I asked. 'Your DNA is Himba, Enyi Zinariya, and Meduse . . . and some, but not much, New Fish . . . this blend is what makes you, you. So you are different from what you were born as, certainly. But as I said before, you're healthy.'"⁵² The good news is that she can fulfill Himba expectations by having children, but it is Okwu rather than Binti who would carry a child. Any children, however, will be parented by a polyamorous cyborg assemblage, as she is paired with New Fish and Okwu and attracted to Mwinyi. The doctor reassures Binti: "'Your family is bigger than any Himba girl's ever was. And twice, you were supposed to die. And here you stand healthy and strong . . .' She chuckled and then added, 'And strange. There is no person like you at this school.'"[53]

## TRANSFORMATIVE RESPONSE-ABILITY

Sentient ships teach us that there is no innocent position; futurity hinges not on getting beyond personal discomfort but in working with it to do better. Futurity hinges on paying attention to the differences and how they matter, even when dealing with uncomfortable histories: "We are all responsible to and for shaping conditions for multispecies flourishing in the face of terrible histories, and sometimes joyful histories too, but we are not all response-able in the same ways. The differences matter—in ecologies, economies, species, lives."[54]

In conversation between Breq and her ship Mercy of Kalr, Ship observes: "there are two parts to reacting, aren't there. How you feel, and what you do. And it's the thing you do that's the important one, isn't it?"[55] Futurity requires not just uniting feeling and thinking, but also action, even though the ability to respond is shaped by individuals who are companionably infected with each other. Both have been drone-like in the past, but in the present both have chosen to respond to Radch imperialism by making change, according to their abilities. These changes create futures that the ships could not have imagined possible.

From the companionable infection between ancillary and ship in Leckie to the companionable infection between ship's AI and human, Sidra and Owl have the freedom to determine how they will be response-able for themselves and their companion species like Pepper, Blue, and Tak. To avoid falling afoul of GC law, Owl is installed in Sidra's café Home. Sidra helps Owl, who as Pepper's mother is like Sidra's grandmother, rewrite any protocols she wishes. The basement is full of memory banks that create two virtual apartments, one for each ship. Although Owl and Sidra have separate spaces, they are connected by a node that either can touch if they wish to communicate. Sidra can flow into her part of the AI space at Home, through six pet bots, or she can inhabit her core body.

Binti's body modifications, including her becoming-ship upgrade her harmonizing skills, with a real chance to shape the future in her war-torn home. Drawing on deep Himba culture as well as Meduse, Enyi Zinariya, and Miri 12 technology *with* at least one other master harmonizer Mwinyi, Binti can better navigate and possibly harmonize liberation and futurity where it seems there is no future but war.

## CONCLUSION

At several points in each trilogy Breq, Sidra, Owl, and Binti could have ended up dead and alone, like NASA's Opportunity rover or like the folkloric Little Match Girl. Instead of gathering around to watch futurity flicker out, Leckie, Chambers, and Okorafor look past the ends directed by social habits and political constructs toward new possible futures. With affect praxis like Tsing's "arts of noticing," Barad's "spacetimemattering," and Haraway's "cyborg writing," the sentient spaceships become resurrection machines. Brought to life by women sf authors, these sentient spaceships remind us to that non-exploitative relations with landscapes, bodies, and worlds is how one survives and (possibly) thrives in/with/through precarity, flipping limitations into liberation and futurity.

## NOTES

1. Science Column, "'My Battery Is Low and It's Getting Dark': Mars Rover Opportunity's Last Message to Scientists," February 14, 2019, https://abc7chicago.com/science/my-battery-is-low-and-its-getting-dark-opportunitys-last-message-to-scientists/5137455/.

2. Ann Leckie, *Ancillary Justice* (2013), *Ancillary Sword* (2014), *Ancillary Mercy* (2015); Nnedi Okorafor, *Binti* (2015), *Binti: Home* (2017), *Binti: The Night Masquerade* (2018); Becky Chambers, *The Long Way to a Small, Angry Planet* (2014), *A Closed and Common Orbit* (2016), *Record of a Spaceborn Few* (2018).

3. Chambers, *A Closed and Common Orbit*, 5402.

4. Ann Leckie, *Ancillary Mercy* (New York: Orbit, 2015), 1812–16. This title is cited by Kindle location throughout.

5. Fieldwork, *This Is Not the End*, 2013, https://www.youtube.com/watch?v=32eywT-bQhQ.

6. Science Vet, "Oppy Story Thread," Twitter, February 14, 2019, https://twitter.com/ScienceVet2/status/1096058154708881409.

7. Sara Ahmed, *Queer Phenomenology: Orientations, Objects, Others* (Durham: Duke University Press, 2006), 57.

8. Jean Hersholt, trans., "The Little Match Girl," The Hans Christian Andersen Centre, A Translation of Hans Christian Andersen's "Den lille Pige med Svovlstikkerne," 1949, https://andersen.sdu.dk/vaerk/hersholt/TheLittleMatchGirl_e.html.

9. Donna Haraway, *Simians, Cyborgs, and Women: The Reinvention of Nature* (New York: Routledge, 1991), 59.

10. See Rosi Braidotti, *The Posthuman* (Cambridge, UK; Malden, MA: Polity Press, 2013), 13–16; Karen Barad, *Meeting the Universe Halfway: Quantum Physics and the Entanglement of Matter and Meaning* (Durham: Duke University Press, 2007), 374–81.

11. Karen Barad, *Meeting the Universe Halfway: Quantum Physics and the Entanglement of Matter and Meaning* (Durham: Duke University Press, 2007), 381.

12. Drezz, *It's Time to Go*, February 13, 2019, February 13, 2019, https://pbs.twimg.com/media/DzS7P1TUUAEY1Fc.png:large; Maryne Lahaye, *Rescue Mission*, February 15, 2019, February 15, 2019, https://www.facebook.com/DoctorFreedom1/photos/a.303635196410534/2059361650837871/?type=3&theater.

13. Sunny Singh, "@sunnysingh_n6," January 21, 2019, https://twitter.com/ShaulaEvans/status/1087453543794200576.

14. Daniel Heath Justice, "On Mars Rover," Twitter, *@justicedanielh* (blog), February 13, 2019, https://twitter.com/justicedanielh/status/1095737207862640640.

15. Sandra Styres (Kanien'kehá:ka), "Literacies of Land Decolonizing Narratives, Storying, and Literature," in *Indigenous and Decolonizing Studies in Education: Mapping the Long View*, ed. Linda Tuhiwai Smith, Eve Tuck, and K. Wayne Yang (New York: Routledge, 2019), 27.

16. Kelsey Dayle John (Diné), "Rez Ponies and Confronting Sacred Junctures in Decolonizing and Indigenous Education," in *Indigenous and Decolonizing Studies in Education: Mapping the Long View*, ed. Linda Tuhiwai Smith, Eve Tuck, and K. Wayne Yang (New York: Routledge, 2019), 52.

17. Erin Marie Konsmo (Métis) and Karyn Recollet (Urban Cree), "Meeting the Land(s) Where They Are At: A Conversation Between Erin Marie Konsmo (Métis) and Karyn Recollet (Urban Cree)," in *Indigenous and Decolonizing Studies in Education: Mapping the Long View*, ed. Linda Tuhiwai Smith, Eve Tuck, and K. Wayne Yang (New York: Routledge, 2019), 239.

18. Audre Lorde, *Sister Outsider: Essays and Speeches* (Berkeley, Calif: Crossing Press, 2007), 9.

19. Haraway, *Simians, Cyborgs, and Women*, 6–7.

20. Gilles Deleuze, *Spinoza, Practical Philosophy* (San Francisco: City Lights Books, 1988), 17.

21. Deleuze, Gilles and Guattari, Félix, *A Thousand Plateaus: Capitalism and Schizophrenia*, trans. Brian Massumi (Minneapolis: University of Minnesota Press, 2011).

22. Brian Massumi, *Politics of Affect* (Cambridge, UK; Malden, MA: Polity, 2015), 17.

23. Anna Lowenhaupt Tsing, *The Mushroom at the End of the World: On the Possibility of Life in Capitalist Ruins* (Princeton, NJ: Princeton University Press, 2015), 37.

24. Tsing, *The Mushroom at the End of the World* 33.

25. Karen Barad, "No Small Matter: Mushroom Clouds, Ecologies of Nothingness, and Strange Topologies of Spacetimemattering," in *Arts of Living on a Damaged Planet*, ed. Anna Tsing et al. (University of Minnesota, 2017), G103–20.

26. Haraway, *Simians, Cyborgs, and Women*, 55.

27. Donna J. Haraway, *Staying with the Trouble: Making Kin in the Chthulucene* (Durham, NC: Duke University Press, 2016).

28. Deborah Bird Rose, "Shimmer When All You Love Is Being Trashed," in *Arts of Living on a Damaged Planet*, ed. Anna Tsing et al. (University of Minnesota Press, 2017), 63.

29. Heading from Hats Off Gentlemen It's Adequate, *When I Was a Ship*, 2018, https://hatsoffgentlemen.bandcamp.com/track/when-i-was-a-ship.

30. Leckie, *Ancillary Mercy*, 9–10.

31. Chambers, *A Closed and Common Orbit*, 2.

32. Chambers, *A Closed and Common Orbit*.

33. Nnedi Okorafor, *Binti*, 66–71.

34. Okorafor, *Binti*, 719.

35. Okorafor, *Binti: Home*, 1204–09.

36. Okorafor, *Binti*, 2018, 82.

37. Okorafor, *Binti*, 2018.

38. Leckie, *Ancillary Sword*, 1040–41.

39. Sandra Styres (Kanien'kehá:ka), "Literacies of Land Decolonizing Narratives, Storying, and Literature," 4.

40. Leckie, *Ancillary Justice*, 3875.

41. Leckie, 88.

42. Leckie, *Ancillary Mercy*, 3688.

43. Chambers, *Long Way to a Small Angry Planet*, 1700.

44. Michael Rymer, "Resurrection Ship (Part 1)," *Battlestar Galactica, 2004–2009*, January 6, 2006; Michael Rymer, "Resurrection Ship (Part 2)," *Battlestar Galactica, 2004–2009*, January 13, 2006.

45. Lorde, *Sister Outsider*, 38.

46. Okorafor, *Binti*, 2018, 151.

47. Sara Ahmed, *Living a Feminist Life* (Durham: Duke University Press, 2017). This title is cited by Kindle location throughout.

48. Erin Marie Konsmo (Métis) and Karyn Recollet (Urban Cree), "Meeting the Land(s) Where They Are At: A Conversation Between Erin Marie Konsmo (Métis) and Karyn Recollet (Urban Cree)." 242.
49. Erin Marie Konsmo (Métis) and Karyn Recollet (Urban Cree), 242.
50. Chambers, *A Closed and Common Orbit*, 80–96.
51. Chambers, 5361, 5385–98.
52. Okorafor, *Binti: The Night Masquerade*, 2203–15.
53. Okorafor, 2249.
54. Haraway, *Staying with the Trouble: Making Kin in the Chthulucene*, 29.
55. Leckie, *Ancillary Mercy*, 1875–76.

# BIBLIOGRAPHY

Ahmed, Sara. *Living a Feminist Life*. Durham: Duke University Press, 2017.
———. *Queer Phenomenology: Orientations, Objects, Others*. Durham: Duke University Press, 2006.
Barad, Karen. *Meeting the Universe Halfway: Quantum Physics and the Entanglement of Matter and Meaning*. Durham: Duke University Press, 2007.
Braidotti, Rosi. *The Posthuman*. Cambridge, UK; Malden, MA: Polity Press, 2013.
Chambers, Becky. *A Closed and Common Orbit*. London: Hodder, 2017.
———. *Record of a Spaceborn Few*, 2019.
———. *The Long Way to a Small, Angry Planet*. London: Hodder, 2015.
Daniel Heath Justice. "On Mars Rover." Twitter. *@justicedanielh* (blog), February 13, 2019. https://twitter.com/justicedanielh/status/1095737207862640640.
Deleuze, Gilles. *Spinoza, Practical Philosophy*. San Francisco: City Lights Books, 1988.
Deleuze, Gilles, and Guattari, Félix. *A Thousand Plateaus: Capitalism and Schizophrenia*. Translated by Brian Massumi. Minneapolis: University of Minnesota Press, 2011.
Drezz. *It's Time to Go*. February 13, 2019. https://pbs.twimg.com/media/DzS7P1TUUAEY1Fc.png:large.
Fieldwork. *This Is Not the End*, 2013. https://www.youtube.com/watch?v=32eywT-bQhQ.
Haraway, Donna J. *Staying with the Trouble: Making Kin in the Chthulucene*. Durham, NC: Duke University Press, 2016.
———. *Simians, Cyborgs, and Women: The Reinvention of Nature*. New York: Routledge, 1991. https://warwick.ac.uk/fac/arts/english/currentstudents/undergraduate/modules/fiction-nownarrativemediaandtheoryinthe21stcentury/manifestly_haraway_----_a_cyborg_manifesto_science_technology_and_socialist-feminism_in_the_....pdf.
Hats Off Gentlemen It's Adequate. *When I Was a Ship*, 2018. https://hatsoffgentlemen.bandcamp.com/track/when-i-was-a-ship.
Hersholt, Jean, trans. "The Little Match Girl." The Hans Christian Andersen Centre. A Translation of Hans Christian Andersen's "Den lille Pige med Svovlstikkerne," 1949. https://andersen.sdu.dk/vaerk/hersholt/TheLittleMatchGirl_e.html.
John, Kelsey Dayle (Diné). "Rez Ponies and Confronting Sacred Junctures in Decolonizing and Indigenous Education." In *Indigenous and Decolonizing Studies in Education: Mapping the Long View*, edited by Linda Tuhiwai Smith, Eve Tuck, and K. Wayne Yang, 50–61. New York: Routledge, 2019.
Konsmo, Erin Marie (Métis), and Karyn Recollet (Urban Cree). "Meeting the Land(s) Where They Are At: A Conversation Between Erin Marie Konsmo (Métis) and Karyn Recollet (Urban Cree)." In *Indigenous and Decolonizing Studies in Education: Mapping the Long View*, edited by Linda Tuhiwai Smith, Eve Tuck, and K. Wayne Yang. New York: Routledge, 2019.
Lahaye, Maryne. *Rescue Mission*. February 15, 2019. https://www.facebook.com/DoctorFreedom1/photos/a.303635196410534/2059361650837871/?type=3&theater.
Leckie, Ann. *Ancillary Justice*. New York: Orbit, 2013.
———. *Ancillary Mercy*. New York, NY: Orbit, 2015.
———. *Ancillary Sword*. New York: Orbit, 2014.

Lorde, Audre. *Sister Outsider: Essays and Speeches*. Berkeley, Calif: Crossing Press, c2007, n.d.

Massumi, Brian. *Politics of Affect*. Cambridge, UK; Malden, MA: Polity, 2015.

Okorafor, Nnedi. *Binti*, 2015.

———. *Binti*, 2015.

———. *Binti: Home*. First edition. Binti 2. New York: Tom Doherty Associates, 2017.

———. *Binti: The Night Masquerade*. First edition. Binti 3. New York: Tom Doherty Associates, 2018.

Rose, Deborah Bird. "Shimmer When All You Love Is Being Trashed." In *Arts of Living on a Damaged Planet*, edited by Anna Tsing, Heather Swanson, Elaine Gan, and Nils Bubandt, G51–63. University of Minnesota Press, 2017.

Rymer, Michael. "Resurrection Ship (Part 1)." *Battlestar Galactica, 2004–2009*, January 6, 2006.

———. "Resurrection Ship (Part 2)." *Battlestar Galactica, 2004–2009*, January 13, 2006.

Science Column. "'My Battery Is Low and It's Getting Dark': Mars Rover Opportunity's Last Message to Scientists." February 14, 2019. https://abc7chicago.com/science/my-battery-is-low-and-its-getting-dark-opportunitys-last-message-to-scientists/5137455/.

Science Vet. "Oppy Story Thread." Twitter, February 14, 2019. https://twitter.com/ScienceVet2/status/1096058154708881409.

Singh, Sunny. "@sunnysingh_n6," January 21, 2019. https://twitter.com/ShaulaEvans/status/1087453543794200576.

Styres, Sandra (Kanien'kehá:ka). "Literacies of Land Decolonizing Narratives, Storying, and Literature." In *Indigenous and Decolonizing Studies in Education: Mapping the Long View*, edited by Linda Tuhiwai Smith, Eve Tuck, and K. Wayne Yang, 24–38. New York: Routledge, 2019.

Tsing, Anna Lowenhaupt. *The Mushroom at the End of the World: On the Possibility of Life in Capitalist Ruins*. Princeton, NJ: Princeton University Press, 2015.

## Chapter Twelve

# What Do We Lose When We Become Posthuman?

*"The People of Sand and Slag" and the Politics of Recognition*

## Michael Uhall

Paolo Bacigalupi's "The People of Sand and Slag" (2008) is a science fiction short story that obliquely addresses the difficult relationship between material conditions and political subjectivity.[1] In particular, the story presents us with a series of implicit questions about the politics of the ecological crisis and the posthuman turn: What does it mean to be human, or posthuman? Are interdependence and vulnerability predicaments to be overcome, or are they normatively valuable conditions? How do environmental constraints affect our capacities and judgments? Do we have an ethical obligation to perceive suffering? What are our obligations to the numerous forms of life that surround and sustain us? What do the limitations of our ecological vision prevent us from registering affectively or politically, and how can such limitations foreclose upon possible pathways of action?

Briefly, the story follows several characters in the distant future who encounter a strange beast, what today we call a dog. The characters are posthumans, and they have been genetically engineered to be maximally adapted to their environment, which is an ecologically devastated Earth. The ocean is contaminated, free of natural life, and the landscape is punctuated by post-industrial ruins, covered in toxic waste. After the encounter, the posthumans decide to keep the dog as a pet, and they view him with a mixture of alienation and pity, for he clearly no longer fits into the brave new world where they frolic and reside. The characters eat broken glass, oily sand, and rusty metal. Their bodies feel no pain. By contrast, the dog struggles even to navigate the landscape itself without grievous injury. Eventually, the mutual incomprehension between the posthuman characters and the dog becomes too much for them to maintain, so they decide to kill and eat him, albeit with some mild regret.

I argue that Bacigalupi's story provides us with an excellent opportunity to consider the tensions between some normative political and theoretical claims—that is, the idea that we exist within, or may enter, a posthuman condition, or that politics is founded in recognition—and the ways in which material conditions can affect our capacities as thinking, feeling subjects. Bacigalupi's story is not merely a cautionary parable, but a generative, interactive site in which the questions I pose above intersect and refract one another. I use Bacigalupi's story to explore the degree to which the concept of posthumanism allows or even requires us to reflect on the relationship between the human and the various modes of recognition available to us as the ecological crisis intensifies.

Accordingly, Bacigalupi's story speaks directly to the core concerns of environmental political theory. Often, discussions of this crisis focus extensively or even exclusively on climate change. Although the effects of climate change are very important, the ecological crisis does not reduce to climate change alone. Indeed, climate change is arguably a symptom of a much deeper crisis. The ecological crisis is a fundamentally political problem because it is, at root, a crisis of relationality, which means that at stake in it is how we relate to each other politically and how we relate to the natural world that we occupy and share with many other forms of agency. A majority of scientific reports indicate that our planet is undergoing catastrophic changes. If we do not alter our attachments and change our practices, then we face catastrophe as well. This is one significant point of contact between the politics of the ecological crisis and the politics of the posthuman turn. Our modes of political action and relation and even our very existence as humans are now dramatically in question.

First, I will provide a short primer on the concept of posthumanism—the idea that the human condition is, in some fashion, giving way to a distinctly posthuman condition. Posthumanists maintain that something about us is changing, or has changed. It may be that what is changing is the manifest image of the human, or it may be that posthuman divergence will initiate a radical ontological break with the category of the human altogether. If either of these options is true, then it is plausible to expect political consequences to follow. At the very least, we need to start asking sharper theoretical questions, like "What is a posthuman politics?" and "How is a posthuman politics different than a human politics?" As I will show, it is not clear that we can answer these questions directly—unless, perhaps, we already are posthumans. Accordingly, inquiries such as these last two necessarily operate within a strange epistemological gap. Either we do not know what we are, or we are becoming something that we do not know.

Next, I will turn to a relatively close, if necessarily fragmentary reconstruction of Bacigalupi's story in order to illustrate how it both draws upon and reflects some of the questions that arise for posthumanism. It is important to note that a literary text differs from a theoretical argument in significant ways (e.g., affectively, interpretively, and structurally). My intention in reading Bacigalupi's story is not to reduce a literary text to a theoretical argument, therefore, but, rather, to sketch and extrapolate lines of interpretive flight from the story in order to clarify and sharpen the wide range of questions with which I first began. As mentioned, posthumanism operates within a strange epistemological gap, and the broad affective spectrum of Bacigalupi's story allows us to explore that gap in highly generative ways. Literature may contain arguments, but it does not reduce to mere argumentation. As such, I rely on the methodological claim that working through this literary text on its own terms introduces and opens up affective insights that can inform, or possibly transform, how we theorize both the posthuman condition and its political consequences.

In conclusion, I will situate Bacigalupi's story in the context of political theoretical arguments about the politics of recognition—the idea that human politics, at least, entails various processes of recognition as its fundamental mode. Specifically, recognition indicates the process by means of which actors get integrated into the matrix of politics, as loci of agency or as subjects of law and of rights, as actors for whom decisional, material, or moral relevance obtains. Georg Wilhelm Friedrich Hegel gives this idea one of its most memorable formulations in the well-known passage on the master-slave dialectic in his *Phenomenology of Spirit*, but we can also find contemporary variations on the thematic of political recognition in theorists as diverse as Judith Butler, Axel Honneth, and Charles Taylor.[2] All of these theorists elaborate complex theoretical structures of recognition that directly inform questions of political action and social identity and that allow political actors to interact, negotiate, and reconcile. By contrast, Bacigalupi's story emphasizes the degree to which ecological and material conditions constrain the limits of what it is possible to recognize, which serves to underscore not only our ultimate implication in those conditions but also the need for us to consider how shifts in subjectivity affect appraisals of ontological possibility and political value alike.

In "The People of Sand and Slag," this insight refuses to take voice only in terms of arguments or observations about the ways that historical practices of recognition have circumscribed the set of legitimate actors, or about how reifying recognition can exclude anything—or anyone—deemed incommensurable with the regime of existing norms. Rather, Bacigalupi skillfully uses tools of literary world-building to evidence the degree to which adaptation to environmental changes and circumstances (adaptations that exist, of course, in varying economic, historical, and political contexts) comes with affective and perceptual effects that alter the range of what it is possible to feel, to know, and to witness. As mentioned, the posthumans in the story ultimately kill and eat the dog they temporarily adopt. Yet something about their encounter with this obsolete creature—in all its shaggy boundedness and woundedness—worries at the periphery of their own highly adapted ecological vision. Dead or alive, the dog figures as an affective specter, or a mournful glimmer of the world they have lost in the very process of gaining the world they now occupy. We can resituate Bacigalupi's insight in terms of yet another question, then. As we proceed into the strange new futures of the Anthropocene, futures increasingly inflected by ecological crisis and mass extinction, what will we take with us, and what will we leave behind?

## THE POSTHUMAN QUESTION

Despite the plethora of attention it has received recently, it remains true that the political implications of the posthuman condition are underdetermined. In part, this is because posthumanist theorists typically emphasize the defeasibility or plasticity of category of the human. This means that we do not, or perhaps cannot, yet know conclusively what it means to be—or to become—posthuman. Are we posthumans already, by dint of changes in our epistemological, material, or technological self-constitution? Or, alternatively, does "the posthuman" indicate a radical ontological break with the category of the human altogether, thereby inaugurating new and fundamentally distinct forms of life? In either case, what does it mean for us to exist in a posthuman condition, as humans or as something like them?

Michel Foucault famously suggests that the historical emergence and eventual dissolution of the category of the human itself is but "the effect of a change in the fundamental arrangements of knowledge."[3] If so, then posthumanism assumes a critical dimension or expression, in which the manifest image of what it means to be human shifts significantly. It shifts away from the false categories and illusory constraints of modern, humanist subjectivity—that is, apperception, interiority, rationality, and self-transparency—and toward the antinomies of the flesh and the defeasible, multiphasic productivity of mediated, technical supplementation. Where the modern humanist subject is a disembodied rational agent, or the self-contained master of her own domain, the posthuman subject is a hybrid becoming, porous to the world, traversed by radical intensities, and susceptible to alien transformations.

As such, critical posthumanism characterizes posthuman subjectivity in terms of its immanence, its materiality, and its plasticity. This brand of the posthuman subject is immanent to a spatiotemporal locality, and, therefore, it is irreducibly ecological and historical. Such relations are constitutive. It is staunchly material, which is to say that it is stubbornly corporeal—embodied, with all the plurality, potentiality, and vulnerability that taking form in a material body entails. And it is plastic, loosed from the gendered, ideological, and metaphysically normative constraints that were heavily refined in the early modern period.

For critical posthumanists like Donna Haraway or Rosi Braidotti, modern humanism is therefore a conceptual and historical cul-de-sac that we need to leave behind in order to explore new, unknown territories. Modern humanism yokes the category of the human to a range of pernicious dichotomies propagated by Cartesian or Christian dualism. These include the distinction between the animal and the human, or the rational and the irrational, or matter and mind. Furthermore, these dichotomies operationalized and sustained concrete political and social norms, like the exclusion of women from public life or the violent subordination of colonial subjects.[4] By contrast, for a critical posthumanism, humans are always already cyborgs, hybrids, or nomads.[5] As Braidotti purports, the posthuman subject is "a connection-making entity [. . .] not abstract but, rather political. It suggests how we should go about re-thinking about the unity of the human being."[6] For critical posthumanism, the human is a developmental trajectory of becoming otherwise. On this account, insofar as the category of the human has been captured by the logic of modernity, we could say, echoing both Haraway and Bruno Latour, that we have never been human.[7] To the contrary, we have always already been posthuman. Hence, we lose ourselves only to find ourselves again—replete in our newly rediscovered posthuman strangeness.

However, it would be a mistake to characterize critical posthumanism only or primarily in terms of its gestures toward the concept of radical becoming. For example, Haraway's work emphasizes the degree to which a genuinely critical posthumanism not only celebrates the vagaries of process ontology, but simultaneously roots itself both in the concrete revision of the manifest image of the human and in the robustly materialist resources of bodies, places, and things. Consider her turn to the theorization of companion species. For her, companion species consist of all the fellow travelers and significant others that accompany us as we make passage through the world. Indeed, this accompaniment is so intimate that we—we "humans," or posthumans, or whatever we are, and the numerous companions upon which we rely for our continued existence—interpenetrate one another at every level, even genetically. Haraway uses the relatively common example of the dog as a companion animal, proceeding to show how dogs and humans inform, mold, and shape each other. As Haraway begins, writing of her own dog: "Ms. Cayenne Pepper continues to colonize all my cells. [. . .] I bet if you checked our DNA, you'd find some potent transfections between us."[8] Here she refers attention to genetic mosaicism, perhaps microchimerism, prevalent phenomena in which we bear cells expressing genotypes that are distinctly not our own—those of mothers, pets, and distant lovers.[9]

Here some of the more directly political theoretical implications suggested by the discourse of critical posthumanism rise further into the foreground. For example, in her account of humans as biocultural creatures, Samantha Frost endeavors to rebuild the category of the human, using resources obtained from biology and the life and physical sciences and taking critical posthumanism as "an instructive point of departure."[10] Although she refuses to identify as a posthumanist (and neither does Haraway, for that matter), Frost situates her reconstruction of the human at the juncture between critical posthumanism and the speculative and theoretical opportunities that it opens up. In other words, if we are to take the interventions of critical posthumanism seriously, then our task becomes the task of inquiring into and producing a new image or theory of the human, or a new philosophical anthropology that refuses the commonplaces of both ideology and scientism. This entails asking not only what bodies *can* do, but also asking what bodies actually do already—what bodies are like when we disarticulate our conception of biological and material embodiment from false, inhibiting modern dogmas of genetic or sociobiological determinism, as well as various ideologically powerful yet empirically illegitimate apprehensions of aptitude, behavior, disability, environment, health, intelligence, and race.

For Frost, after the posthuman turn comes the possibility of developing new, or renewed, ontologies. This possibility occurs only as the underbrush of old manifest images of the human is excised from the posthuman clearing. In this regard, Frost, beyond Braidotti and Haraway, breaks the ground for modes and practices of material speculation that open up a second, speculative dimension or expression of posthumanism.[11] She does this by showing the degree to which bodies are both cultured and material—that is, that to be a material body is to be cultured, cultured in the sense of being affected, cultivated, developed, and dynamic. The truth of this becomes especially evident when viewed through a biological lens, such that bodies are accurately perceived as indices of their environments in every sense, from the chemical, epigenetic contexts of developmental biology to the complex social, symbolic environments of contemporary art, culture, and politics.[12] How speculative posthumanism operationalizes material speculation remains to be seen—but it also rises to the foreground as a question of tremendous existential and political importance.

By material speculation, I intend to transpose our received sense of speculation—that is, that speculation is hypothetical, insubstantial, or ungrounded, that it breeds fantasies and courts nightmares—into a register of material efficacy. This requires that we expand our understanding of speculation in two ways. First, speculation can be a mode of material practice. Consider technical practices of salvage and tinkering, or, better yet, of repurposing artifacts of whatever kind. To repurpose an artifact entails an experiment insofar as it is an attempt to test what an artifact is able to do beyond its manifest purpose. No artifact exists as an isolate, and we tend to forget or obscure the reality that artifacts only exist as temporally extended complexes that emerge within machinic networks. Even the most independent, privileged artifact relies necessarily upon networks of maintenance, production, and support. Consequently, to repurpose an artifact means that we transform its purpose into another purpose, *materially*. This requires the intervention of imagination, or speculative reason—that is to say, of positing a different world than the world we think is given to us. Second, even the mere exercise of imagination or speculative reason itself is a material practice insofar as it functions as kind of ontological mapping, or what Braidotti often calls cartography. Speculative reason maps modal distributions. A modal distribution is a set of alternative possibilities, and possibilities exist, even if they exist in a different way than do actualities. Because thinking is not a ghostly operation that supervenes upon the world without touching it, speculation remains a form of action—or, put differently, it irreducibly accompanies what we identify as action in every case.

Accordingly, speculative posthumanism entails the possibility and perhaps even the demand for material speculation. In this regard, speculative posthumanism exceeds the purview of critical posthumanism insofar as the former takes shape in conceptions of posthuman divergence conceived as a radical ontological break with the human as such. For a speculative posthumanist like David Roden, posthuman divergence requires a meaningful degree of disconnection between us humans and our posthuman descendants.[13] While we might characterize the category of the human in any number of ways—that is, as clever animals or immortal souls, as brains or bodies, as patterns or processes of "data made flesh"—Roden underscores the fact that the category of the posthuman may well embody or signal an analytic shift in the range of what is conceivable or intelligible to us. In other words, speculative posthumanism entertains the distinct possibility that anything genuinely posthuman will exceed, transform, or diverge from whatever we currently are to such an extent that conceptualizing it, much less communicating with or mutually recognizing each other, becomes very difficult, if not impossible.

Roden calls this idea the disconnection thesis. The disconnection thesis relies on a distinction between what Roden calls "Wide Humans" and posthumans. He writes,

> An entity is a Wide Human just so long as it depends for its continued functioning on WH [Wide Human] while contributing to its operations to some degree. Members of the biological species *Homo sapiens*, on the other hand, are *narrowly* human. Thus, domesticated animals, mobile phones and tooth-

brushes are Wide Humans while we obligatory biologicals are both *narrowly* and *widely* human.[14]

Posthumans, therefore, would be "cases of former Wide Humans *becoming feral*: becoming able to fulfill an independent career as an agent outside the human socio-technical assemblage WH."[15] Accordingly, the disconnection thesis clarifies the nature of the radical ontological break in question. In no small part, speculative posthumanism gives even more analytic clarity to the operative nature of the distinction between the categories of the human and the posthuman. This is certainly true for Roden's emphasis on the disconnection thesis, but it is also true for Frost's reclamation and refiguration of hard biology and the life sciences. However, it would be injudicious to avoid observing that critical posthumanists also often tarry with or valorize modes and practices of material speculation, as well. For example, Braidotti's recurrent fascination with insects allows her to explore different ways of mapmaking and navigation, while Haraway's study of the oncomouse intersects with numerous epistemologies and technologies, not to mention the historical associations and material generativity of its flesh.[16]

Note furthermore that Roden's argument is not an appeal to the transhumanist imaginary both Braidotti and Haraway derogate, for he rejects the teleological content of transhumanism, as well. By contrast, Roden's form of speculative posthumanism retains both an element of caution about the risks of posthuman divergence and an incitement to the modes and practices of material speculation that generate the very possibility of such divergence. On the one hand, he strikes a precautionary note when he acknowledges the possibility of posthuman divergence as an "ontological catastrophe."[17] If the posthuman is absolutely unintelligible to us, then there is no assurance that it will be able to accommodate, communicate with, or recognize us. Put this way, these consequences may sound rather minimalist in kind, but consider the possible array of existential threats modeled both by existential risk theorists and in science fiction, as well as posed by our ongoing global experiments with artificial intelligence and biosecurity, to name only two credible vectors.[18] On the other hand, Roden maintains that "there is no basis for concluding that posthumans would have to be beyond evaluation" in principle.[19] This is because assessing the material and normative implications of posthuman divergence is possible only if the divergence in question has already taken place. Caution gets outweighed by epistemological or experimental need. He concludes, "[W]e have an interest in contributing to the emergence of posthumans or *becoming posthuman* ourselves where this is liable to mitigate the interpretative problems posed by disconnection."[20]

Bacigalupi's story, to which I turn in the following section, takes up the issues and questions raised by critical and speculative posthumanists alike, and it opens up for analysis and inquiry some of the same registers of concern. Recall that for critical posthumanism, it is the manifest image of the human that undergoes deconstruction or revision. Once upon a time, we—that is to say, the hegemons of early European modernity—told a story about the human, and that story now lies in ruins, vulnerable to capture and reconstruction. As Haraway writes, "Cyborg writing is about the power to survive, not on the basis of original innocence, but on the basis of seizing the tools to mark the world that marked them as other."[21] By contrast, speculative posthumanism indicates the analytic nature of the divide between the human and the posthuman. In other words, it is not just a descriptive or narrative shift that differentiates the latter from the former, but a radical ontological break with material consequences.

For both critical and speculative posthumanism, then, the posthuman condition is posed not as a determined set of coordinates, but as a question: What *is* the posthuman, and what can, or will, it do? As we have started to see, this is a fundamentally political question, one that directs attention to the processes of collective action and collective imagination that identify, perform, and revise pathways of action for collectives of the human and the posthuman alike. The politics of recognition are especially at issue here. Insofar as the nature of the distinction between the human and the posthuman carries no normative guarantees, posthumanism of any sort remains underdetermined. This suggests that posthumanism is a site of vigorous contestation, both in terms of its theoretical constitution, which is to say, it's very referent, and in terms of its practical implications for our form of life. It is worth noting further the degree to which both dimensions or expressions of posthumanism situate the category of the human as a locus of prime interest—as that which is to be discarded, surpassed, or transformed.

This leads us to the following question, a question that Bacigalupi's story sharpens almost unbearably: *What do we lose when we become posthuman?* A purely critical posthumanist might answer this question by saying that we lose primarily what is undesirable, namely, the vicious conceptual and descriptive constraints inherited from modernity. Consider the posthuman turn as an unqualified emancipation from the human condition, one way or another. In this regard, however, it may be more useful to adopt the stance of speculative posthumanism in order to explore more fully what we lose, or stand to lose, in becoming robustly posterior to ourselves. This question does not need to entail mere reactionary anxiety, however, such as what we find voiced by figures like Francis Fukuyama and Jürgen Habermas in their critiques of posthumanism.[22] Rather, we can pose it in terms of the politics of recognition, to which I turn in my conclusion.

# EATING SAND FOR DINNER: RECONSTRUCTING "THE PEOPLE OF SAND AND SLAG"

To recap, the basic narrative structure of "The People of Sand and Slag" is relatively simple. Several posthuman characters in the distant future encounter an extremely rare specimen of a formerly common species—a dog. As one of the characters, Jaak, observes, finding a dog is like finding a dinosaur, an extinct and outmoded form of life from the distant past. After debating what they should do with the dog—another character, Lisa, lobbies for eating it immediately—they decide to accommodate Jaak's desire to keep it as a pet for a while. However, the dog is maladapted to the landscape in which the posthumans reside. It struggles even to navigate that landscape without injuring itself constantly. Eventually, their incomprehension of the dog's form of life and the inconvenience of caring for it and meeting its needs becomes overwhelming. So the posthumans finally kill and eat it, an option they started debating since first encountering it.

Much of Bacigalupi's story operates by means of descriptive implication. There is relatively little direct exposition, except insofar as characters discuss events incidentally, or as Chen, the protagonist, reflects on the affective disturbance occasioned by the dog's arrival. For example, the Montana landscape in which the story takes place is devastated, albeit devastated in ways we can already detect in fracked regions of our own contemporary Montana. Bacigalupi characterizes this future landscape as ragged and toxic, populated by acid pits, catchment lakes, old mines, tailings, oil-saturated seas, rusting scrap, and ruins. The posthumans reside in a vast wasteland undergoing intense mining operations by their employer, SesCo, but there is good reason to think that the entire planet itself is utterly polluted. It is a post-ecological landscape, an utterly dominated space, in which considerations of ecological health or environmental impact are moot. Late in the story, one of the characters, Jaak, lights the ocean on fire in order to provide mood lighting for a relaxing vacation. The story repeatedly emphasizes the degree to which the posthumans have aesthetic and recreational preferences that their environment now complements:

> Outside the security bunker, the mining robots rumbled back and forth, ripping deeper into the earth, turning it into a mush of tailings and rock acid that they left in exposed ponds when they hit the water table, or piled into thousand-foot mountainscapes of waste soil. It was comforting to hear those machines cruising back and forth all day.[23]

The three main characters are also rather different than we might assume, although nothing signals at first that they are biologically or physically transformed. They are posthumans of some variety, however—although Bacigalupi leaves open the possibility that, ironically, they may be something like uplifted dogs themselves. Occupationally, they work as incredibly efficacious security guards, tasked with proactively defending SesCo's automated mining operations against hostile incursions. It is easy to imagine aspects of this future, in which corporate soldiers raid and repress indigenes or objectors, visiting extreme violence upon those whose interests do not align with various corporate imperatives. How and to what degree these posthumans are, in fact, posthuman becomes increasingly apparent throughout the story. Yet because, for them, their posthuman condition is utterly quotidian, the characters rarely provide much exposition upon their own nature.

What is made clear is that the world Bacigalupi suggests has been transformed by what he calls weeviltech, in which post-biological organisms such as the main characters and their servitors exist symbiotically with "microweevils," genetically engineered or nanotechnological agencies that allow organisms to consume and process any raw material in the environment around them—oil, rock, sand, tar. "We can eat anything. We're the top of the food chain."[24]

Furthermore, the posthumans appear to be utterly impervious to pain or physical suffering. Injury is treated as a joke or a recreational activity. "After dinner we sat around and sharpened Lisa's skin, implanting blades along her limbs so that she was like a razor from all directions."[25] Such a relationship to injury is given special emphasis when, at the story's end, the characters play with vulnerability itself. Chen amputates all of Lisa's limbs in order for her to experiment with what it feels like to be disempowered. "Already, her limbs were regrowing. [. . .] By morning, she would be whole, and ravenous."[26] Because the process of recovery is so accelerated due to the efficient and rapid action of weeviltech, the very idea of injury seems obsolete, and the characters do not register pain except as an annoyance or a distant possibility afflicting lesser biological creatures. For example, when they first encounter the dog in the wastelands, it bites Jaak's arm in fear, but Jaak merely cuts his own arm off with amusement. It rapidly regrows. "The sucker threw up my arm almost right after he ate it. [. . .] I don't think we're compatible for it. [. . .] Weird how it can't eat us."[27]

The degree to which eating figures in the story is also noteworthy. After all, it is by consuming the landscape itself, in all its wrack and ruin, that the posthumans ingest the resources necessary to recuperate any accumulated damage. Jaak invokes the cost of dog food as no small part of its ultimate inconvenience. The dog's inability to eat sand, as it were, functions as a synecdoche for its dependence and vulnerability. "It pawed up a chunk of red plastic rubbed shiny by the ocean and chewed on it briefly. [. . .] I wondered if it had poisoned itself again."[28]

The extreme physical resilience of the posthumans therefore strongly affects their perception of the dog and its inherent biological fragility. At first, the posthumans are skeptical that the dog is even what it appears to be. "'It doesn't have any hands.' [. . .] 'What kind of sick bastard makes a bio-job without hands?'"[29] "It's pretty beat up. Maybe it's the real thing. [. . .] It can't be. It would be dead, if it were a real dog."[30] Indeed, their often rather inhumane or violent treatment of the dog is more a function of their inability to recognize or remember what suffering is than it is due to any inherent cruelty. "I think I might have broken it when I put it in the cage. [. . .] It's not moving like it was before. And I heard something snap when I stuffed it in."[31] Bacigalupi emphasizes the physical damage the dog incurs throughout the story—again and again, as it navigates both the landscape and its time as companion to the posthumans. The dog is constantly bleeding and marked with chemical burns. As the characters remark, "I never thought an animal would be so fragile."[32] "Must be a bummer to wake up and find you're at the end of your evolutionary curve."[33]

After the posthumans capture the dog and report their find, SesCo dispatches a biologist to come and inspect it. "'There's a dead-end job,'" they scoff.[34] The biologist arrives and takes a sample. When the posthumans ask the biologist what to do with the dog, he has no further use for it at all, having taken a sample of its DNA: "A live one is hardly worth keeping around. [. . .] *Recreating the web of life isn't easy. Far more simple to release oneself from it completely than to attempt to re-create it.*[35] Around the biologist's arrival, the characters discuss the exotic and outmoded nature of his largely forgotten discipline. Biology is about life, and they know little about life in any familiar sense.

Their incomprehension of the dog's form of life does not improve, even as they spend time coexisting with it. A crucial scene involves Jaak successfully teaching the dog how to shake hands. Jaak is delighted, but Lisa remains skeptical, surprised at the possibility or the suggestion that perhaps it even thinks. Chen is curious, but when he gets the dog to perform its trick—shaking his hand—his ambivalence only intensifies: "It stuck out its paw. My hackles went up. *It was like sending signals to aliens.*"[36]

As such, Chen's ongoing ambivalence about the dog figures prominently, reflecting all of the posthumans' curiosity and skepticism about this old-fashioned and strange form of life. As Lisa states later in the story, "If you want animals around you, go to a zoo. Or get some building blocks and make something [. . .]."[37] However, Chen's ambivalence takes on a different tenor than Jaak's amusement with the novelty of a real, live animal, or Lisa's derogatory hostility. For Chen is uniquely cognizant that the fact that he and his friends used to be like the dog in some way must mean something, although he is never sure what. Chen makes a comment that reveals the degree to which his awareness of the dog's pathetic and shaggy otherness unsettles him deeply: "*It looks at us, and there's something there, and it's not us.* I mean, take any bio-job out there, and it's basically us, poured into another shape [. . .]."³⁸ Yet Chen remains unable to articulate the inchoate insight lurking underneath this observation, or the feelings that produce it. When the dog licks his face, the limit of his ability to recognize intent rises to the foreground: "It was a funny thing to have this animal licking me, like it wanted to talk, or say hello or something."³⁹ Note how he uses a simile to distantiate his apprehension of the dog's intentions. It is *like* it wants to communicate, *or something*, because he cannot imagine that it is actually doing so, or what it would mean for it to do so. This dog is an atavism to which he can no longer relate, or relate directly.

Ultimately, the inconvenience of the dog overwhelms the posthumans' desire to continue caring for it, and the novelty of the situation dissipates. During a vacation trip to Hawaii, they decide the dog is no longer worth keeping alive. Chen raises a few halfhearted objections to Jaak's proposal that they eat the dog. Nevertheless, Jaak and Lisa overrule Chen's objections, pointing out how expensive the dog is. So they arrive at their final decision.

> Lisa roasted the dog on a spit, over burning plastics and petroleum skimmed from the ocean. It tasted okay, but in the end it was hard to understand the big deal. [. . .] Still, I remember when the dog licked my face and hauled its shaggy bulk onto my bed, and I remember its warm breathing beside me, and sometimes, I miss it.⁴⁰

Throughout Bacigalupi's story, the posthumans reflect on the difference between their posthuman condition and the dog's mortal condition. Repeatedly, the dog's fragility and otherness receives special emphasis, although Chen, Jaak, and Lisa do not seem able to recognize fully what this might mean. They are baffled by the dog's maladaptedness to the landscape where they fight and frolic, and they reflect on numerous occasions upon the apparent uselessness of such a creature as the dog in a world where everything living is designed and instrumentalized. Chen comments, "If someone came from the past, [. . .] would they even call us human? [. . .] No, they'd call us gods."⁴¹ In this regard, at least, they are indeed radically posthuman, disconnected from the conditions of our current existence as ecologically interdependent and fragile animal bodies. And yet they are haunted by the marginal and ragged figure of the dog, as future posthumans of the sort Roden imagines might one day be haunted by us.

While reflecting on the dog's appearance, Chen shares several lines of verse with Lisa, penned by one of the last human poets in their history. The lines emphasize the revolutionary material effects of weeviltech, but also the cost of such transformation. The verse thereby gestures toward what is at issue here, namely, the failures of recognition that such isolated superempowerment and consequent perceptual reengineering can entail.

> Cut me I won't bleed. Gas me I won't breathe.

Stab me, shoot me, slash me, smash me
I have swallowed science
I am God.
Alone.[42]

## CONCLUSION: POSTHUMANISM HAUNTED BY THE POLITICS OF RECOGNITION

Central to Bacigalupi's story is the affective and perceptual gap between the posthuman characters and the dog. Bacigalupi builds the world of the story in such a way that this gap is especially or uniquely apparent to the contemporary reader in two ways. The first involves our likely familiarity with dogs and their behavior and general comportment, and the second involves the figuration of dogs both as beloved pets (i.e., at least in contemporary Western culture) and as valued companions and highly functional domesticated servitors (i.e., in human culture more generally, at least since approximately 12,000 to 15,000 years ago). However, it is not merely a sentimentalist narrative about the tragedy of cruel or uncomprehending characters who heartlessly kill a dog.

For Bacigalupi integrates self-reflective moments into the narrative by means of Chen's affective responses to the dog and to the general ambivalence about its form (that it lacks hands), function (that it is not designed for any clearly instrumental purpose), and significance (that its consciousness is enigmatic or partially occluded) in the world of the story. Jaak may lobby for adopting the dog, but he also initiates the final decision to eat it after its ongoing presence becomes tiresome. By contrast, it is Chen who views the dog as another form of life in its own right—atavistic, perhaps, but nevertheless a distinctly agential subjectivity. This is precisely what disturbs Chen, namely, his cloudy awareness that the dog is something other: "It looks at us, and there's something there, and it's not us."[43] He compares communicating with the dog to sending signals to aliens in outer space. In this regard, Chen evidences a fragmented sense of the need for, or the value of, something like recognition, as well as the strangeness of ecological encounter, although he remains unable to articulate or operationalize that need. Bacigalupi's story becomes especially relevant to political theory at this point.

In much contemporary political theory, the politics of recognition figure prominently, either positively or negatively. For a theorist like Honneth, relations of recognition figure positively, as absolutely necessary for the formation of political agency and social identity alike, as well as the function and health of democratic practice. The point is not merely that identity is contextual or self-interrupting (although it is both), but that, precisely because the identity of the subject always is performed in relation to the other, indeed, to others, the structure of that relationship levies a wide range of affects, contradictions, obligations, and oppositions. For Honneth, the very autonomy of the subject depends upon the social conditions of identity formation, as well.[44] Individuation and socialization are aspects of the same formative process, and the multimodality of this process strongly inflects both the (moral, even structural) integrity of the subject and the conditions of collective well-being or political decay that inform political action as such. By contrast, a theorist like Butler characterizes recognition more negatively, although it might be more accurate to say that Butler is ambivalent about recognition.[45] For Butler, recognition is intimately intertwined with power, which means that the function of recognition is attended by schematic elements of misrecognition or nonrecognition. In this regard, recognition grants intelligibility to a subject, yes, but such a dispensation often entails forms of biopolitical categorization and violent exclusion that consign minoritarian or subaltern subjects to political erasure and social death.[46]

In either case, at issue for theorists like Butler and Honneth is the degree to which the action and performance of recognition distinctly figures for political life. In political theory more generally, this insight is extremely important insofar as questions about what we can recognize as political structure the field of possible actions, issues, and concerns. Regarding the posthuman turn, then, we can reformulate the question I have been considering—*What do we lose when we become posthuman?*—in terms of what we can and cannot recognize as the humans that we are, or as the posthumans of whatever variety that we may become or engender. As such, Bacigalupi's story is not a fable about the dangers of misrecognition, but a speculative fragment about failures of recognition due to environmental and material constraints. And here, what is environmental and material consists not only of the context or the frame—that is, the world—in which the characters exist and act, but also their own natures, or nature-cultures (to use Haraway's neologism). In other words, the posthuman characters may have a greatly expanded range of physical agency, but they are phenomenologically blinkered. They cannot consciously recognize the dog as anything more than an atavism, a bad biojob, botched by nature and displaying the ineluctable vulnerability of biological life. Yet they remain haunted by its agency, its fragility, and its natural purposelessness. This, ultimately, is why Chen finds the dog disturbing, and why Lisa responds to its presence with such casual hostility.

The politics of recognition haunt both Bacigalupi's story and the posthuman condition itself, however the contours of that condition are resolved. They haunt us because they are placed into question. What will we become unable to recognize as we undergo various posthuman transformations, and what things of value might we lose? Apropos of Bacigalupi's story itself, how might we lose the capacity even to perceive or recall the things of value that changes in our condition might efface? If the broad analogy I am posing—between, on the one hand, the dog and the people of sand and slag and, on the other hand, humans and posthumans—obtains at all, then we must start asking new and riskier questions as we theorize ourselves and endeavor to map and understand the posthuman turn we are facing.

## NOTES

1. Paolo Bacigalupi, "The People of Sand and Slag," in *Pump Six and Other Stories* (San Francisco: Night Shade Books, 2008), 49–68.
2. See Judith Butler, *Subjects of Desire: Hegelian Reflections in Twentieth Century France* (New York: Columbia University Press, 1987), especially 1–59, and her more recent *Senses of the Subject* (New York: Fordham University Press, 2015), as well as Axel Honneth, *The Struggle for Recognition: The Moral Grammar of Social Conflict*, trans. Joel Anderson (Cambridge: The MIT Press, 1995) and Charles Taylor, "The Politics of Recognition," in *Multiculturalism: Examining the Politics of Recognition*, ed. Amy Gutmann (Princeton: Princeton University Press, 1994), 25–74.
3. Michel Foucault, *The Order of Things: An Archaeology of the Human Sciences*, trans. Alan Sheridan (New York: Vintage Books, 1994), 387.
4. See Donna Haraway, *Simians, Cyborgs and Women: The Reinvention of Nature* (New York: Routledge, 1991) and Val Plumwood, *Feminism and the Mastery of Nature* (New York: Routledge, 1993).
5. See Rosi Braidotti, *Nomadic Subjects: Embodiment and Sexual Difference in Contemporary Feminist Theory* (New York: Columbia University Press, 2011, 2nd edition) and Donna Haraway, "A Cyborg Manifesto: Science, Technology, and Socialist-Feminism in the Late Twentieth Century" in *Manifestly Haraway* (Minneapolis: University of Minnesota Press, 2016), 3–90.
6. Rosi Braidotti, "Posthuman, All Too Human: Towards a New Process Ontology," *Theory, Culture & Society* 23:7–8 (2006): 200.
7. Donna Haraway, "When We Have Never Been Human, What Is to Be Done?: An Interview with Donna Haraway," *Theory, Culture, & Society* 23:7–8 (2006): 135–58 and Bruno Latour, *We Have Never Been Modern*, trans. Catherine Porter (Cambridge: Harvard University Press, 1993).
8. Donna Haraway, "Companion Species Manifesto," 93.
9. See James R. Lupski, "Genome Mosaicism—One Human, Multiple Genomes," *Science* 341 (2013): 358–59 and Carl Zimmer, "A Pregnancy Souvenir: Cells That Are Not Your Own," *New York Times*, September 10, 2015 accessed March 3, 2020, https://www.nytimes.com/2015/09/15/science/a-pregnancy-souvenir-cells-that-are-not-your-own.html?_r=0.
10. Samantha Frost, *Biocultural Creatures: Toward a New Theory of the Human* (Durham: Duke University Press, 2016), 159.
11. See David Roden, "Speculative Posthumanism" in *Posthuman Glossary*, eds. Rosi Braidotti and Maria Hlavajova (London: Bloomsbury Academic, 2018), 398–401.
12. See *Carnal Knowledge: Towards a 'New Materialism' through the Arts*, eds. Estelle Barrett and Barbara Bolt (New York: I. B. Tauris, 2013) and *The New Politics of Materialism: History, Philosophy, Science*, eds. Sarah Ellenzweig and John H Zammito (New York: Routledge, 2017).
13. David Roden, *Posthuman Life: Philosophy at the Edge of the Human* (New York: Routledge, 2015).
14. Roden, *Posthuman Life*, 112, emphasis in original.
15. Roden, *Posthuman Life*, 113, emphasis in original.
16. Rosi Braidotti, "The Cosmic Buzz of Insects," in *Nomadic Theory: The Portable Rosi Braidotti* (New York: Columbia University Press, 2011), 98–123 and Donna Haraway, *Modest_Witness@Second_Millennium. FemaleMan_Meets_OncoMouse: Feminism and Technoscience* (New York: Routledge, 2018).
17. Roden, *Posthuman Life*, 52.

18. See *Global Catastrophic Risks*, eds. Nick Bostrom and Milan Ćirković (Oxford: Oxford University Press, 2011). On artificial intelligence, see Nick Bostrom, *Superintelligence: Paths, Dangers, Strategies* (Oxford University Press, 2016).
19. Roden, *Posthuman Life*, 121.
20. Roden, *Posthuman Life*, 121, emphasis in original.
21. Haraway, "A Cyborg Manifesto" in *Manifestly Haraway*, 55.
22. See Francis Fukuyama, *Our Posthuman Future: Consequences of the Biotechnology Revolution* (London: Picador, 2003) and Jürgen Habermas, *The Future of Human Nature* (Cambridge: Polity Press, 2003).
23. Bacigalupi, "People of Sand and Slag," 53–54.
24. Bacigalupi, "People of Sand and Slag," 55.
25. Bacigalupi, "People of Sand and Slag," 54.
26. Bacigalupi, "People of Sand and Slag," 65.
27. Bacigalupi, "People of Sand and Slag," 55.
28. Bacigalupi, "People of Sand and Slag," 65.
29. Bacigalupi, "People of Sand and Slag," 51.
30. Bacigalupi, "People of Sand and Slag," 53.
31. Bacigalupi, "People of Sand and Slag," 55.
32. Bacigalupi, "People of Sand and Slag,"
33. Bacigalupi, "People of Sand and Slag," 53.
34. Bacigalupi, "People of Sand and Slag," 56.
35. Bacigalupi, "People of Sand and Slag," 59, emphasis mine.
36. Bacigalupi, "People of Sand and Slag," 62, emphasis mine.
37. Bacigalupi, "People of Sand and Slag," 63.
38. Bacigalupi, "People of Sand and Slag," 64, emphasis mine.
39. Bacigalupi, "People of Sand and Slag," 64.
40. Bacigalupi, "People of Sand and Slag," 67.
41. Bacigalupi, "People of Sand and Slag," 66.
42. Bacigalupi, "People of Sand and Slag," 62.
43. Bacigalupi, "People of Sand and Slag," 64.
44. See Axel Honneth, "The I in We: Recognition as a Driving Force of Group Formation," *The I in We: Studies in the Theory of Recognition*, trans. Joseph Ganahl (Malden: Polity Press, 2012), 201–16.
45. See Paddy McQueen, "Honneth, Butler and the Ambivalent Effects of Recognition," *Res Publica* 21 (2015): 43–60.
46. See Judith Butler, *Giving an Account of Oneself* (New York: Fordham University Press, 2005).

# BIBLIOGRAPHY

Bacigalupi, Paolo. 2008. "The People of Sand and Slag." In *Pump Six and Other Stories*, 49–68. San Francisco: Night Shade Books.
Barrett, Estelle and Barbara Bolt, eds. 2013. *Carnal Knowledge: Towards a 'New Materialism' through the Arts*. New York: I. B. Tauris.
Bostrom, Nick. 2016. *Superintelligence: Paths, Dangers, Strategies*. Oxford: Oxford University Press.
Bostrom, Nick and Milan Ćirković, eds. 2011. *Global Catastrophic Risks*. Oxford: Oxford University Press.
Braidotti, Rosi. (1994) 2011. *Nomadic Subjects: Embodiment and Sexual Difference in Contemporary Feminist Theory*. New York: Columbia University Press.
———. 2006. "Posthuman, All Too Human: Towards a New Process Ontology." *Theory, Culture & Society* 23 (7–8): 197–208.
———. 2011. "The Cosmic Buzz of Insects." In *Nomadic Theory: The Portable Rosi Braidotti*, 98–123. New York: Columbia University Press.

Butler, Judith. 1987. *Subjects of Desire: Hegelian Reflections in Twentieth Century France*. New York: Columbia University Press.
———. 2005. *Giving an Account of Oneself*. New York: Fordham University Press.
———. 2015. *Senses of the Subject*. New York: Fordham University Press.
Ellenzweig, Sarah and John H Zammito, eds. 2017. *The New Politics of Materialism: History, Philosophy, Science*. New York: Routledge.
Foucault, Michel. (1966) 1994. *The Order of Things: An Archaeology of the Human Sciences*, Translated by Alan Sheridan. New York: Vintage Books.
Frost, Samantha. 2016. *Biocultural Creatures: Toward a New Theory of the Human*. Durham: Duke University Press.
Fukuyama, Francis. 2003. *Our Posthuman Future: Consequences of the Biotechnology Revolution*. London: Picador.
Habermas, Jürgen. 2003. *The Future of Human Nature*. Cambridge: Polity Press.
Haraway, Donna. 1991. *Simians, Cyborgs and Women: The Reinvention of Nature*. New York: Routledge.
———. 2006. "When We Have Never Been Human, What Is to Be Done?: An Interview with Donna Haraway." *Theory, Culture, & Society* 23 (7–8): 135–58.
———. (1985) 2016. "A Cyborg Manifesto: Science, Technology, and Socialist-Feminism in the Late Twentieth Century." In *Manifestly Haraway*, 3–90. Minneapolis: University of Minnesota Press.
———. (1997) 2018. *Modest_Witness@Second_Millennium. FemaleMan_Meets_OncoMouse: Feminism and Technoscience*. New York: Routledge.
Honneth, Axel. 1995. *The Struggle for Recognition: The Moral Grammar of Social Conflict*. Translated by Joel Anderson. Cambridge: The MIT Press.
———. 2012. "The I in We: Recognition as a Driving Force of Group Formation." In *The I in We: Studies in the Theory of Recognition*, 201–16. Translated by Joseph Ganahl. Cambridge: Polity Press.
Latour, Bruno. 1993. *We Have Never Been Modern*. Translated by Catherine Porter. Cambridge: Harvard University Press.
Lupski, James R. 2013. "Genome Mosaicism—One Human, Multiple Genomes." *Science* 341: 358–59.
McQueen, Paddy. 2015. "Honneth, Butler and the Ambivalent Effects of Recognition." *Res Publica* 21: 43–60.
Plumwood, Val. 1993. *Feminism and the Mastery of Nature*. New York: Routledge.
Roden, David. 2015. *Posthuman Life: Philosophy at the Edge of the Human*. New York: Routledge.
———. 2018. "Speculative Posthumanism." In *Posthuman Glossary*, 398–401. Edited by Rosi Braidotti and Maria Hlavajova. London: Bloomsbury Academic.
Taylor, Charles. 1994. "The Politics of Recognition." In *Multiculturalism: Examining the Politics of Recognition*, 25–74. Edited by Amy Gutmann. Princeton: Princeton University Press.
Zimmer, Carl. 2015. "A Pregnancy Souvenir: Cells That Are Not Your Own." *New York Times*, September 10, 2015. https://www.nytimes.com/2015/09/15/science/a-pregnancy-souvenir-cells-that-are-not-your-own.html.

# Index

adaptation, 55, 67n3, 189, 237–238
Adorno, Theodor, 1, 135, 138
affect, affecting futurity, 55–56, 59, 60, 83, 86, 139, 211, 222, 223, 231, 235–238, 240, 244, 245, 248–249
Africa, 93, 94, 96–107
African Americans, 7, 94, 95, 98, 99, 102, 105, 205, 206
Afrofuturism, 94, 96, 97, 102, 107
Agamben, Giorgio, 200
Ahmed, Sara, 220, 228
ancillary, 223–224, 230
animals, 4, 6, 21, 29, 43, 44, 63, 159, 161, 165, 199–213, 221, 223, 239, 241, 246, 247
Anthropocene, 4, 6, 64, 113–116, 118, 125–126, 200, 238
anthropological machine, 200–202, 209, 212
apocalypse, 15, 19, 23, 25, 55, 66, 67n5, 82, 115
Apollonian, 42, 44, 47, 48
Arendt, Hannah, 116
artificial intelligence, 242
Atwood, Margaret, 13–14, 16–17, 21–22, 24–29, 95

Bacigalupi, Paolo, 235–238, 242–249
Ballard, J.G., 16, 113–116, 118–120, 123, 126, 127, 128n9, 128n17, 128n23
Barad, Karen, 231

*Battlestar Galactica*, 228
Bendell, Jem, 67n3
Berardi, Franco, 54
Bezos, Jeff, 175, 176, 178–180, 186, 190
biocapitalism, 209, 212
bioethics, 73, 79, 80
biology, 73, 80, 84, 183, 201–203, 213, 240, 242, 246
biotechnology, 74, 76–78, 84
"Black Atlantic," 100–101, 103
*Black Mirror*, 13, 20
Black nationalism, 99
*Black Panther*, 93–94, 97–108
Black political thought, 94, 98, 99, 106
Braidotti, Rosi, 239–242
*Brave New World*, 17
Breakthrough Institute, 125, 126
Brecht, Bertolt, 3
Butler, Judith, 249
Butler, Octavia, 4, 82, 209

capitalism, 1–3, 6, 7, 57–58, 60–61, 64, 65, 80, 136, 138, 142, 149, 156, 167, 175–177, 180, 181, 183, 189, 191, 192, 209–213
Capitalocene, 6
care (or ethics of care, or care ethics), 79, 85–87, 116, 126–127, 164, 179, 183, 206, 208, 210–211, 226–227, 242
catastrophe, 7, 18, 54–61, 64–66, 107, 114–117, 119, 121–123, 125, 185, 236,

## Index

242
clones, 13, 19, 21, 73, 74, 83–86
colonialism, 95–99, 103, 104, 199, 201, 204
colonization, 98, 122, 123, 175, 176, 178, 180, 182, 183, 186, 187, 189–191, 202
Conway, Erik, 65–66
critical theory, 1–3, 135–139, 149, 150
Crutzen, Paul, 6
cyborg, cyborg families, "cyborg writing" (haraway), 80, 199, 202, 222, 223, 228, 229, 231, 239, 243

Dayle John, Kelsey, 222
Debord, Guy, 2
Delany, Samuel R., 140–141, 143–149
democracy, 57, 60, 114, 116, 184, 187
diaspora, 102–108
Dick, Philip K., 16, 85, 176, 185, 189, 190
Dionysian, 33, 42–46, 48
disability, 7, 73, 76–82, 86, 87, 201, 203, 205, 206, 221, 240
domestication, 205, 211
drones, 219–221, 223, 225, 226, 230
dystopia, 3–4, 13–21, 26, 28, 34, 60–61, 64, 81, 137, 141, 144

Edelman, Lee, 208
Enlightenment, 2, 16, 53, 57, 62, 63, 64
entangled, entanglements, 80, 126, 140, 204, 220–223, 225, 229
eugenics, 73–76, 78–80, 83–87, 208

*Fahrenheit 451*, 4
Foucault, Michel, 5, 127, 144, 201–203, 238
future, 13, 15–18, 20, 22, 23, 25, 26, 28, 37, 41, 53–57, 60–61, 64–66, 74, 75, 77–79, 81–82, 84–87, 95–96, 114, 115, 120, 124, 125, 137, 139, 145, 176, 181, 185–186, 191, 199, 201, 204, 205, 207–212, 220, 225, 226, 230, 231, 235, 238, 244, 247

gender, 5–7, 76–81, 87, 95, 98, 150, 200–202, 204, 206, 208–211, 213, 221, 239, 249
Ghosh, Amitav, 182, 184–185, 188
Goddard, Jean-Luc, 3

Hall, Stuart, 3, 100
Haraway, Donna, 80, 201, 209, 221, 222, 231, 239–240, 242–243, 249
Harvey, David, 2–3, 179
Heath Justice, Daniel, 221–222
Heidegger, Martin, 22, 27
heteronormativity, 59, 61, 66, 136, 207
heterotopia, 141, 144–150
Hobbes, Thomas, 15, 53, 63, 119, 120
Honig, Bonnie, 113–116, 125, 127
Honneth, Axel, 248–249
Horkheimer, Max, 1, 138
humanism, human, 4, 6, 22, 64, 199, 203, 205, 207, 236–243

ideology, 20, 76, 81, 84, 98, 142, 149, 158, 240
inequality, 82, 101, 142
instrumentalization, 19–21
international relations (IR), 7, 33
intersex, 76–79
Ishiguro, Kazuo, 13, 19–20

Jameson, Frederic, 1, 67n4, 176, 182
Jonas, Hans, 14, 18

kinship, 85, 106, 201, 205, 208–210, 212, 220

Lang, Fritz, 5
Latour, Bruno, 113, 114, 120, 239
Le Guin, Ursula K., 14, 16, 26–27, 135, 140–142, 147–150
Lebow, Richard Ned, 35–37, 40
liberation, 178, 210, 220, 222–223, 225, 226, 230, 231
Lorde, Audre, 222, 228

*Maddaddam*, 14, 21–23, 28–29
Marcuse, Herbert, 2, 68n9, 136, 138–140, 147–149
Mars, 114, 175, 176, 178, 180–191, 219, 222
Marx, Karl, 4–5, 16, 135, 138, 148, 169, 180
Massumi, Brian, 223
McCarthy, Cormac, 13, 22, 24–26, 28, 55
*Metropolis*, 5

Index                                                                  255

modernity, 3, 15–16, 18, 27, 57, 61, 96–98, 104, 107, 126, 199, 200–202, 204–206, 208, 212, 213, 239, 243
Musk, Elon, 5, 175–176, 179–182, 186–188, 190, 191

NASA, 175, 181, 182, 219, 220, 231
neoliberalism, 2–3, 65, 79, 125, 177, 179, 183, 187
*Neuromancer*, 4
Nietzsche, Friedrich, 33, 42–49, 121
*1984*, 4, 17
Nussbaum, Martha, 53, 63

Oreskes, Naomi, 65–66
*Orphan Black*, 73–74, 76–77, 82–87
*Oryx and Crake*, 4, 16, 21, 26–27, 29

*Parable of the Sower*, 4, 82
post-apocalyptic, 13, 15, 18–19, 21, 23, 25, 115
posthumanism, 4, 236–243
privacy, 5, 20, 79

queer, 7, 74, 76, 80–82, 86, 87, 208, 219, 229

racism, 34, 95, 97, 98, 101, 199, 203, 205
rationality, 2, 39, 191, 238
Rawls, John, 53, 62–63, 67n2
recognition, 5, 25, 26, 36, 63, 148, 161, 165, 184, 227, 236, 237, 243, 247–249
reproduction, 3, 5, 74–76, 101, 140, 181, 201, 204–212
resistance, 3, 4, 7, 17, 60, 74, 80, 85, 94, 97, 101, 103, 113–114, 116, 120, 124, 158, 188, 213
resurrection, 228, 229, 231
Robinson, Kim Stanley, 15, 64, 176, 182–185, 187, 191
Roden, David, 241–242, 247
Rodenberry, Gene, 34, 41
Rousseau, Jean-Jacques, 28, 53, 62, 63

sentient, 13, 46, 95, 155, 161–163, 189, 190, 220, 222, 223, 225–228, 230, 231
sexuality, 81, 95, 141–143, 145, 201, 202, 207, 209
Silicon Valley, 5, 20, 175–180, 182, 184, 186, 188, 191–192
Singh, Sonny, 221
Situationists, 2
slavery, 19, 95, 98, 101, 103, 104, 106
*Snow Crash*, 4
*Solaris*, 185, 186, 189, 190
speculative fiction, 4, 13, 60–61, 74, 80–82, 94, 135, 154, 168, 170, 175, 182, 183, 200, 202
Starfleet, 34, 35, 37–41, 45–49, 50n27
state of nature, 62, 119, 120
sterilization, 75–77, 83
Styres, Sandra, 222, 226
surveillance, 17, 20, 83, 86

technology, 20, 29, 41, 61, 74–78, 80, 84, 85, 93, 97, 102, 115, 125, 175, 177, 183, 185, 202, 221, 224, 229, 230
techno-optimism, 58, 118, 183
Terrans, 37, 39–40, 45
transformation, 3, 7, 46, 87, 115, 139, 147, 153–154, 159, 164, 166, 169, 223, 238, 247, 249
Tsing, Anna, 231

utopia, 3, 14–16, 34, 36, 55–57, 60, 61, 64, 66, 81, 85, 135–150, 159, 163, 177, 182, 183, 200

Vulcans, 38, 40

Wark, McKenzie, 5
*Whole Earth Catalog*, 177–179
Winnicott, D.W., 116

*The Year of the Flood*, 21, 26

# About the Contributors

**Ira J. Allen** is assistant professor of rhetoric, writing, and digital media studies at Northern Arizona University, and formerly assistant professor of rhetoric and composition at the American University of Beirut. He publishes on rhetoric, democracy, ethics, and writing, and has translated works by Nietzsche, Walter Benjamin, and Werner Hamacher, among others. His book *The Ethical Fantasy of Rhetorical Theory*, published by University of Pittsburgh Press, explores the meanings and utility of rhetorical theory for scholars across the humanistic disciplines. Allen's recent publications include articles in journals such as *Political Research Quarterly*, *enculturation*, *Theory and Event*, *College Composition and Communication*, and *SubStance*. He is assistant editor of the film and media studies journal *Screen Bodies: An Interdisciplinary Journal of Experience, Perception, and Display*.

**Libby Barringer** is the Klemens Von Klemperer Post-Doctoral Fellow at the Hannah Arendt Center for Politics and Humanities at Bard College, where she also teaches with the Bard Prison Initiative. Previously she taught as a lecturer at UCLA. Her written work focuses on the dialogue between ancient and modern political thought and literature, particularly classical tragedy, and considers how their interaction can be productive for rethinking contemporary political problems. She is currently working on a manuscript project titled *Mortal Democracy*, examining how different political narratives of death work to enable or suppress democratic capacities for action and recognition. She has also published work examining heroic (and superheroic) narratives as a site of political imagination.

**Matthew Benjamin Cole** is a preceptor of expository writing in the Harvard College Writing Program. His research focuses on modern and contemporary political theory and the history of political thought. He is currently working on a book manuscript titled *Fear the Future: Dystopia and Political Imagination in the Twentieth Century*.

**Caleb Gallemore** is an assistant professor in the International Affairs Program at Lafayette College. He holds a Ph.D. in geography and a master's degree in political science with a concentration in International Relations, both from The Ohio State University. Previously, he was an assistant professor in the Department of Geography and Environmental Studies at Northeastern Illinois University. His research interests include transnational networks, global land use and land cover change, global commodity chains, and the anthropocene.

**Judith Grant** is a professor in political science at Ohio University in Athens, Ohio. While at Ohio University, she has chaired political science and has been the director of gender studies and the director of the Center for Law, Culture and Justice. Her research and teaching interests include contemporary feminist theories, cultural studies, law and popular culture, and posthumanism. She is the author of the book *Fundamental Feminism (*Routledge*)*, and coeditor of the book, *Political Theory and the Animal Human Relationship* (SUNY Press, 2016). A revised second edition of *Fundamental Feminism* is forthcoming (Routledge). An avid horsewoman, dog trainer and scholar/activist, Dr. Grant resides in Columbus Ohio.

**Chase Hobbs-Morgan** (Ph.D., University of Minnesota) is a visiting assistant professor of politics at the University of California, Santa Barbara. Their work, which has appeared in *Political Theory* and the *Tulsa Law Review*, looks to democratic theory, critical legal studies, contemporary social and political thought, and film and literature for insights about how to rethink and reinvigorate democratic politics in light of ongoing environmental degradation and injustice.

**Michael Lipscomb** is a professor of political science at Winthrop University, where he teaches political theory and environmental politics. His research and teaching interests include the roles of desire, temporality, and aesthetics in political thought and practice. His work has appeared in *New German Critique and Administrative Theory* and *Praxis*. He also is the coauthor, with Karen M. Kedrowski, of *Breastfeeding Rights in the United States*.

**Sean Parson** is an associate professor in the departments of Politics and International Affairs and the Masters Program in Sustainable Communities at Northern Arizona University. He is the coeditor of the book *Superheroes and Critical Animal Studies: Heroic Beats of Total Liberation* and the author of the book *Cooking Up Revolution: Food Not Bombs, Homes Not Jails, and Resistance to Gentrification.* Interested in an every growing range of topics, he is currently exploring the intersection of environmental political theory and horror, science fiction, and dystopian fiction. He has written on a range of topics from social movement theory and climate justice, to film studies, comic studies, and critical animal studies. Now that he has tenure this long time comic book and science fiction nerd can find a way to fuse his dorky passions with his academic work.

**Claire E. Rasmussen** is associate professor in the Department of Political Science and International Relations and Gender and Women Studies at the University of Delaware. She specializes in late modern and contemporary political theory with particular interest in theories of political subjectivity. Her work has appeared in *Signs: A Journal of Women in Culture and Society, Environment and Planning D* and other interdisciplinary journals. Her first book *The Autonomous Animal* was published by the University of Minnesota Press.

**Emily Ray** is an assistant professor at Sonoma State University. Her expertise is in environmental political theory with a particular interest in land-use conflicts and the political economic dimensions of environmental destruction. She is the coauthor of "Sustainable Colonization: Tar Sands and Resource Colonialism" (published in *Capitalism, Nature, Socialism*) and "Re-imagining Radical Environmentalism" (published in the *Oxford Handbook of Environmental Political Theory*), and is currently working on projects about the treatment of women in the oil sands, and the intellectual and political underpinnings of Silicon Valley and their climate change interventions.

**Laurie Ringer**, heretically, puts her late medieval/early modern skillsets to work in interdisciplinary, transmedial, and paratextual entanglements with affect theory and speculative fiction, broadly encompassing gothic, science fiction, dystopic, apocalyptic, and post-apocalyptic texts. Because Western thought habits are always already teratologies and hauntologies masquerading as benevolent, civilizing, objective forces, she studies how intersectional feminist updates to affect theory decolonize (gender, race, sexuality, disability) and innovate academic writing through the study of diverse speculative fiction. Part of her work includes collecting terminologies and finding ways to describe what affect theory does, in academic writing and in the university classroom. Another part of her work explores blindspots in normative thought habits because not seeing problems is part of the problem. Although she is professor of English at Burman University, her research is less an evolutionary progress narrative and more involutionary experimentation, colliding canon (literary) and fandom (popular), theory and text, material and digital, and text and image in scholarly articles, chapters, and a forthcoming book.

**Debra Thompson** is an associate professor of political science at McGill University, specializing in race and ethnic politics. Her award-winning book, *The Schematic State: Race, Transnationalism, and the Politics of the Census* (Cambridge University Press, 2016) is a study of the political development of racial classifications on the national censuses of the United States, Canada, and Great Britain. She is currently writing a book that explores the transnational dynamics of the Black Lives Matter movement.

**Michael Uhall** is a PhD candidate in political theory at the University of Illinois at Urbana-Champaign, where he is completing a dissertation on the relationship between concepts of nature, the ecological crisis, and political subjectivity. Ultimately, the goal of the project is formulate a novel theory of the ecologically conditioned subject and to propose a creative biopolitics that reconfigures some long-standing concerns about biopower, freedom, and normativity. Live research interests include the history of ecology, process philosophy, risk management, and security studies. Publications can be found in *Configurations*, *Dialogue*, *Environmental Critique*, *Extrapolation*, and *Kritik*. His website and blog, Noir Materialism, can be found at https://www.michaeluhall.com/.

**Andrew Uzendoski** is a visiting assistant professor in the Department of English at Lafayette College in Pennsylvania. He received his PhD in English with a graduate portfolio in Mexican American studies from the University of Texas at Austin. His research and teaching interests encompass ethnic American literature, science fiction, global indigenous studies, Latinx and Chicanx studies, human rights rhetoric and law, and global Anglophone literature. He is especially interested in representations of colonialism and decolonization in ethnic American and postcolonial science fiction. Dr. Uzendoski has published work in *Aztlán*, *Extrapolation*, *Western American Literature*, *American Indian Quarterly*, *Altermundos: Latin@ Speculative Literature, Film, and Popular Culture*, and *Critical Ethnic Studies: An Anthology*.

**Jess Whatcott** (they/them/theirs) studies and teaches about formations of gender, sexuality, disability, race, and capitalism in the United States as an assistant professor of women's studies at San Diego State University. Dr. Whatcott currently researches California's late-nineteenth- and early-twentieth-century eugenics policies, focusing on the institutionalization of gender non-conforming, sexually deviant, and disabled women and girls. Dr. Whatcott connects this history to current practices in state prisons and other places of detention, and to speculative fiction of possible futures. Dr. Whatcott's work has appeared or will soon appear in *Signs: A Journal of Women in Culture and Society*, *NOTCHES: (re)marks on the history of sexuality*, and the *Routledge Handbook of Disability and Sexuality*.